MIGRATION INTO
RURAL AREAS

MIGRATION INTO RURAL AREAS
THEORIES AND ISSUES

Edited by

PAUL BOYLE

Lecturer in Geography at the University of Leeds
and

KEITH HALFACREE

Lecturer in Geography at the University of Wales, Swansea

JOHN WILEY & SONS

CHICHESTER • NEW YORK • WEINHEIM • BRISBANE • SINGAPORE • TORONTO

Other Wiley Editorial Offices

John Wiley & Sons, Inc., 605 Third Avenue,
New York, NY 10158-0012, USA

VCH Verlagsgesellschaft mbH, Pappelallee 3,
D-69469 Weinheim, Germany

Jacaranda Wiley Ltd, 33 Park Road, Milton,
Queensland 4064, Australia

John Wiley & Sons (Asia) Pte Ltd, 2 Clementi Loop #02-01
Jin Xing Distripark, Singapore 129809

John Wiley & Sons (Canada) Ltd, 22 Worcester Road,
Rexdale, Ontario M9W 1L1, Canada

Library of Congress Cataloging-in-Publication Data

Migration into rural areas: theories and issues / edited by
Paul Boyle & Keith Halfacree.
p.   cm.
Includes bibliographical references and index
ISBN 0-471-96989-3 (alk. paper)
1. Urban-rural migration—Congresses.   I. Boyle, P. J.
II. Halfacree, Keith.
HB1956.M54 1998
307.2'6—dc21   97-50257 CIP

British Library Cataloguing in Publication Data

A catalogue record for this book is available from the British Library

ISBN 0-471-96989-3

Typeset in 10/12pt Garamond from the author's disks by Vision Typesetting, Manchester
Printed and bound in Great Britain by Biddles Ltd, Guildford and King's Lynn

This book is printed on acid-free paper responsibly manufactured from sustainable forestry, in
which at least two trees are planted for each one used for paper production.

CONTENTS

PREFACE

In spite of having quite a turbulent history and geography, the residential migration of people from what can loosely be termed 'urban' areas to 'rural' areas has established itself as something of a social fact over the past few decades within much of the so-called developed world. Numerous studies have documented this situation in considerable descriptive detail, although for many academics researching migration this trend was initially quite an unexpected turn of events. The general tendency towards urbanisation, which had persisted for very many decades before, had reversed and, understandably, the factors underlying this 'counterurbanisation' became of central concern to those interested in population redistribution. Subsequently, various explanations were composed to explain these migration flows, from those which emphasised the importance of economic factors such as the ever-changing space economies of capitalism to those which focused more on the quality of life motivations of the migrants themselves. Overall, however, it is perhaps true to say that theorisation of this migration trend has still some way to go to catch up the body of knowledge provided by more empirical accounts of this phenomenon. Indeed, the relative lack of theoretical debate within their sub-discipline has elicited general concern amongst population geographers in particular (for example, Findlay and Graham 1991).

Situations change, however, and the contributions in this book reflect something of the revival of interest in theoretical issues within population geography. Thus it was that when we organised a conference entitled 'Migration issues in rural areas' at the University of Wales, Swansea, not only did it attract a good number and range of speakers, most especially from the sub-disciplines of rural and population geography, but we also found many of the contributions to be rooted strongly in theoretical considerations. Subsequent to the conference, most of these 'theoretical' papers were extracted (willingly) from the conference delegates with the intention of publication. However, in order to broaden the scope and to extend the appeal of the book, we also invited contributions from a number of internationally distinguished 'migration experts'. In combination, we hope that we have a book which presents a contextualised insight into some of the many ways in which theory can prove heuristically useful in understanding just why it is that so many people each year migrate from the urban environment to some kind of life in the country or in small towns. In this respect, the book is targeted at all those social science academics with an interest in both population migration and the changing rurality of the developed world, as well as at students from higher levels of undergraduate study upwards who are taking related courses.

Numerous people merit special thanks for the completion of this book. Firstly, we would like to show our gratitude to all of those who made the conference such a success, most notably all of the speakers, Emma James and Guy Lewis, whose help with the organisation was invaluable, and the support provided by the Population Geography and Rural Geography Study Groups. Although perhaps it goes without saying, we should also like to thank the individual chapter contributors (and all those who contributed papers at the conference which, although worthy in their own right, did not fit neatly into the theme of this book), noting how the invited authors produced new material for us at quite short notice. Thirdly, there are those who painstakingly put together our final artwork: most notably Alistair French and Helen Durham at Leeds and Nicola Jones and Anna Ratcliffe at Swansea. Special thanks also goes to Phil Rees at Leeds. Fourthly, our gratitude goes out to Wiley's former editor, Iain Stevenson, who commissioned the book, and the current editor Tristan Palmer, who had the dubious honour of inheriting us. Finally, Paul and Keith would particularly like to acknowledge all those 'still on *that* book. . .' commentators – got there in the end!

REFERENCE

Findlay, A. and Graham, E. (1991) 'The challenge facing population geography', *Progress in Human Geography*, **15**, 149–162.

I

MIGRATION, RURALITY AND THE POST-PRODUCTIVIST COUNTRYSIDE

KEITH HALFACREE and PAUL BOYLE

INTRODUCTION

There are four main sections to this introductory chapter. First, we note the ongoing debate over the conceptualisation of migration. Second, we explore the concept of the rural, noting how areas so labelled have changed to the extent that some commentators talk of an emerging 'post-productivist countryside'. Thirdly, the two previous sections are linked in an account of how migration is implicated significantly in the creation of a post-productivist countryside. By problematising the terms 'migration' and 'rural', and yet by demonstrating their contemporary significance, especially when viewed in combination, this chapter opens the terrain which is explored in the book's substantive chapters, namely some of the theories and issues which surround migration into the rural areas of the developed world. These chapters are flagged explicitly in the fourth section, which provides a short overview of the individual contributions.

MIGRATION: THE QUESTION OF DEFINITION

At first glance, human migration appears to be a very straightforward concept – it is the movement of a person from point A to point B, usually involving a change in one's place of permanent residence so as to distinguish the idea from simple spatial mobility. Depending on the goals of the research, some may also use the distance of the move to separate short distance residential mobility from longer distance migration, the majority of which is assumed to be linked to employment factors. However, if we are to understand and to explain migration then these apparently simple definitional distinctions soon reveal a number of more difficult issues. Fundamental amongst these is the issue of how migration is conceptualised (Boyle *et al.* 1998: Chapter 3). Unfortunately, until relatively recently, contemporary migration research tended to concentrate on questions of methodology and technique, rather neglecting the philosophical debates which preoccupied many in geography regarding the 'correct' way in which patterns and processes should be studied and explained. However, this situation has recently changed (for example, Findlay and Graham 1991; White and Jackson 1995), with population geographers, and migration researchers, in particular, showing a renewed interest in theory.

An example, of this interest comes from the current authors, who have put forward the idea that migration should be regarded more as a 'biographical' experience (Halfacree and Boyle 1993) than as a tightly circumscribed instrumental action. Rooted in structuration theory's emphasis upon the contexts and cultures (Giddens 1984) in which any act of migration occurs, the biographical approach emphasises the contextual processes through which the structuration of migration takes place (see also Thrift 1996). Crucially, it goes beyond the humanist bias suggested by many previous uses of the term biographical, to allow explicit recognition of the structural constraints and enablements moulding migration.

Lin-Yuan and Kosinski (1994: 50) have noted that migration 'is generally viewed as goal-directed behaviour', exemplified most clearly in behavioural models of migration. The biographical approach questions this assumption and qualifies it substantially through developing the critique of the 'intellectual fallacy' (Harré 1983), whereby people's behaviour is 'reduced to episodes of theoretical reasoning' (Thrift 1996: 126) – in the model of academic work – and its social character is ignored. Thus, instead of stressing the purposeful and calculating character of migration, the biographical approach emphasises its location within the individual migrant's entire biography (see Boyle and Halfacree, Chapter 16, this volume). Overall, the biographical approach seeks to demonstrate the complexity of the seemingly simple act of migration and its embeddedness within the everyday context of daily life for those involved. Migration is a highly cultural experience for all those involved (Bottomley 1992; Fielding 1992). Hence, we have Chapman's powerful warning against an un-biographical formalised approach to understanding migration. Drawing upon previous work on Pacific island migration, he argues:

> 'Counting people who left island communities produced a numerical skeleton that was replicated by tabulating their personal characteristics and demographic profiles. A complex social process was reduced to a mechanical sequence of discrete events, abstracted from the broader structural contexts of environment, history, culture, society, economy, and polity. ...the ferment of island mobility does not merge easily into a scholarly tapestry woven with the threads of dichotomized thinking and dualistic models' (Chapman 1991: 267, 287).

Perhaps taking the contextual nature of migration still further than the biographical approach, it has also been recognised that research into migration can be used to investigate the human condition (White 1995). For example, migration and its associated experiences of dislocation and marginality can serve to undermine the stability of our cultural identities and our sense of place in the world (Chambers 1994; Gilroy 1993). This is demonstrated in the experiences of migration and the expressions of what it is like to be a migrant contained in works of literature (for example, King *et al.* 1995) and other artistic media. As Gilroy (1993) and others (for example, Massey 1991) note, the results and experiences of such dislocation need not be negative, the issue here being that migration is much more than just the simple movement from A to B that it may appear to be on the ground.

THE RURAL: NETWORKS IN THE 'POST-PRODUCTIVIST COUNTRYSIDE'

Defining the Rural

Finding a satisfactory way of defining the rural has been, and remains, a perennial issue within the social science literature (Cloke and Thrift 1994; Gilbert 1982; Halfacree 1993). All that has been agreed, it seems, is that such a task proves to be extremely difficult! Whilst there are those who regard this effort as being largely a waste of time and an unwarranted distraction (Copp 1972; Hoggart 1990), the issue retains its interest for many, since:

> 'For a subject repeatedly dismissed as a figment of our analytical imagination..., the *rural* world has an unruly and intractable popular significance and remains a tenaciously active research domain' (Whatmore 1993a: 605).

Moreover, as this chapter shows, 'definitions' of the rural have assumed an increasingly central role in the restructuring of areas dominated by an extensive agricultural land-use.

In an exploration of the ways of defining the rural, Halfacree (1993; cf. Cloke and Thrift 1994) identified four principal approaches. The first of these was to attempt to 'fit' retrospectively a definition of rurality, using statistical and other indicators (for example, Cloke 1977; Cloke and Edwards 1986). Here, the aim was to locate the 'correct' tools and data to express the popular understanding of what the rural is. Therefore, this 'definition' is misnamed, as it does not define the rural at all but simply attempts to express it. Secondly, there are attempts to define the rural by arguing that it is characterised by a given set of socio-cultural relations. Such a perspective is best represented in the traditional 'community studies' literature (for reviews, see Bell and Newby 1971; Lewis 1986; Wright 1992). The key problem with this approach is that it draws upon both theoretically and empirically outdated notions of environmental determinism, as it is weak in explaining *why* certain places should have a 'rural' socio-cultural composition. Thirdly, in line with issues raised in the work on 'localities' (for example, Bagguley *et al.* 1990; Cooke 1989), we can attempt to define the rural as a distinct form of locality. The two key criteria for this to be effective are that there are significant local scale structures within society and that 'mapping' these structures consolidates what can be termed an urban–rural distinction (Hoggart 1990: 248). It is from the failure of such an effort that Hoggart (1988, 1990) calls for us to 'do away' with the rural concept altogether, since, as a 'chaotic conception' (see also Urry 1984), it confuses more than it enlightens.

The various flaws and insufficiencies of the previous three attempts at defining the rural promote the status of a fourth means of definition. This approach draws on the work of Moscovici and others influenced by the symbolic interaction school (for example, Mormont 1983, 1987, 1990) to suggest that the rural can fruitfully be described as a 'social representation of space'. Defined in this way, the rural refers to socially defined cognitive means of organising, understanding and mediating the world. These representations link concrete images and more abstract concepts in a loose and dynamic structural arrangement held together by a 'figurative nucleus' (Moscovici 1984). Crucially, if the rural is defined in this way it becomes a 'virtual' structure – in the manner of Giddens's (1984) understanding of structure. Hence, the rural experienced in the countryside is the mediated (see below) physical expression of one or more of these social representations; the rural is 'out there', with only its imprint on the landscape, as a result of the structure being used as a set of rules and resources, being 'visible'.

The mediated expression of the structure of rurality draws attention to the problematic relationship between sign (rurality), signification (meanings of rurality) and referent (the rural locale). Indeed, from such a post-structuralist angle, other researchers have also called for the de-materialisation of the rural. In particular, Murdoch and Pratt (1993) have reviewed academic work in British rural studies over the period since the 1930s. They conclude that the majority of this work can be regarded as modernist, in that it assumes that the rural and the urban are bound together in a dualism inscribed upon contiguous spaces. In an attempt to get away from the search for this essence of rurality, Murdoch and Pratt promote a rival concept, the 'post-rural'. The aim here is to stress how concepts of the rural are 'reflexively deployed'; the rural is 'a complex and multidimensional sign' (Whatmore 1993b: 544) which is practised; it is not some stable referent. Places are not simply rural or urban, therefore.

Networks of the Rural

Understanding the production of different social representations of the rural and the ways in which these structures are practised can be related to the heterogeneous networks of relations through which agency is expressed. To make this connection, the social representation's dynamic character is emphasised, with 'representational *effort*... always firmly embedded in a contextually specific process of social negotiation' (Thrift 1996: 8). Specifically, we are drawing upon 'actor-network theory' (for example, Latour 1987; Law 1986, 1992) and its emphasis on the associations forged between human and non-human resources.

A network emerges when social links acquire 'shape and consistency and therefore some degree of longevity and size' (Thrift 1996: 24). In order for this to occur, actors must define and position one another through their intermediaries (humans, texts, technical artefacts, natural objects, money, and so on). Moreover, these acts of enrolment into the network, whereby 'behaviour [is] stabilized and channelled in the direction desired by the enrolling actor' (Murdoch 1995: 747), are not just done by human beings since, in actor-network theory, all types of intermediary can be agents (Enticott 1996). For example, texts and tools 'speak' of the roles played by others in the network when they have acquired a place within the network. Thus, there is a fundamental discursive recursiveness between the components of a network.

From the actor-network perspective, both structure and power are emergent properties rather than pre-given. On the one hand, a network becomes powerful with respect to other (potential) networks when it achieves stability and becomes 'heavy with norms' (Callon 1991: 151). In order to achieve such stability it is likely to have enrolled many entities (both human and non-human) into the network, with considerable overdetermination of the roles which develop within the network. On the other hand, the network itself is likely to be structured in terms of what Bhaskar (1979: 51) has called elsewhere a 'position-practice system', defined as:

> '*positions* (places, functions, rules, tasks, duties, rights, etc.) occupied (filled, assumed, enacted, etc.) by individuals [or other intermediaries], and of the *practices* (activities, etc.) in which in virtue of their occupancy of these positions (and vice versa) they engage'.

Thus, individuals can be seen as having greater or lesser power within the network by virtue of their position within it. Again, actor-network theory sees the positioning of the individual within the network in dynamic discursive terms:

> 'those who are powerful are not those who "hold" power but are those able to enrol, convince, and enlist others into networks on terms which allow the initial actors to "represent" the others. Powerful actors speak for all the enrolled entities and actors, and control the means of representation. . . The controlling actor grows by borrowing the force of others. . . Power is, therefore, the composition of the network' (Murdoch 1995: 748).

A social representation of the rural can be contextualised as an entity enrolled into a network. Within such a network, any 'objective' definition of the rural becomes lost (if it ever existed) as the rural intermediary is integrated into the highly socially defined set of associations which comprise the network. Practising the rural becomes embedded within the totality of the network. Moreover, by observing that the rural can act as an agent, we can appreciate better the claim that social representations serve to organise, understand and mediate the world; in short, specific social representations of the rural can position individuals within a (rural) network in terms of their behaviour, expectations, norms, and so on. Finally, given the centrality of power to actor-network theory, we are immediately drawn to the need to consider the power relations implicated in practising the rural.

Towards the 'Post-productivist Countryside'

The concept of the 'post-productivist countryside' has been developed mostly in the context of recent changes which have affected what are generally under-stood to be the rural areas of Britain (for example, Lowe *et al.* 1993; Marsden *et al.* 1993: 58–68). However, although the British example is drawn upon most heavily here, Marsden (1997) and Ilbery and Bowler (1998) have stressed the wider relevance of the concept, especially in the rest of northern Europe, North America, Australia and New Zealand. In order to understand the emergence of the post-productivist countryside we must focus first on the changing fortunes of the agricultural industry.

A 'productivist' era for agriculture lasted from the post-1945 reconstruction until the late 1970s. This period was characterised by a sense of security for those engaged in agriculture and related industries – albeit within the confines of some Faustian concessions, such as those represented in the 'agricultural treadmill' (Ward 1993) – with respect to land rights, land-use, finance, politics and ideol-ogy. Rooted in memories of wartime hardships and of the pre-war failures of land-use planning, a 'progressive rural ideology' (Marsden 1998) saw all of these components mesh together to promote agriculture as a progressive, expansion-ist and food production orientated force. Furthermore, the space for this benign constellation was the countryside, so that the rural was defined very much in terms of agriculture. This was the productivist countryside, whereby a degree of stability or 'structured coherence' was maintained 'based on the central position of agriculture... in local society, economy and politics' (Cloke and Goodwin 1992: 327). In addition, a close association was forged between agriculture and the rural in popular consciousness, facilitating the 'agricultural exceptionalism' (Newby 1979: 233) which characterised the post-war land-use planning regime.

However, the productivist era has been coming to an end at least since the 1970s, due to the inability of the state to control the economic and other contradictions in the Atlanticist food order (Marsden *et al.* 1993). Rural areas' local structured coherences (Cloke and Goodwin 1992) have been shattered, and rural space is now very much caught up within an *international*, even global, political economy (for example, Goodman and Redclift 1991; Le Heron 1993), whereby nationally defined and regulated rural distinctions have been overtaken and have become increasingly outmoded (Marsden 1998). The secur-ity of the agricultural industry has been reduced, assailed most strongly by the forces of 'free market' competition, on the one hand, and by ecological con-cerns, on the other. Thus, we have the 1992 reforms of the EU's Common Agricultural Policy, the 1993 GATT world trade agreement and the global environmental concerns raised most prominently at the 1992 Earth Summit in Rio de Janeiro (Ilbery and Bowler 1998).

The resultant 'post-productivist countryside' is very much a nascent entity but its emerging form reflects the breakdown of the productivist hegemony. In the agricultural sphere it is characterised by extensification, dispersion and diversification (Ilbery and Bowler 1998). The latter, in particular, is signified by pluriac-tivity (Evans and Ilbery 1993; Fuller 1990; MacKinnon *et al.* 1991) and the growing role of farmers in activities not traditionally associated with the produc-tion of food, such as diversification into bed and breakfast accommodation or rural leisure activities. More 'environmentally sensitive' forms of farming are also important here. Farmers are also often adopting strategies to convert unused agriculturally productive capital assets into other forms of asset, re-commoditis-ing former agricultural resources (barns, cottages, land) for new uses (Kneale *et al.* 1991; Murdoch and Marsden 1994, Chapter 6). Moreover, some of these activities involve persons from 'non-farming' backgrounds – possibly including the 'hobby farmers' identified in the work of Gasson (1988) and Ilbery (1991) – many of whom are also recent migrants into rural areas.

It is important to stress that the idea of a post-productivist countryside does *not* mean a countryside in which agriculture is either no longer present or in which it has been eclipsed in significance by other land uses (Ilbery and Bowler 1998). Instead, the diversity of rural change suggests a divergence within agri-culture, between those farmers concentrating on subsistence, those combining agriculture with 'other gainful activities' in order to make a decent living and those shifting to a more agribusiness mode of operation; a number of distinctive 'pathways' for farm business development are emerging (Bowler 1992; Ilbery and Bowler 1993). Overall, post-productivism suggests that agriculture will remain the principal land use in rural areas but that its hegemonic cornerstone position in the rural economy, local society and politics will no longer be assured and will increasingly be highly localised to certain rural areas. An agriculturally based structured coherence will be more spatially selective. Thus, for example, the growth of agribusiness on the one hand signifies the conver-gence between agriculture and other more 'usual' capitalist enterprises (What-more *et al.* 1987), but this more purely 'economic' role for agriculture also reflects the retreat of agriculture from the spheres of local society and politics. It also reflects the 'leakage' of agriculture from the rural context, given the increas-ing importance of upstream and downstream economic sectors to the industry (Flynn and Marsden 1992; Ward 1990).

Hand-in-hand with these changes in the productive position of the country-side, the post-productivist era also suggests an enhanced role for exchange and consumption interests, with both vying with productive interests for local pre-dominance (Marsden 1998). This conflict is especially well reflected in the changing ideological constitution of the countryside, as expressed in social representations of the rural (see below). This is expressed further in attempts to find new ways of governing the changing rural spaces, not least in the deregula-tion/reregulation dynamic (Marsden 1998). Thus, on the one hand, there have been formal government attempts to deregulate the economic sphere and encourage 'free trade', whilst at the same time there has often been reregulation through the private sector (especially with regard to food) and an enhancement of local planning control (see also Flynn and Marsden 1995; Munton 1995).

Overall, the ongoing productivist-to-post-productivist transition suggests the creation of a much more heterogeneous countryside, whether this is seen in terms of land-use, localised 'real regulation' (Clark 1992), structured coherence or social composition (see below). If place is understood as the localised 'meeting and weaving together' (Massey 1991: 244) of social, economic, political and cultural relations, often defined at a global or at least international level, it seems that the post-productivist countryside is very much about a 'global sense of place' (Massey 1991). Nonetheless, in spite of this diversity, 'ideal types' of locally embedded rural landscapes can often be identified. Four have been suggested for Britain (Flynn and Lowe 1994; Marsden 1998; Marsden *et al.* 1993: 185–191; see also Cloke and Goodwin 1992):

- Preserved countryside – scenic areas with long-established preservation, anti-development, local decision-making; yet agricultural diversification and increasingly contested development for consumption uses, especially with respect to middle-class in-migrants.
- Contested countryside – areas beyond the core commuter zones; landowners and developers dominate but with increasing challenges from in-migrants.
- Paternalistic countryside – typified by the estates of large private landowners; some conversion of redundant agricultural assets but less development pressure; stewardship ethos.
- Clientelist countryside – remote, marginal zones; agriculture dominant but only through state welfare support; corporatist development.

The post-productivist opening-up of the countryside to new interests has promoted various dimensions of dispute and conflict, their specific local manifestations having been suggested a little by the ideal types presented above. For example, there are major disputes over land-use in the preserved and contested countrysides, which have been linked into this discussion by Marsden *et al.* (1993: 68):

> 'the putative surplus of millions of hectares of agricultural land has opened a wider debate on the access of non-agricultural interests to rural land, thereby allowing a wider range of interests to stake claims, and further compromising the productivist ideology which is now so obviously in disarray. . .'.

As these authors also recognise, these material struggles very much involve contrasting representations of rurality; the shift from productivism involves highly 'contested transitions' (Marsden and Flynn 1993). Thus, Lowe *et al.* (1993: 219) argue that the post-productivist differentiation of the countryside is not being achieved via a Conservative 'New Right' unleashing of market forces in rural areas but through various actors attempting to impose their respective representations of the rural over others. This very much suggests the sort of processes at the heart of actor-network theory.

LINKING MIGRATION AND THE POST-PRODUCTIVIST COUNTRYSIDE

Migrants' Social Representations of the Rural

Migration of people to the more rural areas of the developed world – captured at least in part by the concept of counterurbanisation – forms perhaps *the* central dynamic in the creation of any post-productivist countryside (Marsden 1998; Murdoch and Marsden 1994; see also Gorton *et al.*, Chapter 12, this volume). These migration streams involve the introduction or enhancement of relatively novel networks incorporating specific social representations of the rural, many of which come into conflict with other networks as they each try to strengthen their associational hold upon the countryside. In order to consider these networks and their associated struggles, we must first consider the character of the social representations of the rural held by migrants.

Social representations of the rural vary considerably throughout the developed world but can be classified initially according to whether they regard the countryside as a backward relic of the past to be escaped from at all costs or whether they see it as a haven of sanity and security in a world where the city represents the uncertain mayhem of Babylon rather than the ordered progress of Jerusalem (Short 1991). Concentrating on the second of these perspectives, the historical legacy of a long-standing anti-urbanism – an 'image that will not die' (Hadden and Barton 1973) – is manifested in strong pro-rural ideologies: from agrarian Jeffersonianism in the United States (Marx 1964) and other countries of the New World (Short 1991) to a slightly less harsh pastoral vision in the nations of Western Europe (Williams 1973). Moreover, this nostalgic idealisation of the rural has been joined in more recent years by a growing feeling in some quarters that the countryside is not just the negation of the city and a reservoir of fundamental and honest social values but provides the spatial blueprint for a more progressive future. Such an imagination is often underpinned by environmentalist beliefs:

'Rurality is claimed not only as a space to be appropriated... but as a way of life, or a model of an alternative society inspiring a social project that challenges contemporary social and economic ill. . . . Peasant autarky, village community and ancient technique are no longer relics, but images which legitimize this social project of a society which would be ruralized... The aim is not to recreate a past way of life but to develop forms of social and economic life different from those prevailing at present...' (Mormont 1987: 18).

Thus, we move from the rural as anti-urban to more pro-rural representations.

A more specific example of the idealisation of the rural comes from the British or more strictly English 'popular discourse' (Jones 1995) of the 'rural idyll'. Adoption of this representation, which links into environmental ideologies of Englishness (Short 1991), leads to an understanding of 'real' England as physically consisting of small villages joined by narrow lanes and nestling amongst a patchwork of small fields where contented (and certainly not mad!) cows lazily graze away the day. Socially, this is a tranquil landscape of timeless stability and community, where people know not just their next door neighbours but everyone else in the village. This, of course, is thus a representation without in-migration (Jedrej and Nuttall 1996: 180) and, as such, belies the often long-term 'objective' experience of rural areas (for example, Pooley and Turnbull 1996). Furthermore, and somewhat paradoxically, in spite of representations such as the rural idyll showing little appreciation of migration, it is crucial to note that migration to the rural environment is informed to a greater or lesser extent by such representations (for example, Halfacree 1994; Hughes 1997; Jedrej and Nuttall 1996). As we shall see below, this has considerable implications regarding the behaviour of migrants in rural areas.

A further point which arises concerns the selectivity of social representations such as the rural idyll. In short, such representations tend to be associated with the interests of certain sections of the middle class, notably the service class (Murdoch and Marsden 1994; Thrift 1987), even if the ideas might be held more broadly (Halfacree 1995). Looked at slightly differently, when combined with migration, the migrants' positions within the network of the rural idyll's position-practice system tend to be at odds with those of other rural residents, who are either left out or who assume a marginalised position (Cloke and Little 1997; Murdoch and Marsden 1994) – Philo's (1992) 'neglected rural geographies'. For example, it has been argued that both black people (for example, Agyeman and Spooner 1997; Kinsman 1995) and 'New Age' travellers (for example, Halfacree 1996; Sibley 1997) have no 'place' within the rural idyll.

Migrants' Rurality Within the Post-productivist Countryside

Migration to rural areas has been strongly associated with the increasingly hegemonic success of idyll-type social representations of the rural within such areas. In short, the network of the rural idyll has become very powerful. Nowhere has this been more clearly demonstrated than in Murdoch and Marsden's (1994) study of the ways in which rurality is being 'reconstituted' within Aylesbury Vale in Buckinghamshire. Through struggles over the development of housing, golf courses, land-fill tips, industrial units, and so on, this rural area has increasingly assumed the middle class image of the countryside expressed by the rural idyll (see also Cloke and Goodwin 1992: 328). Starting with the houses to which the migrants move, these sites soon 'impose their cultural aspirations beyond the boundaries of the village' (Murdoch and Marsden 1994: 225). As the authors conclude:

> 'the locality comes to assume an increasingly middle-class shape. As this process accelerates, so other aspects of local life become imbued with middle-class connotations. . . . As certain representations increasingly 'win out' over others, the locality

comes to take on a coherent shape and this provides the structure of enablement and constraint for future action' (Murdoch and Marsden 1994: 227–228).

One particular consequence of these migrations is that the migrants' experienced reality of the rural environment is often perceived to be at odds with their representational blueprint. Such dissonance is reflected in an increasing number of disputes between farmers and incomers unhappy with the sights, sounds and smells of the countryside (see *Guardian* 12/05/1992, 01/06/1993, 18/08/1994 on the noise pollution saga of Corky the cockerel). A 'social' conflict may also occur, reflected clearly in the 'cultural' debates over (English) 'White Settlers' in rural Wales and Scotland (Allan and Mooney, Chapter 15, this volume; Boyle *et al.* 1998: Chapter 9; Jedrej and Nuttall 1996). Two potential responses to experiences such as these follow. On the one hand, migrants may become self-reflexive of their own role in changing the rural, through social and/or physical change. For example, they may observe how, if they are from the higher social classes, they have helped to gentrify the area moved into or how, if they are still in employment, their commuting work patterns serve to undermine any sense of a distinct rural economy. On the other hand, the migrants more commonly look away from themselves and observe the impacts of other migrants and become concerned about the threats to 'their' countryside. Such semi-reflexivity can typically be channelled into pressure group politics and other attempts to maintain or create a grounding of a particular representation of the rural. In other words, efforts are made to increase the power of the rural idyll's network – to represent the space of the rural in that particular way – the success of such struggles leading Murdoch and Marsden (1994: 231) to suggest that the change from a productivist to a post-productivist countryside is symbolised by a shift from an 'agricultural veto' to an in-migrant dominated 'preservationist veto'. Indeed, it has been argued that:

> 'The different levels of power of development and anti-development networks and the pursuance of interests through the forward-planning system currently is one of the most pervasive processes which are reshaping rural space, both materially and sociopolitically' (Marsden 1996: 253).

Finally, the fact that there are these struggles taking place at all emphasises that middle class rural in-migrants are not having things all their own way. Hence, the dangers of too blandly talking about a 'middle class countryside' (Urry 1995). On the one hand, there are some people among the migrants who do not generally subscribe to networks incorporating the rural idyll. Such people include business interests concerned with the heightened commoditisation of the countryside – although much of this commoditisation is likely to be tailored to the distinctive taste of the middle class in-migrants – and those migrants with more 'alternative' or counter-cultural ideas of the countryside (for example, see Fairlie 1996 on 'low impact' settlers). On the other hand, there is the 'established' rural population which, although it may not be as unified as was once assumed, can present quite divergent understandings of the countryside and be incorporated into associated networks (for example, see Cox *et al.* 1994 on hunting). In conclusion, the post-productivist countryside, of which the experience of migration forms so central a part, is very much a contested and even paradoxical space.

THE ORGANISATION OF THE BOOK

The processes, changes and examples introduced above suggest immediately a wide range of theoretical issues which need to be addressed if we are to gain an understanding of the links between migration and the creation of any post-productivist countryside. It is clear that migration as a process and the networks, representations and general activities of the migrants themselves are playing a central role in constructing this countryside. However, it is also important that the various elements of this reconstruction are interrogated from a range of theoretical perspectives.

In Chapter 2, *Tony Champion* adds to the context presented in this chapter by giving an overview of the 'counterurbanisation story' – first identified by Calvin Beale in the United States in the 1970s – within which accounts of rural-to-urban migration must be set. Concerned less about the impacts of in-migration on rural areas, this chapter examines the various forces that have encouraged the trend towards rural living in the last few decades. Noting cautiously that the excitement of the 'migration turnaround' must not blind us to the complexities of the counterurbanisation phenomenon, Champion draws our attention to the need to clarify the geographical framework in which research is set and to disentangle the role played by in-migration as compared to natural changes and out-migration. Moreover, he also flags the varied ways in which rural in-migration has been studied and explained, the latter ranging from individual-level, often survey-based accounts to more structural overviews.

As one of the most noted social scientists to explore the processes behind counterurbanisation in critical detail, *Tony Fielding*, in Chapter 3, looks back over his own and other work in a powerful advocacy of the need to maintain a class perspective on the migrations involved. Capturing the excitement suggested by Champion with respect to counterurbanisation research, Fielding draws on the materialist European tradition of anchoring explanations of counterurbanisation within changing capitalist class relations and the 'spatial fix' involved in much economic restructuring. Drawing on evidence from southern England derived from the census-based Longitudinal Study, he then goes on to assess the contribution of counterurban migration to the changing class structures of non-metropolitan regions and, finally, to suggest a classification of the 'winners' and 'losers' of the urban-to-rural migration experience.

Whilst the first two chapters have largely drawn on material from Britain and the United States, the geographical net is widened in Chapter 4, where *Thomas Kontuly* presents an overview of the experience of and explanations for counterurbanisation in a wide range of European countries. Excluding the heavily studied example of Britain enables him to assess the wider significance of the phenomenon. He notes a tension in the literature between efforts to explain counterurbanisation through reference to a few distinct and overarching causal factors and those explanations which emphasise the need to provide a more geographically and temporally subtle explanatory context. From the European evidence, the key explanatory role has been given to economic structural change as the motor of counterurbanisation but this may reflect the legacy of the 1970s data upon which this importance has been constructed. Conditions in the 1990s, in contrast, may have opened the door to a wider range of interpretations.

Changes in the rate and context of urban-to-rural migration from the 1970s through to the 1990s are examined with respect to the United States by *William Frey* and *Kenneth Johnson* in Chapter 5. Focusing on the proximate causes of this migration, the authors argue that explanation for metropolitan region-to-non-metropolitan region movement in the 1970s tends to emphasise period effects, regional restructuring or deconcentration. However, by the 1990s, when the United States saw a substantial return to net non-metropolitan migration from a downturn in the 1980s, the scope of the first two explanations had been dampened. Instead, they posit that an emphasis on the importance of deconcentration based on residential preference is bolstered by the response of low-skill, United States born residents in certain key port-of-entry cities to the substantial rise of immigration to those cities. Out-migration takes place as these established residents are economically displaced by the newcomers, such that 'selective' deconcentration characterises the contemporary United States migration situation.

Whilst the previous chapter suggested the potential importance of national-scale urban-to-rural migration's links to more international migration networks, Chapter 6 returns to a more domestic focus. Here, *Graeme Hugo* and *Martin Bell* discuss in detail their hypothesis of welfare-led migration to rural Australia. Inspired by the evidence of welfare led migration to non-metropolitan parts of the country in the Depression of the 1930s, the authors wish to add a welfare component to the acknowledged diverse explanations of the rural population growth through migration. The spatial portability of welfare benefits within Australia, it is suggested, encourages those out of work to move to non-metropolitan areas to take advantage of factors such as cheaper and more available low-cost housing, a lower cost of living and the ability to obtain casual employment. In addition, better off retired and other lifestyle migrants, also in receipt of various transfer payments, are also migrating to rural Australia, adding to the complex mix which characterises the contemporary socio-cultural geography of rural areas.

Questions of culture are taken further in Chapter 7, where *Paul Cloke, Mark Goodwin* and *Paul Milbourne* draw upon more qualitative material from their work on 'rural lifestyles' within England and Wales to explore the extent to which many of the social conflicts which often appear commonplace within village life are rooted in differences between residents' cultural expectations and practices. The authors argue that different groups are likely to carry different portfolios of 'cultural competences' with respect to what village life actually *is*. Thus, the problematics of rural life can be based upon experiential issues as well as the more broadly acknowledged normative issues of income, and so on. Grounding division within the village within contrasting 'knowledges' of how to behave in the rural setting – knowledges constructed at national, regional and local levels – takes us beyond simple xenophobic interpretations of cultural conflict.

There are varied ways in which the 'cultural competences' of rural residents can be expressed, and a contrasting approach to that presented by Cloke, Goodwin and Milbourne is given in Chapter 8. Here, *Shaun Fielding* considers the extent to which ideas originating in the 1970s 'Fourth World' theory of George Manuel have and can 'travel' to illuminate the experience of 'indigenous' identity within Swaledale in the Yorkshire Dales. Drawing on Manuel's central themes of land and culture, Fielding suggests that although Swaledalers might talk in terms reminiscent of Native Americans from British Columbia, they are unable to mobilise politically around any single, coherent Swaledale identity. Indeed, any united political front on the part of indigenous Swaledalers would require them to accept and reify the social *status quo ante*. Thus, in terms reminiscent of Murdoch and Pratt's (1993) critique of any 'postmodern' rural studies, Fielding concludes his chapter with a call not to forget the class-related structuring which is evident even *within* Swaledale indigenous society.

Issues of class and culture are also brought together in Chapter 9, where *Paul Cloke, Martin Phillips* and *Nigel Thrift* explore the usefulness of some of the work of Klaus Eder in our investigations of migration to rural areas. Eder's central theme is that of 'cultural texture', by which he means the way in which culture mediates or intervenes between class and collective action. This idea is illustrated by Cloke, Phillips and Thrift with respect to migration to the Gower peninsula in south Wales. Firstly, with respect to middle class colonisation of Gower, the role of rurality is clear in terms of a cultural embedding of socio-economic bases of migration; class-based strategies are clearly culturally legit-imated and directed. Secondly, when detailing the lifestyle strategies employed by these migrants, they were shown to reflect – to varying degrees – Eder's class-specific ethoses of individualism, achievement and materialism.

When the cultural textures of rurality are explored in greater detail they are likely to yield a strong association between the countryside and visions of 'community' and 'nature'. This association is addressed directly in Chapter 10 by *Jonathan Murdoch* and *Graham Day*. The authors explore how mobile middle class incomers to rural areas of Britain bring with them constructs of rurality which incorporate strong ideas about the normative communal relations of such places. Following Lash and Urry, Murdoch and Day argue that an explicit (postmodern) reinvention of community is a key response to the globalisation of daily life and, with the countryside being emblematic of community, the rural is where this reinvention is most strongly practised. However, this reinvention is by no means unproblematic and often has to be actively constructed and defended, whereby the selectiveness of this vision becomes apparent. As Murdoch and Day conclude, the net result is that many parts of rural Britain – at least – are becoming the 'almost exclusive domain of the white middle class'.

The idea of a postmodern reinvention of community, both within a rural context and incorporating an articulated sense of what the rural is (or should be), is also considered in Chapter 11. Here, *Keith Halfacree* examines how Maffesoli's concept of 'neo-tribalism' can be applied to illuminate the current contestation between different groups over the future shape and content of the countryside. Neo-tribes are defined as groups rooted in individual self-reflexive acts of identification, a precarious existence reliant upon the construction of space – as suggested by Murdoch and Day's chapter – for their longer term survival. Within the post-productivist countryside a contest is envisaged between neo-tribal middle class in-migrants and more tribal (i.e. less reflexive) established groups of residents, as well as between different neo-tribal fractions within the in-migrant population.

Chapter 12 explores the increasing diversity and the consequent ability to order the post-productivist countryside through the lenses of modes of political change and theories of justice. After a detailed restatement (after the present chapter) of the importance of diversity in respect of counterurbanisation, agricultural change and economic change in the countryside, *Matthew Gorton, John White* and *Ian Chaston* discuss Marquand's distinction between command, exchange and preceptoral modes of political action. Whilst the former two, rooted in top-down orders and (monetary) exchange relations respectively, are seen to be appropriate to the productivist era, the current diversity of rural spaces and actors points to the rise of the preceptoral mode, rooted in persuasion and network building. However, it is difficult to identify a core element around which this persuasive work can coalesce. This is because the rural idyll, so central to migration to rural areas, has both individualistic and communitarian normative elements which, as theories of justice have long suggested, tend to be mutually incompatible.

Staying with the sphere of political action, Chapter 13 explores the issue of rural governance. Specifically, *Simone Abram, Jonathan Murdoch* and *Terry Marsden* investigate the role of statistical calculations and representations within the planning system. Numbers are shown to be central to modern forms of governance and this is equally true in the rural context of Buckinghamshire in England which is discussed here. The chapter describes the way in which numbers – specifically, household projections – become absorbed into the planning hierarchy such that they become very hard to challenge without recourse to 'appropriate' technical discourses. Indeed, in the Examination-in-Public which accompanied the Structure Plan process, challenges to the likely future population of the county which did occur, especially by the house building interest, strongly emphasised 'hard facts' over more qualitative issues. Besides questions about underlying social assumptions and accuracy which a reliance on such 'facts' tends to overlook, this example of governance-by-numbers also disguises underlying power relations reflected, for example, in the Plan's promotion of development in the north rather than the south of the county.

Much greater attention has recently been paid to the importance of incorporating issues of gender as a central theme for understanding the rural and migration issues in general. Consequently, in a substantial contribution, *Jenny Agg* and *Martin Phillips* in Chapter 14 examine what they see as some of the neglected gender dimensions of rural social restructuring, drawing upon field-work in the English counties of Leicestershire and Warwickshire. A key theme in this chapter concerns the degree to which rural class analysis has been rather gender-blind. This theme is reflected, for example, in the 'household gender–class asymmetry' – with women typically located in more proletarian positions than their male partners – which makes any emphasis on the middle class character of counterurbanisation fundamentally gendered. Agg and Phillips also demonstrate strong gender divisions of labour in both the official and unofficial (domestic) economies of rural areas, how gender identities are central to determining both the propensities and the motivations of households to move, and how colonisation (re)composes the gender order of rural areas. Images of gender are of central concern in all of these fields, with the authors drawing upon Connell's distinction between 'hegemonic masculinity' and 'emphasised femininity' to explore these images. As an example, within the 'official public sphere' of leisure, women are shown to engage in 'emphasised feminine' activities, often centred on the village. This leads on to the especially interesting finding that migrants' association with 'heritage' and 'nature' activities is not just reflexive of (service) class identity but also proves to be a highly feminised association.

Reflection on the meaning of the term 'counterurbanisation' and upon its causal complexity are important themes running through many of the chapters in this book. Such salutary reflexivity is taken further in Chapter 15, where *Jane Allan* and *Elizabeth Mooney* unpack some of the terminology employed in investigations of the impacts of counterurbanisation in rural Scotland. This chapter is symptomatic of moves within social science more generally to problematise the relationships between researchers, their fieldwork, the subjects of the research and the resulting textual products. Particular attention is given to the ambiguities surrounding the terms 'local' and 'incomer', in spite of their widespread use by academics, rural residents themselves and through politically-fecund synonyms such as 'White Settlers' by groups such as 'Settler Watch' and 'Scottish Watch'. Allan and Mooney show how language tends to polarise, fix and oversimplify the processes of social change which are taking place within rural Scotland. For example, the term 'incomer', even when brought to the fore in local festivals, is often used as much by rural residents to signify a rural 'Other', characterised by some negative ascribed characteristics of difference, as it is to define a clear-cut category of person on the basis of kinship or birthplace. Moreover, the term incomer can also be used inclusively to suggest a person accepted into the local social milieu. Taking things further still, Allan and Mooney also draw attention to the need to consider their own positionality in their writing: exploring their preconceptions, reflecting upon their fieldwork experiences and techniques, and drawing to the surface their motivations, and so on.

Chapter 16, by *Paul Boyle* and *Keith Halfacree*, has two major goals. Firstly, it explores the potential of using the previously neglected concept of collective behaviour to understand the phenomenon of migration into rural areas. The chapter achieves this first goal partly by drawing together many of the ideas expressed throughout this volume. Secondly, the chapter extends some of the authors' previous work (Halfacree and Boyle 1993) by advocating an approach to migration research that integrates the biographical more fully with ideas drawn from social psychology. Indeed, the empirical case of migration into rural areas seems particularly appropriate for the use of such a methodology. The chapter is not, therefore, a simple summary of the main conclusions reached by each of the contributors, but is in part an attempt to address some theoretical concerns that we feel have yet to be addressed adequately in previous conceptions of migration.

REFERENCES

Agyeman, J. and Spooner, R. (1997) 'Ethnicity and the rural environment', in P. Cloke and J. Litt'e (eds.), *Contested countryside cultures*, Routledge, London, 197–217.
Bagguley, P., Mark-Lawson, J., Shapiro, D., Urry, J., Walby, S. and Warde, A. (1990) *Restructuring. Place, class and gender*, Sage, London.
Bell, C. and Newby, H. (1971) *Community studies*, George Allen and Unwin, London.
Bhaskar, R. (1979) *The possibility of naturalism*, Harvester, Brighton.
Bottomley, G. (1992) *From another place: migration and the politics of culture*, Cambridge University Press, Cambridge.
Bowler, I. (1992) 'Sustainable agriculture as an alternative path of farm business development', in I. Bowler, C. Bryant and M. Nellis (eds.), *Rural systems in transition: agriculture and environment*, CAB International, Wallingford, 237–253.
Boyle, P., Halfacree, K. and Robinson, V. (1998) *Exploring contemporary migration*, Longman, Harlow.
Callon, M. (1991) 'Techno-economic networks and irreversibility', in J. Law (ed.), *A sociology of monsters: essays on power, technology and domination*, Routledge, London, 132–161.
Chambers, I. (1994) *Migrancy, culture, identity*, Routledge, London.
Chapman, M. (1991) 'Pacific island movement and socioeconomic change: metaphors of misunderstanding', *Population and Development Review*, **17**, 263–292.
Clark, G. (1992) "Real regulation': the administrative state', *Environment and Planning A*, **24**, 615–627.
Cloke, P. (1977) 'An index of rurality for England and Wales', *Regional Studies*, **11**, 31–46.
Cloke, P. and Edwards, G. (1986) 'Rurality in England and Wales 1981: a replication of the 1971 index', *Regional Studies*, **20**, 289–306.
Cloke, P. and Goodwin, M. (1992) 'Conceptualizing countryside change: from post-

Fordism to rural structured coherence', *Transactions of the Institute of British Geographers*, **17**, 321–336.

Cloke, P. and Little, J. (eds.) (1997) *Contested countryside cultures*, Routledge, London.

Cloke, P. and Thrift, N. (1994) 'Introduction: refiguring the "rural"', in P. Cloke, M. Doel, D. Matless, M. Phillips and N. Thrift, *Writing the rural. Five cultural geographies*, Paul Chapman Publishing, London, 1–5.

Cooke, P. (ed.) (1989) *Localities: the changing face of urban Britain*, Unwin Hyman, London.

Copp, J. (1972) 'Rural sociology and rural development', *Rural Sociology*, **37**, 515–533.

Cox, G., Hallett, J. and Winter, M. (1994) 'Hunting the wild red deer: the social organization and ritual of a 'rural' institution', *Sociologia Ruralis*, **34**, 190–205.

Enticott, G. (1996) 'Non-human actors in actor-network theory: an emotive issue', unpublished paper.

Evans, N. and Ilbery, B. (1993) 'The pluriactivity, part-time farming, and farm diversification debate', *Environment and Planning A*, **25**, 945–959.

Fairlie, S. (1996) *Low impact development: planning and people in a sustainable countryside*, Jon Carpenter, Chipping Norton.

Fielding, A. (1992) 'Migration and culture', in A. Champion and A. Fielding (eds.), *Migration processes and patterns. Volume 1. Research progress and prospects*, Belhaven Press, London, 201–212.

Findlay, A. and Graham, E. (1991) 'The challenge facing population geography', *Progress in Human Geography*, **15**, 149–162.

Flynn, A. and Lowe, P. (1994) 'Local politics and rural restructuring: the case of the contested countryside', in D. Symes and A. Jansen (eds.), *Agricultural restructuring and rural change in Europe*, Agricultural University Wageningen, Wageningen, 247–259.

Flynn, A. and Marsden, T. (1992) 'Food regulation in a period of agricultural retreat: the British experience', *Geoforum*, **23**, 85–93.

Flynn, A. and Marsden, T. (1995) 'Rural change, regulation and sustainability', *Environment and Planning A*, **27**, 1180–1193.

Fuller, A. (1990) 'From part-time farming to pluriactivity: a decade of change in rural Europe', *Journal of Rural Studies*, **6**, 361–373.

Gasson, R. (1988) *The economics of part-time farming*, Longman, Harlow.

Giddens, A. (1984) *The constitution of society*, Cambridge University Press, Cambridge.

Gilbert, J. (1982) 'Rural theory: the grounding of rural sociology', *Rural Sociology*, **47**, 609–633.

Gilroy, P. (1993) *The black Atlantic. Modernity and double consciousness*, Verso, London.

Goodman, D. and Redclift, M. (1991) *Refashioning nature: food, ecology and culture*, Routledge, London.

Guardian (12/05/1992) 'Victory leaves Corky cockerel crowing'.

Guardian (01/06/1993) 'Corky is cock-a-hoop as he finds new life in wide open spaces'.

Guardian (18/08/1994) 'Corky the torturer – now the book and the bankruptcy'.

Hadden, J. and Barton, J. (1973) 'An image that will not die: thoughts on the history of anti-urban ideology', *Urban Affairs Annual Review*, **7**, 79–116.

Halfacree, K. (1993) 'Locality and social representation: space, discourse and alternative definitions of the rural', *Journal of Rural Studies*, **9**, 23–37.

Halfacree, K. (1994) 'The importance of "the rural" in the constitution of counterurbanization: evidence from England in the 1980s', *Sociologia Ruralis*, **34**, 164–189.

Halfacree, K. (1995) 'Talking about rurality: social representations of the rural as expressed by residents of six English parishes', *Journal of Rural Studies*, **11**, 1–20.

Halfacree, K. (1996) 'Out of place in the countryside: travellers and the "rural idyll",

Antipode, **29**, 42–72.

Halfacree, K. and Boyle, P. (1993) 'The challenge facing migration research: the case for a biographical approach', *Progress in Human Geography*, **17**, 333–348.

Harré, R. (1983) *Personal being*, Blackwell, Oxford.

Hoggart, K. (1988) 'Not a definition of rural', *Area*, **20**, 35–40.

Hoggart, K. (1990) 'Let's do away with rural', *Journal of Rural Studies*, **6**, 245–257.

Hughes, A. (1997) 'Rurality and "cultures of womanhood". Domestic identities and moral order in village life', in P. Cloke and J. Little (eds.), *Contested countryside cultures*, Routledge, London, 123–137.

Ilbery, B. (1991) 'Farm diversification as an adjustment strategy on the urban fringe of the West Midlands', *Journal of Rural Studies*, **7**, 207–218.

Ilbery, B. and Bowler, I. (1993) 'Land diversion and farm business diversification in EC agriculture', *Nederlandse Geografische Studies*, **172**, 15–27.

Ilbery, B. and Bowler, I. (1998, forthcoming) 'From agricultural productivism to post-productivism', in B. Ilbery (ed.), *The geography of rural change*, Longman, Harlow.

Jedrej, C. and Nuttall, M. (1996) *White settlers. The impact of rural repopulation in Scotland*, Harwood Academic Publishers, Luxembourg.

Jones, O. (1995) 'Lay discourses of the rural: developments and implications for rural studies', *Journal of Rural Studies*, **11**, 35–49.

King, R., Connell, J. and White, P. (eds.) (1995) *Writing across worlds. Literature and migration*, Routledge, London.

Kinsman, P. (1995) 'Landscape, race and national identity', *Area*, **27**, 300–310.

Kneale, J., Lowe, P. and Marsden, T. (1991) 'The conversion of agricultural buildings: an analysis of variable pressures and regulations towards the post-productivist country-side', *ESRC Countryside Change Initiative Working Paper*, **29**, Department of Agricultural Economics, University of Newcastle upon Tyne.

Latour, B. (1987) *Science in action: how to follow scientists and engineers through society*, Open University Press, Milton Keynes.

Law, J. (ed.) (1986) *Power, action and belief: a new sociology of knowledge?*, Routledge and Kegan Paul, London.

Law, J. (1992) 'Notes on the theory of the actor-network: ordering, strategy and hetero-geneity', *Systems Practice*, **5**, 379–393.

Le Heron, R. (1993) *Globalised agriculture: political choice*, Pergamon Press, Oxford.

Lewis, G. (1986) 'Welsh rural community studies: retrospect and prospect', *Cambria*, **13**, 27–40.

Lin-Yuan, Y. and Kosinski, L. (1994) 'The model of place utility revisited', *International Migration*, **32**, 49–70.

Lowe, P., Murdoch, J., Marsden, T., Munton, R. and Flynn, A. (1993) 'Regulating the new rural spaces: the uneven development of land', *Journal of Rural Studies*, **9**, 205–222.

MacKinnon, N., Dryden, J., Bell, C., Fuller, A. and Spearman, M. (1991) 'Pluriactivity, structural change and farm household vulnerability in western Europe', *Sociologia Ruralis*, **31**, 58–71.

Marsden, T. (1996) 'Rural geography trend report: the social and political bases of rural restructuring', *Progress in Human Geography*, **20**, 246–258.

Marsden, T. (1998 forthcoming), 'Rural restructuring: economic perspectives', in B. Ilbery (ed.), *The geography of rural change*, Longman, Harlow.

Marsden, T. and Flynn, A. (1993) 'Servicing the city: contested transitions in the rural realm', *Journal of Rural Studies*, **9**, 201–204.

Marsden, T., Murdoch, J., Lowe, P., Munton, R. and Flynn, A. (1993) *Constructing the countryside*, UCL Press, London.

Marx, L. (1964) *The machine in the garden*, Oxford University Press, New York.

Massey, D. (1991) 'A global sense of place', *Marxism Today*, June, 24–29.

Mormont, M. (1983) 'The emergence of rural struggles and their ideological effects', *International Journal of Urban and Regional Research*, **7**, 559–575.

Mormont, M. (1987) 'Rural nature and urban natures', *Sociologia Ruralis*, **27**, 3–20.

Mormont, M. (1990) 'Who is rural? Or, how to be rural: towards a sociology of the rural', in T. Marsden, P. Lowe and S. Whatmore (eds.), *Rural restructuring*, David Fulton, London, 21–44.

Moscovici, S. (1984) 'The phenomenon of social representations', in R. Farr and S. Moscovici (eds.), *Social representations*, Cambridge University Press, Cambridge, 3–69.

Munton, R. (1995) 'Regulating rural change: property rights, economy and environment – a case study from Cumbria, UK', *Journal of Rural Studies*, **11**, 267–284.

Murdoch, J. (1995) 'Actor-networks and the evolution of economic forms: combining description and explanation in theories of regulation, flexible specialization, and networks', *Environment and Planning A*, **27**, 731–757.

Murdoch, J. and Marsden, T. (1994) *Reconstituting rurality*, UCL Press, London.

Murdoch, J. and Pratt, A. (1993) 'Rural studies: modernism, postmodernism and the "post-rural"', *Journal of Rural Studies*, **9**, 411–427.

Newby, H. (1979) *Green and pleasant land*, Wildwood House, London.

Philo, C. (1992) 'Neglected rural geographies: a review', *Journal of Rural Studies*, **8**, 193–207

Pooley, C. and Turnbull, J. (1996) 'Counterurbanization: the nineteenth century origins of a late-twentieth century phenomenon', *Area*, **28**, 514–524.

Short, J. (1991) *Imagined country*, Routledge, London.

Sibley, D. (1997) 'Endangering the sacred. Nomads, youth cultures and the English countryside', in P. Cloke and J. Little (eds.), *Contested countryside cultures*, Routledge, London, 218–231.

Thrift, N. (1987) 'Introduction: the geography of late Twentieth Century class formation', in N. Thrift and P. Williams (eds.), *Class and space*, Routledge and Kegan Paul, London, 207–253.

Thrift, N. (1996) *Spatial formations*, Sage, London.

Urry, J. (1984) 'Capitalist restructuring, recomposition and the regions', in T. Bradley and P. Lowe (eds.), *Locality and rurality*, Geo Books, Norwich, 45–64.

Urry, J. (1995) 'A middle-class countryside?', in T. Butler and M. Savage (eds.), *Social change and the middle classes*, UCL Press, London, 205–219.

Ward, N. (1990) 'A preliminary analysis of the UK food chain', *Food Policy*, **15**, 439–441.

Ward, N. (1993) 'The agricultural treadmill and the rural environment in the post-productivist era', *Sociologia Ruralis*, **33**, 348–364.

Whatmore, S. (1993a) 'On doing rural research (or breaking the boundaries)', *Environment and Planning A*, **25**, 605–607.

Whatmore, S. (1993b) 'Sustainable rural geographies?', *Progress in Human Geography*, **17**, 538–547.

Whatmore, S., Munton, R., Little, J. and Marsden, T. (1987) 'Towards a typology of farm businesses in contemporary British agriculture', *Sociologia Ruralis*, **27**, 21–37.

White, P. (1995) 'Geography, literature and migration', in R. King, J. Connell and P. White (eds.), *Writing across worlds. Literature and migration*, Routledge, London, 1–19.

White, P. and Jackson, P. (1995) '(Re)theorising population geography', *International Journal of Population Geography*, **1**, 111–123.

Williams, R. (1973) *The country and the city*, Chatto and Windus, London.

Wright, S. (1992) 'Image and analysis: new directions in community studies', in B. Short (ed.), *The English rural community*, Cambridge University Press, Cambridge, 195–217.

2

STUDYING COUNTERURBANISATION AND THE RURAL POPULATION TURNAROUND

TONY CHAMPION

INTRODUCTION

The purpose of this chapter is to set the context for the collection of essays which form the remainder of this book. It can hardly be emphasised too strongly that the study of migration into rural areas should not be undertaken in a vacuum, either purely descriptively in geographical and demographic terms or, even less, from a more theoretical perspective. Behind the process of rural in-migration, there is implicit the idea of urban out-migration, though research (for example, Halfacree 1994) also points to the existence of rural-to-rural migration that can lead to depopulation of certain rural localities while others are repopulating. Deeply embedded in migration theory is Ravenstein's (1885, 1889) 'law' that, for every migration stream (for example, migration into a rural area), there will exist a counterstream, the relative strength of which will determine the scale of net migration gains made by an area as well as influence the extent to which the newcomers replace the pre-existing residents (along with the effect of deaths). Furthermore, migration in general is recognised to be a very diverse process, so diverse as to be labelled a 'chaotic conception' (Champion 1992), and rural in-migration is not reckoned to be an exception to this (Halfacree 1994). This complexity is reflected in the fact that rural in-migrants are by no means homogeneous in terms of such features as distance of moves, types of previous environment, the types of rural areas that they have sought out or found themselves channelled towards, the degree of permanence that they attach to this change of residence, motives behind their moves and – no doubt underlying much of this diversity – personal characteristics including stage in their lives.

The following account explores these contextual considerations in four steps. First of all, it briefly outlines the 'counterurbanisation story', describing the discovery of the rural population turnaround and the almost immediate incorporation of this phenomenon into the study of counterurbanisation and wider urban-system change. It then goes on to examine the ways in which counterurbanisation has been recognised 'on the ground', so to speak; i.e. in terms of the empirical evidence drawn upon in order to show whether or not counterurbanisation has occurred at any particular time and place. This section also assesses the part which rural in-migration itself seems to have played in this, thereby emphasising that counterurbanisation and rural in-migration, whilst closely related, are not synonymous. Next, the chapter provides an overview of the various explanations and theories which have been put forward to account for counterurbanisation, demonstrating how varied these actually are and how complicated the task of analysis is. A key theme in this debate is the extent to which those moving into rural areas are motivated by a desire for 'rurality' in terms of a rural living environment and lifestyle – in essence making a 'new start' that represents a 'clean break' from their past – as opposed to choosing (or even being forced) to move because of a geographical redistribution of elements that have always been important to their quality of life such as jobs, housing, services and safety. The final section develops this discussion by assessing the strengths and weaknesses of research focused specifically on rural in-migrants and by pointing to the need for a comparable degree of attention to be given to other aspects of the migration process, including the process of rural out-migration, the factors influencing urban dwellers contemplating a move, and the extent to which both migrants and non-migrants are responding to circumstances which are largely beyond their control. Attention is focused primarily on British experience, both in recognition of the broader international perspectives taken in the next few chapters and so as to provide context for the case studies in the second half of the book.

THE COUNTERURBANISATION STORY

The counterurbanisation debate has now entered its third decade. It was in 1975 that Calvin L. Beale, a researcher in the Economic Development Division of the United States Department of Agriculture, first drew attention to 'the revival of population growth in non-metropolitan America' (Beale 1975). On the other hand, few commentators might be prepared to suggest that the debate has now 'come of age'. There were always some who considered the whole idea as misconceived, perhaps even stillborn, while there have been many others who have treated the phenomenon as a very temporary affair, perhaps as an idea that has aged prematurely! Yet the debate continues, and indeed it looks like experiencing a new lease of life as a result of the latest observations of renewed rural population growth in the United States and elsewhere, as mentioned below.

Beale's discovery was followed almost immediately by a series of further studies of the situation in the United States and by an almost equally rapid mushrooming of international analyses. Among them, Morrison and Wheeler (1976) confirmed the existence of a 'rural renaissance in America', while Berry (1976) rationalised this phenomenon as 'the counterurbanisation process'. The following year, Vining and Strauss (1977) emphasised the historic nature of these developments by their 'demonstration that the current deconcentration of population in the United States is a clean break with the past', and another year on, Vining and Kontuly (1978) extended the debate internationally by finding plenty of evidence of actual or incipient 'population dispersal from major metropolitan regions' for eleven other countries. These results prompted Fielding (1982) to make a closer and more rigorous examination which led him to confirm the widespread nature of 'counterurbanisation in Western Europe'.

Merely a cursory exploration of this early literature, and of the many other contributions over these few years (see Champion 1989 for a fuller review), is sufficient to indicate the sense of excitement which these observations generated. For many, these trends were seen as heralding a new era in population redistribution and as constituting the logical accompaniment of a major societal transformation that was getting underway. Berry (1976: 17) announced that:

'A turning point has been reached in the American urban experience. Counterurbanisation has replaced urbanisation as the dominant force shaping the nation's settlement patterns'.

According to Bourne and Logan (1976: 136), 'Urbanisation in Australia and Canada appears to have entered a new period'. In the words of Vining and Kontuly (1978: 50):

'We seem to be confronted with no less than a breakdown in Clark's "law of concentration", of all laws of population geography, surely the most enduring'.

Moreover, in terms of this phenomenon being part of wider societal developments, Beale (1975: 14) himself referred to the revival of rural areas as:

'another aspect of the demographic transition..., in which the distribution of population is no longer controlled by an unbridled impetus to urbanisation'.

This is an idea that could be developed further, now that the period since the mid 1960s is seen by some as witnessing the 'second demographic transition' and 'the demographic revolution' (McLoughlin 1991; van de Kaa 1987). More generally, these changes fitted in very neatly with contemporary notions of a shift from an industrial to some form of 'post-industrial' society, as they appeared to provide a physical and readily measurable manifestation of more complex and deep-seated changes believed to be taking place in economic and social structures.

Yet this notion of revolutionary change did not go unchallenged at the time, and subsequent events led to doubts about the durability of the phenomenon. The main theoretical challenge came from those who did not recognise the observed trends as being any significant departure from past trends. Early on in the history of the debate, Gordon (1979) challenged the 'clean break' interpretation of United States trends on the grounds that the Vining/Strauss results were not incompatible with continued metropolitan spread, as the highest rates of hinterland growth were found for urban cores experiencing the highest rates of population loss. Meanwhile, European research found rather limited evidence of a specifically rural turnaround and gave more emphasis to the continuity from the 1950s and early 1960s displayed by many of the aspects of urban change recorded in the 1970s, particularly in terms of the relatively faster growth of medium-sized towns and in terms of ideas concerning the evolution of large metropolitan areas through 'stages of urban development' (see, for instance, Hall and Hay 1980; Klaassen *et al.* 1981; van den Berg *et al.* 1982).

The durability of the counterurbanisation tendency was called into question in the 1980s, with the amassing of evidence of a slowdown in the pace of population deconcentration and of a return to faster metropolitan growth for a number of countries. This was most notably the case in the United States, where turnaround turned into 'turnbackaround' (Beale and Fuguitt 1985; Engels 1986; Richter 1985), with the result that by the second half of the 1980s the pattern of population growth rates across the metropolitan/non-metropolitan spectrum more closely resembled that of the 1960s than of the 1970s (Frey 1993). An updating of the Vining and Kontuly study to cover the first half of the 1980s revealed a similar somersaulting of the original 'metropolitan migration reversal' for the majority of the countries covered in the survey (Cochrane and Vining 1988). In the case of Britain, research showed that the rate of rural population growth had peaked in the early 1970s and, although remaining positive, had slumped markedly by the early 1980s (Champion 1987).

These developments did little to resolve the counterurbanisation debate. As outlined in the concluding chapter of Champion (1989), academic commentators were divided on the nature and significance of the phenomenon. For some, the 1970s had constituted a temporary anomaly brought about by a chance combination of events that had nothing to do with a long-term transformation of the settlement system. At the other extreme, for those who subscribed to the revolutionary perspective it was the decade of the 1980s that was anomalous, being viewed as merely an interruption to the new population deconcentration tendency brought about largely by the economic recession gripping the world at that time. Yet others drew on this latter idea to argue for a cycle-based interpretation of recent events, suggesting that settlement systems were now subject to a rather even balance of centripetal and centrifugal forces, with the relative strength of the two altering over time (Berry 1988; Champion 1988; Mera 1988; see also Champion and Illeris 1990).

The latest twist in this saga is provided by evidence of another rural population revival, notably in the United States but also in Britain. In the words of Johnson and Beale (1994: 655):

> 'Population growth was widespread in the nonmetropolitan areas of the United States during the early 1990s. ...it is premature to conclude that the renewed population growth in nonmetro areas first noted in the 1970s has ended'.

According to Nucci and Long (1995), the rate of net migration for non-metropolitan America, using the latest (1993) definition, switched from an annual rate of −0.28 percent for 1980–1990 to one of +0.48 percent for 1990–1994, an impressive scale of renewed turnaround. For Britain it has been shown that a further surge in rural population took place in the mid 1980s until it was strangled by a major collapse in labour and housing markets in 1988/1989 and that the scale of migration out of metropolitan areas rose again subsequently (Champion 1994, 1996). Moreover, the planning debates raging in mid-1990s Britain have largely been provoked by expectations of renewed metropolitan overspill (see, for instance, Breheny and Hall 1996). These developments would seem to ensure the continuation of the counterurbanisation story and to justify further efforts at recording and analysing population redistribution trends within a counterurbanisation framework.

IDENTIFYING COUNTERURBANISATION

While the counterurbanisation debate would still seem to be alive, there is less unanimity about how well it is. Perhaps the key problem is the lack of clear and universally agreed 'rules' about how counterurbanisation should be recognised 'on the ground'. Though researchers have in the past been criticised for giving more attention to describing patterns than to exploring processes (see, for instance, Sant and Simons 1993), it is vital that links should be made between what is considered to be counterurbanisation in conceptual terms and how its existence can be tested operationally. The purpose of this section is to review this specific element of the debate and, in so doing, to examine more closely the relationship between counterurbanisation and migration into rural areas.

Berry's original definition must provide the starting point, not just for reasons of historical narrative but because it strongly shaped the way in which research on this topic developed. According to Berry (1976: 17):

> 'Counterurbanisation is a process of population deconcentration; it implies a movement from a state of more concentration to a state of less concentration'.

Despite the explicit mention of 'process', it is not difficult to understand why many subsequent studies were concerned primarily with measuring trends in the degree of population concentration, nor why measures like the Hoover index of concentration were adopted for some of the earliest tests, notably by Vining and Strauss (1977).

The central weakness of Berry's basic definition is that it provides no guidance as to how concentration and deconcentration are to be recognised and, as such, is no more than a starting point. The most fundamental issue is the spatial scale for which any test of trends in level of population concentration should be measured. Vining and Strauss (1977), in a sense, dodged this problem by looking at several different levels in the United States's geographical hierarchy: broad regional divisions, states, economic subregions, state economic areas, and counties. Berry himself provides some indicators in his seminal paper, but stops short of setting down explicit rules. In recognising the existence of counterurbanisation, he refers most consistently to the metropolitan-area framework, noting the slower growth of metropolitan areas than the nation as a whole, the rapid growth in smaller metropolitan areas, and 'the reversals in migration trends in the largest metropolitan areas and in the furthermost peripheral counties' (Berry 1976: 21). Yet, as part of this depiction of the major dimensions of population change in early 1970s America, he also cites the broad regional shifts to the South and the West, the loss of population from the central cities of the larger metropolitan areas, and the 'rapid growth … in exurban counties located outside SMSAs as currently defined, but with substantial daily commuting to metropolitan areas' (Berry 1976: 21).

Most subsequent work has, either explicitly or implicitly, built on Berry's antithesis of urbanisation and counterurbanisation and adopted a reverse version of the definitions traditionally used by geographers to recognise the population concentration that is associated with urbanisation. Thus counterurbanisation is deemed to be taking place when the proportion of the population living in urban places is falling and/or when the proportion of the urban population living in larger urban places is declining because of the faster growth of medium-sized and small urban places. This approach is embraced by most of the United States studies, helped by the official definitions of metropolitan and non-metropolitan areas, with comparisons being made between these two types of areas and also between metropolitan areas grouped by population size. The same principle was adopted by Fielding (1982) in his study of Western Europe, in which counterurbanisation was recognised as the prevailing tendency in the situations where the measure of regional population change (normally net migration rate) was negatively correlated with the measure of the region's urban status (normally the region's overall population density in the absence of properly defined urban places). Similar approaches were used in the nine national case studies brought together in Champion (1989).

While this definition may seem clear-cut, however, the task of operationalising it comes up against the thorny problem of delineating individual urban places. The task of identifying on the ground where one settlement ends and another begins has proved increasingly difficult even for studies of urbanisation, as the built-up areas of individual towns and cities have spread well beyond their ancient walls and often in discontinuous fashion. In counterurbanisation research, this challenge has taken on much greater significance because it is believed to be necessary to demonstrate the existence of a 'turnaround' or 'clean break' as opposed to the wider geographical spread of the traditional forms of urban growth known as suburbanisation and metropolitan decentralisation.

Studies of the United States begin with the great advantage of the officially defined metropolitan areas. For countries without the benefit of such frameworks defined in functional terms and on a comprehensive basis, it has often been felt necessary to undertake special regionalisations, as in the case of Standard Metropolitan Labour Areas and Local Labour Market Areas for Great Britain (see, respectively, Hall 1971 and Coombes *et al.* 1982) and Functional Urban Regions for Western Europe (Hall and Hay 1980; van den Berg *et al.*

1982). Even then, however, problems can arise due to the fact that on the ground there is usually a transition zone between the metropolitan and the non-metropolitan rather than a clear line. Problems can also occur because the definitions tend to lag behind events on the ground, both in terms of the boundaries round individual metropolitan areas and as a result of the emergence of new metropolitan areas out of formerly non-metropolitan territory. As a result, whilst in theory it is common to draw a distinction between more peripheral growth within metropolitan areas and that outside their boundaries (termed respectively 'decentralisation' and 'deconcentration' by Robert and Randolph 1983), in practice it is extremely difficult to do this in any meaningful way. Similarly, where urban centres are relatively tightly packed and their commuting zones overlap, one cannot confidently assign new population growth to one particular metropolitan area on the basis of it occurring on its side of what must be a rather arbitrary line.

Rather less attention has been given to the problem of distinguishing counter-urbanisation from population redistribution at the other end of the spatial scale, namely broad regional shifts. The crucial point is that population shifts between macro regions can result from counterurbanisation, but the former should not be equated with the latter. In the case of the United States, for instance, it has never been suggested that the westward shift of population from the more heavily populated North East is symptomatic of over a century of counterurbanisation! An equally graphic example is provided by Halliday and Coombes (1995), who argue cogently that not all migration from South East England to Devon can be considered as counterurbanisation, given that many of the newcomers to Devon are moving to its largest city (Plymouth) and a proportion of these will have previously lived in a smaller city or more rural area. Once again, it is vitally important to examine population shifts within a geographical framework which represents the settlement system in functional terms and in this way to identify whether shifts are indeed occurring down the urban hierarchy. In this sense, counterurbanisation can be seen as a process operating at a spatial scale intermediate between local decentralisation within metropolitan areas and population redistribution between macro-economic regions and, as pointed out by Long (1981), it was at this level that the United States experience after 1970 was different to that before then.

The recognition of counterurbanisation as an essentially intermediate-scale phenomenon has an important implication for research that has not been widely appreciated until recently, namely that the process can be expected to take place within each macro region separately and that the latter should form the principal frame of reference. All too often, tests for the existence of counterurbanisation have been undertaken at the national scale, but in the terms just described this makes sense only if the national urban system is highly integrated, as is most likely in a relatively small country or one with a highly centralised pattern of organisation and a single dominant capital city. From the early days of the counterurbanisation debate, most studies of the United States have included an examination of trends separately for at least the three broad regional divisions of North, South and West, though this approach seems to have been adopted more for descriptive purposes than for a more accurate portrayal of the settlement system. Coombes *et al.* (1989) set out with the explicit goal of illustrating differences in population redistribution trends between the various regional urban systems of Britain and Italy, while studies of other countries have also pointed to the uneven geographical incidence of counterurbanisation, notably those on Australia (Hugo 1989; Sant and Simons 1993). This perspective has been incorporated in the 'differential urbanisation' model put forward by Geyer and Kontuly (1993).

The operational definition of counterurbanisation outlined above also has implications for studying rural population change. If the latter is being examined in terms of the counterurbanisation phenomenon, the 'rural' should be taken to refer only to areas lying beyond the boundaries of urban/metropolitan regions, i.e. not forming part of the commuting hinterland of any settlement which is considered urban or metropolitan. In the United States context, these areas were dubbed the 'intermetropolitan periphery' by Berry (1970), while similarly in studies of Britain and Europe led by Peter Hall these areas were either 'unclassified' or treated as 'non-metropolitan' (Hall 1971; Hall and Hay 1980; see also Spence *et al.* 1982). The CURDS Functional Regionalisation of Britain adopted a rather different approach, in that the whole of national space was divided into Local Labour Market Areas (LLMAs) on the basis of employment nodes and commuting flows and LLMAs were termed Urban Regions or Rural Areas according to whether or not they met the criteria specified for being considered 'urban' (Coombes *et al.* 1982). The CURDS approach also differed from previous studies in restricting the term 'metropolitan' to those parts of Britain where two or more Functional Regions were more closely linked together by commuting flows (through the effect of a 'dominant' city) than elsewhere in the country, which was termed 'Freestanding Britain'. In counterurbanisation studies, therefore, the term 'rural' cannot refer to areas that, while having the appearance of countryside in physical terms, are part of the commuting hinterlands of urban centres, but instead is restricted to areas which lie outside these commutersheds and will normally be in locations that are relatively distant from these urban centres. The importance of this point is recognised by Boyle (1995) through distinguishing rural districts lying at least 65 km from a metropolitan county boundary from those which were less remote.

Some of the complexity of identifying counterurbanisation on the ground, hinted at in this discussion of definitions, is well demonstrated by Halliday and Coombes (1995). They distinguish three 'alternative models of counterurbanisation': anti-metropolitan, anti-urban and pro-rural. They use the term 'anti-metropolitan' to refer to movements of people out of the CURDS Metropolitan Regions, i.e. out of LLMAs that are parts of conurbations dominated by a major city and into Freestanding Britain. Meanwhile, 'anti-urban' moves are those involving a move down the urban hierarchy, i.e. from a higher-status

LLMA to a smaller one. Finally, 'pro-rural' is defined as movement between areas distinguished on a more local, 'bricks and mortar' basis; for example, from a densely built-up area into a more loosely developed area – a move that could be considered a form of suburbanisation and could take place within a particular LLMA but not necessarily so. The important point to note here is that these characterisations are not mutually exclusive; on the contrary, any single move can be classified on each of these three sets of criteria. In relation to the foregoing discussion, it is the 'anti-urban' definition that accords with what has been shown above to be the generally accepted approach to counterurbanisation, whereas the 'anti-metropolitan' definition resembles most closely the shift between macro-economic regions and the 'pro-rural' is essentially that of suburbanisation and metropolitan decentralisation, despite not being limited to shorter-distance moves. Though apparently rigorous and clear cut, this three-fold categorisation does serve to highlight the scope for confusion in counterurbanisation studies, not least because the term 'rural' is used here in its physical sense as opposed to the economic sense conveyed when used in the context of LLMAs called Rural Areas and as normally meant in the idea of 'rural population turnaround'.

The reader might be forgiven for thinking that the discussion by now must have exhausted the definitional problems associated with the term 'counterurbanisation', but this is not the case. So far, we have dealt principally with the geographical framework needed to identify counterurbanisation, leaving aside the question of what is to be measured. Note that, during the above discussion, the emphasis has switched away from talking about the redistribution of population between places as measured in terms of differentials in overall population change rates and towards a focus on the migration of individuals between one type of place and another. This prompts questions as to whether it is proper to consider certain types of moves as 'counterurban' or 'counterurbanising' and, if so, what relevance this has to the identification of 'counterurbanisation' as a phenomenon. Closely linked is the issue of how a 'rural population turnaround' is to be recognised, and what role migration into rural areas plays in this.

The most straightforward approach to these issues, to my mind, is to try and disentangle 'pattern' from 'process' and tackle the former first. The majority of the counterurbanisation literature uses aggregate statistics relating to whether the population is becoming more or less concentrated, preferably adopting the recommended geographical framework outlined above. It could be argued that it is overall population change that should be used for measurement rather than merely the migration component. For one thing, this would conform to the approach generally taken in the study of urbanisation where it has been conventional to talk principally in terms of 'rural depopulation' and 'urban population growth'. This is because, as with urbanisation, there are potentially three direct causes: not just migration but also natural change and the redefinition of 'urban areas'. For another, the original terminology did refer specifically to the 'rural *population* turnaround'. Nevertheless, in the counterurbanisation literature, there has been a strong emphasis on the use of migration data, and indeed in most cases an actual turnaround can be found only for the migration component and not for overall population change. In the United States, for instance, natural increase ensured that the non-metropolitan areas were already growing in the 1960s, and this is by no means an isolated case (Champion 1989). It is, however, probably a mistake to allow mere words like 'turnaround' and 'clean break' to determine the research strategy. From the viewpoint of the population geographer, there is merit in seeing overall population redistribution as the starting point – the 'thing' to be explained – and everything else, including migration, as the potential explanations for the observed trends. This also has the advantage of highlighting the primary role of migration in producing these patterns – a role which has become more important as traditionally above-average levels of natural increase in rural areas have waned or been replaced by natural decrease, thereby working against counterurban shifts in overall population distribution.

In sum, therefore, the definition of counterurbanisation is by no means a trivial task. If counterurbanisation is to be considered as a process, it is not sensible to provide a definition until its dynamics are fully understood. While a better understanding will no doubt prompt us to change our perspectives on studying population change, nevertheless there is a strong case to be made for adopting interim definitions as the basis for monitoring trends in population distribution. As outlined above, Berry's basic definition of counterurbanisation – couched in terms purely of population deconcentration – needs to be qualified by reference to a geographical framework rooted in urban-systems theory. Counterurbanisation is then to be recognised as the direct opposite of urbanisation, i.e. involving a fall in the proportion of the total population living in urban places and/or a fall in the proportion of the urban population living in the larger cities. In its perfect form, there is a negative correlation between a place's population change rate and its status in the urban hierarchy, where the word 'place' is used in the sense of an area that is relatively self-contained in terms of people's regular daily mobility and will normally be an urban-centred region. The 'rural population turnaround' is thus seen merely as part of a system-wide pattern of change, with the phrase referring to a switch in relative terms from being the slowest to the fastest growing part of this system. In order to minimise confusion between pattern and process, the patterns should be described, initially at least, purely in terms of changing population distribution without reference to migration, the latter being treated as part of the explanation. In this approach, as will be shown below, migration into rural areas is seen as a necessary, but not a sufficient, condition for counterurbanisation.

EXPLAINING COUNTERURBANISATION

Following the distinction drawn above between studying pattern and studying process, this section concentrates on the latter, looking at the several different levels of engaging in the analysis of counterurbanisation, the separate explanations which have been put forward to account for it, and the alternative interpretations which have been made of the nature and significance of counterurbanisation and the rural population turnaround. Because these theoretical and conceptual issues are developed in more detail in later chapters, the treatment here can be relatively brief, with the chief aim being merely to provide a framework within which the themes raised in the subsequent discussions can be situated. Moreover, reflecting the artificial nature of a pattern/process split and the need for conceptual issues to inform the study of the phenomenon on the ground, some of the themes have already been flagged up in the previous section. It will therefore be no surprise to find that the debates over the causes of counterurbanisation are even more varied and complex than the essentially methodological questions described above.

If, as suggested at the end of the previous section, counterurbanisation is defined in terms of population redistribution, then the most direct form of explanation is to analyse it in accounting terms by reference to the components of population change. This task can begin with the demographic components of deaths, births and migration, with the testing of hypotheses that could explain the switch from concentration to deconcentration across the urban system. The logical explanations would be a decrease in deaths at the lower levels of the urban hierarchy relative to the larger metropolitan areas, or an increase in births, or a change in migration patterns away from the latter areas to the former. In practice, research shows that, while natural change has contributed in some instances, it is the migration component that has dominated the phenomenon and, not surprisingly, that has attracted the most attention from researchers (see, for instance, the review in Champion 1989).

The direct accounting approach can also be adopted for the more detailed examination of the migration component of counterurbanisation and the rural population turnaround. There are a number of ways of doing this. The most fundamental point to make is that, while the migratory element of population change is normally expressed in terms of net migration (and often calculated as a residual because of the paucity of data on migration compared with births, deaths and total population), there is no such thing as a 'net migrant'. Net migration is merely the balance between the numbers of newcomers to an area and the numbers quitting it over a given time period. Once individual migrants are recognised, it is but a small step to disaggregate migration flows in terms of some classification. Alternative criteria include distance of move, the motivations for movement and characteristics of the migrants such as age, ethnicity, labour market position and socio-economic indicator.

The vast majority of studies seeking to explain counterurbanisation focus on the characteristics and motivations of people moving into more rural areas. In the British research (see especially Cross 1990), three specific groups of migrants are identified as constituting the largest elements of such in-migration. One is 'retirement migrants', though this heading can be modified to include a wide range of migrations including people who are not working or seeking employment, such as 'drop-outs' and others who have given up the idea of getting a job, at least for the present. Secondly are those in the labour market who are moving to be close to a job in the destination area or who are actively searching for employment there – potentially a wide diversity of people reflecting the variety of local economies, but almost by definition being households headed by people of 'working age' and biased towards more mobile groups, particularly those who can most readily find appropriate housing. The third main group comprises 'commuters' in the sense that, though moving house, they continue to work in their previous home area. This group can, of course, be expanded to include those who have moved over a longer distance to a new job based in a higher-order settlement but who choose to live in a more rural location. It, too, can be very varied, including not just those who have actively sought out a less urban living environment but also commuters who would have preferred a more urban place to live if they could have found suitable housing at a price they could afford. Technically, of course, this third group should not be included if the 'clean break' view of counterurbanisation is taken.

The next step in explanation, moving beyond the accounting-type methods of analysis just described, is to examine the factors which have prompted migratory growth at the lower end of the settlement hierarchy. It is at this stage that the full complexity of the task of understanding counterurbanisation becomes apparent. In the first place, questionnaire surveys of newcomers have discovered a wide range of reasons for moving. Though they can be grouped under headings like housing, employment, environment, and access to new partner/family/ friends or services, each of these categories contains considerable variety and many respondents cite more than one reason (see Halfacree 1994 for a review). At the same time, researchers have uncovered a large number of ways in which changes have taken place in what is probably best termed broadly the 'decision-making environment', including changes in the nature of places (housing, jobs, services, living environment, etc.) as well as changes in the socio-demographic structure of the population and in the sum of personal attitudes and aspirations. Table 2.1 shows a list of the explanations most commonly mentioned in a set of nine national case studies of counterurbanisation undertaken in the late 1980s – 17 in total, though admittedly including some of the 'accounting' type mentioned above.

This two-fold distinction between what may be called 'motivational' and 'environmental' research perspectives in the counterurbanisation literature is reflected in a number of dichotomies recognised by previous studies. In his original study, Berry (1976) placed great emphasis on the role of residential preferences in drawing people into non-metropolitan areas, but he also recognised the importance of facilitating factors which allowed more people to realise their aspirations than in the past, such as improved transport and communication links, the wider spread of services and the changing distribution of employment – factors which are beyond the control of individual people and are, in a sense, imposed by other agencies. These dichotomies include distinctions

TABLE 2.1 Explanations for the migration turnaround

1. Expansion of commuting fields round employment centres.
2. Emergence of scale economies and social problems in large cities.
3. Concentration of rural population into local urban centres.
4. Reduction in the stock of potential out-migrants living in rural areas.
5. Availability of government subsidies for rural activities.
6. Growth of employment in particular localised industries such as mining, defence and tourism.
7. Restructuring of manufacturing industry and the associated growth of branch plants.
8. Improvements in transport and communications technology.
9. Improvement of education, health and other infrastructure in rural areas.
10. Growth of employment in the public sector and personal services.
11. Success of explicitly spatial government policies.
12. Growth of state welfare payments, private pensions and other benefits.
13. Acceleration of retirement migration.
14. Change in residential preferences of working-age people and entrepreneurs.
15. Changes in age structure and household size and composition.
16. Effect of economic recession on rural-urban and return migration.
17. First round in a new cyclic pattern of capital investment in property and business.

Source: Champion 1989: 236–237, reproduced with permission from Edward Arnold.

between 'people-led' and 'job-led' explanations (Moseley 1984), between 'individual' and 'structural' explanations (Perry *et al.* 1986), between 'environmental/ quality of life' and 'economic' explanations (Jones *et al.* 1986), and between 'voluntarist' and 'non-voluntarist' explanations (Grafton and Bolton 1987). In this terminology there is more than a hint that, while recognising that specific moves from one place to another are unlikely to be 'forced' upon people but are the results of decisions made 'freely' by the individuals concerned, a significant part of the aggregate movement is a response to essentially autonomous changes in economy and society at large. There are clearly several alternative ways of viewing the underlying nature of counterurbanisation and, moreover, in each of these perspectives the individual factors do not fall neatly under one or other of the two headings but are ranged across the spectrum from one extreme to the other.

STUDYING MIGRATION INTO RURAL AREAS IN THE CONTEXT OF COUNTERURBANISATION

The underlying message of this chapter is that it is important to situate the results of studying migration into rural areas within the broader context of the counter-urbanisation debate, in order to achieve a balanced and robust understanding of the evolving patterns of population distribution. It is this line of thinking which has stimulated the way in which this book has been put together, beginning with the various perspectives on counterurbanisation itself and then going on to examine the results of recent research on rural in-migration. This final section therefore provides the justification for this form of contextualisation.

The principal argument is that counterurbanisation, as defined in this chapter, is not synonymous with migration into rural areas. The term refers to a change in the distribution of population in which migration into rural areas plays a part. There are two main differences. One is that the existence of migration into rural areas does not mean that counterurbanisation is taking place, because it may be that other factors are outweighing the effect of this migration on population distribution. Even during the days of most rapid rural depopulation, there were usually some people moving into the rural areas, whether newcomers or return migrants. Similarly, people are continuing to move out of rural areas even during the periods of strongest counterurbanisation.

The second difference is that rural population growth forms only part of the population redistribution pattern known as counterurbanisation. The latter refers to the shifts in population down the urban hierarchy from larger places to smaller places, not just to the relative rates of growth of the urban and rural aggregates. These two aspects represent the two parts of the definition of counterurbanisation identified above. In numerical terms, the population shifts between the different parts of the urban system are, in most of the world's more urbanised countries, much larger than the net redistribution between urban and rural areas or between metropolitan and non-metropolitan regions.

Recent research on Great Britain (Champion and Atkins 1996) can be used to illustrate these two points. Using Boyle's (1995) classification of local authority districts into 13 types, extended to include Scotland, this analyses the data on migration within Britain provided by the 1991 Census. In rather crude terms, this classification can be treated as a representation of the national settlement hierarchy, ranging from Inner London boroughs at one end to most remote rural districts (MRRDs) at the other. The latter comprise those 'remoter mainly rural districts' that are situated more than 65 km from metropolitan areas (these being defined as Greater London, the six English metropolitan counties and the Central Clydeside Conurbation) and is the category which is of prime interest for counterurbanisation-oriented studies of migration into rural areas.

On the basis of this framework, the research reveals a clear counterurbanisation relationship in net migration rates for the year leading up to the Census (Table 2.2). In particular, the greatest relative and absolute net loss in migrants for 1990/1991 was for Inner London (−1.24 percent and −31 009 people) and the greatest gain was for the MRRDs (+0.77 percent and +36 450 people). There is a clean break between the aggregate losses of the six most urban types comprising the metropolitan areas and the non-metropolitan cities and the net gains of the remaining seven non-metropolitan district types. There is also a fairly clear negative relationship between the net migration rates for the district types and their position in the settlement hierarchy, with progressively lower rates of net loss for Inner London, the principal metropolitan cities and non-metropolitan cities and generally rising rates of net gains through the bottom seven types shown (Table 2.2).

At the same time, however, it should be noted that the total picture is much

TABLE 2.2 Population changes resulting from within-Britain migration, 1990–1991, by district types

District type	Population 1991	Net migration 1990–1991	%
1 Inner London	2 504 451	−31 009	−1.24
2 Outer London	4 175 248	−21 159	−0.51
3 Principal metropolitan cities	3 922 670	−26 311	−0.67
4 Other metropolitan districts	8 427 861	−6 900	−0.08
5 Large non-metropolitan cities	3 493 284	−14 040	−0.40
6 Small non-metropolitan cities	1 861 351	−7 812	−0.42
7 Industrial districts	7 475 515	7 194	0.10
8 Districts with new towns	2 838 258	2 627	0.09
9 Resort, port and retirement	3 591 972	17 736	0.49
10 Urban/rural mixed	7 918 701	19 537	0.25
11 Remote urban/rural	2 302 925	13 665	0.59
12 Remote rural	1 645 330	10 022	0.61
13 Most remote rural	4 731 278	36 450	0.77

Note: 'metropolitan' includes the Central Clydeside Conurbation.
Source: Champion and Atkins 1996. Calculated from 1991 Census SMS and LBS/SAS (ESRC/JISC purchase), Crown copyright.

more fluid than these net migration statistics suggest. The MRRDs' net gain of 36 450 migrants shown in Table 2.2 represents the balance between 140 481 newcomers and 104 031 people leaving during the year. In other words, for every four people moving into this lowest level of Britain's settlement hierarchy, there were approximately three leaving it for places further up the hierarchy. The analysis also finds that the 140 481 arrivals in the MRRDs comprised less than one in five of all moves down the settlement hierarchy (numbering 771 274) and that the net gain of 36 450 by the MRRDs accounted for only 22.4 percent of the net down-the-hierarchy migration shifts (amounting to 162 822 in all). Clearly, any analysis of counterurbanisation must recognise that the overall shift of population into the most rural areas is much smaller than the number of people moving into these areas, and also note that in both net and gross terms the movements into the MRRDs form only part of the wider counterurbanisation tendency.

This complexity can be highlighted by a more detailed examination of the migration links between these rural areas and the rest of Britain (Champion and Atkins 1996). Given the fact that the greatest net losses and gains are recorded by the two ends of the settlement hierarchy, there is a clear temptation to link the two and conclude that the main element in counterurbanisation comprises migrants moving directly from large cities into rural areas, but this is not the case. As shown in Table 2.3, only one in five (19.8 percent) of the people moving into the MRRDs in 1990–1991 had moved from an address in 'metropolitan Britain' (as defined above), with a further one-fifth moving out of the non-metropolitan cities and fully three-fifths hailing from lower levels of the hierarchy including

TABLE 2.3 Sources of gross and net in-migration to Britain's most remote rural districts, 1990–1991

Origin district type	Gross in-migration		Net in-migration	
	Number	% total	Number	% total
Metropolitan Britain	27 856	19.8	12 472	34.2
Inner London	5 019	3.6	2 009	5.5
Outer London	8 246	5.9	4 617	12.7
Principal metropolitan cities	5 186	3.7	2 055	5.6
Other metropolitan districts	9 405	6.7	3 791	10.4
Non-metropolitan cities	27 184	19.3	5 011	13.7
Large non-metropolitan cities	16 061	11.4	3 513	9.6
Small non-metropolitan cities	11 123	7.9	1 498	4.1
Other non-metropolitan districts	85 441	60.8	18 967	52.0
Industrial districts	16 629	11.8	4 807	13.2
Districts with new towns	7 589	5.4	2 484	6.8
Resort, port and retirement	14 557	10.4	947	2.6
Urban/rural mixed	26 953	19.2	9 065	24.9
Remote urban/rural	12 430	8.8	585	1.6
Remote rural	7 283	5.2	1 079	3.0
All origin types	*140 481*	*100.0*	*36 450*	*100.0*

Note: 'metropolitan' includes the Central Clydeside Conurbation.
Source: Champion and Atkins 1996. Calculated from 1991 Census SMS and LBS/SAS (ESRC/JISC purchase), Crown copyright.

mixed urban/rural districts and rural districts within 65 km of a metropolitan area. Even in terms of net migration, metropolitan Britain was contributing barely a third of the MRRDs' net gain, with the remaining two-thirds coming through balances with the other non-metropolitan areas. The migratory growth of rural Britain is thus seen to be merely part of a rather general 'cascade' of population down the settlement hierarchy, characterised by a very complex interlinkage of individual migrations up as well as down the scale (Champion and Atkins 1996).

Results such as these (see also Boyle 1995) help us to appreciate both the strengths and the weaknesses of using studies of migration into rural areas for obtaining a better understanding of the counterurbanisation tendency in population redistribution. In-migrants clearly form the most important single component of counterurbanisation, so examination of their characteristics and motivations can provide much insight into the process, particularly if studies look back at their previous residential histories and the circumstances which led to departure from their previous addresses. Moreover, in the context of the cascading pattern noted above, there is great potential value in following these linkages further back in order to see how the moves into the rural areas related to other moves down the hierarchy, i.e. those made by the people who moved into the spaces that they vacated and the nature of this relationship in terms of choice and constraints on both out-migrants and in-migrants.

At the same time, however, there are two aspects vital to the understanding of counterurbanisation trends and processes that the study of the rural in-migrants cannot tackle. Out-migration from rural areas is one of these for, given the considerable numbers of out-migrants relative to in-migrants noted above, this could be a major determinant of trends in the overall rate of rural population growth. Here, too, valuable insights could be achieved by identifying the linkages between in-migration and out-migration; for instance, comparing the characteristics and reasons for moving of the two streams and also looking at the nature of the relationship in terms of the extent to which the departures were prompted or facilitated by the inward movement.

The other crucial, but largely neglected, aspect of counterurbanisation studies is the phenomenon of non-migration, which by definition cannot be explored by surveys of people moving into rural areas. In recent years opinion polls have been recording that between 70 and 85 percent of British people would prefer to live in the countryside, yet at any one time only a relatively small proportion do live in the countryside (the proportion varying according to the definition of countryside adopted) and in any one year only a small fraction of those not living in the countryside manage to move there. The obvious conclusion to draw is that people vary in their ability to indulge their preferences, either because there are strong ties which bind them to their existing area or because they are constrained in their freedom of movement, notably by the limited openings for migration and by weaknesses in their competitive position (including inadequate information). Research on the areas of origin further up the settlement hierarchy would help to explain the characteristics of rural in-migrants and also improve our understanding of why the number of people moving into rural areas fluctuates considerably over time. Similar arguments can be made for the study of people who are not moving out of rural areas, given the importance of the out-migration component and the extent to which variations in its level could affect the scale and nature of rural population change.

CONCLUSION

The aim of this chapter has been to provide the counterurbanisation context for the study of migration into rural areas. Arising from this discussion, three points, in particular, need to borne in mind in approaching the rest of the book. In the first place, the counterurbanisation debate is still very much alive, not least because of the evidence of renewed rural revival. Secondly, leading on from this, is the apparent complexity of the counterurbanisation phenomenon, reflected in the plethora of explanations that have been suggested for it and the continuing disagreements about its nature and significance. Finally, while migration into rural areas is the most obvious feature of counterurbanisation, a full understanding of the latter cannot be achieved without reference to all the migration linkages between the various levels of the settlement hierarchy nor without discovering the factors that influence whether or not any particular form of migration takes place. As the next chapters of this book confirm, the counter-urbanisation story is still unfolding, though at present it is difficult to conjecture whether or not it will eventually have a happy ending!

ACKNOWLEDGEMENTS

This chapter includes results generated by the ESRC Census Programme project on migration between metropolitan and non-metropolitan areas in Britain (award reference number H507255132), using data from the 1991 Census Special Migration Statistics and Local Base Statistics, both Crown copyright, and accessed from the ESRC/JISC Census purchase held at Manchester Computing. The data extraction was performed by David Atkins, of Newcastle University Geography Department, using software developed by Oliver Duke-Williams, of Leeds University Geography Department. David Atkins was also responsible for most of the data manipulation.

REFERENCES

Beale, C. (1975) 'The revival of population growth in non-metropolitan America', *Report*, ERS 605, Economic Research Service, United States Department of Agriculture, Washington DC.

Beale, C. and Fuguitt, G. (1985) Metropolitan and non-metropolitan growth differentials in the United States since 1980, *Working Paper*, 85–6, Center for Demography and Ecology, Madison, Wisconsin.

Berry, B. (1970) 'The geography of the United States in the year 2000', *Transactions of the Institute of British Geographers*, **51**, 21–54.

Berry, B. (1976) 'The counterurbanisation process: urban America since 1970', in B. Berry (ed.), *Urbanisation and counterurbanisation*, Sage, Beverly Hills, California, 17–30.

Berry, B. (1988) 'Migration reversals in perspective: the long-wave evidence', *International Regional Science Review*, **11**, 245–252.

Bourne, L. and Logan, M. (1976) 'Changing urbanisation patterns at the margin: the examples of Australia and Canada', in B. Berry (ed.), *Urbanisation and counterurbanisation*, Sage, Beverly Hills, California, 111–143.

Boyle, P. (1995) 'Rural in-migration in England and Wales, 1980–1981', *Journal of Rural Studies*, **11**, 65–78.

Breheny, M. and Hall, P. (1996) 'Four million households – where will they go?', *Town and Country Planning*, **65**, 39–41.

Champion, A. (1987) 'Recent changes in the pace of population deconcentration in Britain', *Geoforum*, **18**, 379–407.

Champion, A. (1988) 'The reversal of the migration turnaround: resumption of traditional trends?', *International Regional Science Review*, **11**, 253–260.

Champion, A. (1989) (ed.) *Counterurbanisation: The Changing Pace and Nature of Population Deconcentration*, Edward Arnold, London.

Champion, A. (1992) 'Migration in Britain: research challenges and prospects', in A. Champion and A. Fielding (eds.), *Migration processes and patterns. Volume 1: research progress and prospects*, Belhaven, London, 215–226.

Champion, A. (1994) 'Population change and migration in Britain since 1981: evidence for continuing deconcentration', *Environment and Planning A*, **26**, 1501–1520.

Champion, A. (1996) 'Migration to, from and within the United Kingdom', *Population*

Trends, **83**, 5–16.

Champion, A. and Atkins, D. (1996) 'The counterurbanisation cascade: an analysis of the 1991 Census Special Migration Statistics for Great Britain', *Seminar Paper*, **66**, Department of Geography, University of Newcastle, Newcastle upon Tyne.

Champion, A. and Illeris, S. (1990) 'Population redistribution trends in Western Europe: a mosaic of dynamics and crisis', in M. Herbert and J. Hansen (eds.), *Unfamiliar territory: the reshaping of European geography*, Avebury, Aldershot, 236–253.

Cochrane, S. and Vining, D. (1988) 'Recent trends in migration between core and peripheral regions in developed and advanced developing countries', *International Regional Science Review*, **11**, 215–244.

Coombes, M., Dixon, J., Goddard, J., Openshaw, S. and Taylor, P. (1982) 'Functional regions for the population Census of Great Britain', in D. Herbert and R. Johnston (eds.), *Geography and the urban environment: progress in research and applications*, 5, Wiley, Chichester, 63–112.

Coombes, M., Dalla Longa, R. and Raybould, S. (1989) 'Counterurbanisation in Britain and Italy: a comparative critique of the concept, causation and evidence', *Progress in Planning*, **32**, 1–70.

Cross, D. (1990) *Counterurbanisation in England and Wales*, Avebury, Aldershot.

Engels, R. (1986) 'The metropolitan and non-metropolitan population at mid-decade', paper presented at the Population Association of America Annual Meeting, San Francisco, California, March.

Fielding, A. (1982) 'Counterurbanisation in Western Europe', *Progress in Planning*, **17**, 1–52.

Frey, W. (1993) 'The new urban revival in the United States', *Urban Studies*, **30**, 741–774.

Geyer, H. and Kontuly, T. (1993) 'A theoretical foundation for the concept of differential urbanisation', *International Regional Science Review*, **17**, 157–177.

Gordon, P. (1979) 'Deconcentration without a 'clean break'', *Environment and Planning A*, **11**, 281–289.

Grafton, D. and Bolton, N. (1987) 'Counterurbanisation and the rural periphery: some evidence from North Devon', in B. Robson (ed.), *Managing the city*, Croom Helm, London, 191–210.

Halfacree, K. (1994) 'The importance of 'the rural' in the constitution of counterurbanisation: evidence from England in the 1980s', *Sociologia Ruralis*, **34**, 164–189.

Hall, P. (1971) 'Spatial structure of metropolitan England and Wales', in M. Chisholm and G. Manners (eds.), *Spatial policy problems of the British economy*, Cambridge University Press, Cambridge, 96–125.

Hall, P. and Hay, D. (1980) *Growth centres in the European urban system*, Heinemann, London.

Halliday, J. and Coombes, M. (1995) 'In search of counterurbanisation: some evidence from Devon on the relationship between patterns of migration and motivation', *Journal of Rural Studies*, **11**, 433–446.

Hugo, G. (1989) 'Australia: the spatial concentration of the turnaround', in A. Champion (ed.), *Counterurbanisation: the changing pace and nature of population deconcentration*, Edward Arnold, London, 62–82.

Johnson, K. and Beale, C. (1994) 'The recent revival of widespread population growth in nonmetropolitan areas of the United States', *Rural Sociology*, **59**, 655–667.

Jones, H., Caird, J., Berry, W. and Dewhurst, J. (1986) 'Peripheral counterurbanisation: findings from an integration of census and survey data in northern Scotland', *Regional Studies*, **20**, 15–26.

Klaassen, L., Molle, W. and Paelinck, J. (1981) *Dynamics of urban development*, Gower, Aldershot.

Long, J. (1981) *Population deconcentration in the United States*, Special Demographic

Analysis CDS-81-5, United States Government Printing Office, Washington DC.

McLoughlin, J. (1991) *The demographic revolution*, Faber and Faber, London.

Mera, K. (1988) 'The emergence of migration cycles?', *International Regional Science Review*, **11**, 269–278.

Morrison, P. and Wheeler, J. (1976) 'Rural renaissance in America?', *Population Bulletin*, **31** (3), 1–27.

Moseley, M. (1984) 'The revival of rural areas in advanced economies: a review of some causes and consequences', *Geoforum*, **15**, 447–456.

Nucci, A. and Long, L. (1995) 'Spatial and demographic dynamics of metropolitan and nonmetropolitan territory in the United States', *International Journal of Population Geography*, **1**, 165–181.

Perry, R., Dean, K. and Brown, B. (1986) *Counterurbanisation: international case studies of socio-economic change in rural areas*, Geo Books, Norwich.

Ravenstein, E. (1885) 'The laws of migration', *Journal of the Royal Statistical Society*, **48**, 167–227.

Ravenstein, E. (1889) 'The laws of migration', *Journal of the Royal Statistical Society*, **52**, 241–301.

Richter, K. (1985) 'Non-metropolitan growth in the late 1970s: the end of the turnaround?', *Demography*, **22**, 245–263.

Robert, S. and Randolph, W. (1983) 'Beyond decentralisation: the evolution of population distribution in England and Wales, 1961–81', *Geoforum*, **14**, 75–102.

Sant, M. and Simons, P. (1993) 'The conceptual basis of counterurbanisation: critique and development', *Australian Geographical Studies*, **31**, 1113–1126.

Spence, N., Gillespie, A., Goddard, J., Kennett, S., Pinch, S. and Williams, A. (1982) *British cities: analysis of urban change*, Pergamon, Oxford.

van de Kaa, D. (1987) 'Europe's second demographic transition', *Population Bulletin*, **42**, 1–57.

van den Berg, L., Drewett, R., Klaassen, L., Rossi, A. and Vijverberg, C. (1982) *Urban Europe volume 1: a study in growth and decline*, Pergamon, Oxford.

Vining, D. and Kontuly, T. (1978) 'Population dispersal from major metropolitan regions: an international comparison', *International Regional Science Review*, **3**, 49–73.

Vining, D. and Strauss, A. (1977) 'A demonstration that the current deconcentration of population in the United States is a clean break with the past', *Environment and Planning A*, **9**, 751–758.

3

COUNTERURBANISATION AND SOCIAL CLASS

TONY FIELDING

INTRODUCTION

This chapter has four sections: the first goes right back to the beginnings of the counterurbanisation debate. It reflects on the attempt at that time to forge links between the analysis of migration trends, carried out by demographers and population geographers, and the emerging literature on the political economy of urban and regional development. An emphasis on such links forced researchers for the first time to consider that counterurbanisation was a phenomenon rooted in capitalist class relations and a product of the fundamental changes that were occurring in those relations in the late 1960s and early-mid-1970s. The second section modifies and extends our understanding of those links by adding new arguments about what happened during this 'high period' of counterurbanisation, and by examining the processes affecting inter-regional migration in the 1980s and early 1990s. Thus both sections are concerned with the nature and causes of counterurbanisation. The third and fourth sections, in contrast, are concerned with the consequences of counterurbanisation. The third section uses data from the Longitudinal Study (LS) to measure the social class consequences of migration to and from the non-metropolitan regions of southern England[1]. The fourth section speculates on the significance of the resulting changes in the class structures and class relations of rural areas affected by counterurbanisation[2]. A short conclusion summarises the main arguments of the chapter.

THE ORIGINAL ARGUMENT ABOUT THE NATURE AND CAUSES OF COUNTERURBANISATION[3]

It was exactly twenty years ago that Brian Berry published his analysis of population redistribution trends in the United States. In this he concluded that a fundamental shift had occurred about 1970 when counterurbanisation came to replace urbanisation as the dominant trend (Berry 1976). At about the same time the European Commission in Brussels was funding research on migration trends in the countries of the European Community (ERIPLAN 1978). This showed that a similar turnaround had occurred in most of the countries of Western Europe at about the same date. What is interesting now, however, is not only that the turnaround was found to be common to virtually all advanced capitalist countries, but that, despite the many links between them, the rather different academic traditions in North America and Western Europe resulted in explanations and interpretations of the turnaround which differed in important respects. For Berry and most of his colleagues, the fundamental cause of the switch from urbanisation to counterurbanisation was to be found in the individual preferences of ordinary people. These were said to have suddenly shifted in favour of rural and small-town environments and against the large metropolitan city. The 'great American dream' that the United States is a land of freedom and democracy, in which the ordinary person 'calls the tune' as voter and consumer, seems to have insinuated itself into social science discourse, to produce a socially benign and idealistic explanation of counterurbanisation – one that simply (i.e. in an unmediated way) translates the will of ordinary people into the systemic properties of metropolitan decline and non-metropolitan growth – that is, counterurbanisation.

In Western Europe a wholly darker, more hard-edged, materialistic and realistic explanation of counterurbanisation emerged. Its roots are to be found in the perspectives reflected in the widely read publications on regional development by Doreen Massey (1979) in Britain and Alain Lipietz (1980) in France. This explanation puts class relations and class conflict centre-stage. What determines the differential ('uneven') development of cities and regions, and therefore the geography of employment and the migration of people, is the search for profitability ('the logic of capital accumulation'). This search for profit forces firms to restructure their activities in such a way as, among other things, to minimise their labour costs and maximise their control of labour. After the 25 years of rapid post-war growth, located mostly in the large metropolitan cities, employees in these cities were in short supply, they were far too expensive to employ to remain competitive in international markets, and being well versed in the struggle between labour and capital, they were extremely difficult to manage. The obvious solution to the problem was to decentralise routine production of goods and services to branch plants and back offices in regions where reserves of 'green' labour (previously non-employed women and young people) were to be found. These reserves were located in old industrial regions, in the urbanised countryside around the large metropolitan cities, in former resort towns, and, more generally, in rural and peripheral regions. I tried to condense this argument in the conclusion to my own survey of counterurbanisation trends in Western Europe:

'It is in continuing to do something that they have always done – i.e. make changes in what, how and where to produce goods and services in such a way as to remain profitable – that firms have acted as the major agents of change in the distribution of population – i.e. as the prime generators of counterurbanisation' (Fielding 1982: 32).

I have found no empirical evidence or theoretical argument since that time to make me question this judgement. What are the implications of adopting this view of the counterurbanisation process? There are implications both for other explanations of migration trends and for the role of social class structures and relations in rural areas in the counterurbanisation process. First, however, let me emphasise what this approach does not imply. To say that something is the prime cause of the thing that you are trying to explain is not the same as saying that it is the only cause. A migration flow is the product of multiple processes and contingencies (Champion 1989). There never was a conflict between the position outlined above and the argument that, for those who had the means to do so (such as the wealthy retired), their migration might reflect an attempt to realise their 'village in the mind' by migrating to rural or small-town environments.

Accepting this perspective does, however, imply that other arguments occupy secondary positions – quite rightly so, in my opinion. It was remarkably naive to ignore the strong bonds of economic necessity which tie people to certain locations, or to argue that in some mysterious way increased household incomes in the 1960s and early 1970s had significantly loosened these bonds (except in the banal sense of allowing longer commuting distances). It was also naive to think that state redistribution policies had produced counterurbanisation. Some researchers employing a faulty logic (dependent on the increasingly useless shift-share analysis) to predict what would have happened in the absence of policy, made grossly inflated claims about the role of regional policy in job creation in British Development Areas (Moore et al. 1986). A more sober analysis of state regulation effects would emphasise the many ways in which governments counteracted their own regional redistribution policies (for example, through defence procurement), and yet (unwittingly) during the same period encouraged dispersal of economic activity or stability of settlement structures through the standardisation of public service and utilities provision and by means of transfer payments (social welfare policy). Similarly, the nearest we get to a serious claim to an explanation for counterurbanisation from standard (neoclassical) economics is that the turnaround was caused by economic recession. Besides the fact that the timing is wrong (the downturn in the economy in the 1970s occurred after counterurbanisation had become well established), we now know (see below) that, due to turnover rates in the housing and labour markets, counterurban migration is highest during booms and lowest during recessions (i.e. exactly the opposite of that suggested by the economists).

What role then do rural social class relations play in this perspective? The argument is that inherited rural social relations were important because they produced good opportunities for profitable production. For generations the populations of rural areas had accustomed themselves to a shortage of non-farm jobs and to the low pay and subservience of farm work. With low expectations and a deferential attitude towards those who command the local economy, it is hardly surprising that incoming employers enjoyed a period of good working relations with a grateful and largely well-satisfied workforce. As I argued earlier:

'A company is best placed when it can be "mobile" in its investment, in the sense that it can adjust quickly to changing labour market and other cost-affecting factors, and at the same time be employing labour that is immobile. The workers are best placed when the reverse of this situation prevails, that is, when the labour is "mobile" in the sense that it can find alternative employment locally, ... and when ... the employer is immobile and committed to the continuation of production at that site. ... The importance of this line of argument is that *different urban and regional contexts produce very different outcomes in these employer/employee relations*. In general, in metropolitan areas and in areas that already have large concentrations of manufacturing industry, the balance of advantage is tipped *against the employer*. ... [In] small and medium-sized towns in rural and peripheral regions [however,] ... the balance of advantage is generally tipped *against the worker*. There is a low density of job locations so that few alternative employers exist in the district, and ... the employers operating in such areas are the ones whose production can ... be carried out at [relatively small] scales. .. [W]ith modest commitments ... of labour, land and buildings ..., the probability of closure accompanied by investment elsewhere is high. In such circumstances the workers are stuck and the employers are mobile ..., [enhancing] the authority of the employer over the employee ... [For a recent paper that emphasises the significance of metropolitan/urban/rural context for job creation, see North and Smallbone 1996.] ... From this perspective, counterurbanisation is seen as a product of the rapid deindustrialisation of the largest cities and old industrial regions ... accompanied by a stabilisation of rural population levels following the long process of "restructuring" of agriculture, and by a growth of manufacturing in small and medium-sized towns in rural and peripheral regions' (Fielding 1982: 30–31).

EXTENSIONS TO THE ORIGINAL ARGUMENT

With the benefit of hindsight, it is possible to see the advantages of linking counterurbanisation to the reorganisation of production in advanced capitalist countries in the context of the wider processes of economic and social change which occurred in the late 1960s and early 1970s. It helps, in particular, to see these population redistributions in the context of debates about changing spatial divisions of labour; and Fordism and post-Fordism.

First, it should be said that an awareness of the concept of 'spatial divisions of labour' was present in the original argument:

'there has emerged during the period 1950–80 a new regional division of labour: an increased separation of ownership and control from production; a heightened concentration of the former in the major administrative and commercial centres ...; a clustering of related research and development establishments and ... [high] technology industries in the nearby rural and amenity regions; and a dispersal of routine production to rural and peripheral regions ...' (Fielding 1982: 31).

Nonetheless, at that time it was only possible to envisage two post-war spatial divisions of labour – regional sectoral specialisation (RSS) and the new (or hierarchical) spatial division of labour (NSDL), and to relate changing migration patterns to the transition from the former to the latter. Under regional sectoral specialisation (which dominated in the early 1950s) there was inter-regional migration of all kinds of workers as one branch of the economy grew and another declined; the South East region, with its highly favourable employment structure, experienced net migration gains at this time. Under the new spatial division of labour (which dominated in the early 1970s) the inter-regional migration of professionals and managers became more important (particularly as a result of intra-organisational transfers) and the migration of manual workers became less important; a major de-industrialisation of London, combined with 'counterurban' shifts in both manufacturing and service sector employment led to net migration losses in the South East region.

Now it is sensible to add a third spatial division of labour – regional functional disconnection (RFD). When RSS dominated there were strong inter-regional economic linkages arising from sectorally specialised production for the national market – most goods and services were produced in one region of the country and consumed by those living in another region. Under NSDL there were also strong inter-regional linkages, but this time they were linkages within production organisations, as decisions taken at one location were carried out at another. With RFD (emerging since the mid-1970s) the emphasis is on the weakening of inter-regional linkages as production at one location within a country like Britain becomes more and more connected with suppliers and customers located in other countries, and the production system becomes more likely to be commanded from outside the country. Inter-regional labour migration is reduced by divergence in regional housing and labour markets, resulting in a pattern of low net inter-regional gains or losses. Whether a region gains or loses from migration now depends on neither the market relations between regions (as under RSS) nor the planned relations between regions (as under NSDL) within the country, but on the success or failure of the region to attract capital and labour which is globally mobile (see Marsden et al. 1990: 9–10 for a discussion of this point in relation to rural change).

Secondly, it helps to see the counterurbanisation of the late 1960s and early 1970s as related to the 'last fling' of Fordism. Firms involved in the mass production of goods and services were attempting to use a 'spatial fix' (i.e. industrial decentralisation) to maintain their profitability in the face of increasing international competition and a trend towards a globalisation of operations. With hindsight, we know that in Britain many of those adopting this strategy failed to survive the deep recession of the early 1980s.

This emphasis on the link between counterurbanisation and Fordism helps in another way. The high period of counterurbanisation did not last very long. By the mid-1970s it was beginning to wane in most advanced capitalist countries (although in some countries a weak counterurbanisation continued into the 1980s). What replaced it? Not a return to urbanisation, that is certain. It is true that European rural peripheries in the 1980s and early 1990s are more likely than not to be losing population again. Furthermore, it is well known that capital cities and major financial centres 'bounced back' in terms of population and net migration in the mid-to-late 1980s as the boom in producer services ran its course. However, the main feature of post-1970s population redistribution has been the stability of the system. On average, the rates of net gain and loss have decreased over time, so that although many people are moving from one region to another, the net redistributive effect of these movements is relatively small.

What might these developments have to do with Fordism and post-Fordism? First, along with the mass production of standardised products for mass markets, Fordism was also associated with universal health and education services, the public sector provision of power and transport/communications services and the welfare state. The legacy of that development is a spatial (near) equalisation of the 'social wage' and of the 'general conditions of production' (that is, of the context for profitable production). In the years since the mid-1970s there have been attempts to break this spatial equalisation (especially through privatisation), but much of the structure remains intact and, through both employment and transfer payments, it helps to maintain people in places that would otherwise suffer poverty and mass out-migration.

Secondly, much of the literature on post-Fordism emphasises the endogenous nature of the growth processes of the 1980s and 1990s. I have recently summarised the argument as follows:

> 'For the regions containing new industrial spaces, growth has for the most part been without urbanisation. New factories and new offices have been attached to an existing settlement system, typically consisting of an urbanised countryside of small and medium-sized free-standing towns set in a largely rural environment. In part, the explanation for this lies in the socially-embedded nature of the development of these industrial districts. This means that the special skills, mentalities and dispositions of the people living there have been major factors explaining the successful development of industries and services. Research on new industrial spaces repeatedly emphasises the *endogenous* nature of this form of development – since the early 1970s investments related to locationally-fixed *physical* resources such as raw materials or harbours (the important exception perhaps is North Sea oil) have had far less effect on the geography of production, while those related to locationally-fixed *social* resources have come to have a far greater effect. Hence the spatial stability of the population system in comparison with the dynamics of the production system' (Fielding 1994: 702, emphasis in original).

However, perhaps the most significant extension to the original argument lies not in the reformulation of the restructuring thesis through concepts of spatial divisions of labour or Fordism/post-Fordism, but through an awareness of the fact that the changing political economy shapes migration flows at a number of levels. Counterurban migration flows are then seen as being affected by processes that operate over very different timescales, economic restructuring being only one of these. Specifically, there are processes that work themselves out at rates which are much faster than restructuring (those associated with the business cycle), and there are processes that work themselves out at rates which are much slower than restructuring (those connected to the underlying economic geography of the country).

How then is counterurban migration affected by the business cycle? From recent research on migration to and from South East England (the main source region for counterurban migration flows in Britain) it seems that the main features of the relationship are as follows[4]:

- At the peak in the cycle, even when it is the South East economy which is central to national economic growth (as in the late 1980s), the South East region experiences not net migration gain but net migration loss. Conversely, when the national economy is in recession, the South East region experiences net migration balance or even a small net migration gain (as in the early 1980s). Figure 3.1 shows how this comes about. When the economy is booming, the number of people migrating to the South East goes up signifi-cantly, but at the same time the number migrating from the South East goes up even more significantly; so that a very much higher level of out-migration exceeds higher in-migration. At the subsequent trough, even though it may well be the South East economy which is instrumental in producing the downturn, the lower level of in-migration is surpassed by an even lower level of out-migration thus producing the tendency towards net gain.

- It can be argued that both housing and labour market processes contribute to this situation. In downturns or recession, job and housing moves (some of which will take the household out of the South East region) are postponed, partly because of uncertainty about the near future, but mostly because of the difficulties experienced in disposing of property, land and housing. When turnover in both job and housing markets begins to increase as the economy improves and business confidence rises, these intended moves are actualised. As far as housing and land are concerned this means that individuals can sell their homes and firms can sell their premises. In this way assets are realised in anticipation of new investments in other parts of the South East, in other regions of southern England, or outside southern England. A strong speculat-ive element tends to contribute to the sharp rise in housing and land prices. However, when the ratio of house prices to incomes becomes so great that entry into the market is essentially choked off, the process turns round and moves into reverse. The decline in transactions leads to a marked downturn in the regional economy, equity release dries up, house prices fall (in real if not also in absolute terms), sellers withdraw their properties from the market, and mobility is brought to a sudden halt by the inability of people and firms to dispose of their properties (even when, as often happens, they are desperate to do so). Mobility in the labour market is similarly checked by the risk-avoidance behaviours of individuals and firms. Thus the South East region is prone to periodic bursts of out-migration and net migration loss followed by periods of low population turnover and net migration balance.

This argument has a practical significance in our analysis of counterurbanisa-

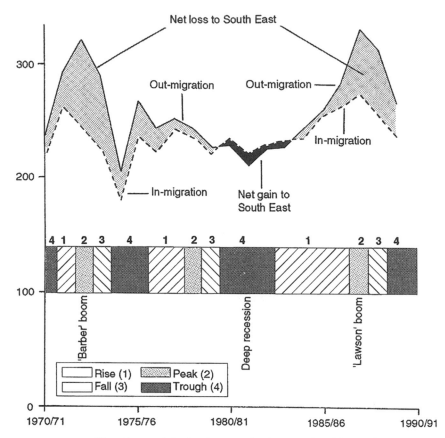

FIGURE 3.1 Migration and the business cycle: inter-regional in- and out-migration for South East England (figures in thousands) Note: the data for 1970/71 are based upon the Census, are for April to April, and are flows to and from GB only. Source: NHSCR (Crown copyright reserved)

tion. It implies that the presence or absence of counterurbanisation is affected by the choice of time interval over which the migration flows are studied. Choose one set of dates (for Britain, say 1977–1982), and you might convince yourself that counterurbanisation had come to an end. Choose another set (say 1982–1987) and there it is back again! Clearly, any analysis of population redistribution trends must take this short-term variability in the size and directional components of migration flows into account.

There is another interesting feature of Figure 3.1. The migration flows to the South East region are remarkably stable over time. Admittedly, they fall suddenly during the oil crisis recession in 1973–1974, and they rise throughout London's 'bubble economy' years of the late 1980s. However, rarely do they wander outside the range of 20 000 migrants above or below the annual average of about 240 000. We shall see below that a very high proportion of these migrants are young people moving to the South East at around the time that they are entering the labour market. This encourages us to view the migration flows within Britain as being in part a reflection of the underlying and almost unchanging economic geography of the country. Certain regions are now, and have been for a very long time, particularly rich in opportunities for social promotion and for the creation of middle class careers; others are particularly poor in such opportunities (Fielding 1992a). Young adults will tend to gravitate towards the former and away from the latter. Older people, some of them in-migrants as young adults, will tend to migrate away from the former and towards the latter. One would expect that the reasons for this out-migration by older people would include the fact that places that are rich in opportunities are also the places where the costs of living are highest, the work pressures greatest, and the pace of life the fastest. Whatever the explanation, the important point for our argument is that the social compositions of flows towards metropolitan city-regions differ from the social compositions of flows away from such regions. This means that if we wish to understand the high level of counterurban migration flows we would be wise to investigate the particular economic and social forces and circumstances affecting those people who are in the mid-career, near-retirement and early retirement stages of their lives.

THE SOCIAL CLASS CONSEQUENCES OF MIGRATION TO AND FROM THE NON-METROPOLITAN REGIONS OF SOUTHERN ENGLAND

We can gain some understanding of the social class effects of counterurbanisation by focusing on the social compositions of migration streams to and from the two non-metropolitan regions of southern England (East Anglia and the South West – that is, the regions most affected by counterurban flows from the South East region), during the intercensal period 1971–1981. This section of the chapter will not concern itself with the general issue of the relationships between migration and social class (Fielding 1992b), nor with the advantages and disadvantages of using the Longitudinal Study (LS) data set in migration research (Fielding 1989). It does need to be said, however, that the LS is a very large sample (of about 500 000 individuals), and that for each LS member we have information obtained at two (now three) census dates (by means of matching census records). What follows will be concerned solely with the impact of migration on the social class structures of these two non-metropolitan regions during the 'high period' of counterurbanisation.

The East Anglia and South West regions together had 9131 LS members living there in 1981 who were living in other regions of England and Wales in 1971. Since the LS is a 1.096 percent sample this represents an in-migrant population of about 830 000. For the same dates the out-migration from these two regions to the rest of England and Wales was 4877 LS members, or about 445 000 people. So the first point to emphasise is the massive net migration gain to these regions.

We know from the LS and from other data sources, notably the National Health Service Central Register data, that between a half and two-thirds of the in-migration flows and the out-migration flows of these regions is accounted for by the South East region alone. So it is exchanges with the London city-region (virtually co-extensive with the South East region) which dominate the migration situations of the non-metropolitan south of England.

The next stage is to examine the social class compositions of the in-migration and out-migration flows. To do this, the migrants' socio-economic group (SEG) has been used, and the SEGs have been grouped into four classes plus the unemployed. The two middle classes are the service class, made up of professional, technical and managerial workers, and the 'petite bourgeoisie', that is, the self-employed and the owners of small and medium-sized businesses. The two working classes are the white-collar (non-manual) working class and the blue-collar (manual) working class. To throw into relief the distinctiveness of particular migration flows, the class composition of the flow under consideration is compared with that of all inter-regional migrants in England and Wales. This is done by means of location quotients – where a value of 1.00 means that the class-specific flow concerned is of equivalent importance to that class-specific flow amongst all migrants in England and Wales.

If we analyse the out-migration flow from these two regions we find that its class composition is not very different from the general situation. There is a slight bias towards those leaving East Anglia and the South West to be drawn from the ranks of the unemployed and from those in full-time education, and an even slighter tendency for them to enter low level white-collar jobs and service class jobs in their region of destination (predominantly the South East). In contrast, the migration flow to these regions is very distinctive. This is shown in Figure 3.2 which gives the location quotients for all the non-trivial social class transitions amongst those who migrated to the two regions between 1971 and 1981 (excluding, of course, re-migrations and deaths of in-migrants). In this figure, the widths of the columns are proportional to the importance of these transitions among all inter-regional migrations in England and Wales.

Figure 3.2 has a number of very interesting features. First, the highest plus values among flows within or into the labour market are for those entering the petite bourgeoisie. The highest value of all is for those who were previously members of the service class, but who enter the petite bourgeoisie as they migrate into the East Anglia and South West regions. The other plus values (for example, service class to white-collar) suggest the possibility that there is a 'bumping down' process affecting women who migrate to these regions. This might arise from the poorer employment prospects facing women who live in two-career households when, for reasons related to their partner's career, they leave the South East for the non-metropolitan south of England (for a fuller development of this theme see Fielding and Halford 1993; also Cloke *et al.* 1995b: 229). Secondly, the highest values for those not in the labour market in 1981 were for entries into retirement, especially from those who were previously

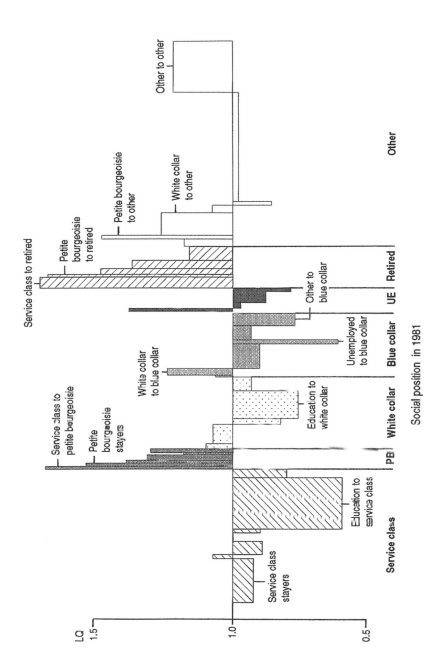

FIGURE 3.2 The social composition of migration flows to the South West and East Anglia regions from elsewhere in England and Wales, 1971–1981. LQ: location quotient; PB: petite bourgeoisie; UE: unemployed. Source: Longitudinal Study (Crown copyright reserved)

in middle class jobs. It is also interesting to see how important the category 'other' is as a destination. This reflects the tendency for non-metropolitan areas to be associated with family formation (rather as a mirror-image to the metropolitan areas, which are, of course, associated with career formation) (Little and Austin 1996). Finally, the minus values show how poorly represented in the flows to the East Anglia and South West regions are those who are transferring from full-time education to jobs in the service class or to white-collar employment.

So far, so good. However, these data do not tell us in quantitative terms what the contribution of counterurban migration is to the changing social class structures of non-metropolitan regions. To do this we need to use the full LS regional occupational class data to construct a social class 'balance sheet' for non-metropolitan regions. Such a balance sheet will need to place migration figures in the context of all of the transitions that affect the social class structures of the regions over a ten-year period. These include the effects of entries and exits from the labour market and the complex shifts from one occupation to another which take place within the regions. These social class balance sheets have been constructed for both East Anglia and the South West regions (though only the latter is shown here in Table 3.1.)

To help interpret this table let us concentrate attention on the first column, that is, the balance sheet for those in the service class of professional, technical and managerial employees. In 1971 there were 2917 LS members in this class (representing a population of about 266 000). A total of 2734 LS members were added to this class over the next ten years, of whom 1119 (41 percent) were in-migrants (and 623 of these came, incidentally, from the South East region alone). A total of 1659 were subtracted from the South West's service class, of whom only 355 (21 percent) were out-migrants. The net change in the size of this class, therefore, was +1075, of which +764 was due to net migration.

The next step in the analysis is very simple. One divides the contribution of net migration by the average of the class sizes in 1971 and 1981 to produce the percentage contribution of migration to that class's change over the ten-year period. For the service class in the South West this figure is +22.1 percent – the service class in this region was increased by more than one-fifth by migration between 1971 and 1981. This is a remarkable figure and is higher than the figures for other groups in employment. The petite bourgeoisie was increased by 14.4 percent due to migration, white-collar workers by 8.5 percent and blue-collar workers by just 4.8 percent. Of the total net migration gain in the South West region's labour market of +1944 LS members (equivalent to 177 000 people), 1028 LS members (53 percent) were in the middle class categories of service class and petite bourgeoisie. These middle class categories, however, accounted for only 27.8 percent of the region's economically active population in 1971. The picture is crystal clear – migration was a major contributor to the sharp shift in the South West region's class structure towards the middle classes.

The data for East Anglia yield similar results. The contribution of migration to

TABLE 3.1 A social class 'balance sheet' for the South West region

	Social classes					
	Service class	Petite bourgeoisie	White-collar working class	Blue-collar working class	Unemployed	Total
Total in class X in SW in 1971	2917	1779	4681	6985	541	16903
Additions:						
Transfers into X within SW	856	548	643	772	476	3295
Entries from education within SW	524	147	1254	1378	416	3719
Other entries within SW	235	108	809	506	58	1716
In-migrants from England & Wales	1119	332	755	559	262	3067
of which:						
In class X in 1971	459	65	219	208	9	960
In other class in 1971	243	198	135	138	125	839
In education in 1971	339	31	246	173	102	891
In other in 1971	78	38	155	80	26	377
Total additions	2734	1135	3461	3255	1212	11797
Subtractions:						
Transfers out of X within SW	499	394	965	1264	173	3295
Deaths	205	171	304	625	56	1361
Retirement within SW	397	269	503	1051	107	2327
Other exits within SW	202	124	1043	547	81	1998
Out-migrants to England & Wales	355	68	346	274	80	1123
of which:						
In class X in 1981	221	13	102	120	6	462
In other class in 1981	62	23	114	105	42	346
In retirement in 1981	32	18	24	21	9	104
In other in 1981	40	14	106	28	23	211
Total subtractions	1659	1026	3161	3761	497	10104
Net change 1971–1981	+1075	+109	+300	−506	+715	+1693
Net migration 1971–1981	+764	+264	+409	+325	+182	+1944
Total in Class X in SW in 1981	3992	1888	4981	6479	1256	18596

Note: the data include migration to and from the rest of England and Wales but not to and from the rest of the world. Untraced records are also excluded. 1.0% sample.
Source: OPCS Longitudinal Study (Crown copyright reserved).

the expansion of the service class in East Anglia was of the same order as for the South West but slightly higher at +25.1 percent. The values for other groups in employment were +11.6 for the petite bourgeoisie (rather lower than in the South West), +9.2 for white-collar workers, and +6.0 percent for blue-collar workers. In summary:

> 'These results for East Anglia confirm those for the South West. Taken together, they show that the non-metropolitan regions of southern England experienced a very specific set of social class changes as a result of their migration exchanges with the rest of England and Wales. They saw their numbers of unemployed people increased, but more significantly, they witnessed a sharp shift towards professional, technical and managerial employment as a result of migration, and especially in the case of the South West region, a further shift towards the expansion of the (already unusually large) petty bourgeoisie' (Fielding 1991/2: 407–408).

THE IMPACT OF COUNTERURBAN MIGRATION ON THE SOCIAL CLASS RELATIONS OF RURAL AREAS

It has been argued above that an awareness of social class relations and class interests over the past thirty years is essential for an explanation of the phenomenon of counterurbanisation. Such an awareness is no less essential, in my opinion, when it comes to an analysis of the effects of counterurbanisation (a position apparently supported by Cloke 1989). We have seen that the non-metropolitan regions of southern England have experienced a marked in-migration of middle class people, and that a high proportion of those who were retired by 1981 were also from middle class backgrounds. What does this imply for class relations in the rural areas and areas of 'urbanised countryside' that have witnessed this in-migration?

The LS, of course, cannot answer this kind of question, nor can most kinds of aggregate analysis. These impacts can only be discovered through detailed empirical study, and perhaps only with the help of ethnographic research. It is not quite enough simply to ask people about the social class changes brought about by the arrival of the 'townie' in-migrants (incidentally, many of the migrants to East Anglia and the South West do not come directly from London, but have already migrated into the outer metropolitan area or the semi-rural outer South East before migrating out of the region altogether; see Boyle 1995: 73). Responses to inquiries of this kind are likely to reflect, firstly, the strong tendency for people to object to, or at least feel uncomfortable about, discussing the people they know in terms of social class; and, secondly, the power of certain popular, incomplete, and often very superficial, impressions about the nature of these changes (sometimes expressed in apocalyptic language such as 'the destruction of the English countryside' or 'the loss of a rural way of life') (for discussion of the popular impressions, see Halfacree 1992, 1995).

To avoid an unfruitful engagement with these discourses (of which there have been many!), this last section speculates in a rather general analytical way on the social class effects of counterurbanisation, drawing selectively upon a large and diverse literature. It does this by asking the question 'which social groups gain by this in-migration, and which social groups lose by it?'

The social groups whose members gain from counterurbanisation include the following:

- The local working class – opportunities for employment, perhaps especially for women and for farm workers, expanded considerably as a result of the arrival of the wealthy retired, and of the influx of middle class people that accompanied the decentralisation of employment. Female activity rates increased almost everywhere during the 1960s and 1970s, but the growth was especially fast in rural areas (Cloke and Thrift 1990: 172; see also Gilligan 1984: 108–109, for interesting comments on the changes in social class and gender relations consequent upon the arrival of industry in a rural area).
- Owners of land and property – many a small fortune was made from the sale of land for housing development. More substantial owners benefited from their involvement in speculative land development (for example, for shopping centres and industrial estates).
- Owners of local small and medium-sized businesses – they saw an increase in their market as service class customers with money to spend moved into the small towns and rural areas. In-migrants setting up businesses in these areas also benefited. Some even realised their dream, entertained no doubt while they sat at their desks in city offices, of owning and running a restaurant or a pub in an attractive rural area of southern England.
- The in-migrant working class – it should not be forgotten that nearly half of the net migration gain in the non-metropolitan south of England came not from the middle classes but from those in low-level white-collar and blue-collar jobs. These people gained from the lower living costs in non-metropolitan areas, and from working in smaller establishments where there was less industrial conflict.
- The in-migrant service class – not only did these people achieve their preferred environment in which to work, live (Halliday and Coombes 1995) and enjoy their rural leisure activities (Urry 1995), they gained financially from the fact that many of them were on nationally negotiated pay rates, while living in areas where housing and commuting costs were much lower than in the city. Early in-migrants also saw large increases in the value of their properties as others followed in their footsteps. Often the members of the service class took on local social leadership roles (especially on matters relating to the 'preservation of the countryside'), despite the fact that in many cases their careers would require them to move again in a few years time (Murdoch 1995: 1226).
- The retired – they benefited from the slower pace of life, lower perceived risk of crime (and those associated in their minds with crime, i.e. ethnic minorities), lower perceived noise and pollution levels (for a discussion of rural areas as 'white space' see Murdoch and Marsden 1991: 48). Many achieved

equity release through the sale of their suburban houses in the metropolitan city (Cloke *et al.* 1995b: 231). An increasing proportion of the 'middle class' retired also enjoyed significant income from company pension schemes.

- Last, but not least, the major investor:

  'those who invested in the small and medium-sized towns in the rural and peripheral regions found many of the things they had hoped for: reliable, manageable
  workforces untainted by the work practices of the large factory or office, prepared
  to work hard and cooperatively for wages which were well below what would
  have had to be paid in a metropolitan region; land for modern buildings in
  spacious surroundings, providing decent car parking space and room for expansion; and helpful and interested local authorities, keen to attract and retain new
  businesses. In short, for a time at least, counterurbanisation was the 'spatial fix'
  which allowed major firms to achieve profitability and growth in the face of
  sharpening international competition' (Fielding 1990: 236).

More generally, it might be suggested that as counterurban migration undermined the deference of people towards those formerly in control, notably the
major landowners and farmers, people in rural and small-town areas enjoyed a
more liberal cultural environment and a greater fluidity in local class relations. At
the same time, employment structures were shifted sharply towards growth
sectors and towards high-status occupational groups. So, in short, there were
many benefits and many beneficiaries from counterurbanisation.

Is that all that needs to be said? No, of course not. Counterurbanisation also
created losers, many of them drawn from the same social groups that were just
now seen as gainers. The losers include the following:

- Members of the working class – in rural and small town areas the arrival of
  predominantly middle class in-migrants had a dramatic effect on the housing
  market, forcing prices up to levels that were way beyond the means of those
  who were not already home owners in the area (see Murdoch and Marsden
  1994: 63). This problem was experienced in particular by young people trying
  to enter the housing market. They were often unable to compete even for
  houses that were being bought as second homes. However, it was not only in
  the housing market that the in-migrants affected the opportunities open to
  local working class people. The high levels of car ownership of the newcomers, and their ability to use privatised forms of health and education
  services, left those who were not so prosperous dependent upon services
  which were becoming less available, such as village shops and post offices,
  public transport, state schools and public health services (many of these
  problems are discussed in Cloke *et al.* 1995a). Furthermore, those new jobs
  were not always a godsend. For women the change often meant the substitu-
  tion of one form of subordination (for example, as a farm worker's wife) by
  another (as a low-level worker in a factory or office) (Little 1987). Moreover,
  when, as frequently happened, the rural branch plants were closed down, the
  service class employees would typically be redeployed within the organisation, but the rest would not.

- Owners of local businesses – they did well for a time, but then they faced the problem that the expansion of local markets for goods and services had attracted not only competing in-migrant small businesses but the attentions of larger commercial capital. In the situation where the threshold size of the business needed to achieve profitability was increasing, many local small owners fell by the wayside.
- Members of the service class – the problem for these people is that the nature of local labour markets in non-metropolitan areas adversely influences their chances of upward social mobility. Professionals need to build up 'cultural capital', but this is often acquired by the kinds of social contacts available, not in rural areas, but in the metropolitan city. Managers need to demonstrate more and more ability in organising the work of others, but typically, the managerial challenges of small businesses or small establishments in rural and small-town environments are unimpressive to those who can offer them advancement. Perhaps it is only those who merit the rather unkind label of 'spent spiralists' who can settle easily to non-metropolitan service class careers.
- The wealthy retired, perhaps most surprisingly, because however amenable the area was to the retired couple when they were still active, it became less and less attractive as they became older, less active, less healthy, less independent, more liable to be living on their own, and above all, less mobile. Then, for all their wealth, they join the rural poor in experiencing the many limitations arising from 'mobility deprivation'.
- Major investors – with the benefit of hindsight we can see that the 'spatial fix' of decentralisation was, like all fixes, very temporary in the enjoyment that it provided. For many companies the problems posed by sharper international competition were a whole order more serious than those that were earlier met by an internal relocation within the country.

More generally, there were negative impacts on rural social relations. The old leadership had been self-seeking and openly class-conscious, but its paternalism had helped to cement a certain kind of social solidarity. With the newcomers came the destruction of that solidarity, and the loss of distinctive localisms in culture, dialect and work traditions (Newby 1979:165). With the counterurban movement came the 'banalisation' of non-metropolitan space; the in-migrants carried with them the messages, rules and practices of cosmopolitan middle class taste, mass society and popular culture (for an interesting commentary on an earlier expression of this concern, see Matless 1994). However, above all, the significant effects of counterurbanisation on social class relations lie in the rapid extension of the external control of Britain's non-metropolitan regions. The inhabitants of these areas had even less command over the economic circumstances of their lives in the 1980s than those that had lived there in the 1950s.

CONCLUSION

This chapter has re-examined the literature on the relations between counterurbanisation and class. It has done so by reassessing and developing the argument that a political economy perspective is an indispensable asset in coming to terms with the causes of counterurbanisation. Of fundamental importance was the shift in manufacturing and service sector investment in favour of freestanding cities and small and medium-sized towns, set in rural regions or in areas of 'urbanised countryside'. In addition, the chapter has used Longitudinal Study data to explore the class content of counterurban migration flows, and has taken a tentative step in the direction of assessing the social class consequences of counterurbanisation in non-metropolitan areas. It was found that the non-metropolitan regions of southern England were not only the recipients of middle class retirement migrations but were also major destinations for migrants who were in the labour market. Moreover, it was shown that prominent amongst these labour market in-migrants were members of the three middle classes – professionals, managers and the petite bourgeoisie.

NOTES

1. This section draws heavily upon material first published in Fielding (1991/2). I want to thank the editor for permission to use some of the tables and figures from this article.
2. This section draws heavily upon material discussed in the final section of my chapter in Fielding (1990).
3. Debates about definitions are not discussed here. For an extended treatment of the complexities surrounding the term 'counterurbanisation', see Fielding (1998).
4. This section draws upon material presented in a report commissioned by the Department of the Environment, published (in part) in Fielding (1993).

REFERENCES

Berry, B. (1976) 'The counterurbanisation process: urban America since 1970', in B. Berry (ed.), *Urbanisation and counterurbanisation*, Sage, Beverly Hills, California, 17–30.

Boyle, P. (1995) 'Rural in-migration in England and Wales 1980–81', *Journal of Rural Studies*, **11**, 65–78.

Champion, A. (1989) (ed.) *Counterurbanisation*, Edward Arnold, London.

Cloke, P. (1989) 'Rural geography and political economy', in R. Peet and N. Thrift (eds.), *New models in geography, volume 1*, Unwin Hyman, London, 164–197.

Cloke, P. and Thrift, N. (1990) 'Class and change in rural Britain', in T. Marsden, P. Lowe and S. Whatmore (eds.), *Rural restructuring*, David Fulton, London, 165–181.

Cloke, P., Goodwin, M., Milbourne, P. and Thomas, C. (1995a) 'Deprivation, poverty, and marginalization in rural lifestyles in England and Wales', *Journal of Rural Studies*, **11**, 351–365.

Cloke, P., Phillips, M. and Thrift, N. (1995b) 'The new middle classes and the social constructs of rural living', in T. Butler and M. Savage (eds.), *Social change and the middle classes*, UCL Press, London, 220–238.

ERIPLAN (1978) *Migration*, Report for the EEC's CREST programme, Brussels.

Fielding, A. (1982) 'Counterurbanisation in Western Europe', *Progress in Planning*, **17**, 1–52.

Fielding, A. (1989) 'Inter-regional migration and social change: a study of South East England based upon data from the Longitudinal Study', *Transactions of the Institute of British Geographers*, **14**, 24–36.

Fielding, A. (1990) 'Counterurbanization: threat or blessing?', in D. Pinder (ed.), *Western Europe: challenge and change*, Belhaven Press, London, 226–239.

Fielding, A. (1991/2) 'Social and geographical mobility in the non-metropolitan south of England', *Espaces-Populations-Societes*, 395–408.

Fielding, A. (1992a) 'Migration and social mobility: South East England as an "escalator" region", *Regional Studies*, **26**, 1–15.

Fielding, A. (1992b) 'Migration and social change', in J. Stillwell, P. Rees and P. Boden (eds.), *Migration processes and patterns. Volume 2: population redistribution in the 1980s*, Belhaven Press, London, 225–247.

Fielding, A. (1993) 'Migration and the metropolis', *Progress in Planning*, **39**, 71–166.

Fielding, A. (1994) 'Industrial change and regional development in Western Europe', *Urban Studies*, **31**, 679–704.

Fielding, A. (1998, forthcoming), 'Urbanization and counterurbanization: reflections on an 'unresolved debate", in L.-E. Borgegard, P. Hall and S. Musterd (eds.), *Migration, mobility and metropolitan change in a dynamic society*, John Wiley, Chichester.

Fielding, A. and Halford, S. (1993) 'Geographies of opportunity: a regional analysis of gender-specific social and spatial mobilities in England and Wales 1971–81', *Environment and Planning A*, **25**, 1421–1440.

Gilligan, J. (1984) 'The rural labour process: a case study of a Cornish town', in T. Bradley and P. Lowe (eds.), *Locality and rurality: economy and society in rural regions*, Geo Books, Norwich, 91–112.

Halfacree, K. (1992) *The importance of spatial representations in residential migration to rural England in the 1980s*, unpublished PhD thesis, Department of Geography, Lancaster University, Lancaster.

Halfacree, K. (1995) 'Talking about rurality: social representations of the rural as expressed by residents of six English parishes', *Journal of Rural Studies*, **11**, 1–20.

Halliday, J. and Coombes, M. (1995) 'In search of counterurbanisation: some evidence from Devon on the relationship between patterns of migration and motivation', *Journal of Rural Studies*, **11**, 433–446.

Lipietz, A. (1980) 'The structure of space, the problem of land, and spatial policy', in J. Carney, R. Hudson and J. Lewis (eds.), *Regions in crisis: new perspectives on European regional theory*, Croom Helm, London, 60–75.

Little, J. (1987) 'Gender relations in rural areas: the importance of women's domestic role', *Journal of Rural Studies*, **3**, 335–342.

Little, J. and Austin, P. (1996) 'Women and the rural idyll', *Journal of Rural Studies*, **12**, 101–111.

Marsden, T., Lowe, P. and Whatmore, S. (1990) 'Introduction: questions of rurality', in T. Marsden, P. Lowe and S. Whatmore (eds.), *Rural restructuring*, David Fulton, London, 1–19.

Massey, D. (1979) 'In what sense a regional problem?', *Regional Studies*, **13**, 233–243.

Matless, D. (1994) 'Doing the English village, 1945–90: an essay in imaginative geography', in P. Cloke, M. Doel, D. Matless, M. Phillips and N. Thrift, *Writing the rural: five cultural geographies*, Paul Chapman, London, 7–88.

Moore, B., Rhodes, J. and Tyler, P. (1986) *The effects of Government regional policy*, HMSO, London.

Murdoch, J. (1995) 'Middle class territory? Some remarks on the use of class analysis in rural studies', *Environment and Planning A*, **27**, 1213–1230.

Murdoch, J. and Marsden, T. (1991) 'Reconstituting the rural in an urban region: new villages for old?', *Countryside Change Working Paper Series*, 26, School of Geography and Earth Sciences, University of Hull, Kingston upon Hull.

Murdoch, J. and Marsden, T. (1994) *Reconstituting rurality*, David Fulton, London.

Newby, H. (1979) *Green and pleasant land? Social change in rural England*, Hutchinson, London.

North, D. and Smallbone, D. (1996) 'Small business development in remote rural areas: the example of mature manufacturing firms in northern England', *Journal of Rural Studies*, **12**, 151–167.

Urry, J. (1995) 'A middle class countryside?', in T. Butler and M. Savage (eds.), *Social change and the middle classes*, UCL Press, London, 205–219

4

CONTRASTING THE COUNTERURBANISATION EXPERIENCE IN EUROPEAN NATIONS

THOMAS KONTULY

INTRODUCTION

A migration 'turnaround' occurred in European nations during the 1960s and 1970s. Then in the 1980s a number of these countries experienced a 'turn-backaround', while counterurbanisation or regional deconcentration continued unabated in other nations. Currently, research on the United States indicates the possibility of a 'new turnaround' during the first half of the 1990s. The continuation of counterurbanisation tendencies in Denmark, France, Great Britain and Italy, and the possibility of renewed regional deconcentration in the United States, stimulates interest in the reasons for or explanations of the phenomenon.

Numerous explanations have been suggested for the turnaround in European countries. By comparing and contrasting the different reasons for counterurbanisation, this chapter will attempt to determine if the phenomenon can be explained by one or two theories pervasive throughout the developed world or if there are numerous geographically distinct causes which suggest that the phenomenon is a complex feature of contemporary society. This chapter will rank the relative importance of the different explanations as determined from a survey of the published literature on the topic.

Several studies evaluate and explain the counterurbanisation phenomenon in Britain. These explanations are discussed by Champion in Chapter 2 and therefore are not included in this chapter. This chapter is intended to provide a comparison to the primarily British-based explanations reviewed by Champion.

CHARACTERISING COUNTERURBANISATION TRENDS IN EUROPE

Defining counterurbanisation is not an easy task. Studies attempting to identify the existence of the phenomenon in European countries are either comparative across countries and strive to identify counterurbanisation utilising a single definition, or focused on single countries and test for the existence of counterurbanisation using several definitions. Four comparative studies utilise different approaches for identifying the counterurbanisation phenomenon in European countries.

First, Illeris (1988) evaluates population growth rates of national capital regions and other major metropolitan areas relative to the national average; major metropolitan areas are those with economies based on high level services. Urbanisation or a spatial concentration of the national population occurs when major metropolitan regions experience growth rates above the national average, while counterurbanisation or deconcentration is evident when these major centres show growth rates below the national average.

The second approach, used by Cochrane and Vining (1988), starts with a core–periphery subdivision of each country, with the core defined as one or more large urban/metropolitan areas and the periphery defined as the remaining regions of the country. For example, the core area of Sweden is defined as the three urban regions of Stockholm, the Southern metropolitan and the Western metropolitan areas, and the periphery is defined as Mid-Sweden, the South East, Mid-Sweden forest, the Central-North and the North. Temporal variations in core–periphery net migration rates are used to characterise whether national populations show a trend of increasing or decreasing spatial concentration. A trend of net in-migration to national core areas translates into spatial concentration (urbanisation), while net out-migration means deconcentration (counterurbanisation).

The third approach, used by Champion (1992), defines counterurbanisation as a negative relationship between the net migration rates of urban regions and regional population density and defines urbanisation as a positive association. Champion summarises the findings of Fielding's earlier research (1982, 1986, 1990) and supplements this information with data supplied by national statistical offices. The fourth definition, used by Schön (1995), is similar to that of Champion; a statistically significant negative relationship between the regional population change rate and regional population density identifies counterurbanisation, and a statistically significant positive relationship signifies urbanisation.

Other studies of the counterurbanisation phenomenon in individual European countries also utilise either regional population and/or internal migration data, and employ one or more of the approaches suggested above.

As a first step in a comparison of the different explanations given for the counterurbanisation phenomenon in European countries, urbanisation (U) and counterurbanisation (CU) trends starting in the 1960s and continuing into the 1990s are summarised in Table 4.1. The information presented in Table 4.1 represents a distillation of the findings gathered from the published literature on the topic; the objective of this author was to include everything written on European counterurbanisation, excluding the extensive work done on Britain. Table 4.1 also includes the literature source or reference from which this information was gathered. In summary, the published literature which directly or indirectly discusses the topic of counterurbanisation includes studies which

TABLE 4.1 Urbanisation (U) or counterurbanisation (CU) trends in European countries during the 1960s, 1970s, 1980s and 1990s

Country	Reference	Trend
Austria	Champion 1992	U 1970s; CU 1980–1984; U 1984–1988
Belgium	Illeris 1988	CU 1970–1986
	Cochrane and Vining 1988	U 1970–1972; CU 1973–1980; U 1983–1985
	Champion 1992	CU 1970–1984; U 1984–1988
	Schön 1995	CU 1985–1990
Czechoslovakia	Cochrane and Vining 1988	U 1970–1986
Denmark	Illeris 1988	CU 1970–1987
	Cochrane and Vining 1988	CU 1971–1980; U/CU 1981–1985
	Court 1989	CU 1970–1986
	Champion 1992	CU 1970–1979; U/CU 1980–1986
	Schön 1995	CU 1985–1990
Finland	Illeris 1988	U (slowing) 1970–1979; U 1980–1987
	Cochrane and Vining 1988	U (slowing) 1970–1977; U 1978–1984
	Vartiainen 1989	U (slowing) 1975–1985
	Champion 1992	U 1980–1988
	Irmen 1995	U 1980–1990
France	Cochrane and Vining 1988	CU 1962–1982
	Illeris 1988	CU 1970–1986
	Champion 1992	CU 1970–1988
	Winchester and Ogden 1989	U 1954–1968; U/CU 1968–1975; CU 1975–1982
	Winchester 1993	CU 1975–1982
	Jones 1991	CU 1982–1990
Germany (East)	Cochrane and Vining 1988	U 1970–1986
	Schön 1992	U 1971–1986
	Kontuly and Schön 1995[a]	U 1981–1990; U 1990–1991
Germany (West)	Kontuly and Vogelsang 1988, 1989	U 1950–1960; U/CU 1960–1968; U/CU 1970–1979; CU 1980–1984
	Illeris 1988	CU 1970–1985
	Cochrane and Vining 1988; Kontuly 1992	CU 1970–1985; CU 1986–1987
	Champion 1992	CU 1970–1984; U/CU 1984–1988
	Kanaroglou and Braun 1992	CU 1978–1983
	Kontuly 1992	CU 1980–1903
	Schön 1991	CU 1980–1984; U/CU 1985–1989
	Kontuly and Schön 1994	CU 1980–1984; U/CU 1985–1989
	Irmen 1995	CU 1980–1990
	Irmen and Blach 1994	CU 1980–1992
	Kontuly and Schön 1995[b]	CU 1981–1990; CU 1990–1991
Greece	Schön 1995	CU 1985–1990
Iceland	Illeris 1988	CU 1970–1980; U 1980–1987

continued overleaf

TABLE 4.1 (*continued*)

Country	Reference	Trend
Ireland	Champion 1992[c]	U 1970–1980; CU 1980–1990
	Cawley 1994	U 1971–1991 (population data); U 1971–1981 (migration data); U/CU 1981–1986 (migration data)
	Cawley 1990	U 1981–1986
	Cawley 1991	U 1981–1986
	Walsh 1991	U 1986–1991
Italy	Cochrane and Vining 1988	U 1970–1981; CU 1982–1985
	Champion 1992	U/CU 1970–1984; CU 1984–1988
	Coombes *et al.* 1989	U 1971–1981
	Dematteis 1986	CU 1974–1980
	Dematteis and Petsimeris 1989	CU 1975–1985
Netherlands	Cochrane and Vining 1988	CU 1970–1981; U/CU 1982–1985
	Illeris 1988	CU 1970–1980; U 1980–1986
	Champion 1992	CU 1970–1980; U/CU 1980–1984; U 1984–1988
Norway	Cochrane and Vining 1988	U 1970–1971; U/CU 1972–1974; U 1975–1978; U/CU 1979–1980, U 1981–1985
	Illeris 1988	CU 1970–1980; U 1980–1987
	Champion 1992	U (weak) 1970–1980; U 1980–1988
	Hansen 1989	U 1970–1985
	Myklebost 1984	U (stopped) 1970–1980
Portugal	Champion 1992	U 1970–1986
Spain	Cochrane and Vining 1988	U 1970–1979; U/CU 1980–1985
Sweden	Oberg 1991	U (strong)1960–1970; CU 1970–1980; U (weak) 1980–1989
	Illeris 1988	CU 1970–1980; U 1980–1987
	Cochrane and Vining 1988	CU 1971–1980; U 1981–1986
	Champion 1992	CU (weak) 1970–1980; U/CU 1980–1984; U 1984–1988
	Borgegård *et al.* 1995	CU 1972–1981; U 1982–1987; CU 1988–1992
Switzerland	Schaeffer 1992	CU 1970–1980
	Illeris 1988	CU 1970–1987
	Champion 1992	CU 1970–1984; U/CU 1984–1988
	Irmen 1995	CU 1980–1990

[a] Trends are identified for the old German Democratic Republic between 1981 and 1990 and for the eastern part of unified Germany between 1990 and 1991.
[b] Trends are identified for the old Federal Republic of Germany between 1981 and 1990 and for the western part of unified Germany between 1990 and 1991.
[c] Because of the small number of regions (nine in number) Champion's results for Ireland are not statistically significant at the five percent level.

search for a slowing down of urbanisation tendencies in European countries as well as a reversal of this urbanisation trend. An exploration of this literature found that the topic had been evaluated in 18 European countries.

Based on the trends identified in Table 4.1, the 18 countries can be divided into the following groups:

- Strong urbanisation tendencies during the 1970s, 1980s and 1990s – Czechoslovakia, Germany (East) and Portugal.
- Slowing urbanisation during the 1970s – Finland, Ireland and Norway.
- Slowing urbanisation during the 1980s – Spain.
- Counterurbanisation during the 1970s – Belgium, Denmark, France, Iceland, the Netherlands, Sweden and Switzerland.
- Counterurbanisation during the first half of the 1980s – Austria, Germany (West) and Italy.
- Counterurbanisation during the second half of the 1980s – Greece.

Looking more closely at trends after 1985, the situation appears complex:

- A return to strong urbanisation tendencies during the 1980s – Finland, Ireland and Norway.
- A return to urbanisation from an earlier counterurbanisation tendency – Austria, Iceland and the Netherlands.
- Continued counterurbanisation – Denmark, France, Greece and Italy.
- Unclear post-1985 trends – Belgium, Germany (West), Spain, Sweden and Switzerland; four of these five countries exhibited counterurbanisation tendencies during the 1970s or 1980s (Belgium, Germany (West), Sweden and Switzerland), while Spain showed a slowing of urbanisation tendencies during the 1980s.

From another perspective, most of the studies investigating counterurbanisation in Europe focus on data from the 1970s, because the phenomenon was first identified in the United States during this time period. However, two studies search for the existence of the phenomenon during the 1950s and 1960s, and attempt to identify stages in the evolution from urbanisation to counterurbanisation (France – Winchester and Ogden 1989; Germany (West) – Kontuly and Vogelsang 1989).

A CLASSIFICATION OF COUNTERURBANISATION EXPLANATIONS

Several studies have provided useful listings of explanations for the counterurbanisation phenomenon (Borgegård *et al.* 1995; Borgegård and Håkansson 1996; Champion 1992; Frey 1987; Geyer 1996; Hugo and Smailes 1985; Sant and Simons 1993b). Additional explanations were also found in the individual country studies evaluated for this chapter. Using this body of literature, it is possible to construct a six-part classification of explanations into the following

TABLE 4.2 Explanations of the counterurbanisation phenomenon

1. Economic cyclical factors
   1a. Business cycle fluctuations – a temporary fluctuation in rural-to-urban and return migration as a response to the economic recessions of the 1970s.
   1b. Regional boom and bust experiences – caused by the growth of employment in localised industries such as mining, defence and tourism, in favoured non-metropolitan locations.
   1c. A new cyclic pattern of capital investment in property and business – a phase in which the potential returns of urban investments in residential property are depleted and the focus moves to small settlements and rural areas.

2. Economic structural factors
   2a. Structural economic change is occurring as the proportion of tertiary and quaternary employment increases relative to secondary employment. Also, the decline in primary employment has almost run its course, so there is a reduction in the stock of potential out-migrants living in rural areas. Older industrial countries have been going through a process of deindustrialisation that has had a strong negative impact on larger cities, especially on their central areas. Fielding (1989) expands on this explanation by emphasising the evolution of a new spatial division of labour. He argues that the growth of companies into multi-plant, multi-product and multi-national enterprises was accompanied by disinvestment in high-wage areas in favour of low-wage reserves of labour within national territories. The deconcentration of jobs was followed by population migration.

3. Spatial and environmental factors
   3a. Agglomeration diseconomies – the emergence of scale diseconomies in large urban areas, combined with social (urban decay and large numbers of foreign migrants) and environmental (air and water pollution) problems serve to increase the push factor from metropolitan areas.
   3b. Housing availability and costs.
   3c. Environmental amenities – such as favourable climatic conditions or locations near to seacoasts, mountains or lakes – a pull factor.
   3d. Expansion of tourism and employment growth in resort and recreation industries.

4. Socio-economic and socio-cultural factors
   4a. A change in residential preferences or in the ability to act on such preferences – a basic change either in the preferences of the working-age population or in their ability to act on such preferences, in favour of residences in rural or small-town environments and against large cities.
   4b. State welfare payments – the growth of state welfare payments, private pensions and other benefits free a larger proportion of the population from the constraints of living near their jobs.
   4c. Changing socio-demographic compositions – the influence of relative age cohort sizes such as the proportion of the population in the Baby Boom generation and the proportion of the population which is elderly. The emergence of large birth cohorts during the 1950s and early 1960s impacted on labour markets and the spatial structure of young adult migration flows became more geographically focused. The ageing of the population has meant a rapid increase in the numbers of economically inactive people and a growing pool of potential migrants. Retirement enables those with sufficient resources to realise long-held desires for more relaxed lifestyles in attractive, uncongested surroundings.

TABLE 4.2 (*continued*)

4d. Attitudinal changes – social values undergo changes that are sufficient to cause noticeable geographical shifts.

4e. Regional entrepreneurial skills – regionally specific historical, cultural and social conditions which adjusted to the needs of deconcentrated industrial production.

5. Implicit and explicit government policies

5a. Planned (industrial) deconcentration initiatives – occurred where governments perceived that either infrastructure costs of large cities or the problems of regional decline warranted new policies to redistribute jobs and people.

5b. Improvements of education, health and other social infrastructure in rural/peripheral areas.

6. Technological innovations

6a. A reduced friction of distance associated with transportation and communications technology improvements which allowed an extension of urban residences and employment into widely dispersed areas – one outcome of these innovations is telecommuting.

---

categories: economic cyclical factors, economic structural factors, spatial and environmental factors, socio-economic and socio-cultural factors, implicit and explicit government policies, and technological innovations. Their classification is detailed in Table 4.2.

Two different opinions exist in the literature concerning the specific set of explanations needed to understand the counterurbanisation phenomenon. Several authors (Frey 1987, 1988, 1989; Geyer 1996; Hugo and Smailes 1985; Kontuly and Vogelsang 1988; Moseley 1984) argue that two or three major explanations provide the basis for understanding counterurbanisation throughout the developed world, while Sant and Simons (1993a) contend that specific locational or environmental disparities between places rather than general factors explain the phenomenon.

Moseley (1984) argues that the explanations given for counterurbanisation can be grouped into two general classes, that is, one which is consumption based or people-led and the other which is production based or job-led. For people-led explanations, the expression of popular preferences is the prime dynamic, whereas the redistribution of employment opportunities forms the basis for job-led explanations. The people-led explanations are included in the socio-economic and socio-cultural factors (explanation 4) in Table 4.2, while job-led explanations are found under economic structural factors (explanation 2).

A similar dichotomy was proposed by Frey (1989), who suggested that the two theoretical perspectives of 'deconcentration' and 'regional restructuring' can be used as basic explanations for the counterurbanisation phenomenon. Deconcentration corresponds with explanation 4a in the table, while regional restructuring is covered by explanation 2. The two perspectives suggested by

Frey are also similar to the 'behavioural' and 'structural' explanations of counter-urbanisation proposed by Hugo and Smailes (1985). They argue that these two explanations are particularly significant because they come closest to providing a coherent causal mechanism for understanding counterurbanisation. However, Kontuly and Vogelsang (1988) contend that government policy must be added to the two major explanations suggested in the literature; they argue that government policies are important explanations of counterurbanisation.

Geyer (1996) points out that most of the explanations given for the counterur-banisation phenomenon can be seen as causes of both spatial deconcentration and concentration (see also Borgegård and Håkansson 1996). According to him, only two factors are fundamental for contrasting these processes: 'production-ism' and 'environmentalism'. Productionism refers to the phase in people's lives when improved job opportunities, education and income are more important than living conditions, and during this phase movement is toward large metro-politan regions. During the environmentalism phase, the need to improve one's living conditions becomes as important as earning a living, and migration shifts toward smaller sized, sparsely populated areas containing environmental amenities[1]. Productionism and environmentalism can be thought of as refine-ments of the explanation referring to the residential preferences of individuals (explanation 4a), which has been suggested as one of the major causal mechan-isms for understanding the counterurbanisation phenomenon (Frey 1989; Hugo and Smailes 1985).

In contrast to all of these accounts, Sant and Simons (1993a) offer a different approach to understanding counterurbanisation. They suggest that reasons for counterurbanisation may lie in the geographical disparities in economic and environmental conditions relative to the residential qualities sought by house-holds and the locational attributes sought by expanding industries. For without such disparities there would be little incentive for counterurbanisation, whether it is people-led or job-led. Consequently, they imbed residential preferences within a broader conceptualisation of counterurbanisation as a behavioural filter and as the outcome of individual decision-making. As a precondition for counterurbanisation, change must take place in either the utility of a place or in the set of enabling factors that make population shifts possible. Place utility includes residential preferences and the trade-offs between locational attributes, while enabling factors include the conditions that affect the ability of people to move, the assets and wealth of retired people, and innovations affecting the linkages between work and home.

Nonetheless, according to Sant and Simons (1993a), changes in place utility or enabling factors are not sufficient to cause counterurbanisation. As the final condition, locational or environmental disparities (explanations 3a – agglomer-ation diseconomies, 3b – housing costs and availability, and 3c – environmental amenities) must be sufficiently large to make a move worthwhile. They bring the evaluation of reasons for counterurbanisation down to the individual decision-making level and, in so doing, suggest that several factors or explanations are

TABLE 4.3 Explanations given for the counterurbanisation phenomenon in European countries

Country	Reference	Explanation[a]
Belgium	Ahnström 1986	2a
	Keeble *et al.* 1983	2a
Denmark	Keeble *et al.* 1983	2a
	Court 1989	2a, 5b, 1c, 3b, 5a
Finland	Ahnström 1986	2a
	Kontuly and Bierens 1990	1a
	Vartiainen 1989	2a
France	Ahnström 1986	2a
	Keeble *et al.* 1983	2a
	Winchester and Ogden 1989	3b, 2a, 5a
	Winchester 1993	3b, 4a, 2a
Germany	Keeble *et al.* 1983	2a
(West)	Kontuly and Vogelsang 1988	4a
	Kontuly and Vogelsang 1989	2a, 4a, 3c, 5b, 3b, 4d
	Kontuly 1991	2a
Iceland	Kontuly and Bierens 1990	1a
Ireland	Cawley 1991	5b
	Keeble 1989	5a
Italy	Keeble *et al.* 1983	2a
	Kontuly and Bierens 1990	1a
	Dematteis 1986	1c, 3b, 2a, 4f, 5b, 6a
	Dematteis and Petsimeris 1989	2a, 3b, 5a, 5b, 4f
Netherlands	Keeble *et al.* 1983	2a
Norway	Myklebost 1984	2a, 4a, 3a, 5a, 6a
Spain	Kontuly and Bierens 1990	1a
Sweden	Kontuly and Bierens 1990	1a
	Ahnström 1986	2a
	Borgegård *et al.* 1995	5a, 5b
Switzerland	Schaeffer 1992	1a, 2a, 4a

[a] When more than one explanation is given, the factors are listed in the order given by the author(s).

necessary to understand the phenomenon. Sant and Simons thus believe that an explanation of counterurbanisation lies in the specific locational factors important to households and to businesses.

EXPLANATIONS GIVEN FOR EUROPEAN COUNTERURBANISATION

Numerous studies, in addition to identifying the beginning of counterurbanisation or a reduction of urbanisation tendencies in European countries, suggest reasons for this change. Using the classification scheme developed in Table 4.2, these explanations are listed in Table 4.3 by individual European country. Table

4.3 also includes the literature source or reference from which this information was collected.

As we have seen above, several authors (Frey 1989; Hugo and Smailes 1985; Moseley 1984) contend that the counterurbanisation phenomenon may be explained by the two major factors of economic structural change (explanation 2a) and residential preferences (explanation 4a). The literature summarised in Table 4.3 provides little support for the importance of residential preferences as a major factor. Instead, economic structural change (explanation 2a) is the most widely cited European explanation for the counterurbanisation phenomenon. Explanation 2a is found to be important for 10 of the 18 countries included in this chapter: Belgium, Denmark, Finland, France, Germany (West), Italy, the Netherlands, Norway, Sweden and Switzerland. Also, several different authors investigating the phenomenon in Belgium, Denmark, Finland, France, Germany (West) and Italy independently confirm the importance of this explanation. For example, Ahnström (1986), Keeble *et al.* (1983) and Winchester and Ogden (1989) each conclude that economic structural change is an important explanation for France.

Government policies (explanation 5) and economic cyclical factors (explanation 1) were found to be the second most important set of explanations of European counterurbanisation, based on the number of times these factors were listed in Table 4.3. Government policies were found to be important in seven countries (Denmark, France, Germany (West), Ireland, Italy, Norway and Sweden); both planned deconcentration initiatives (explanation 5a) and improvements in education, health and other social infrastructure (explanation 5b) were cited as important in four of these seven countries. Economic cyclical factors were cited as important in seven nations (Denmark, Finland, Iceland, Italy, Spain, Sweden and Switzerland).

Socio-economic and socio-cultural factors (explanation 4) and spatial and environmental factors (explanation 3) were found to be the third most important sets of explanations. The residential preference explanation (4a) was listed as being important in only four countries (France, Germany (West), Norway and Switzerland). In fact, considering the other socio-economic and socio-cultural explanations listed in Table 4.3, attitudinal change (explanation 4d) and regional entrepreneurial skill (explanation 4e) were found to be important only in Germany (West) and Italy. In total, socio-economic and socio-cultural factors were important in only five countries. Spatial and environmental factors (explanation 3) were important in Denmark, France, Germany (West), Italy and Norway. Within this factor, housing availability and costs (explanation 3b) were listed as important in four of these five countries. In particular, Winchester (1993) states that for France, the demand for and supply of good quality housing is the most important explanation of counterurbanisation. Finally, technological innovations (explanation 6) was the least important category, being cited as important in only Italy and Norway.

For many of the European countries included in this chapter, several explanations were necessary to explain their counterurbanisation experience. Indeed, numerous authors cited in Table 4.3 explicitly stated that an understanding of European counterurbanisation required a set of explanations (Court 1989 – Denmark; Dematteis and Petsimeris 1989 – Italy; Kontuly and Bierens 1990 – Finland, Iceland, Italy, Spain and Sweden; Kontuly and Vogelsang 1989 – Germany (West); Schaeffer 1992 – Switzerland; Winchester 1993 – France). The need for multiple explanations of European counterurbanisation was also voiced by other authors (for example, Champion 1989; Illeris 1979).

If several explanations are needed to understand counterurbanisation in Europe, then the question arises as to whether the individual factors reinforce one another or conflict with each other. From the Australian experience, Hugo and Smailes (1985) contend that the two major explanations of counterurbanisation (their behavioural and structural factors) are to some extent competing. On the other hand, Champion (1995) suggests that the deconcentration and regional restructuring perspectives were reinforcing one another in the 1970s and 1980s. During the 1970s, strong population deconcentration forces coincided with the dispersal of economic activity to peripheral regions. In the 1980s, the forces causing population deconcentration weakened as difficult economic times reduced investments in the housing and public sectors of peripheral areas. Economic restructuring continued with a deconcentration of manufacturing activity to peripheral areas and a concentration of high-order services in the centres of large metropolitan regions.

Unfortunately, none of the authors listed in Table 4.3 were able to comment on whether the multiple factors causing counterurbanisation reinforced or competed with one another, but several suggested that multiple factors appear to be at work simultaneously. Attesting to the empirical difficulty of determining whether different explanations reinforced or competed with one another, it was found that only one author (Winchester 1993) was able to specify the most important factor in a set of multiple explanations.

Moving away from a focus on the national picture, several authors concluded that geographic variations in counterurbanisation tendencies can be found within individual countries and it may be necessary to develop a regionally sensitive approach to better understand and explain the phenomenon in Europe. Winchester (1993) points out that, in France, counterurbanisation trends are spatially differentiated between the core, the periphery and the remote regions of the country. Coombes et al. (1989) conclude that because of the vast regional differences that exist in Italy, it is impossible to generalise counterurbanisation trends within the country. Dematteis and Petsimeris (1989) solve this problem by subdividing Italy into three parts, and find early counterurbanisation in the North West, more recent counterurbanisation in the North East and Centre and continued urbanisation in the South. They emphasise the importance of subdividing a country into separate regions based on different levels of economic development. Sant and Simons (1993a: 117) emphasise this point by noting succinctly that 'not all places experience the same trends at the same time';

Australian counterurbanisation shows a strong contrast between coastal and inland non-metropolitan areas.

In a discussion of the counterurbanisation of manufacturing activity in Europe, Keeble (1989) states that recent empirical research on the processes of industrial change in different European countries suggests that the nature of recent rural industrialisation varies so greatly in the different regions of the European Community as to demand a regionally sensitive approach. The need for such an approach is also evident in the results of Kontuly and Bierens (1990). They find business cycle fluctuations (explanation 1a) to be an important explanation of counterurbanisation for the Barcelona, Bilbao and Valencia metropolitan areas of Spain but not for Madrid, and also an important explanation for the Southern metropolitan area of Sweden but not for the Stockholm and Western metropolitan areas.

COUNTERURBANISATION IN WEST GERMANY

This section focuses on West Germany because this author specialises in the study of German counterurbanisation. Research points to the usefulness of generating age-specific explanations, the importance of identifying the counterurbanisation phenomenon at several geographical scales and the need to disaggregate total migration into an internal and foreign component.

Two studies by Kontuly and Vogelsang (1988, 1989) disaggregate urbanisation/counterurbanisation tendencies by age and then offer age-specific explanations for the changing patterns of movement. They discover the filtering-down of a counterurbanisation direction of migration from the 50 and over age-groups to both the 30–49 and the 25–29 years olds. They conclude that a deconcentration of employment opportunities to small-sized, less densely populated regions combined with an increasing preference for residential locations in areas with abundant natural amenities explains the counterurban movements of the 30–49 year olds. Employment deconcentration and return migration explain the filtering down of a counterurban direction of movement to the 25–29 year olds. By contrast, the movement of the 18–24 year olds remained in an urbanisation direction due to the availability of educational, employment and on-the-job-training opportunities in large metropolitan regions.

Different geographical processes become evident at different spatial scales. Thus, Vining and Strauss (1977) argued that in order for a dominant counterurbanisation trend (a clean break) to exist in the United States, it must be evident at all spatial scales from the county level through to the Census Geographic Division level. Such a condition was satisfied in West Germany during the 1970s and 1980s. Counterurbanisation was found to exist at several spatial scales, that is, at the county (*kreise*) level (Kanaroglou and Braun 1992), at the Federal Planning Region level (Kontuly and Schön 1994), at the functional urban region scale (Kontuly and Vogelsang 1988, 1989) and at the macro-region or urban systems level (Kontuly 1992). Identifying counterurbanisation in West Germany at several spatial scales provided strong evidence for the broad consolidation of the phenomenon.

Direct linkages exist between foreign migration and counterurbanisation because international migration may counterbalance the counterurbanisation phenomenon. Indeed, Kontuly and Vogelsang (1988) found that immigration disguised the extent of the counterurban movement of the West German population and the same situation appears to be true for Australia (Sant and Simons 1993b) and Sweden (Borgegård et al. 1995). Foreign in- and out-migration can also affect the counterurbanisation phenomenon by impacting on the direction of internal migration. Frey (1995a) argues that recent immigration to the United States (Frey 1995b) and other developed countries (Champion 1994) is affecting internal migration in unprecedented ways. In particular, immigration impacted on internal migration into and out of the high immigration states of the United States and altered the national internal migration system. In short, states showing a large influx of immigrants also show internal (net) out-migration. A similar pattern is also evident in western Germany during 1991 (Bucher et al. 1994); several regions which experienced a large influx of foreign migrants also showed high rates of internal (net) out-migration. These regions included small- and medium-sized areas such as Kiel, Osnabrück and Göttingen, as well as the large industrial centre of Dortmund.

CONCLUSION

Contrasting the explanations provided for counterurbanisation in Europe does not provide a clear-cut answer to the question of whether the phenomenon can be explained by a few general theories which are pervasive throughout the developed world or whether there are numerous, geographically distinct reasons. The information gathered in this chapter suggests that the former is more appropriate for Europe.

The single most widely cited explanation of European counterurbanisation was economic structural change; it was cited as important in 10 of the 18 countries evaluated above. Government policy and economic cyclical factors were second in importance. Changes in residential preferences or in the ability to act on such preferences appear to be of minor importance in understanding European counterurbanisation. Nonetheless, even though economic structural change or manufacturing deconcentration was the most widely cited reason for European counterurbanisation, it was not clear whether the impact of this factor was restricted to the 1970s or whether its importance continued through the 1980s. Many of the studies evaluating the significance of this explanation were published during the 1980s and analysed data from the 1970s, so it is too early to know the answer to this question. If the importance of manufacturing employment deconcentration waned during the 1980s and 1990s, then it may be possible that this change was only temporary in nature and the predictions of the regional restructuring perspective (Frey 1987, 1988, 1989) will become true. This perspective agues that after a transitional period in which the economies of developed nations adjust to deindustrialisation, spatial concentration will return as certain large metropolitan centres become command and control centres and the preferred locations for high-order producer and corporate business services, and for research and development.

Champion (1992) suggested that, based on the fluctuations of the pace of counterurbanisation during the 1970s and 1980s, the phenomenon may be cyclical in nature and caused by changing economic conditions and the effects of variations in the sizes of different age groups. Dematteis (1986) argues that the 1990s and 2000s will show irregular fluctuations of urbanisation (concentration) and counterurbanisation (diffused growth). Berry (1988) and Mera (1988) also suggest the emergence of migration cycles in developed countries. Geyer and Kontuly (1993) continue this line of thought by arguing that urban/metropolitan areas progress through a first cycle of spatial development in which urban areas go through a phase of spatial concentration and then a phase of deconcentration. When this first cycle of urban development is completed, national urban systems are hypothesised to pass through sequential phases of spatial concentration and deconcentration. If Geyer and Kontuly's systemic maturation theory is appropriate, then it is reasonable to expect that national settlement systems in developed countries will be influenced in the future by countervailing processes of concentration and dispersion (Elliott 1997).

Geyer and Kontuly (1993) also argue that, as a country passes from the first into the second cycle of urban development, national level changes will be subtle and regional level changes will be more significant. During this advanced second cycle of urban development, analysis and explanation should be undertaken within regions or within subregions (such as urban systems) of a developed country rather than at the national level.

Lastly, Sant and Simons (1993a) make the point that many reasons were put forward to explain counterurbanisation but that there still is no satisfactory explanation for why certain countries were affected more than others. This chapter suggests that, in order to understand better the counterurbanisation phenomenon in Europe, it may be necessary to begin disaggregating population and migration data by social-economic factors (such as by age, education, gender and income), by regional differences (such as coastal versus interior) and by metropolitan characteristics (such as old industrial versus high-tech regions, or capital regions versus new growth poles).

NOTES

1. Productionism and environmentalism, as with all deterministic indicators, are 'not water tight and should, therefore, be treated with caution' (Geyer 1996: 11).
2. The specification of the West German metropolitan size hierarchy developed by Kontuly (1992) provides an alternative to the core–periphery delimitation used by Cochrane and Vining (1988).

REFERENCES

Ahnström, L. (1986) 'The turnaround trend and the economically active population of seven capital regions in western Europe', *Norsk Geografisk Tidsskrift*, **40**, 55–64.

Berry, B. (1988) 'Migration reversals in perspective: the long-wave evidence', *International Regional Science Review*, **11**, 245–251.

Borgegård, L.-E. and Håkansson, J. (1998) *Population concentration and dispersion in Sweden since the 1970s*, Cerum, * (forthcoming).

Borgegård, L.-E., Håkansson, J. and Malmberg, G. (1995) 'Population redistribution in Sweden – long term trends and contemporary tendencies', *Geografiska Annaler*, **77B**, 31–45.

Bucher, H., Kocks, M. and Siedhoff, M. (1994) *Die künftige Bevölkerungsentwicklung in den Regionen Deutschlands bis 2010: Annahmen und Ergebnisse einer BfLR-Bevölkerungsprognose*, Informationen zur Raumentwicklung, 12, Bundesforschungsanstalt für Landeskunde und Raumordnung, Bonn.

Cawley, M. (1990) 'Population change in the Republic of Ireland 1981–1986', *Area*, **22**, 67–74.

Cawley, M. (1991) 'Town population change 1971–1986: patterns and distributional effects', *Irish Geography*, **24**, 106–116.

Cawley, M. (1994) 'Desertification: measuring population decline in rural Ireland', *Journal of Rural Studies*, **10**, 395–407.

Champion, A. (1989) 'Conclusion: temporary anomaly, long-term trend or transitional phase?', in A. Champion (ed.), *Counterurbanisation: the changing pace and nature of population deconcentration*, Edward Arnold, London, 230–244.

Champion, A. (1992) 'Urban and regional demographic trends in the developed world', *Urban Studies*, **29**, 461–482.

Champion, A. (1994) 'International migration and demographic change in the developed world', *Urban Studies*, **31**, 653–677.

Champion, A. (1995) 'Internal migration, counterurbanization and changing population distribution', in R. Hall and P. White (eds.), *Europe's population: towards the next century*, UCL Press, London, 99–129.

Cochrane, S. and Vining, D. (1988) 'Recent trends in migration between core and peripheral regions in developed and advanced developing countries', *International Regional Science Review*, **11**, 215–243.

Coombes, M., Dalla Longa, R. and Raybould, S. (1989) 'Counterurbanisation in Britain and Italy: a comparative critique of the concept, causation and evidence', *Progress in Planning*, **32**, 1–70.

Court, Y. (1989) 'Denmark: towards a more deconcentrated settlement system', in A. Champion (ed.), *Counterurbanisation: the changing pace and nature of population deconcentration*, Edward Arnold, London, 121–140.

Dematteis, G. (1986) 'Urbanization and counter-urbanization in Italy', *Ekistics*, **316/317**, 26–33.

Dematteis, G. and Petsimeris, P. (1989) 'Italy: counterurbanization as a transitional phase in settlement reorganization', in A. Champion (ed.), *Counterurbanisation: the changing pace and nature of population deconcentration*, Edward Arnold, London, 187–206.

Elliott, J. (1997) 'Cycles within the system: metropolitanization and internal migration in the US, 1965–1990', *Urban Studies*, **34**, 21–41.

Fielding, A. (1982) 'Counterurbanisation in Western Europe', *Progress in Planning*, **17**, 1–52.

Fielding, A. (1986) 'Counterurbanisation in Western Europe', in Findlay, A. and White, P. (eds.), *West European population change*, Croom Helm, London, 35–49.

Fielding, A. (1989) 'Migration and urbanization in Western Europe since 1950', *Geographical Journal*, **155**, 60–69.

Fielding, A. (1990) 'Counterurbanisation: threat or blessing?', in D. Pinder (ed.), *Western Europe: challenge and change*, Belhaven, London, 226–239.

Frey, W. (1987) 'Migration and depopulation of the metropolis: regional restructuring or rural renaissance', *American Sociological Review*, **52**, 240–257.

Frey, W. (1988) 'Migration and metropolis decline in developed countries: a comparative national study', *Population Development Review*, **14**, 595–628.

Frey, W. (1989) 'United States: counterurbanization and metropolis depopulation', in A. Champion (ed.), *Counterurbanisation: the changing pace and nature of population deconcentration*, Edward Arnold, London, 34–61.

Frey, W. (1995a) 'Immigration and internal migration 'flight' from US metropolitan areas: towards a new demographic balkanisation', *Urban Studies*, **32**, 733–757.

Frey, W. (1995b) 'Immigration impacts on internal migration of the poor: 1990 Census evidence for US States', *International Journal of Population Geography*, **1**, 51–67.

Geyer, H. (1996) 'Expanding the theoretical foundation of the concept of differential urbanization', *Tijdschrift voor Economische en Sociale Geografie*, **87**, 44–59.

Geyer, H. and Kontuly, T. (1993) 'A theoretical foundation for the concept of differential urbanisation', *International Regional Science Review*, **15**, 157–177.

Hansen, J. (1989) 'Norway: the turnaround which turned around', in A. Champion (ed.), *Counterurbanisation: the changing pace and nature of population deconcentration*, Edward Arnold, London, 34–61.

Hugo, G. and Smailes, P. (1985) 'Urban-rural migration in Australia: a process view of the turnaround', *Journal of Rural Studies*, **1**, 11–30.

Illeris, S. (1979) 'Recent developments of the settlement system of advanced market economy countries', *Geografisk Tidsskrift*, **78**, 49–56.

Illeris, S. (1988) 'Counterurbanization revisited: the new map of population distribution in Central and Northwestern Europe', in M. Bannon, L. Bourne and R. Sinclair (eds.), *Urbanization and urban development*, University College Press, Dublin, 1–16.

Irmen, E. (1995) 'Intraregional employment patterns and dynamics', paper presented at the 7th annual Rural Policy Conference of the Canadian Rural Restructuring Foundation, Coaticook, Québec, Canada, October.

Irmen, E. and Blach, A. (1994) *Räumlicher Strukturwandel: konzentration, dekonzentration und dispersion*, Informationen zur Raumentwicklung, 7/8, Bundesforschungsanstalt für Landeskunde und Raumordnung, Bonn.

Jones, P. (1991) 'The French census 1990: the southward drift continues', *Geography*, **76**, 358–361.

Kanaroglou, P. and Braun, G. (1992) 'The pattern of counterurbanization in the Federal Republic of Germany, 1977–85', *Environment and Planning A*, **24**, 481–496.

Keeble, D. (1989) 'The dynamics of European industrial counterurbanization in the 1980s: corporate restructuring or indigenous growth?', *Geographical Journal*, **155**, 70–74.

Keeble, D., Owens, P. and Thompson, C. (1983) 'The urban–rural manufacturing shift in the European Community', *Urban Studies*, **20**, 405–418.

Kontuly, T. (1991) 'The deconcentration theoretical perspective as an explanation for recent changes in the West German migration system', *Geoforum*, **22**, 299–317.

Kontuly T. (1992) 'National-, regional- and urban-scale population deconcentration in West Germany', *Landscape and Urban Planning*, **22**, 219–228.

Kontuly, T. and Bierens, H. (1990) 'Testing the recession theory as an explanation for the migration turnaround', *Environment and Planning A*, **22**, 253–270.

Kontuly, T. and Schön, K. (1994) 'Changing western German internal migration systems during the second half of the 1980s', *Environment and Planning A*, **26**, 1521–1543.

Kontuly, T. and Schön, K. (1995) 'Regional demographic change in unified Germany', *Proceedings*, 1994 International Geographical Union Regional Conference, Prague, Czech Republic.

Kontuly, T. and Vogelsang, R. (1988) 'Explanations for the intensification of counterurbanization in the Federal Republic of Germany', *Professional Geographer*, **40**, 42–54.

Kontuly, T. and Vogelsang, R. (1989) 'Federal Republic of Germany: the intensification of the migration turnaround', in A. Champion (ed.), *Counterurbanisation: the changing pace and nature of population deconcentration*, Edward Arnold, London, 141–161.

Mera, K. (1988) 'The emergence of migration cycles', *International Regional Science Review*, **11**, 269–275.

Moseley, M. (1984) 'The revival of rural areas in advanced countries: a review of some causes and consequences', *Geoforum*, **15**, 447–456.

Myklebost, H. (1984) 'The evidence for urban turnaround in Norway', *Geoforum*, **15**, 167–176.

Oberg, S. (ed.) (1991) *National atlas of Sweden. The population*, Stockholm, Statistics Sweden.

Sant, M. and Simons, P. (1993a) 'The conceptual basis of counterurbanisation: critique and development', *Australian Geographical Studies*, **31**, 113–126.

Sant, M. and Simons, P. (1993b) 'Counterurbanization and coastal development in New South Wales', *Geoforum*, **24**, 291–306.

Schaeffer, P. (1992) 'Deconcentration, counter-urbanization, or trend reversal? The population distribution of Switzerland, 1900–1980', *Socio-Economic Planning Science*, **26**, 89–102.

Schön, K. (1991) 'Urbanisation – counterurbanisation – reurbanisation: where is Germany today?', *Internal Working Paper*, Bundesforschungsanstalt für Landeskunde und Raumordnung, Bonn.

Schön, K. (1992) 'Recent trends in cities and urban agglomerations in Germany', in K. Strohmeier and C. Matthiessen (eds.), *Innovation and urban population dynamics*, Avebury, Aldershot, 137–167.

Schön, K. (1995) Personal communication, Bundesforschungsanstalt für Landeskunde und Raumordnung, Bonn.

Vartiainen, P. (1989) 'The end of drastic depopulation in rural Finland: evidence of counterurbanisation?', *Journal of Rural Studies*, **5**, 123–136.

Vining, D. and Strauss, A. (1977) 'A demonstration that the current deconcentration of population in the United States is a clean break with the past', *Environment and Planning A*, **9**, 751–758.

Walsh, J. (1991) 'Changing Ireland. The turn-around of the turn around in the population of the Republic of Ireland', *Irish Geography*, **24**, 117–125.

Winchester, H. (1993) *Contemporary France*, Longman, Harlow.

Winchester, H. and Ogden, P. (1989) 'France: decentralization and deconcentration in the wake of late urbanization', in A. Champion (ed.), *Counterurbanisation: the changing pace and nature of population deconcentration*, Edward Arnold, London, 162–186.

FURTHER READING (not referenced in the text)

Pandit, K. (1997) 'Cohort and period effects in US migration: how demographic and economic cycles influence the migration schedule', *Annals of the Association of American Geographers*, **87**, 439–450.

Plane, D. (1992) 'Age composition change and the geographical dynamics of interregional migration in the US', *Annals of the Association of American Geographers*, **82**, 64–85.

Plane, D. and Rogerson, P. (1991) 'Tracking the Baby Boom, the Baby Bust, and the Echo Generations: how age composition regulates US migration', *Professional Geographer*, **43**, 416–430.

Rogers, A. and Hemez-Descryve, C. (1993) 'Changing patterns of interregional migration and population redistribution in the United States: a cohort perspective', *Espace, Populations, Societes*, **1**, 35–46.

5

CONCENTRATED IMMIGRATION, RESTRUCTURING AND THE 'SELECTIVE' DECONCENTRATION OF THE UNITED STATES POPULATION

WILLIAM H. FREY and
KENNETH M. JOHNSON

INTRODUCTION

Explaining Non-metropolitan Population Change

The important interplay between theory development and empirical observation is no better illustrated than with the quest to 'explain' recent changes in the growth and decline of the United States non-metropolitan population. The unprecedented, widespread 1970s 'turnaround' from decline to growth in America's non-metropolitan areas was a subject of widespread theorising on the part of demographers, sociologists and geographers (Frey and Speare 1988; Fuguitt et al. 1989; Long and DeAre 1988). Similar counterurbanisation patterns and theories arose in other developed countries as well (Champion 1989, 1995). However, just as the finishing touches were put on these theories, new patterns of metropolitan gains and non-metropolitan decline emerged over the 1980s – suggesting a re-evaluation of earlier deconcentration theories (Frey 1993, 1995a). Now, new post-1990 population estimates show that, once again, non-metropolitan population change has shifted to a net in-migration vis-a-vis the nation's metropolitan areas (Johnson and Beale 1995a, 1995b). This new reversal in the fortunes of America's rural population requires us to review the theories which have been advanced to explain earlier trends.

This chapter re-evaluates three key theoretical perspectives that have accounted for much of the observed non-metropolitan population shiftings of the 1960s, 1970s and 1980s with an eye toward their possible revision to account for the new 1990s trends. These explanations treat the non-metropolitan population shifts as part of the entire settlement system that both affects and is affected by broader social, economic and demographic forces. We pay particular attention to a demographic force that has heretofore received little mention in discussions of rural population change – international migration. Immigration to the United States has increased substantially since the 1970s. While its direct impact is felt by large metropolitan areas, its interaction with other settlement system forces may be promoting a secondary domestic migration to fuel growth in smaller metropolitan areas and in non-metropolitan territory.

We begin with a review of the theoretical perspectives previously brought to bear on America's counterurbanisation phenomena of the 1970s and selective reurbanisation of the 1980s. We then discuss the relevance of these same perspectives to the 1990s, paying special attention to their interaction with the new immigration to the United States. This section is followed by an in-depth examination of these interactions from a metropolitan perspective, with a special focus on how High Immigration Metropolitan Areas may be propelling a 'selective' deconcentration of longer term resident, native born Americans to smaller and non-metropolitan areas.

Following this, we review the 1990s shifts from a non-metropolitan perspective, focusing on how the 'selective' deconcentration concept may help to explain growth in counties of particular geographic and economic types and consider the implications this has for settlement system theories. This section also points up another demographic force which has shifted direction over the course of the last three decades – the natural increase component. Historically, non-metropolitan areas could count on a natural increase 'cushion' to bolster their population gains. However, recently both metropolitan *and* non-metropolitan fertility has declined. As a consequence, non-metropolitan population growth is even more dependent on migration – especially internal migration – in achieving population gains. The final section of this chapter provides a re-evaluation of the theoretical perspectives in light of the new empirical findings of the 1990s.

Defining metropolitan and non-metropolitan areas

Before proceeding further, a brief discussion of what is meant by 'metropolitan' and 'non-metropolitan' is in order. We employ the officially defined Office of Management and Budget metropolitan and non-metropolitan classification which is periodically updated to take into account changing settlement patterns (see Frey and Speare 1988, Chapter 2; United States Bureau of the Census 1992). The metropolitan population comprises the combined population of all individual metropolitan areas. First used in the 1950 Census, the metropolitan area is a functionally based concept designed to approximate the socially and economically integrated community. As originally defined, individual metropolitan areas included a central city nucleus with a population of at least 50 000 along with adjacent counties (or towns in the New England states) that were economically and socially integrated with that nucleus, as determined by commuting data, population density and measures of economic activity. While most of the nation's present metropolitan areas can still be characterised by this concept, minor modifications to the definition have been implemented to account for special cases and more complex urbanisation patterns. Current metropolitan areas are designated as either Metropolitan Statistical Areas (MSA), stand-alone areas; or Consolidated Metropolitan Statistical Areas (CMSAs), combinations of smaller metropolitan units (Primary Metropolitan Statistical Areas) which show commuting relationships with other such units. In 1995, there were 271 metropolitan areas (MSAs and CMSAs) which housed approximately 80 percent of the United States population; the residual 20 percent was defined as 'non-metropolitan' category.

The present analysis will follow the conventional definitions of metropolitan and non-metropolitan with one minor exception. This occurs in the six New England states, where metropolitan definitions, based on towns, preclude the availability of some population data. For this reason, we follow the convention of earlier research, to employ county-based New England County Metropolitan Areas to define the metropolitan population in these states.

Lastly, it should be noted that while the official classification system relegates the more than 2300 non-metropolitan counties to a single residual category (non-metropolitan area), the scholarly literature has devised more meaningful classifications. One of these distinguishes between counties that lie adjacent to metropolitan areas, sometimes called 'exurban counties', and those that are not adjacent to metropolitan boundaries. The former are typically influenced, to some degree, by the metropolitan area's economy. Another useful classification scheme groups non-metropolitan counties according to a functional or economic typology. Following previous studies which used this approach (Cook and Mizer 1994; Fuguitt et al. 1989; Morrison 1990), we employ the 13-category typology introduced below.

THEORETICAL PERSPECTIVES

Explanations for the 1970s and 1980s

The unprecedented population growth in United States non-metropolitan areas during the 1970s spawned a number of interpretations, speculations and theories' not all of which successfully accounted for the renewed metropolitan growth of the 1980s. We begin by reviewing three different perspectives which attempted to distil these explanations for early shifts in non-metropolitan population change (Frey 1989, 1993).

- *Period effects.* In some ways, the most obvious place to look for fluctuating patterns of growth and decline lies with particular 'period effects' or unique economic and demographic circumstances to which these fluctuations can be directly attributed. Such effects could be identified during the 1970s decade. An important one was the 1973–1974 oil crisis and subsequent recession. These events led to declines in manufacturing employment, especially in northern large metropolitan areas which sustained high energy costs. Yet, they also led to non-metropolitan population gains in south and west 'oil patch' areas where oil and natural resource exploration took place. It was during the 1970s, as well, that significant demographic forces favoured non-metropolitan areas. The large baby boom cohorts were 'coming of age' and entering big universities and colleges that were often located in smaller towns and in non-metropolitan territory. These cohorts continued to locate in smaller south and west areas, in light of the over-saturated metropolitan labour markets of the north. Finally, especially large elderly cohorts, born in the 1900s and 1910s decades, increased the pool of potential migrants to smaller-sized retirement communities which were being developed. In short, there were a number of unique period influences to account for a significant part of the large metropolitan area losses as well as the small, metropolitan and non-metropolitan area gains in the 1970s (Beale 1988; Fuguitt 1985).

- *Regional restructuring.* The regional restructuring perspective saw the 1970s non-metropolitan growth to be the result of largely structural, rather than cyclical, forces. The industrial restructuring of the American economy, according to this view, had a spatial component which led to deindustrialisation-related metropolitan population declines. In the context of the global economy, increasingly dominated by the multinational corporation, traditional heavy industries within the United States became less labour intensive as production jobs were eliminated or exported to other countries. During the interim, some of these jobs filtered down into smaller-sized metropolitan areas and non-metropolitan areas, with less expensive labour costs, and at least temporarily contributed to these areas' growth. In contrast to the 'period effects' perspective, which attributed the 1970s growth reversals to a unique coincidence of circumstances, the regional restructuring perspective saw them to be the culmination of a long-term trend that was merely accelerated by the mid-decade recession. Moreover, this view held that, once the deindustrialisation 'shake-out' had taken place, some metropolitan areas would experience renewed growth – especially corporate headquarters areas and centres of knowledge-based industries or high-tech developments, activities that could benefit from agglomeration economies in a post-industrial age (Noyelle and Stanback 1984).

- *Deconcentration.* Unlike the previous two perspectives which attributed the 1970s small metropolitan and non-metropolitan gains to cyclical or structural forces that would eventually subside, the deconcentration perspective saw the 1970s growth in smaller-sized places as a more fundamental break with the past. Following theoretical statements such as those proposed by Wardwell (1977), this view saw a technological and economic 'loosening of spatial constraints' that permitted both residents and employers to fulfil long-standing preferences for low-density, high-amenity locations. In essence, residential space was less dependent on agglomeration economies of the workplace so that the presumed preferences of working-aged residents to locate in smaller-sized places could now be more easily fulfilled. In addition, there were growing numbers of pensioned retirees and members of 'the leisure class' who are relatively detached from the workforce and more free to follow their residential preferences. In short, deconcentration perspectives saw the 1970s as just the beginning of a much more widespread dispersal of the population.

While each of these three perspectives was consistent with trends observed in the 1970s, they held different predictions for the 1980s. The period perspective predicted a return to more 'normal' redistribution patterns after the severe 1970s recession, oil crisis and demographic developments subsided – although this perspective also allowed for new period influences to develop in the 1980s. The regional restructuring perspective predicted a selective return to metropolitan growth after the deindustrialisation 'shake-out' took place. Only the deconcentration perspective predicted continual dispersal. As we now know, deconcentration theory 'purists' were clearly disappointed with the population declines that non-metropolitan America absorbed during the 1980s at the same time that larger metropolitan areas gained (Beale 1988; Frey 1993).

Yet, the interpretation of the 1970s and 1980s in the context of the three theories above is subject to debate, even between the two authors of this chapter. Frey (1995a) in putting forth a 'postmortem on the rural renaissance' suggested that both the 1970s gains and 1980s declines in small metropolitan and non-metropolitan growth could be attributed primarily to *period* and *regional restructuring* influences and that their coincidence helped to provide the illusion that a new era of dispersed settlement had begun. He cites the fact that the same extractive, low-wage manufacturing and agricultural activities which spawned non-metropolitan growth in the 1970s were each adversely affected by macro-economic forces in the 1980s, prompting commensurate population declines in those same small-town America areas. Moreover, the renewed albeit selective metropolitan area growth, as forecasted by the regional restructuring perspective, once again provided job opportunities for new labour force entrants whose counterparts in the 1970s had to relocate elsewhere. Frey observes that there were really only two types of non-metropolitan areas that continued to grow during the 1980s: resort–retirement areas, and 'exurban counties' that lie adjacent to metropolitan boundaries. However, he indicates that growth in such areas does not provide conclusive evidence that the 'loosening of spatial constraints' tenet of the deconcentration perspective is at work. This is because their primary residents – retirees and largely metropolitan commuters – are not dependent on self-sustaining non-metropolitan economies.

In reviewing the same trends, Johnson is not as dismissive of the *deconcentration* perspective as an explanation for this period's non-metropolitan shifts (Johnson and Beale 1995a). While acknowledging both that significant period effects operated in both decades and that regional restructuring processes had migration-related corollaries, Johnson believes that deconcentration played a significant role in the non-metropolitan trends of the 1970s. This is reflected in pervasive growth of non-metropolitan areas in all regions of the country and especially of counties that do not lie adjacent to metropolitan areas. Moreover, evidence shows that a wide range of demographic groups were drawn to these areas, not simply the elderly or new entrants to the labour force (Fuguitt *et al.* 1989). Hence, irrespective of the proximate economic circumstances that precipitated the 1970s dispersal, the very fact that it occurred on such an unprecedented scale, he believes, lends support to the significance of deconcentration forces. Johnson argues that, if anything, the adverse period effects of the 1980s on non-metropolitan areas tended to stifle an already ongoing process of deconcentration. Moreover, the fact that retirees and commuters select non-metropolitan rather than metropolitan areas only reinforces their strong preferences for small-town living and also generates secondary economic activity in these areas.

Explaining the 1990s

These differing interpretations point up the difficulty in documenting whether, when, how, or where deconcentration of the United States population occurred during the 1970s and 1980s. This is because of the influence during this period of significant exogenous factors associated with the economy, demographic structure, industrial reorganisation and the like. Hence, the happenstance that non-metropolitan areas are rebounding again in the 1990s provides another, and certainly better, occasion to test the deconcentration thesis. This is because neither the period effects nor regional restructuring patterns are nearly as dominating in the 1990s as they were in the two prior decades.

It is also possible that non-metropolitan growth will be less susceptible to period effects in light of increasing diversification of attractions in certain kinds of non-metropolitan areas. Fuguitt and Beale (1995) point out that in contrast to the 1980s losses in counties specialising in extractive activities, recent gains in many western mining areas may represent their recreation potential, rather than mining. They also suggest that many rural counties that relied heavily on manufacturing, in the past, are now growing because of increased numbers of service jobs. The period impacts on metropolitan areas were also more muted during the recession of the early 1990s as contrasted with the recessions of the mid-1970s and early 1980s. This time it was not the heavy manufacturing metropolitan areas that lost jobs and population, but those dependent on defence industries which were downsized as a result of federal government cutbacks.

The regional restructuring scenario has, in broad strokes, played out as predicted in the sense that a distinction can now be made between metropolitan areas which have sustained renewed employment and population growth, in contrast to those whose populations might be labelled as 'steady state' or declining. The shake-outs in jobs and populations from the large and medium-sized heavy manufacturing areas are essentially completed. Growing areas tend to be those associated with advanced services, knowledge-based industries and recreation. A notable subset of these (discussed below) are growing largely from immigration and do provide a source for out-migrating residents in search of smaller-sized communities. But this is less a consequence of industrial restructuring than of new immigration and related social and economic dynamics in these areas.

With somewhat 'softer' period effects and restructuring influences operating in the 1990s, a fairer assessment of the deconcentration perspective can be made. The conditions for deconcentration may also be better if, as mentioned above, non-metropolitan areas are becoming more diversified in their economic mix and remain attractive to residents wishing to reside within or near high amenity or recreation areas. The individual whose only tie to the workplace is his modem and laptop computer is still rare. But, with improved transportation and communication systems, the constraints on location for both residents *and* *firms* further diminish. This increases the opportunities in newly diversifying non-metropolitan areas for both workers and smaller 'startup' companies involved in software design or other high tech activities.

Moreover, as the baby boom population approach their 50s, many of this generation may elect to relocate employment with an eye toward their later retirement in smaller places. There is also another segment of the population where preference may be a consideration in moving to a small town or non-metropolitan area. It includes members of the younger 'late baby boom' and 'baby bust' generations who find the cost of living, quality of services and longer commuting costs of larger urban areas to be prohibitively expensive from both an economic and quality of life perspective. The rising perception of large urban areas as less hospitable to child-raising may offer a further outword impetus to these cohorts. Employers and developers responding to this group may help to pave the way for their deconcentration-related moves.

Immigration and Selective Deconcentration

In addition to the perspectives offered to account for earlier population dispersal patterns, a new phenomenon associated with some large United States metropolitan areas needs to be considered as a potential factor in prompting the observed dispersal of the 1990s. This is related to the convergence of large numbers of new immigrants on a few selected ports-of-entry metropolitan areas. These areas, to be discussed below, have traditionally been the primary gateways for foreign-born immigrants to the United States. However, changes in United States immigration laws in 1965, 1986 and 1990 have served to increase the volume of immigrants to these areas and to focus their origins more heavily toward countries in Latin America and Asia (Martin and Midgley 1994). It is also alleged that due to changes in countries of origin and because of the preference system which emphasises family reunification rather than skills, the education gap between new immigrants and native-born residents has risen (Borjas 1994).

The new immigration to the United States is relevant toward accounting for the new selective population dispersal. This is not because the immigrants themselves are dispersing; it is because they are prompting a selective dispersal of domestic migrants away from the large immigrant port-of-entry metropolitan areas – a pattern which is also evident in Europe (Champion 1994). This phenomenon can be attributed, in part, to the increasing dual labour market character of high immigration metropolitan areas such as Los Angeles and New York (Waldinger 1996). Low-skilled immigrants, many with at most high school educations, tend to take poorly paying service jobs and work in the informal sector. Because these metropolitan areas also tend to serve as advanced service centres, they attract highly educated professional domestic migrants to activities which complement the informal and low-wage sectors that employ the bulk of new immigrants. In the process, low-skilled and lower-income United States residents see their wages bid down and job prospects reduced at the same time that costs of housing and commuting rise. The increased multi-ethnic nature of these metropolitan areas also leads to the perception that social service costs in these areas are driven up and the potential for inter-ethnic conflict will increase. In response, lower middle class domestic residents of these areas show a propensity to out-migrate (Frey 1995b).

The destinations of these out-migrants are not always to small metropolitan areas or non-metropolitan territory. Often they relocate to growing metropolitan areas which are less ethnic and do not have a dual economy character. However, the coincidence of heavy immigration in Californian metropolitan areas, coupled with increased development and diversification of small towns, located in non-metropolitan and small metropolitan areas in the states surrounding California and in the Rocky Mountain region, has laid the groundwork for selective domestic out-migration into more dispersed settlement areas in the western United States in the early 1990s (Frey 1995c, 1996).

In the sections that follow, we take cognisance of the three perspectives discussed earlier as well as the emerging immigration-related dispersal in evaluating the post-1990 small metropolitan and non-metropolitan growth. We interpret these patterns with an eye toward identifying 'selective' deconcentration as consistent with the theoretical arguments underlying that theoretical perspective. By 'selective' we are referring to selectivity both by demographic groups and by the kinds of geographic areas which are attracting new population growth. The demographic groups, we anticipate, will continue to be elderly populations which had helped to sustain the one strand of deconcentration during the 1970s and 1980s. We would also anticipate some deconcentration of 'footloose professionals' who are attracted to smaller high tech companies which have filtered out into small towns. Lastly, we are on the lookout for the deconcentration of lower-income and less-skilled domestic migrants retreating from large multi-ethnic dual economy metropolitan areas.

From a geographic standpoint, we anticipate small town and non-metropolitan growth to be 'selective' in those areas which have shown signs of greater diversification over the early 1990s. These may be previously mining or extractive counties in the west and south west which have become attractive to businesses or residents for their amenity or recreation value. They may be previously old-line small manufacturing areas which have diversified into a variety of service functions. Finally, we expect a continued growth in re-sort–retirement and exurban non-metropolitan counties, which have continued to attract retirees and commuters since the 1970s. Yet, it is the former, more diversified counties which signal a more viable long-term growth in non-metropolitan areas consistent with the 'loosening of spatial constraints' premise of the deconcentration perspective. The sections that follow examine these tendencies, first, from the perspective of large metropolitan areas and, second, from the point of view of non-metropolitan counties.

SELECTIVE DOMESTIC MIGRATION FROM METROPOLITAN AREAS

Trends

In important ways, the changing fortunes of metropolitan America exert an impact on the population changes in non-metropolitan America. This was especially evident during the 1970s when there was a wholesale downsizing of manufacturing production. As a consequence, some of the largest metropolitan areas in the United States sustained unprecedented population losses during this decade. Eight northeast and midwest metropolitan areas with populations over one million – New York, Philadelphia, Detroit, Cleveland, St Louis, Pittsburgh, Milwaukee and Buffalo – were among the losers during the 1970s. Migration flows, during this period, showed a clear redistribution via migration streams 'down the metropolitan hierarchy' that was especially evident from these hard-hit manufacturing areas. Of course, the availability of employment opportunities in smaller metropolitan and non-metropolitan areas was necessary to attract migrants to smaller-sized places. The point is that there was an accentuated metropolitan area 'push' during this period, as well as a number of non-metropolitan 'pulls'.

During the 1980s, there was a selective rebounding of metropolitan area growth. To a large degree, this growth was consistent with expectations of the regional restructuring perspective discussed earlier. That is, the areas that were most likely to gain were the locations of advanced services activities including corporate headquarters cities, high-tech incubation centres and other places that were able to make the manufacturing-to-advanced services transition, or those that were generally diversified enough to weather the 1970s manufactur-ing 'shakeouts' (Frey 1993). Examples of such metropolitan areas were New York, Boston, Minneapolis–St Paul, Atlanta, Dallas–Fort Worth, Los Angeles and San Francisco. Other metropolitan areas whose economic bases were somewhat less diversified but were able to prosper by attracting vacationers, retirees and the hotel trade also showed growth during the more prosperous 1980s. These include several Florida metropolitan areas such as Miami,

Tampa–St Petersburg and Orlando, as well as several western areas such as Phoenix.

Still, many of the 'heavy industry' metropolitan areas – both large and small – had a difficult time rebounding from the deindustrialisation period of the 1970s. The growth levels of metropolitan areas such as Detroit, Cleveland and Pittsburgh were slow to recover. Finally, the 1980s exerted its own 'period effects' on metropolitan areas that were relatively specialised with respect to particular industries. The best example involved the impact of the mid-decade decline in oil prices on Houston's population growth, which declined metropolitan-wide from 16.8 percent in 1980–1985 to only 2.4 percent in 1985–1990.

Of course, the selective rebounding in metropolitan areas during the 1980s represented only the 'pull' side of the migration equation. As is discussed below, there were several severe period effects which helped to 'push' migrants away from non-metropolitan areas and small metropolitan areas during the 1980s. Among the 150 metropolitan areas with populations under 250 000, only ten showed population declines in the 1970s. But this number increased to 36 in the 1980–1985 period and to 59 in the 1985–1990 period. Many of the same period influences that affected non-metropolitan areas also affected these smaller areas located largely in the interior part of the United States (Frey and Speare 1992).

The 1990s and High Immigration Metropolitan Areas

The 1990s thus far have shown more modest 'period effect' influences on metropolitan growth. Many of the same selective metropolitan gain patterns of the 1980s continue into the 1990s. If anything, several of the areas which were hard hit by the oil price declines and other extractive industry difficulties of the 1980s have become more diversified. Two cases in point are Houston and Denver, whose metropolitan areas have rebounded as their economies have become more broad based. Even several of the old manufacturing centres, including Detroit and Cleveland, have diversified their economies and showed more 'steady state' growth patterns during the first half of the 1990s. If there were adverse 'period effect' influences during the early 1990s recession, it affected metropolitan areas that also had significant United States government defence installations or areas which did much contract work with the United States defence agencies (for example, San Diego, Los Angeles). This contributed to accentuated domestic out-migration from these areas.

Yet, perhaps a more important and long-term phenomenon affecting both the demographics and economies of selected large metropolitan areas is the impact that concentrated immigration imposes on a few port-of-entry areas. What is clear when looking at Table 5.1 is that the eight areas listed as 'High Immigration Metropolitan Areas' are sustaining all or most of their migration-related growth from immigration rather than from domestic, internal migration. These areas are quite distinct from areas which are classed as 'High Internal Migration Metropolitan Areas', or 'High Out-migration Metropolitan Areas'. The latter two kinds of

Table 5.1 Immigration and net internal migration components of change, 1985–1995, for selected large metropolitan areas

Metropolitan area[a]	Immigration ('000s)	Internal migration ('000s)	1995 metropolitan area population (millions)
High Immigration Metropolitan Areas			
Los Angeles	1635	−1270	15.4
New York	1420	−2172	19.7
San Francisco / Oakland	525	−364	6.5
Chicago	377	−565	8.6
Miami	352	41	3.4
Washington / Baltimore	289	12	7.1
Boston	198	−241	5.8
Houston	193	−98	4.2
High Internal Migration Metropolitan Areas			
Atlanta	64	464	3.4
Las Vegas	27	364	1.1
Phoenix	61	311	2.6
Seattle	90	273	3.3
Tampa / St Petersburg	42	237	2.2
Orlando	45	235	1.4
Portland, OR	46	202	2.0
West Palm Beach	37	183	0.9
Raleigh / Durham	16	158	0.9
Charlotte	12	136	1.3
High Out-migration Metropolitan Areas			
Detroit	84	−308	5.3
Cleveland	30	−130	2.9
New Orleans	14	−119	1.3
Pittsburgh	14	−109	2.4
St Louis	23	−73	2.5
Milwaukee	19	−69	1.6
Buffalo	15	−63	1.2

[a]The metropolitan area definitions are consistent with Office of Management and Budget definitions of CMSAs, MSAs and the NECMA counterparts of 30 June, 1995. Official names are abbreviated.
Source: Compiled by the authors from Special 1990 US Census migration tabulations and US Census postcensal estimates.

areas either gain or lose most of their migration-related population change through domestic migration subject to the 'pushes' and 'pulls' of the economy. High Internal Migration Metropolitan Areas such as Atlanta, Seattle, Raleigh–Durham and Charlotte are among the fast-rising national or regional 'command and control' corporate or banking centres with significant advanced service components to their economies. Also on this list are places such as Las Vegas, Phoenix and Orlando – noted retirement and recreation centres – which are also attracting an increasing 'working aged' population lured by new job growth in these areas. At the other extreme, Detroit, Cleveland and other High Out-migration Metropolitan Areas are losing internal migrants due to more sluggish economies.

In contrast to these latter two categories of metropolitan areas, the High Immigration Metropolitan Areas are distinct in a number of respects. First, most of them can be thought of as either global cities or national corporate head-quarters and trade centres. Not only do they attract large numbers of immigrants, mostly from Latin America and Asia, but they are also centres of finance and corporate decision-making at a national or worldwide level. Second, it is plain that there is a strong net out-migration of domestic migrants from most if not all of these areas and especially from those areas which are the largest 'world cities'. This suggests that these areas are taking on a dual city character (Sassen 1991; Waldinger 1996) in that their economic and labour force structures will become highly bifurcated between professionals, on the one hand, and lower-level service workers, on the other. In these areas (in contrast to the High Internal Migration Metropolitan Areas) it appears that the recent immigrant population will be taking over more of the latter jobs, while domestic migrants and longer-term residents will be taking the former.

While immigration to the United States has always been high, it has changed in both magnitude and character in the last two decades as the result of revisions in immigration legislation in the mid-1960s, which were further modified in 1986 and in 1990 (Martin and Midgley 1994). These changes have turned back pre-1965 'national origins' quotas, which favoured immigrants from Europe, in favour of a more open system of origin countries, where 'family reunification' represents the dominant admission criterion. These changes in policy, along with economic pressures in the new origin countries and large flows of illegal immigrants, have served to increase the number of immigrants from Latin America as well as from Asia. This accentuated the concentration of these immigrants into familiar port-of-entry areas where there are like race-ethnic and nationality populations who can provide both social and economic support as well as information about employment in the informal economy. Because the United States immigration preference system favours family reunification to a greater extent than recruitment based on skills, the most recent immigrant cohorts who are of labour force age tend to be comprised, disproportionately, of persons with at most high school educations who are best suited for lower-level service kinds of employment (Briggs 1992). As a consequence, these immigrants provide competition for less-skilled United States residents because they tend to bid down the wages for employment in these large gateway metropolitan areas. This is *part* of the reason that the High Immigration Metropolitan Areas are showing large domestic out-migration. Indeed, it is these areas (rather than the High Out-migration Metropolitan Areas) that are contributing to the large do-mestic out-migration from all large metropolitan areas over the 1990–1995 period. This is illustrated in Figure 5.1.

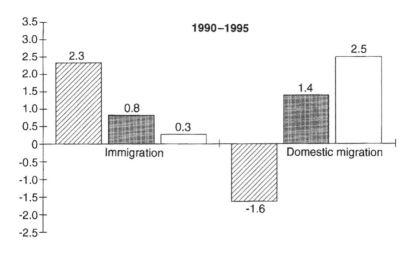

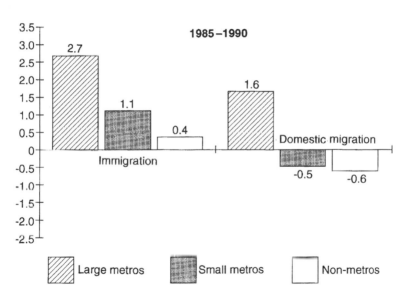

FIGURE 5.1 Rates of immigration and domestic migration

Selective Deconcentration from Large Metropolitan Areas

Because of this competition with the lower-skilled immigrants, the domestic out-migration from Los Angeles, New York, Chicago and most of the other High Immigration Metropolitan Areas is accentuated for United States-born residents with high school educations or less (Frey 1995b, 1996). This kind of internal migration differs from the more conventional 'circulation of elites' model (Frey

T A B L E 5 . 2 Net internal migration exchanges[a] with metropolitan areas and non-metropolitan areas by region in the USA, 1985–1990

| | Total net migration | | Net migration exchanges | | | | |
| | | | Within same region | | With other regions | | |
	Rate	Number ('000s)	Small metropolitan	Non-metropolitan	Large metropolitan	Small metropolitan	Non-metropolitan
North large metropolitan areas – net migration exchanges							
Total	-2.94	-1738	-177	-185	-838	-456	-128
Poverty	-5.00	-350	-92	-60	-100	-63	-35
Non poverty	-2.17	-1212	39	-31	-778	-363	-79
College graduate	-1.47	-147	80	30	-186	-60	-11
Ages 65+	-3.58	-311	-21	-23	-131	-107	-30
South large metropolitan areas – net migration exchanges							
Total	2.31	691	31	-48	527	120	60
Poverty	-1.23	-49	-58	-44	72	-9	-11
Non poverty	3.40	949	178	45	519	136	71
College graduate	5.43	268	86	32	81	47	21
Ages 65+	1.68	65	-28	-16	94	8	5
West large metropolitan areas – net migration exchanges							
Total	1.42	439	-46	-1	310	115	61
Poverty	-1.74	-71	-59	-23	29	-6	-12
Non poverty	1.64	520	20	49	259	124	69
College graduate	4.48	239	43	16	105	54	22
Ages 65+	-0.14	-6	-24	-18	36	–	–
Total USA large metropolitan areas – net migration exchanges with total small metropolitan/non-metropolitan areas							
Total	-0.54	-654	–	–	–	-413	-241
Poverty	-3.11	-471	–	–	–	-286	-184
Non poverty	0.22	257	–	–	–	134	123
College graduate	1.77	360	–	–	–	249	111
Ages 65+	-1.53	-252	–	–	–	-171	-81

Large metropolitan areas have 1995 populations of 1 000 000 or more; small metropolitan areas include all others. Table column 2 equals the sum of columns 3 to 7.
[a] Net internal migration exchanges shown for large metropolitan areas with another area equals the size of the out-migration flow to that area minus the size of the in-migration flow from that area.

1979), wherein it is the *most* skilled and educated residents who tend to respond to employment opportunities or declines, since it is they who are in a national job market and who tend to behave in the most 'economically rational' manner with respect to employment opportunities (Lansing and Mueller 1967; Long 1988). Indeed, domestic in-migrants to the High Internal Migration Metropolitan Areas are disproportionately comprised of college graduates; and those most likely to leave High Out-migration Metropolitan Areas are also the most educated (Frey 1995b). This is not the case with the domestic out-migrants from the large immigrant magnets.

Moreover, there is evidence to suggest that it is these migrants who are especially likely to relocate into smaller-sized metropolitan areas and non-metropolitan areas. This appears to be the case for out-migration from California into surrounding and nearby States of the west (Frey 1995c, 1996). The lure of communities with lower social service costs, less conflict and the availability of employment opportunities all combine to make smaller-sized places more attractive. Another segment of the population which is leaving these High Immigration Metropolitan Areas are elderly migrants and pre-elderly migrants. Many of these out-migrants also tend to select smaller-sized places as destinations. The evidence for this appears in Table 5.2, which shows net internal out-migration *exchanges* between each region's large metropolitan areas with smaller metropolitan areas and non-metropolitan areas in the same region and with other regions.

The data show that, within each region, exchanges with smaller metropolitan areas in the same region are in favour of the dispersal of poverty (rather than non-poverty) populations[1] and persons aged 65 and over. These patterns are especially evident in the north and west regions where High Immigration Metropolitan Areas are located. This suggests an important dynamic between concentrated immigration in the latter areas and a selective deconcentration of lesser skilled and elderly elements of the population. This pattern may become a new source of non-metropolitan area gains. At the same time, it represents a distancing of poorer and lower middle class United States residents from the new immigrant populations.

NEW NON-METROPOLITAN GAINS

Trends

Demographic trends in the less urban areas of the United States have been extremely fluid during the past 30 years (Long and DeAre 1988). Non-metropolitan demographic change has historically been dominated by an excess of births over deaths sufficient to offset the net out-migration of population to the nation's urban areas. This pattern of slow non-metropolitan population gain through an excess of natural increase over migration loss was so consistent that it came to be taken for granted (Fuguitt *et al.* 1989). This changed abruptly in the 1970s with the onset of what came to be called the non-metropolitan population 'turnaround'. During this era of population deconcentration, the population gains in non-metropolitan areas exceeded those in metropolitan areas for the first time in at least 150 years (Beale 1975; Fuguitt 1985; Johnson and Purdy 1980). Net migration to non-metropolitan areas from the nation's urban areas fuelled much of this growth. In contrast, natural increase (the excess of births over deaths) contributed much less to the non-metropolitan population gains of the 1970s than had been the case historically.

Non-metropolitan population redistribution patterns shifted yet again in the 1980s. Most non-metropolitan counties lost population during the 1980s because they had a modest net outflow of population combined with low levels of natural increase (Johnson 1993b). Researchers who believed that period effects were the primary force underlying the turnaround of the 1970s cite the diminished non-metropolitan growth of the 1980s as evidence that United States population redistribution trends had reverted to historical form, with the turnaround of the 1970s just a short-term fluctuation. However, non-metropolitan areas began to show signs of growth again in the late 1980s and this growth rebound has accelerated as the 1990s have progressed (Beale and Fuguitt 1990; Johnson and Beale 1994a). Critical to any understanding of recent population deconcentration trends in the United States is a recognition of the changing role of migration and the selective nature of such migration for different kinds of non-metropolitan counties.

The Increased Importance of Migration

In a reversal of the trend of the 1980s, there was widespread population growth in non-metropolitan areas of the United States during the first half of the 1990s[2]. As Table 5.3 shows, more than 75 percent of the 2304 counties classified as non-metropolitan in 1993 gained population between 1990 and 1995. In all, 720 more non-metropolitan counties gained population than in the 1980s. The estimated non-metropolitan population gain between April 1990 and July 1995 was nearly 2.6 million. In contrast, non-metropolitan areas grew by fewer than 1.3 million during the entire decade of the 1980s. Thus, the non-metropolitan population gain between 1990 and 1995 is already twice as large as that during the entire decade of the 1980s. The non-metropolitan population still grew at a slower pace (5.1 percent) than did the metropolitan population (5.8 percent) between 1990 and 1995, but the gap was much narrower than during the 1980s. The post-1990 population gains occurred in many regions of the country. Gains were most prevalent in the Mountain West, Upper Great Lakes, Ozarks, parts of the south and in rural areas of the north east. Widespread losses occurred only in the Great Plains, Western Corn Belt and Mississippi Delta.

Renewed non-metropolitan growth is due in large part to a recent, mostly domestic migration gain. Such migration gains accounted for 60 percent of the total estimated population increase between April 1990 and July 1995. Non-

TABLE 5.3 Population change with migration and natural increase components by adjacency and metropolitan status, 1980–1990 and 1990–1995

	Number of cases	Initial population ('000s)	Population change			Net migration[a]			Natural increase		
			Absolute change ('000s)	Percent change	Percent growing counties	Absolute change ('000s)	Percent change	Percent growing counties[b]	Absolute change ('000s)	Percent change	Percent growing counties[c]
1980–1990											
All nonmetropolitan	2 305	49 578	1 320	2.7	45.1	−1 370	−2.8	27.3	2 690	5.4	89.6
Nonadjacent	1 298	22 612	134	0.6	36.4	−1 175	−5.2	20.7	1 309	5.8	87.0
Adjacent	1 007	26 966	1 186	4.4	56.3	−194	−0.7	35.8	1 382	5.1	92.9
Metropolitan	836	176 965	20 848	11.8	81.0	6 575	3.7	57.7	14 271	8.1	97.7
Total	3 141	226 543	22 168	9.8	54.7	5 206	2.3	35.4	16 962	7.5	91.8
1990–1995											
All nonmetropolitan	2 304	50 820	2 580	5.1	75.3	1 555	3.1	66.8	1 025	2.0	74.3
Nonadjacent	1 297	22 669	989	4.4	67.5	529	2.3	59.4	460	2.0	67.2
Adjacent	1 007	28 151	1 591	5.7	85.4	1 026	3.6	76.4	565	2.0	83.4
Metropolitan	837	197 893	11 456	5.8	90.7	2 873	1.5	73.7	8 583	4.3	96.3
Total	3 141	243 713	14 037	5.6	79.4	4 429	1.8	68.6	9 608	3.9	80.1

1993 metropolitan status used for 1980–1990 and 1990–1995
[a] Includes internal migration and immigration components, combined.
[b] Indicates percent of counties showing net in-migration.
[c] Indicates percent of counties showing positive natural increase.

metropolitan areas had an estimated total net migration inflow of 1 555 000 people during the period. This compares to a net outflow of 1 370 000 during the 1980s. In fact, the net migration percentage gain (3.1 percent) in non-metropolitan areas between 1990 and 1995 was more than twice as large as the migration gain in metropolitan areas (1.5 percent). This is a sharp contrast to the pattern during the 1980s, when metropolitan areas had net in-migration of 3.7 percent, whereas non-metropolitan areas had a net out-migration of 2.8 percent. As we indicated in the previous section, most of the recent non-metropolitan gain is a domestic (rather than international) migration; and most of the *metropolitan* migration gain accrued in smaller metropolitan areas[3]. Non-metropolitan areas receive very few immigrants; only 164 000 of the 1.5 million migrants to non-metropolitan areas came from outside the United States. Thus, the influx of migrants to non-metropolitan areas since 1990 has been primarily the result of internal migration from United States urban areas. The only other recent period during which non-metropolitan migration gains exceeded those in metropolitan areas was during the population turnaround of the 1970s.

Natural increase accounted for 40 percent of the non-metropolitan population increase between April 1990 and July 1995. In all, births exceeded deaths by 1 025 000 in non-metropolitan areas. The annual gain through natural increase in non-metropolitan areas was somewhat lower between 1990 and 1995 than it had been during the 1980s. In contrast, the annual rate of natural increase accelerated in metropolitan areas during the early 1990s. The extent of the slowdown in natural increase in non-metropolitan areas is reflected in the sharp increase in the incidence of natural decrease to record levels during the early 1990s (Johnson and Beale 1994a, 1995a). The accelerating pace of natural decrease in non-metropolitan America results from several interrelated phenomena (Johnson 1993b; Johnson and Beale 1992). The most important is that the age structure of many non-metropolitan areas has been distorted by decades of out-migration by young adults, coupled with the ageing in place among older adults. In addition, the traditionally higher birth rate of non-metropolitan women has been converging with that of urban women (Fuguitt *et al.* 1991; Long and Nucci 1996). Thus, the natural increase that traditionally fuelled most of the growth in non-metropolitan areas has diminished sharply in recent years and this trend is likely to continue (Johnson 1993b, Johnson and Beale 1992).

Selective Deconcentration Trends in Non-metropolitan America

Non-metropolitan population gains have been widespread since 1990, but there is significant selectivity in the patterns of growth and decline. Consistent with recent trends, non-metropolitan population gains since 1990 have been more common in counties near metropolitan centres. More than 85 percent of these adjacent counties gained population in the early 1990s and 76 percent had net in-migration. In fact, the net migration gain in adjacent non-metropolitan coun-

TABLE 5.4 Population change, migration and natural increase in non-metropolitan counties of different types, 1990–1995

County type	N	Population change		Net migration[a]		Natural increase	
		Percent change	Percent growing	Percent change	Percent growing[b]	Percent change	Percent growing[c]
Retirement	190	13.8	100	12.2	98	1.6	64
Federal lands	269	12.1	94	8.8	87	3.3	84
Recreational	285	9.7	92	7.6	88	2.2	79
Manufacturing	506	4.6	90	2.6	76	2.0	91
Commuting	381	6.9	90	5.0	85	1.9	83
Government	242	5.4	88	1.8	74	3.6	83
Service	323	7.3	85	5.6	76	1.7	74
Non-specialised	484	5.2	81	3.7	75	1.5	74
Transfer	381	4.8	77	3.6	71	1.3	66
Poverty	535	4.3	75	1.6	60	2.7	83
Mining	146	2.7	64	0.4	53	2.3	82
Low density	407	5.9	54	2.8	46	3.1	64
Farming	556	3.2	50	1.6	46	1.6	54
Total non-metropolitan	2304	5.1	75	3.1	67	2.0	74

1993 metropolitan definition; 14 previously metropolitan counties are excluded from analysis.
Percent change is aggregate change for all cases in category.
Recreational counties defined by Johnson and Beale (1995c); Low density counties contain fewer than six persons per square mile in 1990; all other types as defined in Cook and Mizer (1954). Counties are classified into one economic type (farming, mining, manufacturing, government, service and non-specialised). Other types are not mutually exclusive.
[a] Includes internal migration and immigration components, combined.
[b] Indicates percent of counties showing net in-migration.
[c] Indicates percent of counties showing positive natural increase.

ties (3.6 percent) exceeded that in metropolitan areas (1.5 percent) by a substantial margin. Even among more remote non-metropolitan counties, recent population gains were significantly greater than during the 1980s. Growth occurred in 68 percent of counties not adjacent to metropolitan areas in the early 1990s, compared to 36 percent during the 1980s. Such non-adjacent counties had net in-migration (2.3 percent) during the early 1990s, compared to a net loss (−5.2 percent) in the 1980s.

Also, as with recent decades, non-metropolitan counties that were destinations for retirement age migrants or centres of recreation were the fastest growing counties during the early 1990s. All 190 non-metropolitan retirement destination counties gained population and 98 percent had net in-migration between 1990 and 1995. This is shown in Table 5.4. Such areas are located in the Sunbelt, coastal regions, parts of the West and in the Upper Great Lakes (Cook and Mizer 1994). They are attracting retirees while retaining their existing population (Fuguitt and Heaton 1993). Population gains also occurred in 92 percent of the 285 non-metropolitan recreational counties during the early 1990s with a large majority (88 percent) receiving net in-migration. Such counties were prominent growth nodes during the 1970s and 1980s and this trend persisted in the early 1990s (Johnson and Beale 1995a).

What is noteworthy with the 1990s is that non-metropolitan population gains were also widespread in government dependent counties and those with concentrations of manufacturing jobs. Evidence of the increasing non-metropolitan diversification is reflected in the fact that much of the recent growth in manufacturing counties appears to have been fuelled by jobs in sectors other than manufacturing (Fuguitt and Beale 1995). Population gains in these manufacturing and government dependent counties have been smaller than those in recreational and retirement counties and the growth has been more evenly balanced between natural increase and net migration. Yet, to the extent that these areas are diversifying economically, these 1990 patterns portend a longer-term growth scenario. Other county types with high growth rates fuelled by net migration include those with a large proportion of their workforce commuting to jobs in other counties and those with economies dominated by service sector jobs. The importance of small businesses, 'startups', may be responsible for some of these gains.

Counties dependent on farming were the least likely to gain population during the first half of the 1990s. Only 50 percent of the farming dependent counties grew and only 46 percent had net in-migration. Natural decrease was also more common in farming dependent counties than elsewhere. Population

---

FIGURE 5.2 Non-metropolitan population change, 1980–1990 compared to 1990–1995.

Non-metropolitan counties are classed as follows:
Loss = population loss for both 1980–1990 and 1990–1995 periods.
Turn Loss = Population gain for 1980–1990 and loss for 1990–1995.
Turn Gain = Population loss for 1980–1990 and gain for 1990–1995.
Gain = population gain for both 1980–1990 and 1990–1995

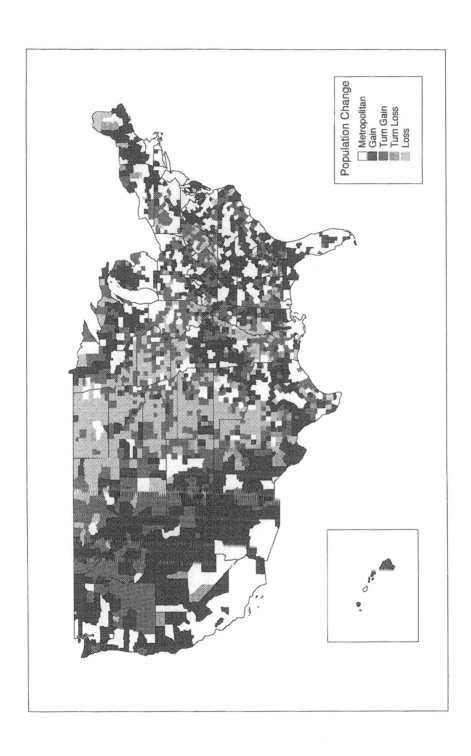

Population Change

Metropolitan
Gain
Turn Gain
Turn Loss
Loss

gains were more widespread in mining counties, but the magnitude of the gains was quite small. Migration gains occurred in only slightly over half of the mining counties. The smaller than average population gains and widespread out-migration from mining and farming dependent counties of the early 1990s represents a continuation of the trends of the 1980s. However, even among these counties the population and migration trends in the early 1990s moderated compared to the 1980s when losses were much more prevalent. Counties with histories of persistent poverty also had low growth rates during the early 1990s and, as in the case of the mining and farming counties, what growth there was came from natural increase. On the whole, however, there was increased in-migration in most types of non-metropolitan counties.

Longitudinal Patterns of Population Change

Comparing growth patterns in non-metropolitan areas in the 1980s to those during the 1990s underscores two important points. First, the renewal of non-metropolitan growth in the 1990s is extremely widespread geographically, as shown in Figure 5.2. Counties shifting from loss in the 1980s to growth in the 1990s (Turn Gain) are prevalent in all regions. Many are on the periphery of existing concentrations of counties that grew consistently through the 1980s and early 1990s (Gain). Second, counties that lost population during the 1980s and continued to do so during the 1990s are concentrated in areas of the country with long histories of population decline.

Comparing non-metropolitan demographic trends between 1990 and 1995 to those during the 1970s and 1980s also underscores important similarities and differences. Growth in non-metropolitan areas during the early 1990s is similar in pattern to that during the turnaround decade of the 1970s, though it is smaller in magnitude. During both periods, net migration and natural increase made significant contributions to the growth of the non-metropolitan population. In contrast, during the 1980s the minimal population gains in non-metropolitan areas occurred because natural increase was sufficient to offset net out-migration. In this regard, the 1970s and early 1990s represents a significant departure from the historical demographic trends in non-metropolitan areas of the United States (Johnson and Beale 1994a). Through most of this century, non-metropolitan population growth has been fuelled by natural increase (Johnson 1989). Net migration has traditionally diminished the non-metropolitan growth rate because more people left such areas than migrated to them. In contrast, during the 1970s and again during the 1990s, the majority of the non-metropolitan population gain came from net in-migration.

Comparing historical growth patterns in non-metropolitan areas to those during the 1980s and 1990s illustrates the complex interplay between deconcentration trends and period effects. While the non-metropolitan growth patterns of the 1970s were strong, there is a debate about whether they were fuelled mainly by deconcentration or by period effects. However, during the 1980s period effects mitigated against non-metropolitan growth. The protracted economic recession of the 1980s hurt non-metropolitan areas more severely than urban areas and agricultural areas were hit hard by the long farm crisis of 1980–1986. In addition, non-metropolitan manufacturing – which employs many more non-metropolitan people than farming – came under increased competitive pressure from offshore firms, with much loss of jobs (Elo and Beale 1988; Henry *et al.* 1986). All these period effects contributed to the slower overall non-metropolitan growth in the 1980s. Only in the late 1980s, as the differential impact of these periodic factors began to subside, did non-metropolitan growth rates begin to rise again (Beale and Fuguitt 1990). For example, the rate of non-metropolitan job growth has exceeded that in urban areas annually since 1990 (Economic Research Service 1994). As a result, non-metropolitan workers have had less economic reason to migrate to urban areas recently. With the 'dampening' of period effects in the 1990s, deconcentration trends appear to be emerging in non-metropolitan areas during the 1990s.

CONCLUSION

Since 1990, growth rates in non-metropolitan areas of the United States have rebounded from the minimal levels of the 1980s. Although these growth rates are slightly lower than those in metropolitan areas, the gap between the relative growth rates is quite small. Overall, the growth patterns in non-metropolitan America during the early 1990s resemble the patterns of the non-metropolitan turnaround of the 1970s more than those of any other period. These findings offer evidence that the growth in non-metropolitan areas that was evident in the 1970s was not just a one-time phenomenon[4].

The turnaround and its aftermath stimulated significant theoretical work as researchers sought to account for the turnaround and then for the diminished growth in non-metropolitan areas during the 1980s. The three theoretical perspectives (period effects, regional restructuring, deconcentration) outlined here each offer a partial explanation for the turnaround of the 1970s, but predicted a somewhat different demographic pattern for non-metropolitan areas in the 1980s and 1990s. There is still disagreement regarding which of these theoretical models, if any, fits the non-metropolitan population trends of recent decades (Lichter 1993; Wardwell 1988). Even the current authors disagree on whether or how much the deconcentration perspective explains the non-metropolitan growth patterns of the 1970s.

Findings from the 1990s reported here and elsewhere (Johnson and Beale 1995b; Nucci and Long 1995) cast doubt on the argument that the turnaround of the 1970s was merely a function of unique demographic and economic period effects, whereas the redistributive patterns of the 1980s represent a reversion to more consistent historical patterns. The non-metropolitan demographic trends of the 1980s were neither a repeat of the non-metropolitan turnaround of the 1970s nor a reversion to the patterns of the 1950s. On the other hand, if deconcentration implies a sustained pattern of dispersed settlement, immune from sharp cyclical influences (Frey 1995a), the evidence is less conclusive.

What is clear is that the sharp 'period effects' of both the 1970s and 1980s do not characterise the 1990s. This means that the non-metropolitan growth patterns of the present decade can be more unambiguously attributed to deconcentration influences as put forth in the original theory. One still needs to take into account the entire settlement system, both metropolitan and non-metropolitan. It is clear that a new factor has entered the metropolitan side of the equation – increasing and concentrated immigration into large dual economy metropolitan areas. This concentrated immigration appears to be triggering an additional exodus of domestic migrants, selective among lower middle income and less educated United States residents, as well as the elderly population. The areas they are moving to are also selective. They include the exurban and non-metropolitan recreation-oriented counties that have continuously attracted metropolitan residents over the last three decades. However, new metropolitan out-migrants are also attracted to diversifying manufacturing and service employment counties, which portends a more viable long-term growth scenario for these places. This evidence of selective deconcentration during the absence of any strong period effects portends a continued dispersed settlement pattern in many parts of the United States.

Speculation about future non-metropolitan population redistribution is perilous given the fluidity of the demographic shifts in non-metropolitan areas of the United States during the past several decades. This reflects the complexity of the forces causing population redistribution. Non-metropolitan demographic trends are likely to continue to be volatile in the future. Recent changes in non-metropolitan fertility rates and age structures are sure to diminish the substantial contribution that natural increase has traditionally made to non-metropolitan population gains. Thus, future non-metropolitan growth or decline is increasingly dependent on net internal migration. And, as the integration of non-metropolitan areas into the national economy continues, non-metropolitan migration patterns are likely to become increasingly sensitive to immigration trends, national and global economic events, political affairs and a variety of social forces.

ACKNOWLEDGEMENTS

William H. Frey acknowledges support from NICHD grant RO1-HD 297525 and NIA grant RO1-AG12291, as well as the computer programming assistance of Cathy Sun. Kenneth M. Johnson acknowledges support from United States Department of Agriculture grant 9237401-8283.

NOTES

1. Poverty status is determined from income earned during 1989 as reported in the 1990 census. Persons in families and unrelated individuals are classified as being above or below poverty, using a poverty index that is based on the Department of Agriculture's Economy Food Plan, which reflects the different consumption requirements of families based on their size and composition. Poverty thresholds are updated annually to reflect changes in the Consumer Price Index. Poverty thresholds for 1989 (used in this study) were $12 675 for a family of four (sliding scale depending on family size) and $6311 for an individual not living in a family (US Bureau of the Census 1992: 426–427).

2. Data on demographic change since 1990 are from the Federal-State Cooperative population estimates series developed jointly by the United States Bureau of the Census and the States. Additional data are from the United States decennial censuses of population for 1980 and 1990. Metropolitan reclassification complicates efforts to compare the trends of various time periods. The 1993 metropolitan definition is used here to classify counties as metropolitan or non-metropolitan. Because counties are reclassified from time to time, as new metropolitan areas are formed or territory is added to existing areas, the demographic implications of using one definition of metropolitan in preference to another are far from trivial (Johnson 1989). There is no simple resolution to the problem of metropolitan reclassification nor is any one approach clearly superior to all others (Fuguitt *et al.* 1988). A net of 92 counties shifted from the non-metropolitan to metropolitan category as a result of using the 1993 metropolitan definition rather than, for example, using the 1985 definition. Using the 1993 definition results in greater non-metropolitan losses during the 1980s and slower non-metropolitan gains during the early 1990s than would have been the case had the earlier metropolitan definition been used.

3. The 1990–1995 non-metropolitan total net migration rates, shown in Table 5.3, are not exactly the sum of the immigration and domestic migration rates shown in Figure 5.1. This is because the figure omits gains for United States residents returning from abroad and a 'residual category' which is part of the Census Bureau's estimates .

4. Further evidence of an upturn in non-metropolitan growth is forthcoming from recent Current Population Survey (CPS) data. Following minimal non-metropolitan migration gains in the 1991 and 1992 CPS, analysis of the 1993 and 1994 CPS indicates a net inflow of approximately 350 000 and 230 000 migrants to non-metropolitan areas between 1992–1993 and 1993–1994, respectively. This is the first significant net in-migration to non-metropolitan areas reported by the CPS in more than a decade. Differences in metropolitan definition and time period preclude direct comparisons of CPS and Federal-State results. However, the substantial net in-migration reflected in the 1993 and 1994 CPS represents additional independent evidence of the growth of the non-metropolitan population after 1990.

REFERENCES

Beale, C. (1975) 'The revival of population growth in non-metropolitan America', *Report*, ERS-605, United States Department of Agriculture, Washington DC.

Beale, C. (1988) 'Americans heading home for the cities, once again', *Rural Development Perspectives*, **4**,(3): 2–4.

Beale, C. and Fuguitt, G. (1990) 'Decade of pessimistic nonmetro population trends ends on optimistic note' *Rural Development Perspectives*, **6**,(3): 14–18.

Borjas, G. (1994) 'The economics of immigration', *Journal of Economic Literature*, **2**, 1667–1717.

Briggs, V. (1992) *Mass immigration and the national labor market*, N.E. Sharpe, Armonk, New York.

Byerly, E. (1994) *Population estimates for counties and metropolitan areas: July 1, 1991*, P25-1108, United States Bureau of the Census, Washington DC.

Champion, A. (ed.) (1989) *Counterurbanisation: the changing pace and nature of population deconcentration*, Edward Arnold, London.

Champion, A. (1994) 'International migration and demographic change in the developed world', *Urban Studies*, **31**, 653–677.

Cook, P. and Mizer, K. (1994) *The revised ERS county typology: an overview*, RDRR-89, Economic Research Service, United States Department of Agriculture, Washington DC.

Economic Research Service (1994) *Rural conditions and trends*, Economic Research Service, United States Department of Agriculture, Washington DC.

Elo, I. and Beale, C. (1988) 'The decline in American counterurbanization in the 1980s', paper presented at the meeting of the Population Association of America, New Orleans.

Frey, W. (1979) 'The changing impact of white migration on the population compositions of origin and destination metropolitan areas', *Demography*, **16**, 219–238.

Frey, W. (1989) 'United States: counterurbanization and metropolis depopulation', in A. Champion (ed.), *Counterurbanisation: the changing pace and nature of population deconcentration*, Edward Arnold, London, 34–61.

Frey, W. (1993) 'The new urban revival in the United States', *Urban Studies*, **30**, 741–774.

Frey, W. (1995a) 'The new geography of population shifts: trends toward balkanization', in R. Farley (ed.), *The state of the union, volume II. Social trends*, Sage Foundation, New York, 271–336.

Frey, W. (1995b) 'Immigration and internal migration "flight" from US metropolitan areas: toward a new demographic balkanization', *Urban Studies*, **32**, 733–757.

Frey, W. (1995c) 'Immigration and internal migration flight. A California case study', *Environment and Planning*, **16**, 353–375.

Frey, W. (1996) 'Immigration, domestic migration, and demographic balkanization in America: new evidence for the 1990s', *Population and Development Review*, **22**, 741–763.

Frey, W. and Speare, A. (1988) *Regional and Metropolitan Growth and Decline in the United States*, Sage, New York.

Frey, W. and Speare, A. (1992) 'The revival of metropolitan growth in the United States: an assessment of findings from the 1990 Census', *Population and Development Review*, **18**, 129–146.

Fuguitt, G. (1985) 'The non-metropolitan turnaround', *Annual Review of Sociology*, **11**, 259–280.

Fuguitt, G. and Beale, C. (1995) 'Recent Trends in Non-metropolitan Migration: Toward a New Turnaround?', *Working Paper*, Number 95-07, Center for Demography and Ecology, University of Wisconsin.

Fuguitt, G. and Heaton, T. (1993) 'The impact of migration on the non-metropolitan population age structure, 1960–1990', unpublished manuscript, Department of Sociology, University of Wisconsin.

Fuguitt, G., Beale, C. and Reibel, M. (1991) 'Recent trends in metropolitan-non-metropolitan fertility', *Rural Sociology*, **56**, 475–486.

Fuguitt, G., Brown, D. and Beale, C. (1989) *Rural and small town America*, Sage Foundation, New York.

Fuguitt, G., Heaton, T. and Lichter, D. (1988) 'Monitoring the metropolitan process', *Demography*, **25**, 115–128.

Heaton, T., Clifford, W. and Fuguitt, G. (1981) 'Temporal shifts in the determinants of young and elderly migration in non-metropolitan areas', *Social Forces*, **60**, 41–60.

Henry, M., Drabenstott, M. and Gibson, L. (1986) 'A changing rural America', *Economic Review*, **71**, 23–41.

Johnson, K. (1989) 'Recent population redistribution trends in non-metropolitan America', *Rural Sociology*, **54**, 301–326.

Johnson, K. (1993a) 'When deaths exceed births: natural decrease in the United States', *International Regional Science Review*, **15**, 179–198.

Johnson, K. (1993b) 'Demographic change in non-metropolitan America, 1980 to 1990', *Rural Sociology*, **58**, 347–365.

Johnson, K. and Beale, C. (1992) 'Natural population decrease in the United States', *Rural Development Perspectives*, **8**, 8–15.

Johnson, K. and Beale, C. (1994a) 'The recent revival of widespread population growth in non-metropolitan areas of the United States', *Rural Sociology*, **59**, 655–667.

Johnson, K. and Beale, C. (1994b) 'Post-1990 demographic trends in non-metropolitan America', *Working Paper*, Demographic Change and Fiscal Stress Project, Loyola University, Chicago.

Johnson, K. and Beale, C. (1995a) 'The rural rebound: the revival of population growth in non-metropolitan America', *Working Paper*, 7, Demographic Change and Fiscal Stress Project, Loyola University, Chicago.

Johnson, K. and Beale, C. (1995b) 'The rural rebound revisited', *American Demographics*, July, 46–54.

Johnson, K. and Beale, C. (1995c) 'Non-metropolitan recreational counties: identification and fiscal concerns', *Working Paper*, Demographic Change and Fiscal Stress Project, Loyola University, Chicago.

Johnson, K. and Purdy, R. (1980) 'Recent non-metropolitan population change in fifty year perspective', *Demography*, **17**, 57–70.

Lansing, J. and Mueller, E. (1967) *The geographic mobility of labor*, Survey Research Center, Institute for Social Research, Ann Arbor, Michigan.

Lichter, D. (1993) 'Migration, population redistribution, and the new spatial inequality', in D. Brown, D. Field and J. Zuiches (eds.), *The demography of rural life*, Northeast Regional Center for Rural Development, University Park, Pennsylvania, 19–46.

Long, L. (1988) *Migration and residential mobility in the United States*, Sage, New York.

Long, L. and DeAre, D. (1988) 'US population redistribution: a perspective on the non-metropolitan turnaround', *Population and Development Review*, **14**, 433–450.

Long, L. and Nucci, A. (1996) 'Convergence or divergence in urban rural fertility differences in the United States?', paper presented at the annual meeting of the Population Association of America, San Francisco.

Martin, P. and Midgley, E. (1994) 'Immigration to the United States: journey to an uncertain destination', *Population Bulletin*, 49, 2, Population Reference Bureau, Washington DC.

Morrison, P. (ed.) (1990) *A taste of the country: a collection of Calvin Beale's writings*, Pennsylvania State University Press, University Park, Pennsylvania.

Noyelle, T. and Stanback, T. (1984) *The economic transformation of American cities*, Rowman and Allanheld, Totowa, New Jersey.

Nucci, A. and Long, L. (1995) 'Spatial and demographic dynamics of metropolitan and non-metropolitan territory in the United States', *International Journal of Population Geography*, **1**, 165–181.

Sassen, S. (1991) *The global city*, Princeton University Press, Princeton, New Jersey.

United States Bureau of the Census (1992) *Statistical abstract of the United States*, United States Bureau of the Census, Washington DC.

Waldinger, R. (1996) *Still the promised city?: African Americans and new immigrants in post-industrial New York*, Harvard University Press, Cambridge, Massachusetts.

Wardwell, J. (1977) 'Equilibrium and change in non-metropolitan growth', *Rural Sociology*, **42**, 156–179.

Wardwell, J. (1988) 'Counter-urbanization in the United States: facts of the 1980s – theories of the 1970s', paper presented at the meeting of the Population Association of America, New Orleans.

6

THE HYPOTHESIS OF WELFARE-LED MIGRATION TO RURAL AREAS: THE AUSTRALIAN CASE

GRAEME HUGO and MARTIN BELL

INTRODUCTION

Over the one and a half centuries for which reliable data are available in Australia there have been only two periods when the non-metropolitan population has grown more quickly than that living within the nation's large urban centres, a trend common in other nations too. The most studied of these is the period since the 1970s when Australia, like many other Euro-American societies, experienced what has come to be known as counterurbanisation or the 'turnaround' (Bell 1992, 1994, 1995; Burnley 1988; Hugo 1986, 1989a, 1989b, 1994, 1996; Hugo and Smailes 1986, 1992; Jarvie 1985, 1989a, 1989b; Salt 1992; Sant and Simons 1993a, 1993b). However, there was also a slackening and short reversal of the longer-term trend toward urbanisation in Australia during the Great Depression of the 1930s when the nation's rural population reached a pre-war peak. The 1933 Census showed, although by then the Depression's effects had begun to slacken, that 2.8 million Australians lived outside of urban areas. The Commonwealth Statistician (Commonwealth Bureau of Census Statistics 1940: 48–49) attributed this 'turnaround' directly to the Great Depression which.

> 'drove many to seek work away from their usual place of residence. Many town dwellers roved the country districts as prospectors for minerals, or as seekers of casual work or as applicants for locally distributed government relief'.

Indeed, one of the most enduring images of the Great Depression in Australia is of 'swagmen' roaming the rural parts of the country seeking a handout or to work in return only for meals and shelter. It was perceived at that time that the chance of obtaining welfare support was greater in rural than in urban areas. Accordingly, much of closely settled rural Australia recorded population growth in the early 1930s. With the virtual full employment which returned in the second half of the 1930s, and which lasted for about two decades, a pattern of increasing urbanisation resumed.

The contemporary turnaround differs in many ways from that of the 1930s both in terms of the politico-economic context in which it is occurring and in the form that it has taken. There have been a number of attempts to account for recent trends (Hugo and Smailes 1986; Jarvie 1984, 1989a, 1989b; Sant and Simons 1993a, 1993b), with most writers concluding that no single theory provides a comprehensive explanation. In common with much of the theoretical literature on counterurbanisation, Australian research has tended to ignore poverty- or welfare-led explanations such as that proposed for the 1930s by the Australian Commonwealth Statistician. However, it has been argued (Hugo 1989a, 1989b) that this should be one element in any comprehensive explanation of population growth in parts of non-metropolitan Australia. The present chapter seeks to explore this proposition in more detail and uses 1991 Census data to test some of the issues inherent in a poverty- or welfare-led hypothesis of the turnaround.

COUNTERURBANISATION IN AUSTRALIA

The 1970s saw a dramatic reversal in population trends in Australia, with growth outside the major capital cities outpacing that within the large cities for the first time during the post-war period. As Table 6.1 shows, this trend has been maintained at the national level throughout the 1980s, unlike the situation in many Western countries which saw a return to increasing urbanisation (Champion 1993). While the differential between metropolitan and non-metropolitan growth rates was less in the 1980s than the late 1970s, the population of the six state capital cities taken as a group grew more slowly than that of their hinterlands.

The major population dynamics in non-metropolitan Australia during the 1970s can be summarised as follows (Hugo and Smailes 1985):

- The long-standing pattern of more than a century of increasing concentration of the national population in large urban areas was reversed.
- There was an inverse relationship between the size category of urban centres and rates of population growth.
- The non-metropolitan 'renaissance' was very spatially concentrated in the well watered and attractive areas of the south east and east coast and the areas at the margins of the commuting zones of the large cities. Most of the dry farming and grazing areas maintained long-standing patterns of population decline, though those declines were much reduced.
- The non-metropolitan turnaround involved both greater retention of established residents and a small net migration gain from major urban areas. The latter was made up overwhelmingly of the Australian-born population and the overseas-born population became increasingly concentrated in major urban areas over this period.
- The turnaround resulted from a number of causes among which structural change in the economy, lifestyle shifts and improved levels of transport,

TABLE 6. I Annual average population growth rates, state capital city statistical divisions and non-metropolitan areas, six states, 1971–1991

	1971–1976		1976–1981		1981–1986		1986–1991	
	Metro.	Non-metro.	Metro.	Non-metro.	Metro.	Non-metro.	Metro.	Non-metro.
Census counts[a]								
New South Wales	0.58	1.06	1.18	1.83	0.98	1.17	1.01	1.49
Victoria	0.79	0.86	0.90	1.25	0.80	1.35	1.06	1.18
Queensland	1.95	2.43	1.44	3.25	2.25	2.57	2.50	3.14
South Australia	1.33	1.79	0.68	0.54	0.98	0.80	0.92	0.47
Western Australia	2.76	0.71	2.21	2.02	2.04	1.94	2.83	1.47
Tasmania	1.13	0.30	0.77	0.80	0.79	0.84	0.76	0.73
Six states	1.09	1.23	1.16	1.90	1.18	1.57	1.39	1.75
Estimated resident population[b]								
New South Wales	1.09	0.76	0.85	1.49	1.15	1.04	1.13	1.57
Victoria	1.60	0.01	0.60	0.97	0.88	1.50	1.24	1.16
Queensland	2.35	2.59	1.84	2.73	1.76	2.72	2.10	2.74
South Australia	1.67	0.03	0.63	0.85	1.03	0.74	1.05	0.52
Western Australia	3.19	0.20	2.06	1.82	2.64	1.56	2.51	1.83
Tasmania	1.43	0.24	0.79	0.66	0.92	0.87	0.88	0.90
Six states	1.65	0.86	0.98	1.60	1.28	1.55	1.42	1.70

Average annual rate of participation growth is calculated by using the compound interest formula to establish population change over time.
[a] Enumerated count of every person who spent census night in Australia, where they were on the night of the census.
[b] Official ABS intercensal estimate of the Australian population based on results of the population census.
Source: Bell 1995: 77.

communications, personal mobility and accessibility were especially important.

• Partly as a result of the turnaround, the non-metropolitan population has become more diverse and there has been a convergence in the economic, demographic and social composition of the metropolitan and non-metropolitan populations. One element in this has been a decreasing reliance of non-metropolitan communities and families on traditional rural primary industries for their income.

While the 1980s saw a continuation of the overall counterurbanisation trend, some crucial differences emerged (Bell 1995; Hugo 1989a, 1989b, 1994, 1996):

• While overall the non-metropolitan population grew faster than that in large cities in the early 1980s, the differential was not as great as in the late 1970s, so there was a slowing down of the turnaround.
• The tendency toward spatial concentration was accentuated so that there was an even sharper clustering of non-metropolitan growth in the 1980s.
• The overseas-born population began to participate in the turnaround to a greater extent, although they tended to be predominantly immigrants of long

TABLE 6.2 Australia: population change in capital city statistical divisions and rest of state, 1989–1994

State	Average annual growth rate		
	Capital city	Rest of state	Total
New South Wales	0.6	1.4	0.9
Victoria	0.7	0.7	0.7
Queensland	2.3	2.7	2.5
South Australia	0.8	0.4	0.7
Western Australia	1.5	1.4	1.5
Tasmania	0.9	0.7	0.7
Northern Territory	0.5	1.8	1.2
Australian Capital Territory	1.7	–	1.7
Total	1.0	1.5	1.2

Source: ABS 1995: 5

standing and mainly from English-speaking backgrounds (Bell and Cooper 1995).

Although 1996 Census data were not available at the time of writing, there are some indications that the pattern of counterurbanisation has continued during the early 1990s. Table 6.2, for example, shows official population estimates for the states and territories for the 1989–1994 period and it is apparent that, overall, the non-metropolitan population has been growing substantially faster than that of the capital cities.

One of the most distinctive features of the turnaround in Australia has been its spatial concentration (Hugo 1989a) and indeed the spatial separation of non-metropolitan areas of growth and decline has become more marked over time. This is seen to some extent in Tables 6.1 and 6.2, which show that at a state level it has primarily been in the eastern mainland states, especially New South Wales and Queensland, where counterurbanisation has consistently occurred. At a finer regional level, analysis has shown a clear spatial divide between non-metropolitan regions recording net gains through migration and those experiencing net losses (Bell 1995; Hugo 1989a, 1989b, 1994, 1996; Hugo and Smailes 1986; Sant 1993). The principal areas experiencing net migration gains were as follows:

• The eastern coast, especially in Queensland and New South Wales, where migration gain formed a more or less continuous coastal band.
• An arc around the major capital cities, around and somewhat beyond the boundaries of their commuting zones.
• The snowfields and some River Murray resort areas.
• The Hume Highway linking Sydney and Melbourne.
• The coast to the north and south of Perth.

- Some of the sparsely settled mining areas of Western Australia and the Northern Territory.

In each of the five mainland states the extensive areas of the wheat–sheep belt in the east, south east and south west were almost universally areas of *net out-migration* in the 1980s.

It is clear (Hugo 1994) that there is a growing dichotomy emerging in Australia's non metropolitan areas with respect to population growth patterns and the economic trends which underlie them. On the one hand are the well watered eastern and south eastern coastal zones and areas around the commuting sheds of each of the major cities. In these areas the population is growing at rates above the national level and the local economies are diversifying and expanding. On the other hand are the heartland dry farming and pastoral areas of rural and remote Australia which cover the bulk of the continent. In these areas net out-migration is continuing such that absolute population decline is common and there is a consequent diminution in both their social and economic potential.

POVERTY/WELFARE-LED EXPLANATIONS OF THE TURNAROUND

Most studies of inter-regional migration in Australia have stressed the pre-eminent role of employment opportunities in shaping the pattern of internal migration and population distribution. A variety of explanatory frameworks have been used including spatial interaction models (Hugo 1971a, 1971b), equilibrium concepts (Rowland 1979), analysis of structural change in the economy (Jarvie 1981, 1985, 1989a, 1989b; McKay 1985) and investigation of the role of employment transfers by large companies and government departments (McKay and Whitelaw 1977). Human capital approaches have also been employed (Flood *et al.* 1991; Langley 1977). Only recently have migration analysts begun to recognise and examine the role of non-economic motives for inter-regional migration (Bell and Maher 1995; Flood *et al,* 1991). Specialised literature on the turnaround, however, has been more broadly based. Hugo and Smailes (1985) listed a number of hypotheses from the wider literature, in ascending order of strength, as follows:

- The turnaround is only a temporary fluctuation in the general trend toward urban concentration in response to the economic recession of the 1970s.
- The turnaround is a demographic effect caused by changes in the particular age and life cycle population mixes of metropolitan/non-metropolitan populations.
- The turnaround is a result of successful public regional development and decentralisation policies, particularly those relating to deconcentration of manufacturing industry from large cities.
- The turnaround is an area-specific effect traceable to employment growth in

particular, localised industries in favoured non-metropolitan regions (for example, mining, defence) rather than a general broad-scale phenomenon.

- The turnaround is a result of the gradual emergence of scale diseconomies in large urban areas, which combine with growing social problems to increase the push factor in migration streams from urban areas.
- Reduced distance friction associated with new transport and communication technology has allowed a further rapid extension of urban commuting fields into widely dispersed but still metropolitan-focused economic networks.
- There has been a basic change either in people's values and lifestyle preferences or in their ability to act on such preferences, acting in favour of residence in rural or small town environments and against large cities.
- The turnaround is primarily a result of structural change in modern Western economies as the proportion of tertiary and quaternary employment increases relative to secondary employment, while the decline in primary employment has almost run its course.

Hugo and Smailes (1985) placed particular emphasis on the last three of the explanations listed, suggesting the need for an eclectic approach which incorporates elements of all three.

It was later suggested (Hugo 1989a, 1989b) that a further hypothesis should be considered in seeking a comprehensive explanation of counterurbanisation in Australia – one which had attracted little attention in the turnaround literature. This hypothesis suggests that a significant component of population growth in Australian non-metropolitan areas is due to the in-migration, and retention, of low income groups. An important element in this movement is of people receiving some form of transfer payments from government which are equally available across the entire nation and totally portable, and a major attraction is the lower cost of living, especially cheaper housing.

The number of Australians receiving some form of welfare benefit has risen sharply over the last two decades. The number of persons receiving the four major types of Commonwealth benefits increased from 1.18 million in 1973 to 3.13 million in 1993 (Australian Bureau of Statistics 1994: 147). Figure 6.1 shows that the proportions of adult Australians receiving an aged pension, unemployment benefit, disability pension or sole parent pension almost doubled from 12.5 percent in 1975 to 23.1 percent in 1993. Moreover, these data do not include recipients of some other special government benefits (for example, those received by some Aboriginal and Torres Strait Islander people)[1] and those receiving private income transfers (for example, through superannuation schemes)[2]. The increasing proportion of Australia's adult population reliant upon income transfers is due to the ageing of the population[3], a trebling of unemployment in the 1970s and 1980s associated with major structural change in the economy[4], introduction of new government benefits in the 1970s (for example, the single parent benefit) and widening of eligibility for benefits in the 1970s. It is important to note that each of the benefits shown in Figure 6.1 is provided by the

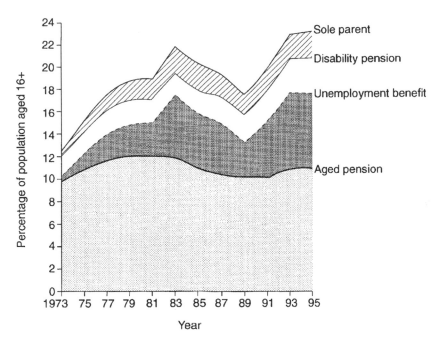

FIGURE 6.1 Australia: proportion of the population aged 16 years and over reliant upon Commonwealth transfer payments, 1973–1995. Source: ABS 1994: 147

federal government out of central revenue and is totally portable. Hence reliance on transfers is not itself a constraint on mobility. Indeed, the unemployed and other groups on welfare benefits have substantially higher rates of inter-regional migration than the employed workforce, or others on private incomes (Bell and Maher 1995, Wulff and Bell 1997).

The hypothesis argues that a major draw-card attracting low income people, among whom transfer recipients are a significant element, from metropolitan to non-metropolitan locations is the lower cost of housing in the latter areas (Budge 1996; Budge *et al.* 1992). Figure 6.2 provides some supporting evidence, indicating a substantial and persistent difference in housing affordability between metropolitan and non-metropolitan areas over the last decade. Moreover, it is notable that housing affordability varies widely between capital cities, with the lowest affordability index in Sydney, the city with the highest rate of net out-migration (ABS 1994: 168). Burnley (1988: 280) argues that a trade-off in housing is occurring in some of the out-migration from Sydney:

'Not only are people 'trading up' to better housing or trading down to accommodate other investments or amenities but there is evidence from studies of movers to Merimbula and Pambula (Byrne 1986), Shoalhaven (O'Dea 1982) and Forster and Tancurry (Brown 1984) that a significant minority of migrants in middle age are purchasing their homes for the first time in their lives'.

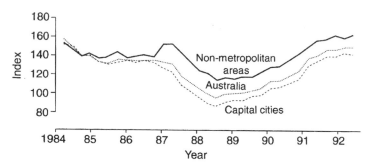

FIGURE 6.2 Australia: housing affordability in Australian capital cities and non-metropolitan areas, 1984–1993. Source: ABS 1994: 167

TABLE 6.3 South Australia: average sale prices of houses, flats and vacant lots in the Adelaide metropolitan area and non-metropolitan towns, March 1992

	Non-metropolitan (Dollars)	Adelaide (Dollars)	Difference (%)
Single unit houses	71 276	121 413	+70
Home units	67 320	97 212	+44
Flats	112 583	184 583	+64
Vacant lots	21 523	40 887	+90

Source: South Australian Department of Lands 1992: 59.

Similarly, in South Australia the average cost of single unit housing in metropolitan Adelaide is 70 percent above that in country towns. This is shown in Table 6.3. In some country towns which have suffered severe population decline in the early post-war years, due to mechanisation in farming, increased centralisation of manufacturing and retailing in Adelaide, and so on, the costs of housing can be very low indeed.

A second factor in the housing equation is the distribution of public housing. A significant proportion (32.8 percent) of the nation's public rental housing stock is located in non-metropolitan parts of Australia. In fact in 1991, 6.0 percent of all housing units in major cities were public rental properties, compared with 7.8 percent in other regional towns and cities[5] and 1.0 percent in rural areas. Invariably the pressure on public housing in the major cities is greater than in non-metropolitan areas so that many groups given priority status in access to public housing (for example, single mothers) are allocated dwellings in non-metropolitan areas. Hence, for some transfer recipients there is little or no choice involved in their housing-related move from metropolitan to non-metropolitan locations. Another dimension of the housing cost issue is the increasing number of Australians living in caravans in non-metropolitan areas. The Australian Census has only differentiated between residents and vacationers in caravans since the 1986 Census. Nevertheless, at the 1991 Census, 127 000

TABLE 6.4 Average weekly household expenditure as a percentage of household expenditure in capital cities, 1993–94

	Other cities	Rural
New South Wales	84.0	73.7
Victoria	80.0	87.5
Queensland	93.9	93.8
South Australia	76.3	91.7
Western Australia	97.0	78.1
Tasmania	87.9	103.1
Total	86.6	83.8

Source: ABS 1996: 130.

Australians were living permanently in 71 000 caravans. Of these, almost three-quarters (73 percent) were located in non-metropolitan areas (ABS 1994: 164), compared with 60 percent of the total population.

Allied to the cost of housing is the generally lower cost of living outside the major cities. This is reflected in Table 6.4, which shows that average household weekly expenditure in rural and provincial Australia is around 15 percent below that in the capital cities. This differential is especially marked in rural New South Wales, with average expenditure 26 percent below that in Sydney.

While living costs and the availability of housing have been important magnets, much of the impetus for counterurbanisation is a product of economic change. The Australian economy has experienced massive structural change over the last two decades. This has resulted in a huge loss of capital-city-based jobs in both blue-collar and white-collar sectors. Overall, the number of manufacturing jobs in Australia's capital cities declined from 1 302 784 in 1971 to 662 069 in 1991 and the job losses have disproportionately affected unskilled and semi-skilled workers. This is also the case with jobs lost in white collar areas, where increased automation and computerisation has displaced large numbers of lower level clerical staff in large cities. Many of the displaced workers find it difficult to make the transition to those sectors of the economy which are expanding – especially the service sector – where both the skill requirements and the organisation of the work (non-union, fractional time, hours predominantly outside of the nine-to-five regime) are difficult to adjust to. Despite these difficulties, non-metropolitan locations clearly represent an attractive alternative to the large cities for many displaced workers (Stilwell 1993: 195–198). Not only are these groups able to obtain significant capital gains from selling their home in the city and purchasing a much cheaper house in the non-metropolitan sector but they also may be able to pick up unskilled work, at least on a part-time basis. Numerous opportunities exist for seasonal work in agriculture or tourism in non-metropolitan areas. Moreover, by their very nature, the income from such jobs is less likely to come to the attention of taxation or social security officials (Bansemer 1987).

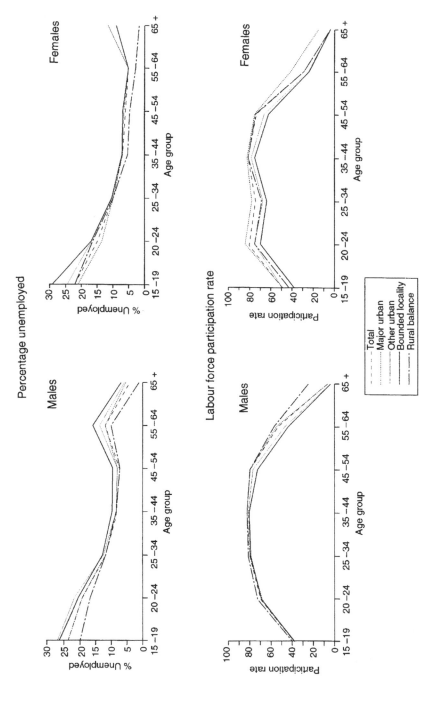

FIGURE 6.3 Australia: proportion unemployed and labour force participation rate by section of state, 1991. Source: ABS 1991 Census

It is difficult to compare levels of well-being between non-metropolitan and metropolitan areas in Australia because of the differences in cost of living as well as in income. However, there are strong indications that the incidence of poverty is greater in non-metropolitan than metropolitan areas. If one considers unemployment, for example, Figure 6.3 shows that unemployment levels are highest in regional cities and bounded rural localities (i.e. centres with 200–99 999 residents), which are the major destinations of non-metropolitan bound migrants from metropolitan areas.

Similarly, it is clear that the incidence of underemployment and discouraged workers is greatest in such areas. Hence labour force participation rates are lower for males aged over 35 in urban areas with less than 100 000 inhabitants than in large cities and this is the case for women of all ages. This is consistent with a pattern of increasing concentration of unemployed, underemployed, low income and recipients of disability, unemployment, single parent and aged pensions in Australia's non-metropolitan urban centres through in-migration of such groups and out-migration of higher income groups. Other indications are the fact that the incidence of students in schools receiving exemption from school expenses, such as purchase of books and payment for excursions, because of the income of their parents is greater in non-metropolitan areas than in the major cities. In South Australia, for example, 44.2 percent of children in non-metropolitan-based schools qualified for the school card compared with 40 percent of their Adelaide counterparts[6]. It would seem then that the incidence of poverty in Australia is greater in non-metropolitan than in metropolitan areas, as is the case in the United States (O'Hare 1985: 15).

The poverty/welfare-led hypothesis should not be seen purely in terms of 'economic push', since there is undoubtedly a contingent of people on low incomes or reliant upon transfer payments who decide to relocate to a congenial environment in non-metropolitan areas for amenity reasons. This is especially the case for transfer recipients at or near retirement age. One of the most clearly documented components of counterurbanisation is the movement of former metropolitan residents in their 50s and 60s to non-metropolitan locations upon retirement or semi-retirement (Drysdale 1991; Murphy 1981; Murphy and Zehner 1988; Neyland and Kendig 1996; Pollard 1996). Figure 6.4, for example, shows that over the 1981–1991 period there was a significant increase in the proportion of Australians aged 50–74 living in the areas designated rural[7] at the respective censuses. Whereas the rural sector's share of the total population increased only from 14.2 to 14.9 percent, increases of over two percentage points were recorded in the 50–64 age categories. Moreover, in the age categories 50–74 the proportions living in rural areas in 1981 were below the average for the total population but by 1991 they were above the average for the total population.

This form of retirement migration to scenically attractive coastal or riverside locations occurs in all states but a major focus is the warmer climate of northern New South Wales and Queensland. Burnley (1996) found that in the north coast

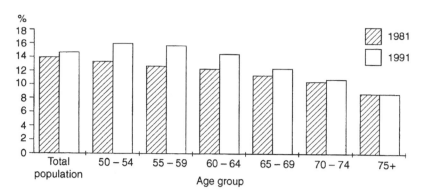

FIGURE 6.4 Australian rural areas: share of total population and population aged over 50 years, 1981 and 1991. Source: calculated from 1981 and 1991 Censuses

region of New South Wales, a prime turnaround region, the 55-and-over age group made up an increasing proportion of net migration gains over the 1971–1991 period. Incomes in this region are well below the state and metropolitan average and the number of low income families has increased significantly (Burnley 1996).

A distinctive feature of this migration is that in many cases it is associated with people moving to a house which was formerly a holiday home or to a place that they regularly visited in the past as vacationers (Brown 1984; Byrne 1986; Cook 1980; Murphy 1981; O'Dea 1982). There is also evidence of retirement migration involving return of people to home areas which they left many decades ago when they left school or were forced to seek work in the city because of a lack of job opportunities (Burnley 1988; Hudson 1987). However, it is not only the older population that are involved in this type of migration to amenity-rich non-metropolitan locations. There are indications that younger unemployed people also tend to gravitate to coastal locations if they are unable to get work in large cities (Burnley 1996; McDonald 1986). Burnley (1988) shows that the unemployed were disproportionately represented in the movement from Sydney to non-metropolitan New South Wales in both 1971–1976 and 1976–1981. This was especially focused on the high net migration gain coastal area. He points out that this was contrary to traditional push–pull, neo-classical migration models which suggest that internal migration occurs from low wage to high wage areas and from high unemployment to low unemployment areas and suggests that:

'It is possible that the transferability of social security payments makes mobility of younger persons possible, but it may be that on finding themselves unemployed in Sydney, members may have moved back to country locations for support from kin. Unemployment would be more bearable in the country than in the metropolis' (Burnley 1988: 270).

The significance of welfare groups in urban to rural flows is also evident from the last Australian Bureau of Statistics sample survey of internal migration conducted in 1987 (ABS 1987). As Wulff and Newton (1996: 435) concluded from their analysis of these data:

> 'The older aged groups (particularly those aged over 65 years and older childless couples) are more likely than other households to make an urban–rural move. Another group with a higher than average rate of urban to rural mobility is the unemployed, with about 10 percent making this type of move compared with 7 percent of all movers'.

Similarly, from his analysis of the 1986 Census, Flood (1992) argued that the key group contributing to net inter-regional migration in Australia were those outside the workforce – the 45 percent of the adult population comprising spouses in single income families, pensioners and beneficiaries, retirees and people on fixed incomes such as owners of shares and residential properties. He concluded that it was this group, along with the unemployed, who were moving out of the cities, towards coastal regions in New South Wales, Victoria and especially Queensland, while the net migration of employed people favoured the large cities.

THE ROLE OF WELFARE GROUPS IN COUNTERURBANISATION

While there is considerable circumstantial evidence that non-metropolitan areas are attractive to the poor, especially to those in receipt of welfare payments, there has been little direct investigation of the precise role of such groups in the process of counterurbanisation. Apart from the work of Flood (1992) mentioned above, which focused primarily on the labour force, most support for the welfare hypothesis has been drawn from small-scale surveys, local case studies and anecdote. Data from the 1991 ABS Census and the 1992 Survey of Families analysed in two recent studies, now provide a much more comprehensive picture (Bell and Maher 1995, Wulff and Bell 1997). We turn first to the overall mobility of welfare recipients and then examine their role in the composition of movements between metropolitan and non-metropolitan regions of Australia[8].

The Australian Census does not collect information on source of income but data of this type from the 1992 Australian Bureau of Statistics Family Survey demonstrates that households reliant on welfare payments (principally the aged pension, invalidity pension, unemployment and single parent benefits) have substantially higher rates of mobility than their counterparts on private incomes (wages, salaries and investments). This is evident from Figure 6.5, which reveals consistently higher mobility among welfare recipients at all ages beyond the mid twenties. Only among young adults, where mobility is universally high and the number of household heads comparatively small, does the variation disappear.

Wulff and Bell (1997) have shown that these variations are even greater if

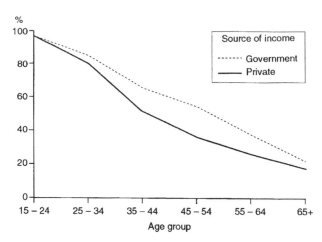

FIGURE 6.5 Australia: age-specific mobility rates by main source of income, household heads, 1987–1992. Source: ABS Family Survey (unpublished data)

mobility is measured in terms of frequency of moves. For example, almost a quarter of unemployed household heads aged 30–44 and 15 percent of sole parents had moved four times or more over the five-year period 1987–1992, compared with only one in ten private income earners. Data on period of residence portray a similar picture: less than half of households headed by an unemployed person or sole parent had been living in their current dwelling longer than two years, compared with more than two-thirds of those earning independent incomes.

Data from the Family Survey refer to all forms of mobility, including intra-urban moves, not simply to long distance migration or counterurbanisation. However, Census data, which enable longer distance moves to be distinguished, provide similar results. As can be seen from Table 6.5, inter-regional migration rates among the unemployed aged 30 and over are well above those for wage and salary earners or people outside the labour force. Similarly, while the Census does not identify welfare recipients directly, Table 6.5 shows that low income households move between regions at substantially higher rates than their counterparts on higher incomes. These differences are masked in the aggregate rates because the majority of low income households are headed by older people, among whom mobility is comparatively low (Wulff and Bell 1997).

It is interesting to note in Table 6.5 that people not in the labour force aged 30–54 were more mobile than those who were employed. This reflects the generally high levels of movement of early retirees, people in receipt of invalidity pensions and discouraged workers. The latter group are people in the working ages who have given up attempting to find work largely because they have been unable to get employment over a long period of time and hence are not classified as unemployed. Also, in 1993 there were 406 572 Australians of

TABLE 6.5 Inter-regional mobility rates (percent) by age and selected character-istics, 1986–1991, 34 regions of Australia

	Age group			
Characteristic	15–29	30–54	55+	Total
Household income[a]				
$0–16 000	22.2	15.3	6.3	10.8
$16–30 000	21.7	12.3	6.4	12.1
$30–50 000	20.4	10.9	4.4	11.3
$50 000+	21.9	9.5	3.3	10.1
Labour force status[b]				
Employed	15.3	10.4	4.4	11.4
Unemployed	16.9	16.9	12.4	16.6
Not in the labour force	14.3	12.7	6.4	9.7

[a] Household heads.
[b] Persons.
Source: Adapted from Wulff and Bell 1997.

working ages receiving disability pensions. There is considerable debate that, especially among older workers, people still able to work are classified as eligible for a disability pension. The higher mobility of early retirees, disability pension recipients and discouraged workers undoubtedly accounts for the higher levels of movement among the 'not in the labour force' group and survey evidence suggests that they are important in counterurbanisation movement.

High mobility itself can be an indicator of vulnerability (Wulff and Newton 1996). Migration is widely viewed as a means of improving life chances but frequent moves are often involuntary, especially among the older aged population (Rowland 1996). However, the level of mobility itself is a poor guide to the spatial impacts of migration. Most migration streams are balanced to a greater or lesser degree by counterstreams in the opposite direction and a high level of mobility does not necessarily generate a correspondingly high level of population redistribution.

One simple summary measure of the extent of this redistribution is the Migration Effectiveness Index (MEI), calculated as the net gain (summed across all gaining regions) as a percentage of the gross inter-regional flows (Shryock *et al.* 1975: 656). The value of the index denotes the amount of redistribution which occurred for every 100 cross-border flows. Thus, high values indicate that migration is an efficient mechanism for redistribution, generating a large redistributional effect for a given volume of movement. Conversely, low ratios denote that the flows are more closely balanced, leading to comparatively little redistribution.

Table 6.6 indicates a clear inverse relationship between household income and the extent of inter-regional redistribution. For the given volume of move-

TABLE 6.6 Gross flows, population redistribution and migration effectiveness between 34 regions of Australia, 1986–1991, persons aged 15 and over by household income and labour force status

Characteristic	Gross flows	Migration Net redistribution	Effectiveness Index	Percent of flows	Percent of net
Household income[a]					
$0–16 000	149 993	42 460	28.3	24.3	32.7
$16–30 000	178 786	41 781	23.4	28.9	32.2
$30–50 000	162 574	27 409	16.9	26.3	21.1
$50 000+	126 628	18 153	14.3	20.5	14.0
Total	617 981	129 803	21.0	100.0	100.0
Labour force status[b]					
Employed	805 446	122 516	15.2	57.1	45.3
Unemployed	153 404	33 936	22.1	10.9	12.6
Not in labour force	452 506	113 715	25.1	32.1	42.1
Total	1 411 356	270 167	19.1	100.0	100.0

[a] Household heads.
[b] Persons.
Source: ABS 1991 Census (unpublished data).

ment, there was significantly greater redistribution of low income households between regions than of those earning higher incomes. For every 100 households earning less than $16 000 per annum that migrated between regions in the 1986–1991 period, there was a net shift of more than 28 households compared with just 14.3 households earning $50 000 or more. As a result, low income households made up a substantially larger share of the net redistribution between regions than they did of the gross flows. Households earning less than $16 000 contributed almost a third of the net redistribution yet they comprised less than a quarter of the gross movement. Conversely, those earning $50 000 or more made up 20 percent of the flows but just 14 percent of the inter-regional shift.

A similar pattern is apparent in the data classified by labour force status. Migration Effectiveness was substantially higher among the unemployed and those outside the labour force than for employed workers. Together these two groups contributed 55 percent of the population redistribution between regions but only 43 percent of the gross flows. Conversely, employed labour is under-represented in the net population shift. This lower Migration Effectiveness among employed workers is readily explained by the strong reciprocal flows of labour between major employment centres as part of the career development process (Bell and Maher 1995; Jarvie 1989a; McKay and Whitelaw 1977). In contrast, the unemployed and those outside the labour force are less strongly tied to fixed nodes of employment.

The MEI reveals the extent of redistribution of particular groups but it does

TABLE 6.7 Non-metropolitan Australia: internal migration flows and net gain / loss from capital cities, 1986–1991, persons aged 15 and over by household income and labour force status

Characteristic	Arrivals	Departures	Net migration	Percent of net	Percent of 1991 non-metropolitan population
Household income[a]					
$0–16 000	79 048	47 958	31 090	50.0	29.7
$16–30 000	89 704	64 379	25 325	40.8	29.9
$30–50 000	79 329	70 805	8 524	13.7	24.3
$50 000+	65 745	68 555	−2 810	−4.5	16.0
Total	313 826	251 697	62 129	100.0	100.0
Labour force status[b]					
Employed	383 808	371 978	11 830	12.7	55.7
Unemployed	76 198	60 048	16 150	17.3	10.3
Not in labour force	230 152	164 741	65 411	70.0	34.0
Total	690 158	596 767	93 391	100.0	100.0

[a] Household heads.
[b] Persons.
Source: ABS 1991 Census (unpublished data).

not identify the regions that are gaining and those that are losing. Table 6.7 extends the analysis, setting out the household income and labour force composition of internal migration flows between Australia's seven major metropolitan centres and the non-metropolitan parts of the country. The results provide considerable support for the poverty/welfare-led hypothesis of counterurbanisation. Households with incomes of less than $16 000 made up half of the non-metropolitan migration gain from the capital cities and this rises to more than 90 percent for households with incomes below $30 000. More striking still is that non-metropolitan Australia recorded a net loss of high income households to the cities. These results clearly conflict with interpretations that see counterurbanisation as a product of the out-migration of highly paid professionals, loosed from their ties to the cities by development in transport and telecommunication and able to move to more congenial non-metropolitan rustic surroundings. While high income households are strongly represented among in-migrants to non-metropolitan Australia, their numbers are more than offset by those moving in the reverse direction.

The labour force data tell a similar story. Although there were substantial flows of employed labour between the capital cities and their hinterlands, the inwards and outwards movements were closely balanced. As a result, the employed workforce accounted for just one-eighth of the net gain by non-metropolitan areas, outnumbered by the unemployed who contributed a further one-sixth, and overwhelmed by people outside the labour force who comprised a massive 70 percent. Again, this profile strongly counteracts the claim that counterurbanisation is primarily an employment-led phenomenon. The image is rather of a mass exodus of 'urban refugees' (Hugo and Smailes 1992) freed from ties to the city or seeking lower living costs or higher amenity in the non-metropolitan parts of the country.

It is important to recognise that a significant segment of the non-metropolitan net gain of low income households and people outside the labour force are older Australians, outside the prime working age groups. However, retirees are by no means the dominant group of counterurban migrants. Indeed, people aged 65 and over made up only 17 percent of the non-metropolitan net gain from capital cities between 1986 and 1991 (Bell 1996). Even if attention is confined to individuals aged 15 to 54, to exclude early and pre-retirement groups, low income households still account for the bulk of the net gain and employed workers remain in the minority. Households on incomes of under $16 000 made up 45 percent of the net gain and those on incomes of $16–30 000 a further 48 percent. Similarly, the proportion of employed workers rises only marginally to 16 percent, while the unemployed rise to 34 percent: people aged 15–54 outside the labour force still account for half of the non-metropolitan net gain (Wulff and Bell 1997). Many of these are almost certainly the spouses or other dependent relatives of principal migrants, but a significant proportion may well be discouraged job-seekers or others on welfare income.

Wulff and Bell (1997) show that outflows of low income earners from city to country were most pronounced in the two most populous states, New South Wales and Victoria, but all Australian states registered net gains of low income earners in some non-metropolitan regions. The majority of the movement is directed towards coastal destinations and the metropolitan peripheries – the primary foci of the turnaround. However, gains of low income households were also recorded in several parts of inland Australia, contrary to the general trend of overall population loss.

The net migration profile for regions of New South Wales, shown in Table 6.8, clearly demonstrates the major role of low income earners in the process of counterurbanisation. Net losses from the Sydney metropolitan area were heavily biased towards low income groups. In contrast, all non-metropolitan regions registered gains of low income households, and all except the Illawarra and South Eastern regions to the south of Sydney lost high income earners. Table 6.8 suggests three distinct groupings of non-metropolitan regions:

- First is the Illawarra, which gained in all income classes. Substantial gains here are readily attributed to the in-migration of higher status households to fringe suburban development within commuting range of metropolitan Sydney.
- A second group, at the other extreme of the income profile, comprises the Central West, Murray–Murrumbidgee and Far West/North Western regions. Together, these regions cover most of inland New South Wales and are experiencing substantial out-migration associated with rural adjustment, recession and deteriorating terms of trade for agricultural products. Yet these

TABLE 6.8   Net internal migration by household income, eight regions of New South Wales, 1986–1991

Region	Household income				
	$0–16 000	$16–30 000	$30–50 000	$50 001+	Total
Sydney	−23 640	−22 217	−11 492	159	−57 190
Hunter	1 926	1 546	898	−248	4 122
Illawarra	1 655	1 424	1 119	571	4 769
North Coast	7 463	6 113	909	−1 280	13 205
Central West	147	−123	−321	−624	−921
South Eastern	1 197	1 472	659	1	3 329
Murrumbidgee/Murray	620	−7	−583	−1 056	−1 026
Far West/North Western	350	166	−533	−351	−368

Source: ABS 1991 Census (unpublished data).

regions actually gained more than 1000 low income households over the 1986–1991 period.

● The third grouping comprises the predominantly coastal regions of the Hunter, South Eastern and North Coast. Although each recorded net in-migration over the period, these gains were strongly biased to the lower end of the income spectrum.

The profile for the North Coast, a prime turnaround region, is especially striking, with the whole of the substantial net gain accounted for by households on incomes of $30 000 or less, and more than half on incomes under $16 000. Analysis of labour force composition reinforces the picture. Over the 1986–1991 period the North Coast region gained almost 10 000 people in the 15–54 age group. Yet 5000 of these were unemployed at the time of the 1991 Census and more than 6000 were not in the labour force: despite its rapid growth, the region actually lost almost 1500 employed workers to other parts of Australia over this period (Wulff and Bell 1997).

Figure 6.6 clearly depicts the widespread dispersal of low income households from Sydney. Not all outflows were directed to non-metropolitan New South Wales: a significant component went to other states, including their capitals which themselves lost similar groups to their non-metropolitan hinterlands. Nevertheless, it is clear that coastal regions were the principal beneficiaries of this movement.

There can be little doubt that the lower housing costs in many non-metropolitan parts of Australia are an attraction to people on low or fixed incomes. The Census does not provide reasons for migration but an Australian Bureau of Statistics Internal Migration Survey in 1985 (ABS 1986) found that almost a quarter of the migrants moving from metropolitan to non-metropolitan locations quoted 'housing' as the reason for their move compared with eight percent among migrants moving in the opposite direction.

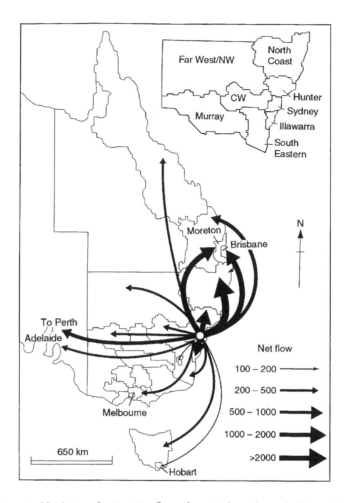

FIGURE 6.6 Net internal migration flows from Sydney, households with incomes of under $16 000 per annum, 1986–1991

At the same time, it is apparent that economic change is the primary force driving each of the four main patterns of migration that are progressively changing the distribution of population in Australia – the movements from the southern 'rustbelt' to the northern 'sunbelt', from the city to the coast, from the inner suburbs to the fringe and away from the inland (Bell and Maher 1995). O'Connor and Stimson (1996) conceptualise these shifts in terms of an increasing disarticulation between demographic trends on the one hand and economic forces on the other, the former leading to dispersal of population, the latter to increased agglomeration of productive investment but dispersal of employment that is based on consumption-related activities. This, in turn, it is argued, is leading to increasing divergence in the types of jobs that are available in different locations. 'Good jobs' that demand high level skills but offer high wages and security are increasingly concentrated in a few locations (primarily the major metropolitan centres), whereas the growing number of 'less desirable' jobs, characterised by lower wages and less security, are dispersing.

The evidence assembled in this chapter supports and extends this view, pointing to the central role of disadvantaged groups, especially low income earners and the unemployed, in the drift away from the cities. As the ageing of the population accelerates, and structural change and microeconomic reform continue, the scene seems set for an ongoing shift in the nature of the Australian space economy, with disadvantaged groups playing an increasingly significant role.

SOME INTERNATIONAL COMPARISONS

In other developed countries internal migration research is increasingly beginning to focus on the mobility of the poor. This is especially the case in the United States where, for example, there is growing recognition of the significance of migration of the poor as an influence upon the level and spatial distribution of rural poverty. On the one hand, it has been convincingly demonstrated that the poor, less educated and least skilled are underrepresented among the people leaving depressed rural areas (Cromartie 1993; Garkovich 1989; Lichter *et al.* 1994). On the other hand, there is also some evidence of the poor being an important element in urban to rural migration (Johansen and Fuguitt 1984; Lichter *et al.* 1994). Fitchen (1995), in a case study of a depressed rural community in New York, shows that this community has become a migration destination for poor migrants from both urban and other rural areas, causing dramatic increases in the poverty rate, welfare rolls and service needs. Her research indicates that cheap housing provided the main attraction to newcomers while the lack of local jobs was not an element since many of the newcomers had limited job skills and would have had trouble getting and keeping a job in any case.

Frey (1994a, 1994b, 1995a, 1995b, 1995c) and Frey *et al.* (1995) have closely analysed the migration of the poor between states in the United States and shown that there is a significant out-migration of the poverty population from states which are experiencing high levels of immigration. The fact that, unlike Australia, the United States welfare system varies between states has led to an important research question being whether states offering more generous or comprehensive welfare programs become magnets for poor migrants from other states which have more limited programs. Early research based on 1960s and 1970s data appeared to lend support to the welfare magnet hypothesis that higher welfare benefit levels were a positive draw to migration (Cebula *et al.* 1973; Glantz 1973; Southwick 1981). However, Hanson and Hartman (1994) addressed this question by examining the Current Population Survey for the 1980s and found no evidence to support the so-called welfare magnet hypothesis. They concluded that in the United States poor people do not move from one state to another to receive more public assistance and that in fact the poor are unlikely to move out of their home state. This is in contrast to the findings of studies in the 1960s and 1970s which suggested that there was a positive influence of welfare benefit levels or generous eligibility criteria on migration of the disadvantaged. Nonetheless, Torrecilha and Sandefur (1990) have demonstrated that these studies suffer from a number of methodological limitations. They used data on Aid to Families for Dependent Children (AFDC) to examine the welfare magnet hypothesis and found that there was no difference between advantaged and disadvantaged groups in their propensities to leave individual states, nor was there any difference between the groups in their likelihood of moving to high benefit states. Friedl (1986) found that movers receiving AFDC payments are able to improve their economic standing more than those who do not move. A study of net migration within New York State found a moderate relationship with public sustenance variables but concludes that:

'manipulating public assistance organisation via public policy changes would probably have less of an effect on net migration than would a change in private sustenance organisation' (Hirschl *et al.* 1990: 15).

Overall, however, as Clark (1989) has pointed out, the research literature in the United States has failed to produce compelling evidence that individuals migrate in order to collect generous welfare payments.

An interesting study was undertaken by Clark (1989) whereby, instead of focusing upon the destination areas of migrants, she examined conditions in the area of origin in her analysis of the relationship between migration and welfare. She focused upon sole mothers and found that the availability of high welfare payments in a state inhibits the migration of both current welfare recipients and non-recipients. From the perspective of the current study, the findings of Rives *et al.* (1983) show that low cost of living at the destination is an important factor shaping the migration of the older population.

CONCLUSION

In the burgeoning literature on internal migration in developed countries the class dimension remains neglected. Part of this neglect is the limited amount of attention which has been devoted to consideration of migration of the poor and its consequences. The present chapter has attempted to make a contribution to this area by examining the role of the low income and welfare recipient population in the counterurbanisation phenomenon in Australia. The Australian case is to some extent a distinctive one since transfers from government are equally available across the entire nation, are totally portable and the extent of their coverage is more extensive among eligible groups than in most OECD nations[9]. Nevertheless, it is apparent that a 'low income/welfare-led hypothesis' has some validity in partially explaining the turnaround in Australia. In contrast, conventional neo-classical models based on wage and employment opportunity differences have only limited validity in explaining the movement of people between Australian metropolitan and non-metropolitan areas. This is consistent with a wider questioning of the power of such theories to comprehensively account for patterns of inter-regional migration (Harkman 1989; Roseman 1983).

The evidence of a significant 'welfare population' group being involved in the turnaround either by virtue of metropolitan to non-metropolitan migration or by staying in non-metropolitan areas after becoming part of the population dependent upon income transfers has many policy implications. These include the possible marginalisation of these people in non-metropolitan areas because of the inferior public infrastructure compared with that available in the metropolitan centres. There are also important issues for local non-metropolitan communities faced with increasing demands to supply infrastructure and services for this population. These issues have yet to be addressed by policy makers and planners of national and regional levels in Australia (Wulff *et al.* 1993). They will, however, become more pressing over the next decade since broader economic, social and demographic trends in Australia – such as the continuation of high levels of unemployment, structural change in the economy, reduction of public housing availability in major urban areas, rapid growth of the older population – would appear to be working toward at least a continuation, and perhaps an expansion, of the 'welfare-led' counterurbanisation which has occurred over the last decade.

NOTES

1. In 1994 some 45.3 percent of adult Aboriginal men stated that their main source of income was a government payment, while the proportion for females was 64.1 percent. The figures were higher in regional cities (52 and 66.5 percent) than in capital cities (41.4 and 59.5 percent), while in rural areas they were slightly lower for men (40.1 percent) but higher for females at 64.8 percent (ABS 1996: 122).
2. In 1992, 11.4 percent of retired Australians relied upon superannuation as their main source of income (ABS 1994: 143).
3. The proportion of the population aged 65 years and over increased from 8.3 in 1971 to 12 percent in 1995 (ABS 1996: 21).
4. The proportion of the workforce unemployed increased from 1.5 in 1971 to 8.5 in 1996.
5. In Australia major cities are urban places with 100 000 or more inhabitants and 'other cities' are urban places with between 10 000 and 99 999 inhabitants.
6. Those living in centres with less than 1000 inhabitants or individual scattered farmsteads.
7. Data provided by South Australian Department for Education and Children Services, July 1995.
8. Data from the 1992 ABS Family Survey and the 1991 Census examined in this report were provided by the Bureau of Immigration, Multicultural and Population Research for other research projects undertaken by the authors, and are analysed in more detail in a number of the reports listed in the bibliography
9. Shaver (1995: 8), for example, shows that the coverage of means tested transfers to aged couples and single females is substantially higher in Australia than in other OECD nations.

REFERENCES

ABS [Australian Bureau of Statistics] (1986) *Internal migration Australia: 12 months ended 31 May 1985,* Catalogue Number 3408.0, Australian Bureau of Statistics, Canberra.

ABS (1988) *Internal migration, Australia,* Catalogue Number 3408. 0, Australian Bureau of Statistics, Canberra.

ABS (1994) *Australian social trends,* 1994, Catalogue Number 4102.0, Australian Bureau of Statistics, Canberra.

ABS (1995) *Regional population growth, Australia 1993–94,* Catalogue Number 3218.0, Australian Bureau of Statistics, Canberra.

ABS (1996) *Household expenditure survey, Australia: States and Territories,* Catalogue Number 6533.0, Australian Bureau of Statistics, Canberra.

Bansemer, O. (1987) 'Work and the welfare state: the Dolesville case', unpublished BA (Hons) Thesis, Flinders University of South Australia, Adelaide.

Bell, M. (1992) *Internal migration in Australia,* 1981–1986, AGPS, Canberra.

Bell, M. (1994) 'Australians on the move: internal migration in Australia, 1981–86', unpublished PhD Thesis, Department of Geographical Sciences, University of Queensland.

Bell, M. (1995) *Internal migration in Australia, 1986–1991: overview report,* AGPS, Canberra.

Bell, M. (1996) *Understanding internal migration,* AGPS, Canberra.

Bell, M. and Cooper, J. (1995) *Internal migration in Australia, 1986–1991: the overseas-born,* AGPS, Canberra.

Bell, M. and Maher, C. (1995) *Internal migration in Australia, 1986–1991: the labour force,* AGPS, Canberra.

Brown, F. (1984) 'Retirement migration and service requirements in Great Lakes Shire', unpublished BA Honours Thesis, School of Geography, University of New South Wales, Kensington.

Budge, T. (1996) 'Population decline in Victoria and Tasmania', in P. Newton and M. Bell (eds.), *Population shift: mobility and change in Australia,* AGPS, Canberra, 192–204.

Budge, T., Hugo, G. and D'Rozario, J. (1992) *The national housing strategy – housing and services in rural and remote Australia,* AGPS, Canberra.

Burnley, I. (1988) 'Population turnaround and the peopling of the countryside? Migration from Sydney to the Country Districts of New South Wales', *Australian Geographer,* **19**, 268–283.

Burnley, I. (1996) 'Migration, well-being and development in coastal New South Wales, 1976–91', *Australian Geographer,* **21**, 53–76.

Byrne, P. (1986) 'The economic importance of tourism to coastal regions and localities in New South Wales', unpublished BSc Honours Thesis, School of Geography, University of New South Wales, Kensington.

Cebula, R., Kohn, R. and Vedder, R. (1973) 'Some determinants of interstate migration of blacks, 1965–1970', *Western Economic Journal,* **11**, 500–505.

Champion, A. (1993) 'Population distribution patterns in developed countries', paper prepared for the Expert Group Meeting on Population Distribution and Migration, Santa Cruz, Bolivia, January.

Clark, R. (1989) 'Welfare and outmigration of solo mothers', in United States Bureau of Census, *Proceedings of the conference on individuals and families in transition,* United States Bureau of Census, Washington.

Commonwealth Bureau of Census Statistics (1940) *Census of the Commonwealth of Australia, 1933, Volume 3,* Commonwealth Bureau of Census Statistics, Canberra.

Cook, B. (1980) 'Migration patterns of the elderly', paper presented to the fifth annual meeting of the Regional Science Association, Australian and New Zealand Section, Tanunda, South Australia.

Cromartie, J. (1993) 'Leaving the countryside: young adults follow complex migration patterns', *Rural Development Perspectives*, **8**, 22–27.

Drysdale, R. (1991) 'Aged migration to coastal and inland centres in New South Wales', *Australian Geographical Studies*, **29**, 268–283.

Fitchen, J. (1995) 'Spatial redistribution of poverty through migration of poor people to depressed rural communities', *Rural Sociology*, **60**, 181–201.

Flood, J. (1992) 'Internal migration in Australia: who gains, who loses', *Urban Futures*, **5**, 44–53.

Flood, J., Maher C., Newton, P. and Roy, J. (1991) *The Determinants of Internal Migration in Australia*, CSIRO, Division of Building, Construction and Engineering, Melbourne.

Frey, W. (1994a) 'Residential mobility among the rural poor', *Rural Sociology*, **59**, 416–436.

Frey, W. (1994b) 'Immigration and internal migration for US States: 1990 Census findings by poverty status and race', *Research Report*, 94–320, Population Studies Center, University of Michigan, Ann Arbor.

Frey, W. (1995a) 'New geography of population shifts: trends toward balkanization', in R. Farley (ed.), *State of the union – America in the 1990s – volume 2: social trends*, Sage, New York, 271–334.

Frey, W. (1995b) 'Immigration impacts on internal migration of the poor: 1990 Census Evidence for US States', *International Journal of Population Geography*, **1**, 51–56.

Frey, W. (1995c) 'Poverty migration for US States: immigration impacts', *1994 Proceedings of the Social Statistics Section of the American Statistical Association*, American Statistical Association, Vancouver, 135–140.

Frey, W., Liaw, K.-L., Xie, Y. and Carlson, M. (1995) 'Interstate migration of the US poverty population: immigration "pushes" and welfare magnet "pulls"', *Research Report, 95–331*, Population Studies Center, University of Michigan, Ann Arbor.

Friedl, E. (1986) 'Migration of the poor', *Population Research and Policy Review*, **5**, 47–61.

Garkovich, L. (1989) *Population and community in rural America*, Greenwood Press, New York.

Glantz, F. (1973) 'The determinants of the interregional migration of the economically disadvantaged', *Research Report*, **52**, Federal Reserve Bank of Boston, Boston, Massachusetts.

Hanson, R. and Hartman, J. (1994) 'Do welfare magnets attract?', *Discussion Paper*, 1028-94, Institute for Research on Poverty, University of Wisconsin-Madison, Wisconsin.

Harkman, A. (1989) 'Migration behaviour among the unemployed and the role of unemployment benefits', *Papers of the Regional Science Association*, **66**, 143–150.

Hirschl, T., Poston, D. and Frisbie, W. (1990) 'The effects of private and public sustenance organisation on population redistribution in New York State', *Working Paper, Series* 2.12, Population and Development Program, Cornell University, New York.

Hudson, P. (1987) 'Processes of adaptation in a changing rural environment: a comparison of four rural communities in New England, NSW', unpublished PhD Thesis, Macquarie University, North Ryde.

Hugo, G. (1971a) 'Internal migration in South Australia, 1961–1966', unpublished MA Thesis, Flinders University of South Australia, Adelaide.

Hugo, G. (1971b) 'Some spatial aspects of the pattern of internal migration in South Australia', paper presented to Section 21 of the 43rd Congress of the Australian and New Zealand Association for the Advancement of Science, Brisbane, May.

Hugo, G. (1986) *Australia's changing population: trends and implications*, Oxford University Press, Melbourne.

Hugo, G. (1989a) 'Australia: the spatial concentration of the turnaround', in A. Champion (ed.), *Counterurbanisation: the changing pace and nature of population deconcentration*, Edward Arnold, London, 62–82.

Hugo, G. (1989b) 'Population transitions in Australia', in R. Heathcote and J. Mabbutt (eds.), *Land, water and people: geographical essays on resource management and the organisation of space in Australia*, Australian Academy of Social Sciences, Canberra.

Hugo, G. (1994) 'The turnaround in Australia: some first observations from the 1991 Census', *Australian Geographer*, **25**, 1–17.

Hugo, G. (1996) 'Counterurbanisation', in P. Newton and M. Bell (eds.), *Population shift – mobility and change in Australia*, AGPS, Canberra, 126–146.

Hugo, G. and Smailes, P. (1985) 'Urban-rural migration in Australia: a process view of the turnaround', *Journal of Rural Studies*, **1**, 11–30.

Hugo, G. and Smailes, P. (1986) 'Migration patterns in the Lower Northern Region of South Australia', paper presented to Third Conference of the Australian Population Association, Adelaide, December.

Hugo, G. and Smailes, P. (1992) 'Population dynamics in rural South Australia', *Journal of Rural Studies*, **8**, 29–51.

Jarvie, W. (1981) 'Internal migration and structural change in Australia, 1966–1976: some preliminary observations', *Papers of the Australian and New Zealand Section Regional Science Association*, Sixth Meeting, Surfers Paradise, August, 25–55.

Jarvie, W. (1984) 'Internal migration in Australia, 1966–71 to 1971–76', unpublished PhD Thesis, School of Social Sciences, Flinders University of South Australia, Adelaide.

Jarvie, W. (1985) 'Structural economic change, labour market segmentation and migration', *Papers of the Regional Science Association*, Eighth Pacific Science Association, Tokyo, 1983, 129–144.

Jarvie, W. (1989a) 'Migration and regional development', in B. Higgins and I. Zagorski (eds.), *Australian regional development: readings in regional experiences, policies and prospects*, AGPS, Canberra, 218–233.

Jarvie, W. (1989b) 'Changes in internal migration in Australia: population or employment-led?', in L. Gibson and R. Stimson (eds.), *Regional structure and change: experiences and prospects in two mature economies*, Monograph Series, Number 8, Regional Science Research Institute, Peace Dale, Rhode Island, 47–60.

Johansen, H. and Fuguitt, G. (1984) *The changing rural village in America – demographic and economic trends since 1950*, Ballinger, Massachusetts.

Langley, P. (1977) 'Interregional migration and economic opportunities in Australia 1966–71', *Economic Record*, **2**, 51–69.

Lichter, D., McLaughlin, D. and Cornwell, G. (1994) 'Migration and the loss of human resources in rural America', in L. Beaulieu and D. Mulkey (eds.), *Investing in people: the human capital needs of rural America*, Westview Press, Boulder, 224–246.

McDonald, H. (1986) 'Integration is the watchword, and it really works', *Far Eastern Economic Review*, 14 August, 53–54, 63.

McKay, J. (1985) 'Internal migration and rural labour markets', in R. Powell (ed.), *Rural labour markets in Australia*, Bureau of Labour Market Research, Monograph Number 10, AGPS, Canberra.

McKay, J. and Whitelaw, J. (1977) 'The role of large private and government organizations in generating flows of inter-regional migrants: the case of Australia', *Economic Geography*, **53**, 28–44.

Murphy, P. (1981) 'Patterns of coastal retirement migration', in A. Howe (ed.), *Towards an older Australia*, University of Queensland Press, St Lucia, 301–314.

Murphy, P. and Zehner, R. (1988) 'Satisfaction and sunbelt migration', *Australian Geographical Studies*, **26**, 320–334.

Neyland, B. and Kendig, H. (1996) 'Retirement migration to the coast', in P. Newton and

M. Bell (eds.), *Population shift – mobility and change in Australia*, AGPS, Canberra, 364–377.

O'Connor, K. and Stimson, R. (1996) 'Convergence and divergence of economic and demographic trends', in P. Newton and M. Bell (eds.), *Population shift – mobility and change in Australia*, AGPS, Canberra, 108–125.

O'Dea, S. (1982) 'Retirement migration to Shoalhaven Shire', unpublished BSc Honours Thesis, School of Geography, University of New South Wales, Kensington.

O'Hare, W. (1985) 'Poverty in America: trends and new patterns', *Population Bulletin*, **40**(3), 1–44.

Pollard, H. (1996) 'Seasonal and permanent moves among the elderly', in P. Newton and M. Bell (eds.), *Population shift – mobility and change in Australia*, AGPS, Canberra, 378–391.

Rives, N., Serow, W., Freeman, G. and McLeod, K. (1983) 'Migration of the elderly: are conventional models applicable?', *Proceedings of the American Statistical Association (Social Statistics)*, 343–347.

Roseman, C. (1983) 'Labour force migration, non-labour force migration and non-employment reasons for migration', *Socio-Economic Planning Science*, **17**(5–6), 303–312.

Rowland, D. (1979) *Internal migration in Australia*, Catalogue Number 3409.0, Australian Bureau of Statistics, Canberra.

Rowland, D. (1996) 'Migration of the aged', in P. Newton and M. Bell (eds.). *Population shift—mobility and change in Australia*, AGPS, Canberra, 348–363.

Salt, B. (1992) *Population movements in non-metropolitan Australia*, AGPS, Canberra.

Sant, M. (1993) 'Coastal settlement systems and counterurbanisation in NSW', *Australian Planner*, **31**(2), 108–113.

Sant, M. and Simons, P. (1993a) 'Counterurbanisation and coastal development in New South Wales', *Geoforum*, **24**, 291–306.

Sant, M. and Simons, P. (1993b) 'The conceptual basis of counterurbanisation: critique and development', *Australian Geographical Studies*, **23**(2), 113–126.

Shaver, S. (1995) 'Who gets means-tested benefits?', *Social Policy Research Centre Newsletter*, **58**, August, 8–9.

Sherlaimoff, T. (1986) *Sunbelt migration: Coffs Harbour Shire immigration survey*, New South Wales Department of Environment and Planning, Sydney.

Shryock, H., Siegel, J. and associates (1975) *The methods and materials of demography*, Two Volumes, United States Department of Commerce, Bureau of the Census, Washington DC.

South Australian Department of Lands (1992) *Department of Lands Annual Report*, 1991–1992, Government Printer, Adelaide.

Southwick, L. (1981) 'Public welfare programs and recipient migration', *Growth and Change*, **12**, 22–32.

Stilwell, F. (1993) *Understanding cities and regions*, Pluto Press, Sydney.

Torrecilha, R. and Sandefur, G. (1990) 'State characteristics and the migration of the disadvantaged', *Working Paper*, 90–19, Center for Demography and Ecology, University of Wisconsin-Madison, Wisconsin.

Wulff, M. and Bell, M. (1997) *Internal migration, social welfare and settlement patterns; impacts on households and communities*, Department of Immigration and Multicultural Affairs, Canberra.

Wulff, M. and Newton, P. (1996) 'Mobility and social justice', in P. Newton and M. Bell (eds.), *Population shift: mobility and change in Australia*, AGPS, Canberra, 426–443.

Wulff, M., Flood, J. and Newton, P. (1993) *Population movement and social justice: an exploration of issues, trends and implications*, AGPS, Canberra.

7

INSIDE LOOKING OUT; OUTSIDE LOOKING IN. DIFFERENT EXPERIENCES OF CULTURAL COMPETENCE IN RURAL LIFESTYLES

PAUL CLOKE, MARK GOODWIN and PAUL MILBOURNE

INTRODUCTION

In this chapter, we discuss some of the ways in which the social conflicts experienced in village life can be accounted for by differences in the cultural expectations and practices of various people in particular places. In particular, we highlight the notion of 'cultural competence' which suggests that rural people, whether long-term residents or in-migrants, will have strong cultural and geographical imaginations of what rural life should be like, and that these imaginations will be associated with particular practices of social relations, lifestyle and consumption. Such practices will variously be constructed within a range from competent to incompetent, and incompetent practices may well contribute to socio-cultural discord in rural places.

In order to discuss these ideas we draw on a programme of research which has been funded by the Economic and Social Research Council (ESRC) and a number of government agencies, and which focuses on changing rural lifestyles in England and Wales (Cloke *et al.* 1994a, 1994b, 1997). Lifestyles were encountered through a series of interviews with rural people, some 250 rural people in each of 16 study areas (12 in England and four in Wales), shown in Figures 7.1 and 7.2. The survey schedules were based on those used by Brian McLaughlin (1985) in his 1980–1981 study of five areas of England. As such, they emphasised normative issues, but we made some at least partially successful attempts to open out more unstructured moments in the interviews wherein respondents' own voices could be heard on broad issues of rural community life. The intersubjective value of these encounters in the English studies was lost because interviews were carried out by a private sector polling organisation, and so the qualitative texts produced in the interviews were frustratingly unsatisfactory compared with the likely yield of carefully constructed ethnographies. Nevertheless, we do attempt to make use of these texts in two ways. First we have

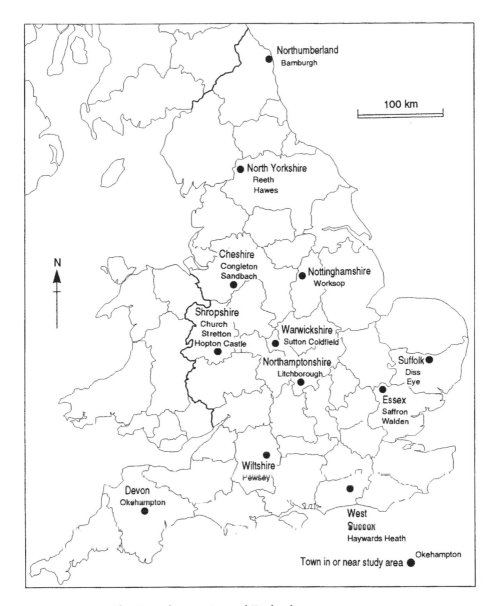

FIGURE 7.1 The 12 study areas in rural England

been anxious to ensure that our respondents' own voices could be heard in the academic and policy-related reporting of our findings (we are, of course, very aware here of the power vested in the researcher to choose which voices are, and are not, heard). Secondly, we have been keen to ensure that our respondents' own constructions of rural life could emerge alongside more orthodox policy-related issues of housing, work, income and accessibility. Interestingly, these constructions tended to link experiential issues to more material ones (for example social change/housing and status/income) as well as reflecting rather different categories of study, such as well-being (a mix of health and enjoyment of living environments, for example community and countryside) and isolation (a mix of mobility issues and experiences of loneliness).

Although the study areas were selected to represent a range of ruralities in England and Wales, and therefore reflect rather different localised rural geographies, for the purposes of this paper we tend to use these qualitative texts more broadly, seeking to pursue the notions of difference within and between the two national sub-sets of interviews in England and Wales.

DISCURSIVE RURAL IDYLLS

In the rural lifestyles programme, we argue that a sensitive understanding of the problematics of rural life is most likely to be reached by combining normative and experiential issues which impinge on the differential experience of rural worlds where opportunity levels and change are often structured from the outside. To some extent we go against the grain of the postmodern and post-structural turns in geography here, but we suggest that both elements remain important. We thereby emphasise *normative issues*, because to reject external-ised and quantified measures of problematics, such as deprivation and poverty, on the grounds that such concepts impose stigmatic labels onto individuals and households who might not accept or experience these labels or their assumed 'states', is a case of throwing out the baby with the bathwater.

The differential structuring of *lifestyle opportunities* such as affordable hous-ing, reasonably paid work, accessible services, and of *living standards*, for example, involving benefit levels, remains a crucial context for the experience of rural life, even if rural people are acknowledged to experience and respond to these structured opportunities and living standards in very different ways. Equally, we emphasise *experiential issues*, because it is increasingly recognised that discursive ruralities will often spawn very different imagined geographies of rural places and rural life. Such imagined geographies may themselves raise expectations about rural lifestyles against which day-to-day life experiences may be reflexively judged. Thus, different people will experience the same rural life-worlds differently and lifestyle should not simply be mapped from the structuring of opportunities and living standards.

In a previous paper (Cloke and Milbourne 1992), we attempted to show how the (re)production and (re)circulation of cultural constructs of rural life tended to occur at different geographical scales. Much of the recent work on rural idylls has tended to suggest mythological and romanticised constructions of pastoral-ism and arcadia laden with implied and signified meanings of happy, healthy bucolic idyll amongst close-knit and problem-free communities and close to the natural environment of the countryside (see Bunce 1994; Mingay 1989a, 1989b,

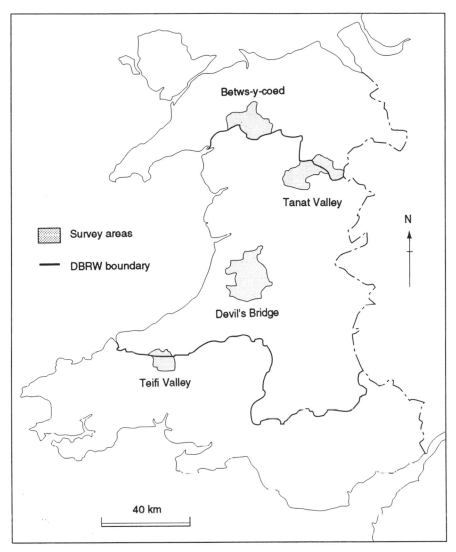

FIGURE 7.2 The four study areas in rural Wales. (DBRW = Development Board for Rural Wales)

1989c; Short 1991). Our interest here in such cultural constructions lies in their relevance to attitudes, behaviours, practices and decisions: the decision to move to or visit the rural; the expectation of a lower level of formal opportunities and facilities, and of a higher level of community self-support and care; the assumptions made about what is 'acceptable' or 'welcome' in village life, including questions of gender, ethnicity, sexuality and the like. Clearly it would again be unsubtle to attempt to 'read off' or map rural lifestyle experiences from these socio-cultural constructs. To do so would be to treat rural people as some kind of character-less surface, devoid of human agency, just waiting to be culturally constructed upon. Nevertheless, we argue that these different scales of idyll, though interconnecting and overlapping, impinge on rural lifestyle experiences in different ways:

- *National-level constructs*: we suggest that the cultures of national identity inherent in rural idylls will filter the acceptability of particular races and ethnicities, ideologies and protests, gender roles and sexual preferences, and village 'problematics'. Different national-level constructs of rurality may clash significantly when one comes into contact with the other, particularly where language, organisational structure, religious affiliation and other historic differences combine to produce culturally distinct ways of life. Thus the idyllistic framework for 'village England' might be expected to offer quite different frames of reference for rural life than idylls associated, for example, with Welsh-speaking rural Wales (for example, Bowie 1993; Cloke *et al.* 1995, forthcoming; Emmett 1982).

- *Regional-level constructs*: we suggest that regional constructs of rurality will also affect the expectations and behaviours of rural people. For example, elements of the north–south debate in England are relevant here to the suggestion that different senses of cultural 'belonging' exist in the rural north from those in the rural south (or 'west country', or East Anglia). In addition, we can point to important regional differences in the intensity and nature of cultural and political identity within rural Wales (Balsom 1985). Indeed, elements of these differences are being reinforced by the place marketing strategies of tourist boards and others whose current concern seems to be to encapsulate regional difference through literary reference (for example, Herriot Country, D.H. Lawrence Country, even Robin Hood Country) and, more recently, through reference to popular television programmes on rural life (for example, three tourist guides to Heartbeat Yorkshire, Emmerdale Country and Peak Practice Country (Ashley and Newley Limited 1994a, 1994b, 1994c) actively conflate the imagined ruralities associated with these programmes with advertisements for tourist boards, hotels and heritage sites). Such literary and television references act to popularise and make conspicuous a range of regional-level cultures of the rural.

- *Local-level constructs*: in addition to both national- and regional-level cultural differences, we suggest that localised constructs of rurality will also apply. Thus, within regions, different rural places (perhaps through particular features of landscape, heritage, organisation or perceived social affiliation) will represent the sites of very different cultural constructs of rurality. Chapman (1993), for example, has highlighted important localised variations in identity within areas of Cumbria, suggesting a 'moral divide' and cultural gulf between western areas of the county and the Lake District. It can again be argued that these localised differences will contribute to differentiated experiences of belonging, placedness and cultural affinity in rural lifestyles in particular places.

We do not suggest that these three scales are either all-embracing or mutually exclusive. Indeed, it can be argued that it is the interplay between these different scales of identity that is important; that in different situations individuals may select a national construct of identity (for example, a Welsh-speaking resident talking to one of our interviewers) or a more localised identity facet. We must also be careful with our use of national-level constructs of Englishness, given Cohen's (1982: 13) criticism that such identity constructs represent merely 'empty receptacles which are filled with *local* and particular experience'. As such, national identity can be seen to be mediated through regional, local and individual experiences, with Englishness understood in very different ways by the English. Indeed, groups of English in-movers to areas of rural Wales are choosing to relocate to the region in order to exclude themselves from dominant notions of English identity. However, even with such complexities, we believe that these different scales of rural identity offer particularly interesting cuts on the understanding of the complexities of idyll-ised lifestyles in rural areas.

CULTURAL EXPECTATIONS AND COMPETENCES IN RURAL LIFESTYLES

It follows from these suggestions about differentiated cultural constructions of rural idyll that people migrating to particular rural areas may, to varying degrees, carry with them particular imagined geographies of rural life which include particular expectations about the lifestyle which will result from the move. Equally, and perhaps in more entrenched ways, the long-standing residents of that place will have their own imagined geographies and expectations about rural life, and cultural conflict can result. Indeed, the arena of conflict will often relate to the 'competences' which arise from translating idyll-ised expectations into actions and attitudes (see Chapter 9 in this volume, which uses Eder's ideas of cultural texture and competence). The emphasis on cultural competence suggests that the interdependence of income/qualifications and moral/aesthetic attributes allows the identification of socially distributed quantities of competences which in turn represent the developing networks of class structure in developed nations. We might therefore suggest that social conflict in rural life will, at least in part, reflect disjunctures between the different cultural competences which inform rural lifestyles.

Here we would raise three immediate caveats. First, we are not proposing any essentialist link between cultural constructs and behaviour. Rather we are seeking to explore some of the (often) hidden complexities in the experience of well-being and/or problematics in rural life. Secondly, we do not seek here to lend support to any dualistic conception of 'locals versus newcomers'. Although such terms do frequently crop up in the lay discourses of rural life encountered in our interviews, we would rather suggest a more complex idea of iterative sedimentations of different in-migrant groups with different aspirations and expectations over different lengths of time. Thirdly, it is clear that expectations and competences are not fixed and unchanging. Not only do rural residents adjust to changing circumstances of opportunity and living standards, but they also are able to learn new competences which may aid their experience of belonging and placedness. Feeling 'local' may not relate to length of residence, or to family or status connections, although these can obviously be important.

The focus on different cultural expectations and competences reflects our wish to understand more of the interconnections between the structuring of material opportunities, and the experiential differentiations within rural communities. So often, commentaries of rural life resort to meta-narratives of xenophobia:

> 'The countryside is not a welcoming or a friendly place. Many people in rural communities display attitudes of intolerance and frequently of xenophobia. It is tempting to discuss these attitudes as racism, but while racism is there, it forms only a component of this broader hostility to and fear of outsiders. Incomers are seen as those people who move into the countryside, who know nothing about the 'real' nature of a locality, but who either interfere with the way things should be done, or seek to maintain a kind of rural idyll – trying to live in the countryside of their dreams and aspirations as opposed to the real countryside. It is clear that there is little chance of reconciliation between locals and incomers, and that acceptance of new residents in rurality is the exception rather than the rule' (Roberts 1992: 1).

There is much in Roberts' statement that we would wish to endorse – particularly the notions of living out an idyll, the potential for rural racism and the discursive potential for the filtering out of the problems encountered in the 'real' countryside. However, to reduce rurality to xenophobia is to obscure the many different nuances of belonging and not belonging which rural residents speak of when they give voice to concerns over social change and changing notions of community. In the remainder of this chapter we seek to highlight some of these differences, and to interconnect them with the imagined expectations and acted-out competences of rural lifestyles.

CHANGING COMMUNITY IN RURAL WALES: NATIONAL-LEVEL CONSTRUCTS OF RURALITY

The rural lifestyles research in Wales presented an opportunity for very strongly voiced views about the links between rural change and cultural change in a context where clashes over national-level rural identities occur due to English migration into Welsh-speaking rural communities. First, our respondents presented a very stark narrative of what they saw as community change over recent years:

> 'Used to be more close-knit. People moving in don't seem so interested in what's happening in the village' (1250 Betws-y-Coed FWS[1]).

'It's not as friendly: a lot of people moving in' (2116 Devil's Bridge FWS).

'There's no community spirit, and individuals are ignored by neighbours. No-one helps each other out anymore' (4916 Teifi Valley NWS).

Such a bemoaning of the loss of 'community' is very little different here to that found in other study areas surveyed as part of our research. The loss of a 'close-knit', 'friendly' community which used to be self-supporting and which had some kind of communal 'spirit' are typical reactions to widespread processes of economic restructuring and social recomposition in the period since the 1970s. Indeed, it can be suggested that such attitudes are present throughout the history of rural areas, as each generation points back to the last in order to identify the time-space of 'ideal' rural life. We would contend that rural idyll is in some part a nostalgia for what has recently been lost by any particular set of rural residents, because such losses give tangible expression to more discursive signals of what constitutes paradisal lifestyles, however mythological such signals might be.

Our respondents in Wales, however, strongly associate community change with cultural change due to the influx of 'foreigners':

'[There has been] an influx of people with no roots here – only use the area for odd homes and periods – people who don't join in the spirit of the community' (1205 Betws-y-Coed WL).

'The foreigners moving in don't have the same community attitude, so the neighbourliness has been diluted' (3200 Tanat Valley WL).

Moreover, there is no doubt that many of our Welsh-speaking respondents, particularly within areas of *Y Fro Gymraeg*, clearly identify the influx of the foreign with an invasion of 'the English'. Here, we can view 'Englishness' as a 'significant other' (Cohen 1985) which is perceived by local Welsh-speaking residents as threatening the existence of their everyday language and culture. As such, individual English in-movers can become labelled as a collective threat and homogenised as 'other':

'There has been a substantial increase in retired English people. They come and destroy the Welshness of the Welsh countryside and are detrimental to the culture of our society' (1222 Betws-y-Coed FWS)

'Loads more English. The whole community is being changed, especially schools – affecting education and language' (2120 Devil's Bridge FWS).

'English immigrants, swamping the village, changing [the] character' (4943 Teifi Valley FWS).

'[There's been] more English migrants, mostly retired. . . these people do not take part or contribute to the social life of the village' (1097 Betws-y-Coed FWS).

'More English coming in. They don't belong here. They would be alright if they were part of the community, spoke Welsh. But they live as if they were still in England' (2066 Devil's Bridge FWS).

This last comment – 'they live as if they were still in England' – seems to us a significant pointer to a process whereby English in-migrants bring with them portfolios of different cultural competences drawn from imagined geographies of English rural life. When such competences are placed and practised in rural Wales they can often lead to distinct cultural conflicts resulting in an experience of 'not belonging' on the part of in-migrants, and experiences of 'a threat to our way(s) of life' on the part of different existing residents. Some elements of 'living as if they were still in England' relate to the obvious inability to speak the Welsh language, which in many cases would also rule in-migrants out of joining local organisations (both church-related and secular) which use the medium of Welsh. Nevertheless they also represent a wider threat to cultural 'identity':

> 'These people are ruining the Welsh identity and are mostly killing the Welsh language' (1112 Betws-y-Coed FWS).

> 'They come and destroy the Welshness of the Welsh countryside and are detrimental to the culture of our society' (1222 Betws-y-Coed FWS).

Other elements of 'living as if they were still in England' are slightly less obvious but equally important. We would suggest that many Welsh residents represent English migrants as having a colonialist ideology, taking over the housing stock, living off the back of the country and trying to dominate proceedings. Indeed, in the following commentaries we see that for some Welsh residents perceptions of cultural recomposition can become conflated with notions of economic power, property relations and affluence associated with the incoming English:

> 'Affluent English people, especially of retirement age... [have] escalated local prices of housing beyond the means of local people' (4198 Teifi Valley FWS).

> 'A lot more English people have moved in – able to buy homes – preventing young people from buying homes. The village is dying' (3029 Tanat Valley FWS).

> 'immigrants... come in and live off the back of the country' (1065 Betws-y-Coed FWS).

> 'some English come here and act like colonials; talk about us as peasants' (4138 Teifi Valley NWS).

> 'English people move in and [are] trying to dominate the bloody country' (3222 Tanat Valley FWS).

Part of the potential clash of cultural competence arises from more microscale practices of 'individualism' and 'not taking part':

> 'people are... more interested in themselves than others' (4944 Teifi Valley FWS).

> 'these people are arrogant selfish bastards who become very snug and have no sympathy at all. They want to turn the place into another Surrey' (2196 Devil's Bridge NWS).

> 'these people do not take part or contribute to the social life of the village' (1097 Betws-y-Coed FWS).

> 'Lot of English moving in... they stay inside. The ones who come in are not used to saying hello like the Welsh' (4146 Teifi Valley FWS).

A further claim from Welsh respondents is that English in-migrants bring with them particular class practices and consumption signals which are out of place in the Welsh village context:

'we've had class from the English – class distinction is an English thing. . . [here] in the pub the professor drinks with the labourer' (4136 Teifi Valley WL).

'[we've had] more ghastly middle class people – the sort who live in these bunga-lows and drive Volvos' (2052 Devil's Bridge NWS).

Clearly we are only touching on some aspects of clashes over cultural compet-ence in these texts, and we should acknowledge at this point that other, much more sympathetic narratives of the impact of English in-migrants were given to us by English and Welsh alike:

'Lots of English people have moved into the villages and buy the houses. [It] keep[s] the school going. I work in the school and most of my friends want work too' (1203 Betws-y-Coed WL).

'The English bring some very good qualities into the area. I am one of them. . . The advent of the English drift has brought a lot of ideas into the area – especially in the area of craft' (2092 Devil's Bridge NWS).

'A lot of English moved in and are doing very well here financially. . . if English didn't come, the place would die. They bring money with them and pay taxes' (3203 Tanat Valley FWS).

Nevertheless, as already suggested, we believe that there is far more to these conflicts than can be explained by mere xenophobia. We suggest that *English* in-migrants are referring to cultural constructs of the *English* village when organising their lifestyle strategies in rural Wales. Although such strategies will differ, many seem to have moved because of the attraction of the surrounding countryside, and are content to live in that environment without any need to 'join in' the local community. Others might wish to join in, but are prevented from doing so because of the assumptions made by existing residents about the cultural strategy employed in their move, or because of their own linguistic or other lack of competence to engage in joining in practices. This issue of competence is very soon detected and made significant by local residents. One of our respondents noted that:

'a lot of English people have come in. . . changed the way of life. The problem with those people is that they're working on a Sunday – you know, cleaning their cars and mowing the lawns. They shouldn't do it on a Sunday – they should be in chapel' (2162 Devil's Bridge FWS).

Another study area resident told one of the authors:

'they [the English] just don't know how to behave. They drive the wrong cars, put up the wrong curtains, and create pretty front gardens that just don't fit in. In the village they don't know how to greet people, how to have a real conversation. Some of them want nothing to do with us, and others would like to be part of the community, but only if they can be in charge of what goes on. They just don't know how to belong, even when they try very hard to fit in' (PC interview with Teifi Valley resident).

We are not suggesting that competence is in any way restricted to Sabbatarianism, or symbolic consumption, or even social graces. There will be many more and complex aspects to cultural competence which are beyond the scope of this study. Equally, we are not suggesting any essentialist version of cultural conflict. Rather we argue, on the basis of the rural lifestyles research, that these issues can contribute significantly to feelings of belonging/not belonging, welcome/not welcome, and marginalisation/ centrality in rural lifestyles. Nor are we suggesting that such competences cannot be learnt, although there certainly were contrasting attitudes amongst our respondents on this theme of 'learning' to fit in:

> 'the girl down the road – she's English but fair play, she's trying to learn the language, but it's hard you know' (2059 Devil's Bridge FWS).

> 'a lot of English people come to live here – joining the community – some learning Welsh, and church-going and Women's Institute' (3202 Tanat Valley FWS).

> 'most of them seem nice enough – so long as they don't meddle in village business' (3057 Tanat Valley FWS).

Detailed studies of organisations such as PONT (bridge) which have been established to ease the transition from (incompetent) English migrant to competent Welsh-speaking resident of Welsh-speaking Wales would reveal a range of different transitional difficulties experienced by different people if different places, and a number of different strategies for coping with such difficulties with varying success. Nonetheless, much more needs to be understood about the polyvocal geographies of cultural competence which draw in very different ways on national-level circulations of cultural constructs of rurality.

CHANGING COMMUNITY IN RURAL ENGLAND: SUB-NATIONAL CONSTRUCTS OF RURALITY

Had we looked more closely at the texts constructed in the Welsh study areas there would also have been the potential for highlighting conflicting cultural competences which draw on sub-national constructs of rurality. In the final part of this chapter, though, we have used some of the findings of our research in different parts of England where, on the whole, cultural conflicts over the nature of rural community did not involve a perceived challenge to one nation/rural/ culture by another. We certainly believe it to be the case that the idyll-ised ideology of village England *does* have a component which privileges English nationhood over 'other' races and ethnicities, resulting in a discursive filtering out of cultural belongings other than 'whiteness' and material manifestations of racism and discrimination. However, in this chapter, we restrict our interpretative gaze to sub-national cultural competences.

First, we should acknowledge that, just as in rural Wales, there was an overall experience of significant change occurring in rural communities in England:

'It was like a big family when we came, but now the youngsters are coming in and taking over' (0530 Northamptonshire).

'Don't know half the people of the village today. Years ago, knew virtually everyone' (3744 Suffolk).

'Everyone has so much going on. There is not the community spirit' (0820 Suffolk).

'The new housing has taken the guts out of the community spirit' (4503 Northamptonshire).

'I think we've lost the village as I knew it' (Parish Clerk, Wiltshire).

Nonetheless, again the sense of lost community was not universal:

'It has changed but not necessarily reduced. We have quite a reasonable community [along our road]. I assume it is similar within the rest of the village' (0436 Northamptonshire).

'Not [lost community] in this village. There are a lot of organisations, and newcomers have organised more things than there were before' (2451 Essex).

'The sense of community is still there – but it is a changed kind of sense of community than existed before – no longer like the traditional sense of the term' (1526 West Sussex).

In these comments, community appears to be understood tacitly, as a negotiated construct which is worked (and re-worked) out in practice at different scales. Respondents variously regard 'the road' and 'the village' as the arena in which the constantly shifting negotiation of ideas, family and friendship networks, and other social relations are being worked out to the satisfaction of some but not others.

Within these reflexive processes of negotiation, there seems to be a strong sense of an 'original', 'indigenous' or even 'native' population who are being disadvantaged or even displaced in the process of social recomposition, especially in terms of changes to local housing markets.

'The original village people and their families cannot find accommodation they can afford' (7983 Cheshire).

'Bad feelings come from the indigenous population who are quite upset about 'incomers' who force the cost of housing up' (0307 Shropshire).

'When new houses were built here for first time buyers, local people felt that young villagers should have priority, and they didn't' (5117 Essex).

The fears, feelings of threat and marginalisation, and 'bad feelings' are polarised in successive rounds of in-migration of 'newcomers' but are also polarised culturally because the new residents come from 'outside the area'. Not only, then, is there the disruption of the 'new', but an additional disruption because the 'new' brings with it 'outside' attitudes and lifestyles which appear to be incompatible with the established local culture of village life:

> 'People from outside the area have moved in – people in council houses have moved from places like Crewe. Can't do anything about it. Some of the tenants just stay for a short while and then move on' (5293 Cheshire).

> 'Great influx of people from the south east where the cost of living is high. Also people from East Midlands and professional people with holiday homes' (7678 Cheshire).

> 'More people moving in from out of the area. [There are] few farm, countryside people left' (2212 Warwickshire).

> 'Commuters live here and travel out each day. No commitment to the area from them, i.e. no hunting wanted, even though it's gone on for years. They are the first to object to new developing – yet they did it in the first place. Newcomers are ruining rural community. [They] put up unsightly buildings and so called renovations' (2292 Shropshire).

> 'People moving from south. . . I don't mind as long as they don't change things – [you must] expect things of the farming area – they complain of manure smells, cows mooing' (7772 Shropshire).

Such texts were constructed in surveys in all of our study areas, and display a range of different 'outsiders' – from places like Crewe, from the south, from the East Midlands and so on – and a range of different cultural conflicts stemming at least in part from 'outsider' cultural competences relating to, for example, hunting, new development, renovations, and coping with the sights and smells of agricultural life.

We should stress at this point that these views from the inside looking out are not the only arena for social and cultural marginalisation in village life. Views from the outsider looking in give us a very different sense of varying imagined geographies of the rural, and of the problematics encountered in rural lifestyles. Here, though, we encounter narratives of how villages can variously be improved during and through social recomposition. Outsiders, then, often thought that their presence and that of others like them had brought changes for the better:

> 'More coloured families moving in like us. It's helped me to be accepted' (1103 Shropshire).

> 'A lot of outsiders like us. It has opened up a slightly feudal area' (3555 Shropshire).

> 'Twenty years ago approximately it changed from a sleepy village to more of a commuter village. . . [I approve because] mainly you need a mix every so often to inject new life and ideas' (0585 Northamptonshire).

Such insider/outsider conflicts in both the material and cultural arenas – although these clearly interconnect – tend to be highly localised in some cases, with particular in-movements generating specific concerns about 'fitting in' with the lifestyles already being acted out in that place. The most extreme case we came across in the lifestyle research programme was in our Nottinghamshire study area, where a large number of respondents saw and disapproved of population changes in terms of the characteristics of, we assume, one small group of people who had moved onto a particular council estate:

'Influx of one parent families and trouble makers into one large council estate. It tends to place all misfits together and breeds trouble' (7059 Nottinghamshire).

'Rough people seem to get houses around here now; unmarried mothers etc. [This] lowers the area that you live in. Makes it a lot noisier' (0629 Nottinghamshire).

'Shady characters, sex offenders, people out of prison, people out of town. Why should we have all the undesirables?' (0432 Nottinghamshire).

'[Population has changed] definitely, even gypsies get houses here. People are not vetted now like they used to be. The council tries to improve the estate but do not teach the tenants to look after it' (2805 Nottinghamshire).

In these voiced responses there are very severe examples of the prejudices which are often implicit in the cultural constructs of idyll which inform the practice of many rural lifestyles. Culturally 'different' people are categorised into 'undesirable' groups – one-parent families, unmarried mothers, sex offenders, ex-prisoners, gypsies – and pilloried for 'lowering (the tone of) the area'. Part of the problem here is the group dynamic of culturally different in-migration into an estate, with distinct geographical as well as socio-cultural boundaries. Another part of the issue, though, seems to involve the suggestion by local residents that 'these people' do not know how to behave properly in a rural area. They are not 'vetted', they have not been 'taught' to look after the place, they are 'rough' and 'noisy' and breed 'trouble'. In this extreme case, then, we can detect the powerful conjoining of discursive marginalisation of particular individuals and groups, with the disapproval of local people of attitudes, practices, 'looks' and characteristics of these individuals and groups who are culturally incompetent in this rural setting. The result is raw prejudice, and socio cultural conflict experienced on both sides of this perceived polarity.

This Nottinghamshire example is the exception in our study. Most discussion about what we are calling cultural competence revolves around issues relating to the 'difference' imposed by 'townies'. Many of our respondents complained that town people had either moved in and taken over, or moved in and not participated in the life of the community. Here, we would want to suggest that part of the issue is that urban in-migrants to rural areas will share a particular national scale vision of village England, but do not bring with them the cultural competences by which means their integration into their new home area might be attempted:

'The town type living here are not true country people and commute to the towns and don't adapt to country life. Because to be a true country person they should respect the countryside and not try to take over social life' (0323 Shropshire).

'They think they own the place – people from large towns. Very few original villagers left now. They don't want to know original villagers. Come in and take over everything. Have put price of homes up so "natives" have to move out' (0201 Warwickshire).

'Immigrants from town, commuters, etc. – now a breakdown in village life. Just have objectives because some take little interest in village life and don't join into enough activities. They give nothing back to the area' (1571 West Sussex).

Clearly, some in-migrants adopt lifestyle strategies which lead them to have very little desire to 'join in'. Others, though, have bought into the idea of community as part of rurality and in their eagerness to join in they are often seen as 'taking over' the social life of the village. While we again encountered the prejudice of some existing residents, there is also a sense in which knowing how to live is important. In an interview with one of the residents in the Devon study area, one of the authors was told:

'The trouble with these new people is that they don't realise that they have to ease themselves into the community. The early days is crucial. If they don't come and say hello, folks says they're stand-offish. If they do make the first move, folks say they're too eager and they want to take over the place... Now don't you go thinking that we're horrible to these new people. Lots of us in the church makes special effort to welcome [them]. The trouble is they don't know how to behave, to act properly. In the church, in the village hall meetings, in the street. When you goes in their homes they're like urban palaces not like country cottages. Its like they're new kids at a school – all lost and don't know the ropes. Except that some try to bully their way out of trouble' (PC interview with Devon resident).

Again we sense here conflict over competence; over how to assess and act out the cultural expectations held by others in the village concerned. It is about the nature of social contact, particularly early on; it is about how people express their lifestyle strategies (often this is 'too eager' or 'stand-offish'); it is about 'acting properly', realising the hidden cultural codes of behaviour in churches and in meetings; it is about how you decorate and furnish your property; and so on. Whether different cultural competences arise from national or sub-national constructs of rurality, or both, they do seem to contribute to reflexivity over the problematics of rural lifestyles as exhibited by the respondents to our surveys.

CONCLUSION

We are not suggesting that social conflict in villages is in any way solely dominated by issues of cultural competence. Matters of gender, ethnicity, sexuality, age, class and income/wealth are all of obvious importance in the differentiation of rural populations and in their reflexivity about rural problematics. Indeed, cultural competences will contain within them characteristics relating to gender, ethnicity and so on. Nevertheless, our belief is that both *material* issues, associated with the differential structuring of lifestyle opportunities, and *experiential* issues, relating to differential experiences of similar rural worlds, contribute to an understanding of changing rural lifestyles. In the interconnecting of the material and the experiential, discursive assumptions will play an important role, but so will different cultural competences which may be drawn from these cultural constructs of rurality which are produced at various scales. These differing scales of cultural construct are capable of being picked up or dropped by individual residents across a range of situations. Within areas of rural Wales, for example, certain Welsh-speaking residents may choose to discuss English in-movement in relation to and as conflicting against national constructs of Welshness; others may draw on more localised constructs of rural life; while others still may draw on components of each in different situations (conversations with an 'outside' interviewer may draw on different level constructs than those utilised amongst Welsh-speaking neighbours). These wider-scale constructs of rural life need to be viewed as shifting, negotiated concepts which become embedded within a variety of localised situations of interaction.

The common thread which can be seen to run through most of the commentaries outlined within this chapter has been cultural change and conflict; that visions of the local from without have, in many cases, clashed with views of local life held by existing residents. In certain situations, opposition to an in-movement of 'outside' groups has involved national-level constructs of rural life (for example, in areas of rural Wales), whilst in others this contestation of cultural change has remained within the realm of regional identity (for example, some of the narratives from our rural study areas in northern parts of England). In other commentaries, however, opposition to population in-movement has been focused on and mediated through different social groupings and issues (for example, our research within Nottinghamshire suggested an opposition of 'problem' groups moving into a particular housing estate). Thus, whether we focus on inside views of the outside, or outside views of the inside, we need to be aware of the ways in which different constructs of rurality interplay within different situations; how localised socio-cultural interactions and conflicts are bound up with wider scale constructs of rurality; and how regional and national identities become permeated by local and the specific experiences. While it is recognised that, in some ways, our lifestyles research methodologies were inappropriate as a means of encountering fully the different cultural competences at work in the places concerned, we would suggest that further, more ethnographic, efforts in these directions will yield important understandings of cultural change and conflict in rural lifestyles.

NOTES

1. In these extracts of text, FWS denotes a fluent Welsh speaker, WL a Welsh speaker and NWS a non-Welsh speaker.

REFERENCES

Ashley and Newley Limited (1994a) *Touring and exploring Heartbeat Country*, Ashley and Newley Limited: Leyburn.

Ashley and Newley Limited (1994b) *Touring and exploring inside Emmerdale*, Ashley and Newley Limited: Leyburn.

Ashley and Newley Limited (1994c) *Touring and exploring Peak Practice Country*, Ashley and Newley Limited: Leyburn.

Balsom, D. (1985) 'The three Wales model', in J. Osmond (ed.), *The national question again*, Gomer Press, Llandysul, 1–17.

Bowie, F. (1993) 'Wales from within: conflicting interpretations of Welsh identity', in S. Macdonald (ed.), *Inside European identities*, Berg Publishers Limited, Oxford, 167–193.

Bunce, M. (1994) *The countryside ideal: Anglo-American images of landscape*, Routledge, London.

Chapman, M. (1993) 'Copeland: Cumbria's best-kept secret', in S. Macdonald (ed.), Inside European identities, Berg Publishers Limited, Oxford, 194–218.

Cloke, P. and Milbourne, P. (1992) 'Deprivation and lifestyles in rural Wales: II. Rurality and the cultural dimension', *Journal of Rural Studies*, **8**, 359–371.

Cloke, P., Goodwin, M. and Milbourne, P. (1994a) 'Lifestyles in rural Wales', *Report to the Development Board for Rural Wales*, Newtown.

Cloke, P., Milbourne, P. and Thomas, C. (1994b) *Lifestyles In rural England*, Rural Development Commission: London.

Cloke, P., Goodwin, M. and Milbourne, P. (1995) ' "There's so many strangers in the village now": marginalization and change in 1990s Welsh rural life-styles', *Contemporary Wales*, **8**, 47–74.

Cloke, P., Goodwin, M. and Milbourne, P. (1997) *Rural Wales: community and marginalization*, University of Wales Press, Cardiff.

Cloke, P., Goodwin, M. and Milbourne, P. (forthcoming) 'Cultural change and conflict in rural Wales: competing constructs of identity', *Environment and Planning A*.

Cohen, A. (1982) 'Belonging: the experience of culture', in A. Cohen (ed.), *Belonging: identity and social organisation in British rural cultures*, Manchester University Press, Manchester, 1–17.

Cohen, A (1985) *The symbolic construction of community*, Routledge, London.

Eder, K. (1993) *The new politics of class*, Sage, London.

Emmett, I. (1982) 'Place, community and bilingualism in Blaenau Ffestiniog', in A. Cohen (ed.), *Belonging: identity and social organisation in British rural cultures*, Manchester University Press, Manchester, 202–221.

McLaughlin, B. (1985) 'Deprivation in rural areas', *Report* to the Department of the Environment, London.

Mingay, G. (ed.) (1989a) *The rural idyll*, Routledge, London.

Mingay, G. (ed.) (1989b) *The unquiet countryside*, Routledge, London.

Mingay, G. (ed.) (1989c) *The vanishing countryman*, Routledge, London.

Roberts, L. (1992) 'A rough guide to rurality', *Talking Point*, **137**, October, 1–6.

Short, J. (1991) *Imagined country: society, culture and environment*, Routledge, London.

8

INDIGENEITY, IDENTITY AND LOCALITY: PERSPECTIVES ON SWALEDALE

SHAUN FIELDING

INTRODUCTION

This chapter focuses upon the relationship between place and the socio-cultural identity of local (some might say 'indigenous') rural people – those who have been in residence for most (if not all) of their lives. Today, there is a whole multitude of ideas about what it means to be a local rural person; ideas which are not constructed by local people themselves, but which are influenced by 'other' identities. People from without the community remotely construct the rural as somewhere nice and quaint, where the landscape is rich and where the romance is rife, and where their purchasing power enables this image to be perpetuated (see the essays in Cloke *et al* 1994a; Cloke and Little 1997). In addition, and as this volume demonstrates, counterurbanisation dramatically alters the fabric within rural communities. This process is interlaced with the operation of internal and external power relations which are accessed by both 'locals' and 'incomers'. As a result, contemporary rural communities have been encountering aestheticisations of their lives and places that emanate from *within* their own midst. Over the course of time, the to-ing and fro-ing of these power relations has created two interesting avenues for rural researchers. Firstly, the definitions of and the boundaries between what it means to be a 'local' and an 'incomer' are increasingly difficult to define (as, indeed, Allan and Mooney, Chapter 15, point out in this volume). Secondly, the identity of people with little access to these power relations is becoming increasingly marginalised.

A similar situation developed with more obviously 'indigenous' communities (such as the First Nations of Canada and the United States, the Aboriginal Peoples of Australia and the Maoris of New Zealand) during the 1960s. Faced with pressures upon them to assimilate into mainstream society, many 'indigenous' leaders began to construct their identity through the shifting focus of the policies which were stripping away their 'indigenous' identity. They had been marginalised on their own ancient lands, spatially and psychologically set-aside by different and more powerful people not 'indigenous' to the lands in question. The 'non-indigenous' identity of these people was bound up with a place other than the one that they currently occupied; a differentiated identity not located 'there' but which nonetheless impacted upon 'indigenous' people and in a sense informed them how to identify with this other place. The powerful could therefore, *dis-locate* 'indigenous' people's identity, forcing them to construct an identity which is conceptually located in an 'other' and foreign place.

A theory known as the 'Fourth World' was developed by 'indigenous' peoples in the mid-1970s to contextualise these processes (particularly in the Western democracies mentioned previously). It describes the experiences of distinct peoples and cultures whose lives, lands and cultures have been physically and psychologically 'invaded', appropriated and exploited (often by force). Fourth Worlders wanted to retain their land and ways of life, to strive to survive as distinctive peoples and cultures. Today, the 'Fourth World' still comprises politically weak, economically marginal and culturally stigmatised minority citizens of a society (the First World) that has overtaken them and their lands. Having encountered the 'Fourth World' during research for my undergraduate dissertation in Canada and having detected similar feelings amongst the Welsh-speaking population of Lampeter[1], I was interested in whether the concept of the 'Fourth World' could connect to the fate of stigmatised but less obviously 'indigenous' people, such as local people in rural England. In addition, as the preservation of a 'local' identity (either by cultural representation or by political dialogue) continues to be a key issue, could the 'Fourth World' illuminate the increasingly fuzzy boundaries between the 'incomer' and the 'local' which curtail this representation?

The crux of this argument is whether a concept such as 'Fourth World' – which was created by the specific circumstances of one place – could travel (migrate even) from there to another place with different contexts, leading to the concept being inflected with new connotations and possibilities. To consider this, I will concentrate on the use of the 'Fourth World' by 'indigenous' people in Canada during the mid-1970s and then contemplate its potential 'travelling' into contemporary English rural communities, specifically Swaledale in North Yorkshire[2]. To talk about the 'travelling' of a concept such as the 'Fourth World' from Canada to Swaledale, I will draw briefly from the ideas of Said (1984).

TRAVELLING THEORY AND THE FOURTH WORLD

According to Said (1984) the travelling of a concept or a theory is both an intellectual and a practical reality and it is carried out in three ways:

- Through conscious influence.
- Through a process of collective borrowing.
- Through wholesale appropriation.

Said encourages the reader to question whether the concept has gained in analytical and representational strength through its travelling and whether the concept in the here-and-now is differentiated from its manifestation elsewhere in the past. In addition, Said indicates four stages of travelling:

- The 'point of origin', the circumstances by which a concept enters the human psyche.
- The 'distance traversed', the passing of a concept from one time to another.
- The conditions of acceptance and/or resistance confronting a concept.
- The transformation of a concept according to its new position.

However, these stages cannot take place unhindered because they require:

'processes of representation and institutionalisation different from the point of origin. This complicates any account of the transplantation, transference, circulation of theories and ideas' (Said 1984: 226).

A sensitivity to travelling theory not only suggests what happens to a particular concept when used in different circumstances, it informs us about the concept itself and its relationship with wider society. Said wanted the reader to understand how a concept may be used uncritically, repetitively and limitlessly by people not 'organic' to its time and place of origin, and how this increases its tendency to be reduced, diluted and parodied. Thus, a concept may degenerate into:

'a theoretical overstatement, a theoretical parody of the situation it was formulated originally to remedy or overcome' (Said 1984: 239)[3].

Specifically, the reader must appreciate that a concept:

'has to be grasped in the place and the time out of which it emerges as part of that time... consequently, that first place can be measured against subsequent places where the [concept] turns up for use' (Said 1984: 241–242).

For the 'Fourth World', this time and place was Canada during the mid-1970s. Whilst the concept has six 'points of origin'[4], I want to concentrate on just one, George Manuel's 1974 text (written with Michael Posluns) *The Fourth World: an Indian reality*. George Manuel was a community leader from the Shuswap Band, a sub-group of the Interior Salish People of British Columbia, who became president of the National Indian Brotherhood (NIB). Manuel's conception of the 'Fourth World' focuses upon the over-running of indigenous land by a modernising nation-state and, hence, upon the subsequent internal colonialism and denying of political autonomy. For Manuel, the people of the 'Fourth World' have a non-technical, non-modern exploitative relationship to the lands they inhabit, but they are effectively (and often literally) disenfranchised by the nation-state they exist within. Talking in terms of the 'Fourth World', nonetheless, is an affirmative action, anticipating a positive future where 'indigenous' people will govern their own social and cultural destiny:

'Our celebration honours the emergence of the 'Fourth World': the utilisation of technology and its life enhancing potential within the framework of the values of the people of the Aboriginal World... The Fourth World is a vision of the future history of North America and of the Indian peoples. The two histories are insepar-able' (Manuel and Posluns 1974: 11–12).

For Manuel, culture was the symbolic glue that held local knowledges in place; allowing Fourth Worlders to understand the richness of their local lives and to experience a sense of identity. Specific 'Fourth World' communities build up an inter-subjective interpretation of how their world functions and connects to their own sustainable identity. Manuel believed that 'indigenous' societies represent vital elements in human understanding and hold countless opportuni-ties for new human relations the world over. These beliefs were grounded in his 'foundational ideas' of people, history and encounter, and also in his underlying themes of land and culture. As I am concerned with the effects of migration on a place-related identity, let me concentrate on these two underlying themes.

UNDERLYING THEMES IN THE FOURTH WORLD. 1: LAND

In Manuel's 'Fourth World', land supposedly brings communities together:

> 'All our structures and values have developed out of a spiritual relationship with the land on which we have lived... The 'Fourth World' emerges as each people develop customs and practices that wed it to the land' (Manuel and Posluns 1974: 6–7).

Different value judgements create different perceptions of different people's relationship with the land. This causes friction between the First and the 'Fourth Worlds':

> 'This is not land that can be speculated, bought, sold, mortgaged ... Those are the things that men [sic] do only on the land claimed by a king who rules by the grace of God... This land from which our culture springs is the Mother Earth. We are part of that creation' (Manuel and Posluns 1974: 6).

Consequently, the First World cannot understand, nor accept the 'Fourth World's' claimed inseparable relationship with the land, particularly as it ham-pers its own vested interests there:

> 'Even the capitalist recognises that the value of land comes from its limited supply. The difference is that he [sic] chooses to exploit this for his own personal ends and finds himself in a society that encourages him to pursue this exploitation' (Manuel and Posluns 1974: 256).

Manuel's counter is to emphasise the inseparability of his people and land by fighting for his people's political representation and by arguing that these moves cannot be separated from the culture of other human beings:

> 'The need to redefine our relationship with the land cannot be separated from our need to find more effective and far reaching ways of re-distributing wealth... A materially comfortable environmentalist cannot tell himself that he is recycling his possessions and avoiding waste, when he uses the poor as the recipients of his

hand me downs without asking why they are poor' (Manuel and Posluns 1974: 257).

This called for an appreciation of the cultural fluidity between the Fourth *and* the First Worlds, a recognition of the importance of re-evaluating not only the people's relationship with the land, but also their relationship with other people and themselves.

UNDERLYING THEMES IN THE FOURTH WORLD. 2: CULTURE

Culture is seen to be inextricably bound up with land and, therefore, Manuel argues that political decisions taken beyond the control of 'indigenous' people must take account of this. He cannot understand the separation of the spiritual and the material in the First World, for in the 'Fourth World', they are (allegedly) inseparable:

'There is no real separation between the cultural artefacts – the drums, the totem poles and moccasins anyone can collect – and the day-to-day life in which culture is evident, through work, family life, words of friendship, and music' (Manuel and Posluns 1974: 69–70).

The key was a common cultural language whereby indigenous people can express themselves as marginal and disconnected components of the West and as people who have to be (re)included in Western society:

'The greatest preservative for racial myths is the difficulty of developing a new language in which the truth can be spoken... Much of the distance we must travel to the Fourth World must be spent developing such a language' (Manuel and Posluns 1974: 224).

In part, Manuel seeks this language through spiritual ties, believing that the Church has a role in bringing the two cultural worlds (First and Fourth) together:

'The church has so long been the treasure-house of values for western European people that it must have a role in the Fourth World... For all its faults, no other institution has a greater potential for building bridges between different societies' (Manuel and Posluns 1974: 263).

By navigating the 'Fourth World' along these roads, Manuel creates a political agenda, paving the way for other 'indigenous' leaders to attack the very foundations of the societies that marginalise and dis-locate them.

Today, the 'Fourth World' has 'travelled' through the conscious influence of 'indigenous' land and culture. In an attempt to reposition it, people have creatively borrowed from George Manuel to shift it away from its point of origin towards another place, the political arena of the First World. This politicisation was part of the third stage of its travels: the conditions of acceptance and/or resistance in new surroundings. I believe that such a set of surroundings have a salience in contemporary Swaledale. I will demonstrate this by operationalising Manuel's underlying themes of land and culture through the terrains of

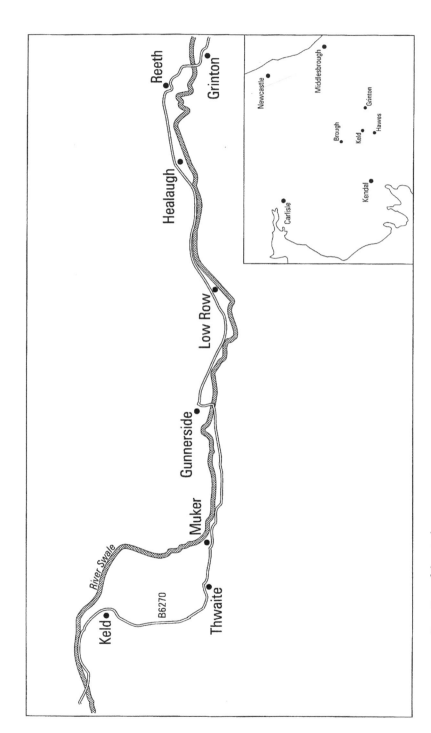

FIGURE 8.1 Location of the study area

experience across and through which a contemporary Swaledale identity is expressed in the present. However, first, the reader must become a little familiar with both Swaledale itself and the issues which local people feel to be important.

SWALEDALE AND THE FOURTH WORLD

The Yorkshire Dales of northern England stretch from the Pennines to the Lake District and across the Lune Valley, with the North Yorkshire Moors to the east. In Swaledale (just one of the dales or valleys), shown in Figure 8.1, sheep farming is the major agricultural activity, and the scenery attracts a large number of tourists, creating a seasonal, low-skilled, low-paid workforce. Usually Swaledale is thought of as divided into an upper and a lower dale. The area beyond the village of Grinton (the upper dale) is the focus of my attention. Today, conversations about what it means to be a 'Swaledaler' are dominated (whether directly or indirectly) by the effects of demographic change and are related to practical concerns such as housing, employment, transport and the Yorkshire Dales National Park.

The empirical material for this investigation was collected during a three-month ethnography in Swaledale between April and June 1992. Participant observation and semi-structured interviews provided the main methodological vision. The observations were carried out in two ways, firstly by working in a local pub and secondly, by working for an annual local cultural festival. These jobs were used to obtain contacts and possible interviewees, which were bolstered by snowball sampling techniques. The interviews themselves were used as an opportunity to encourage people to talk about themselves, the area and how they felt (or did not feel) part of it. Although I never specifically asked people their feelings about 'indigenous' peoples, some of the interviews were structured in such a way that there were opportunities for these connections to be made if people wanted to make them.

In order to explain the possibilities of the 'Fourth World at home', it is instructive to note the presence of parallels with what Manuel says in regard to the underlying themes of land and culture. Having said that, at the same time, it is also important to appreciate the different contexts of the Canadian and Swaledalian examples, principally the ways in which ethnicity shapes the different discourses of 'indigenous' people.

THEMES OF THE 'FOURTH WORLD AT HOME'. I: LAND

Manuel believed that land as the site of marginalisation and dis-location was able to bring 'Fourth World' communities together, as its people were bonded by a common attachment to that land, that stretched beyond economics. Farming families in Swaledale expressed similar feelings regarding their marginal socio-economic situation in terms associated with the 'Fourth World':

'There's so much more to farming than meets the eyes, I get so much more out of it because this is my land, if it was just financial return that would be wrong' (interview, local farmer, Gunnerside, May 1992).

'I agree with some of the teachings of the American Indians because they had a harmony with the land and they were attuned to the environment' (interview, local farmer's wife, Gunnerside, May 1992).

This sense of belonging (Cohen 1982) – of a common cultural and/or spiritual attachment to the land – was also felt by local people who had lived on, but who had not worked the land.

'Rob was thinking the way from his house, and he was picking his way through, and every single patch of land had a name and it was just like the songlines of the Aborigines' (interview, local women, Reeth, June 1992).

'It sounds very fanciful, but you feel for the Red Indians when they talk about their lands being scarred. I would be heartbroken if I saw it all ripped up and something else put in its place' (interview, local farmer's wife, Gunnerside, May 1992).

'I am really touched by the way that the young men sit up in the hills, as if they see the countryside as their life' (interview, local resident, Reeth, June 1992).

The parallels with 'indigenous' communities of the 'Fourth World' are striking. In particular, the final quote evokes something of the Native American rites of passage where young braves leave the community to go off on their own until they have a vision, until they can commune with the land and the animals on it. They then come back to the community and recite their vision to the council, in the hope that they will be declared a man.

These attachments to the land create common bonds amongst the local people and these are in part cemented by the threat of demographic change:

'If migration in and out of the dale continues, then the land and the culture of the dale is really going to be threatened' (conversation with local man in local pub, research diary, June 1992).

These changes are all the more significant when the local people recognise that those people moving into the communities from without imagine the dale in different ways to them:

'It is very upsetting when you see people coming in and not respecting the land and trampling over hayfields, they just do not know that it is a way of life for someone, not money in the wallet, but food in the cow's bellies. . . It would be sacrilege for us to trample across a hayfield' (interview, farmer's wife, Gunnerside, May 1992).

These different imaginations of non-local people, the incomers (or the 'offcum-downs' as they are known in Swaledale) and the threat they pose to a Swaledale identity demonstrate the potential that the Fourth World has – not least if translated into political practice – for unpacking the identity of local people in contemporary Swaledale.

THEMES OF THE 'FOURTH WORLD AT HOME'. 2: CULTURE

According to Manuel, culture and land were inseparable when identifying oneself as an 'Indian'. Whilst this degree of interdependency may not be as advanced in Swaledale, links between land, culture and local identity were visible. One such instance was the strong musical tradition in the dale, stemming from the songs sung by the workers on the land, and by the enthusiasm for musical instruments, particularly brass, amongst the lead-mining communities from the seventeenth century onwards. In contemporary Swaledale, local schools were working with local communities to maintain this by encouraging participation in the local Silver Bands. The two remaining Silver Bands, at Muker and Reeth, gave regular village concerts and were the source of great pride amongst those communities.

Manuel stressed that the artefacts and symbols of a culture cannot be separated from the work, family life or words of friendship of a people – the spiritual and the material worlds were inseparable. In this respect, people must pay just as much attention to the day-to-day lived realities of local people in Swaledale as they do to the cultural and economic systems that facilitate these:

> 'It has always been a tradition that you never get anything for nothing up here, so I guess that is part of the culture' (interview, local man, Low Row, June 1992).

The dangers of neglecting these realities is evidenced in the Swaledale Festival, a month long event set up by two offcumdowns with a view to 'bringing' culture to the dale and of re-invigorating an interest in local cultural issues. As the organisers were offcumdowns, they had difficulty imagining local culture. Consequently, many local people did not take part in the festival because they felt it was irrelevant to their lives.

> 'Most local people do not bother with the festival, either they are too busy or they don't think that it matters to them' (interview, festival workers, April 1992).

What I hoped I have demonstrated (albeit far too briefly) in these two sub-sections is that the underlying themes of Manuel's 'Fourth World' have the potential to travel into the hearts and minds of local people in Swaledale. What the reader must consider now, is whether the 'Fourth World' is consciously accepted or denied by Swaledalers (travelling theory's third stage) and whether it has become transformed in its new position (travelling theory's final stage). For Manuel, this positioning of the 'Fourth World' was carried out in two ways: politically and culturally.

POLITICALLY POSITIONING THE FOURTH WORLD IN SWALEDALE

Manuel's political positioning of the 'Fourth World' in the First World meant ensuring collective political action – the only and obviously shared political feelings – amongst 'indigenous people'. In Swaledale, such collective political action concentrated on the Yorkshire Dales National Park. The composition of the people concerned with directing this 'collective' action, however, were the so-called local agricultural hegemony, an 'indigenous' elite with deep historical and generational roots in the locality. These were the more powerful members of the local community, people whom the less powerful local people have become politically dependent upon, principally because they are experienced in dealing with such 'political' matters. This dependency relationship between them and the more lowly local people stretches beyond politics and is buttressed by a substantial amount of trust, sustained by the more powerful's status and which is bound into (still evident) old style class relations organised around land and property.

The 'Fourth World' in Swaledale has hence become differently nuanced. Unlike Manuel's version, many local people do not (or cannot) challenge the political status quo. If local people or parish councils want to challenge an issue, then the agricultural hegemony has to be left to its own devices, reasserting the dependency relationship between it and 'other' more lowly local people. These people are powerless to do anything about this, because if they did they would have to challenge this accepted social order. There is then the possibility that such a challenge would divide local opinion and open the door for the offcumdowns whom local people do not want making decisions about their community, as they fear that they will change it according to their romanticised vision. In other words, there is not just a local agricultural hegemony, there is also a potential hegemony of the offcumdowns (and hence the overlapping of the local/incomer divide with a working class/middle class divide). The somewhat paradoxical conclusion to this situation is that if a dale community wants to move forwards politically, socially, it must remain stagnant.

Equally – with the benefits of an outsider looking in – local politicians (such as parish and district councillors) do not always, or straightforwardly have the same interests at heart as 'other' local people. Their greater political power allows them greater access to outside political structures where they can create an identity for Swaledale in regional or national political forums. The subsequent discussions that take place with other political representatives from other rural areas within these fora can sow the seeds for imagining Swaledale in different ways and these imaginations are bound to influence that person's identity as a Swaledaler (particularly if they are from someone more powerful than them). In other words, the collective identity of Swaledale – an identity which local politicians are supposed to represent – has the potential to become dis-located, to be conceptually re-located in other parts of the country which, although they may be rural, are not Swaledale. More significantly, the various ways in which this new and transformed identity is acted upon by those representatives when they are back in the dale is going to have implications for other local people there. This is especially the case for the less powerful local people because the control that political representatives have over the local decision-making processes forces them (unwittingly or otherwise) to impose this new and transformed Swaledale identity onto the less powerful, whose own identity as a Swaledaler may be very different. Nevertheless, there is the strong possibility that the less powerful will accept this new and transformed identity because of the dependency relationship discussed previously.

Consequently, many less powerful local people are in an untenable position, a double bind. On the one hand, their local identity is marginalised and dislocated by the socio-economic and socio-cultural cleavages brought by demographic change, and on the other, they are marginalised and dis-located by the socio-political operations of more powerful local people. Their acting out of this relationship in their day-to-day lives creates what I call 'a culture of the powerless'.

In this respect, political-economic analyses of rural power relations (such as those detailed by Cloke 1988; Marsden *et al.* 1990) are still very persuasive when examining identity formation in rural Britain. However, they cannot say it all, and one possible solution, when detailing the 'Fourth World at home', could be to combine political-economic analyses with others which stress the role of culture as the symbolic glue or set of symbolic resources which hold an identity together.

CULTURALLY POSITIONING THE FOURTH WORLD IN SWALEDALE

Unfortunately, culture as a self-aware symbol of identity in Swaledale is easily appropriated. The move to identify culturally with the dale was driven, not by the longer time local non-powerful but by the offcumdowns, like the organisers of the Swaledale Festival:

'The main efforts are building on local culture as far as the festival is concerned, and then, on top of that we do use a high level of mainly Yorkshire artists, particularly musicians. . . There are people up here who could not hope to hear the Lindsay String Quartet or the Grimethorpe Colliery Band' (interview, festival worker, April 1992).

This situation led to many local people staying away from the festival. They criticised it for creating something that was not there: an illusory local culture. This generated tensions amongst the offcumdowns, who criticised local people for being resistant to new ideas and for wanting them to fail.

A crucial factor when considering Swaledale as a possible site for a cultural 'Fourth World' is to recognise that, historically, Swaledale is very different to the interior of British Columbia. Over the course of time, Swaledale has been occupied by a whole host of different peoples, with different cultures, religions, ways of life and identities:

'We have found dances that came from places as far away as Poland and Norway...
and also the old mining song, 'Four Pence a Day', that was not from here but was
brought down by the miners from Teesdale' (interview, festival worker, April
1992).

The result of this demographic transience, is that Swaledale does not have an
obvious and unique cultural tradition of its own to act as the symbolic glue. As a
Fourth World, therefore, it is a much more contested site than that of Manuel's
British Columbia, for its cultural identity is always going to be made up of
someone else's:

'I think that if there was a culture that they could fall back on, then the area would
reassert itself, but one of the problems is that it does not... If I was to make myself
very unpopular I would say that Swaledale is the cultural desert of the north'
(interview, local journalist May 1992).

The upshot of these shifts in Swaledale's cultural identity is that Swaledale
culture appears to be powerless, unable to assert itself because of too many
influences from other places and because its history – both deep history and
more recent – is too fractured, broken up by different peoples from different
places. So a single coherent dale identity is an impossibility; the strategic
Manuelian manoeuvre of asserting a coherent 'Fourth World' identity by mobilising a cultural identity to political ends here falls to the ground.

These political and cultural positionings of the 'Fourth World at home' create a
powerlessness of culture, and a culture of the powerless: a double bind. A
Swaledale identity cannot be seen as singular and fixed, it is a set of *identities* –
multiple constructions of Swaledale – which interact on a range of levels to
scramble any notion of collectivism as envisioned by Manuel. Different local
people create different local identities and multiple imaginations of the rural,
and so a Swaledale identity expressed in 'Fourth World' terms must be seen as a
more hybrid phenomenon. This dilutes its significance in Swaledale, both as a
conceptual tool – for thinking about Swaledale itself – and as a political tool for
local rural people to draw upon.

CONCLUSION: CRITICAL REFLECTIONS ON THE 'FOURTH WORLD AT HOME'

The 'Fourth World' in Swaledale can be seen to be objectively *produced* by the
socio-economic marginalisation of local people through socio-cultural and demographic change. This is more acute if people have no means of transport, no
other employment skills, or they have to live with their families. The 'Fourth
World' is also subjectively *experienced* by Swaledalers in terms akin to Manuel's
underlying themes of land and culture. However, it is not *expressed* in Manuel's
collective political language (a language largely influenced by Manuel's ethnic
and cultural identity) because a Swaledale identity constantly re-defines and
re-contests itself according to the influence and class affiliation of different

people, who move in and out of the dale, at different times, with different ways of identifying with Swaledale. The Swaledale identity which evolves from these interconnections of different but salient class positions is less of a singular unified experience (and so less of a Manuelian 'Fourth World') and more a multiple/hybrid experience founded on multiple constructions of the rural and multiple experiences of marginalisation and dis-location.

The lack of a collective political will to articulate the multiplicity of subjective-ly experienced attachments to land and culture synonymous with the 'Fourth World' means that the 'Fourth World at home' is a less powerful concept than had originally been envisaged. The marginalisation of the 'Fourth World', which in other situations has helped to change national policy, presents an illuminating account about the travelling of a concept and its utility in different places. Not only that, it also provides academics and researchers with a fascinating chal-lenge. On the one hand, we have to sensitise ourselves to the differences and hybridities that emerge from within a fairly simply constructed set of social, economic and cultural relations rooted in a small geographic area such as Swaledale. On the other, we have to realise and plan for the fact that 'on the ground', difference and hybridity are not going to be uppermost in Swaledalers' minds. This is not least because the cultural identity of Swaledale is shaped within a local political climate which subsumes these differences and hybridities and which places less powerful local people in the double bind of the power-lessness of culture and the culture of the powerless. The problem in trying to rectify this double bind – a desire which is a fundamental part of my own identity as a researcher – by, say, stressing the importance of difference and hybridity, is that this initiative would require the political presence of powerful class interests who maintain the collective Swaledale identity and so steamroller over the heterogeneity championed by the academic world.

In this respect, once academic research reaches the political stage – which, if it is to make a difference, it must do – class (and its interconnected power relations) has to become a fundamental issue. This is a significant decision for rural researchers to consider given recent theoretical and cultural shifts (and it is certainly a significant decision for myself after pinning my flag to the mast of rural identity politics). Perhaps the answer continues to lie in the words of Harvey:

> 'If the historical and geographical *process* of class war has feminised poverty, accelerated racial oppression and further degraded the ecological conditions of life, then it seems that a far more united politics can flow from a determination to check *that* process than will likely flow from an identity politics which largely reflects its fragmented results' (Harvey 1993: 64, emphasis in original).

To conclude, I feel that rural studies needs to maintain a sensitivity to culture, difference and hybridity and to take identity politics seriously but, equally, it must recognise that in the step beyond the academy into the 'real' politics of the people concerned, there is a strategic need to incorporate class analysis to clarify *in situ* oppressions that local people may suffer as they struggle to mobilise cultural materials towards political ends. Such an exercise is the stuff of everyday social relations.

ACKNOWLEDGEMENTS

I would like thank all those who worked on the 'Lifestyles' projects at Lampeter, and to the director, Paul Cloke, for allowing me the time to pursue my own ideas. I would also like to thank the Lampeter Social and Economic Research Group for their contribution towards my study visit, and to Chris Philo whose help and guidance as my thesis supervisor has been unquantifiable.

NOTES

1. Some papers at the 'Migration to Rural Areas Conference' investigated these ideas of identity and migration on the Celtic periphery (for example, James 1995; Ni Laoire 1995).
2. This was one of the study areas for the Lifestyles in Rural England project (Cloke *et al.* 1994b) and became the focus of my postgraduate research.
3. One such instance was a theme issue of *Antipode* (1984) on the 'Fourth World'. This academicisation of the 'Fourth World' charts its travels from the thoughts of indigenous people into academic journals. Here, the 'Fourth World' becomes assimilated by (Western) theoretical traditions such as political economy (see Stea and Wisner 1984). However, this chapter pilots a very particular journey: from Manuel's Canada to an assessment of what the concept 'can do' in thinking about the circumstances in Swaledale.
4. For more detailed accounts of these see Berreman (1972); Graburn (1976, 1981); Hamalian and Karl (1976); and Whitaker (1972).

REFERENCES

Berreman, G. (1972) 'Race, caste and other invidious distinctions in social stratification', *Race*, **13**, 383–414.

Cloke, P. (ed.) (1988) *Policies and plans for rural people*, Unwin Hyman, London.

Cloke, P. and Little, J. (eds.) (1997) *Contested countryside cultures*, Routledge, London.

Cloke, P., Doel, M., Matless, D., Phillips, M. and Thrift, N. (1994a) *Writing the rural: five cultural geographies*, Paul Chapman, London.

Cloke, P., Millbourne, P. and Thomas, C. (with contributions from Fielding, S., Hurd, K. and Woodward, R. (1994b) *Lifestyles in rural England*, Rural Development Commission, London.

Cohen, A. (ed.) (1982) *Belonging: identity and social organisation in British rural cultures*, Manchester University Press, Manchester.

Graburn, N. (ed.) (1976) *Ethnic tourist art: cultural expressions from the Fourth World*, University of California Press, Berkeley.

Graburn, N. (1981) '1, 2, 3, 4, . . . Anthropology and the Fourth World', *Culture*, **1**, 66–70.

Hamalian, L. and Karl, F. (eds.) (1976) *The Fourth World: the imprisoned, the poor, the sick, the elderly and the under-aged in America*, Dell, New York.

Harvey, D. (1993) 'Class relations, social justice and the politics of difference', in M. Keith and S. Pile (eds.), *Place and the politics of identity*, Routledge, London, 41–66.

James, E. (1995) 'Great expectations? Inmigration to Welsh rural communities', paper presented at Migration into Rural Areas conference, Swansea, March.

Manuel, G. and Posluns, M. (1974) *The Fourth World: an Indian reality*, Macmillan, Toronto.

Marsden, T., Lowe, P. and Whatmore, S. (eds.) (1990) *Rural restructuring: global processes and their responses*, David Fulton, London.

Ni Laoire, C. (1995) 'The migration experience of people and places in rural Ireland', paper presented at Migration into Rural Areas conference, Swansea, March.

Said, E. (1984) *The world, the text and the critic*, Harvard University Press, Cambridge, Massachusetts.

Stea, D. and Wisner, B. (1984) 'Introduction', *Antipode*, **16**, 3–12.

Whitaker, B. (1972) *The Fourth World: victims of group oppression*, Schocken Books, New York.

9

CLASS, COLONISATION AND LIFESTYLE STRATEGIES IN GOWER

PAUL CLOKE, MARTIN PHILLIPS and NIGEL THRIFT

INTRODUCTION: ACADEMIC AND GEOGRAPHICAL POSITIONINGS

In this chapter we will draw on, and seek to integrate, some 'empirical research' based on an Economic and Social Research Council (ESRC) funded project of the 'Local economic impacts of the middle class in rural areas' (R000231209) and some 'theoretical writings' drawn from what some rural researchers (for example, Miller 1996; Pahl 1995) seem to see as an unwanted or unnecessary 'other' to rural research, namely 'continental social theory'. In particular we wish, firstly, to outline some of the theoretical ideas of Pierre Bourdieu, Michèle Lamont and more specifically Klaus Eder on the relationship between class and culture and, secondly, to demonstrate how these ideas helped us interpret the results of a series of interviews which we undertook as part of the project. As discussed elsewhere (Cloke *et al.* 1995, 1998), the project proceeded through a series of interviews with residents in three contrasting rural locations, alongside a series of contextualising interviews with representatives of local councils, agencies and community groups. In the study we sought not only to explore the implications of a range of different theorisations of class (for example, Goldthorpe 1982; Wright 1978, 1985) but also to investigate the interconnections between class and cultural constructions of rurality and rural life (Cloke *et al.* 1994). The three study areas were the Berkshire Green Belt near Bracknell, the Gloucestershire Cotswolds and the Gower Peninsula in South Wales. In the present chapter we will concentrate on the last of these study areas and on the issue of the interconnection between class and cultural constructions of rurality.

Gower was chosen as a study area for a number of reasons. One reason was practical: at its inception the project was run from two institutions, St David's University College and the University of Bristol, and Gower was easily accessible from both. Another reason behind the choice was that Gower is at the end of the M4 corridor and, hence, potentially at the extremities of socio-economic restructuring associated with the service sector growth. As Day *et al.* (1989: 239–240) have remarked:

'the shifts in occupational structure which have characterised the localities of rural Wales are very different from those of, say, areas adjacent to the London metropolitan area, which have not only been much more affected by commuting patterns... but also by highly distinctive forms of development associated with the growth of technologically-advanced industries in the so-called M4 corridor... as well as substantial changes in the composition of local service employment'.

More specifically it has been suggested that Gower may be affected by a combination of localised economic restructuring of the Swansea Bay economy, the movement of people seeking places with certain degrees of Welshness and/or rurality, tourist-related residential movement, and the westward drift of people working within the M4 corridor (Cloke *et al.* 1991). Lastly, we also felt it important to conduct some research within Wales because one of the institutional centres of the research was Welsh and because we were conscious that the study of the English countryside may have become rather 'hegemonic' within 'British' rural research. Indeed, a number of studies have recently highlighted the relationship between nationalism and rural idyll(s), and Gower has a complex and quite specific relationship to English and Welsh national identities.

BOURDIEU AND DISCIPLES

Perhaps the 'obvious' corpus of theoretical writing from which to draw concepts which inform the interconnection of class and culture is that by Bourdieu (1984). His focus on the interplay between cultural and economic capital suggested the emergence of different social groupings:

- The dominant class – industrialists and managers of large-scale industrial enterprises who have large amounts of economic capital but less cultural capital.
- The new petite bourgeoisie – people in fast developing service sectors (advertising, marketing, public relations, media) with high levels of economic capital and cultural capital. Indeed such people are viewed as the standard-bearers and taste-setters for other groups
- Others – teachers, artistic producers, intellectuals and others with low economic capital and high cultural capital.

Bourdieu's *Distinction* represents an analysis of the relations and struggles between these different groups in France during the 1960s. He suggests an iterative series of 'battles' – although it would seem that such battles were relatively bloodless and perhaps even free from casualties – in which the identity, social position and worth of each group was fought out, particularly in the *cultural* arena.

A number of authors have implicitly or explicitly used Bourdieu's work to argue that a more culturally outgoing middle class has emerged in Britain. For example, Savage *et al.* (1992) describe the formation of middle classes as based around three causal entities – property, bureaucracy and culture. Although organisational assets, property assets and cultural assets are asymmetrical, and classes are only formed in particular historical and spatial circumstances, nevertheless they argue that both property (and therefore place?) and culture have become increasingly important to studies of class in recent years. They point to two rather different types of cultural asset:

> 'First, and most important, is the old cultural distinctiveness associated with the public sector middle class where there is a close reliance on traditional forms of 'high culture', such as classical music, art, literature and so forth. Set against this is the new conspicuous extravagance of the private sector professionals, who indulge in new types of sport and fitness routines along with exotic holidays and luxury consumption' (Savage *et al.* 1992: 212–213).

Their 'placing' of these assets in terms of the relation between particular landscapes/environments/imagined geographies is less distinct, regarding as 'journalistic' some attempts to tie middle or service class consciousness with an endorsement of 'countryside' traditions and habitus:

> 'Meanwhile a popular image emerging from, say, the pages of *Country Life* is that of an older more staid fraction engaging in slower pseudo-rural ways of life; wearing Barbour jackets, green wellingtons and driving spotless four-wheel-drive Land Rovers in pursuit of their children and horses' (Savage *et al.* 1992: 104).

They suggest here that the absence of adequate information leads to the danger of reproducing journalistic stereotypes.

We would support Bourdieu's notion of the habitus as a means of characterising the embodied improvisations through which everyday life is carried forward. However, we are much less sure of Bourdieu's reciprocal mapping of the habitus onto social fields which therefore become areas for a competition of symbolic advantage, with the aim of maximising symbolic capital. Briefly, there are three reasons for this scepticism:

- Bourdieu oversimplifies cultural complexity by recording culture as part of the pursuit of symbolic advantage (Dreyfus and Rabinow 1993). Symbolic advantage is pursued, but this pursuit should not be a totalising principle.
- Bourdieu's emphasis on symbolic advantage takes little account of the cultural 'tactics' employed by different middle class people (de Certeau 1984).
- Bourdieu's account lacks a 'spatiality' of habitus and, in our view, cultural constructions of rurality are themselves intertwined with cultural constructions of class.

SPATIALITY AND RURALITY

In a recent chapter (Cloke *et al.* 1995), we have sought to 'place' the rural into these debates on class and culture. Conventionally, rurality has been discussed in terms of an idyll-ised set of discourses and activity spaces which have been one of many different factors in the way in which the middle classes have identified themselves. We believe that in recent years, the rural in Britain has become more significant than this. We offer five related reasons for this claim:

- The rural as a means of middle class identification has simply become more important, given the decline in respect for other institutions. The affective investment made by middle class people in rural activities has become greater than simply a set of 'leisure activities' or even a form of 'cultural capital'. Affiliation with the rural (along with its cultural and moral constructions) has for some become a more consciously adopted signification of their self.
- The rural has become more important as an arena of middle class action. Just as self-signification has increased, so threats to the arena of that signification have led to a rise in protests and membership of rural pressure groups.
- The rural is now remorselessly circulated as symbol and icon within cultural industries, and therefore its ambit is ever increasing.
- The rural has become a signifier – more so than previously – of a site without social ills; a place of hiding from crime, poverty and the underclass. As such it has become a cultural determinant of class formation and not just something which is identified with particular middle class fractions (for example, the service class).
- Rural areas have increasingly become a preserve of the middle class. Thereby, the rural may have become critical to the constitution of the middle class to the point where the relation between class and the rural has almost been reversed: whereas in the past middle class signified rural, it might now be claimed that the cultural texture associated with the rural has expanded to a point where 'rural' signifies the middle class.

We conclude that the middle class is now discursively constructed to a much greater degree than previously, and that 'the rural' – both spatially and discursively – may be playing key roles in this construction.

KLAUS EDER

Given these suggestions about the importance of spatiality and discourses of the rural, and about its status as a cultural anchor for the middle classes, we choose to draw on the recent work of Klaus Eder for conceptualisations which are more helpful in interpreting what is going on in places like Gower. Eder, more than Bourdieu, problematises the concept of class structure and its relationship with culture and action. Although he is a difficult author in some ways because of the seeming internal contradictions which appear in his work, Eder's *The new politics of class* (1993) proposes a 'culturalist' concept of class. Rather than viewing culture as a bridge between class and action, significant only because of its dependence on class and action, Eder views culture as becoming much more of an 'intervening variable'. Actions are embedded in culturally defined action spaces and so the impacts of class on action are mediated by the 'cultural texture' of that class. He focuses specifically on the constitution of collective action, and proposes a three-layer model:

- Layer 1, Class – class is a structured variable made accessible through probabilistic constructs of aggregates of social positions.
- Layer 2, Cultural texture – the cultural texture of values, identities and knowledge gives meaning to the structural variable of class.
- Layer 3, Collective action – collective action, denoted by preferred structures and orientations, occurs within the context of cultural textures.

Eder thus poses the question of how collective action constitutes and reproduces a symbolically defined action space that is both the condition and the outcome of collective action. He sets forth a model in which collective action events are always situated in culturally defined action spaces; thereby, collective action is embedded in a cultural texture (specifically organised discourses which provide the setting for the motivations of actors to act together, and even overrides those motivations on some occasions); it is cultural texture, which represents those cultural life-forms that allow individuals to act collectively; class has impacts on action through cultural constructions which are produced and reproduced as part of historically specific life-forms. Class comes last. It is the most restrictive variable. It reduces the variability of events that explain what is going on. Class structures generate positions which stand for opportunities (or lack of them) (see Eder 1993: 8–10).

An important element of Eder's work in terms of its applicability to the interconnections between rurality and the middle classes is that in the social struggles of contemporary post-industrial society, the traditional struggles for income have been augmented by struggles for formal and professional qualifications, struggles for taste and struggles for moral excellence. Lamont's (1992) study of French and American upper-middle classes stresses the importance of this latter struggle by emphasising symbolic boundaries (denoting difference between those who have and are, and those who have and are not) in the display and representation of power and inequality within these struggles. She emphasises:

- Socio-economic boundaries – drawn according to judgements relating to people's social position as indicated by their wealth and professional achievements.
- Cultural boundaries – drawn on the basis of education, intelligence, manners, tastes and command of high culture.
- Moral boundaries – drawn according to qualities of honesty, work ethic, personal integrity and consideration for others.

Social groups, and the inequalities between them, are interpretative schemes of social reality, and cognitive representations of social position will take account of a range of *competencies*, which are underemphasised in the work of Bourdieu and others. Eder's argument is that the interdependence of both income/

qualifications and moral/aesthetic competencies allows us to identify the social distribution of the quantities of competence that represent the class structure as it develops as networks in advanced industrial societies. This matter of competence was explored elsewhere (see Cloke, Goodwin and Milbourne, Chapter 7, this volume).

Summarising many of these ideas, in Figure 9.1 Eder offers a three-fold model which links a particular schema of identity and ethos with a particular cognitive representation of the cultural texture of class and with a particular arena of life-world:

- Schema 1 – social equality is seen as the result of differential individual achievements. This interpretative strategy will be common amongst those whose economic and cultural wealth allows them to afford the ethos that it is necessary to ensure that the 'best' people enter the higher social positions. Cultural competence is thus embedded in this notion of 'best' people, and cultural texture is represented predominantly in life-worlds which reflect interests in the cultural, political and public spheres.
- Schema 2 – material inequality is seen as the outcome of different cognitive competence. Here the emphasis is on achievement, and the best positions are reflected by the culture that can be achieved. Hence the predominant life-worlds are those which reflect interests in the private sphere, often the family arena.
- Schema 3 – social position is interpreted in terms of consumption. Here, the representations of status positions in society are reduced to the particular material resources they are tied to, and the predominant life-worlds reflect interests in work areas.

Eder's ideas present us with some very interesting conceptual devices with which to interpret the 'rural' middle classes in our Gower study area.

THE GOWER STUDIES

Our empirical work in Gower focused on the areas centring on Llangennith, Llanmadoc, Reynoldston and Murton (Figure 9.2), and consisted of over 160 interviews with individuals in households, plus interviews with representatives of local councils, agencies and community groups. Alongside the class-orientated information drawn on in this and other papers (Cloke *et al.* 1991, 1995; Phillips 1993), we were also interested in the interconnections between class, gender and ethnicity. As mentioned in the introduction, Gower is peculiarly placed in relation to English and Welsh national identities. From at least the twelfth century Gower, alongside Pembrokeshire, has been described in such terms as 'an English colony in Wales' or 'Little England beyond Wales' (Emery 1971). Bowen (1940, in Emery 1971: 147) has argued that 'one of the outstanding features of the historical geography of Wales' is the 'complete anglization of Pembroke and parts of Gower'. As Emery has documented, Gower was both

FIGURE 9.1 Types of class-specific cultures

Interpratative schema	Cognitive form	Type of life-world
1. Individualistic ethos of personal identity and of the potential equality between people	Idealistic fallacy: what counts is the culture one has.	Predominance of life interests in the cultural, political and public spheres
2. The ethos of achievement, recognition of inequality between people	Ecological fallacy: what counts is the culture one has achieved.	Predominance of life interests in the private sphere (family).
3. The ethos of maximising the chances of consumption, recognition of the division of society into social classes.	Materialistic fallacy: what counts as culture is the goods one has.	Predominance of life interests in the sphere of work, especially the workplace.

Source: Eder 1995: 98

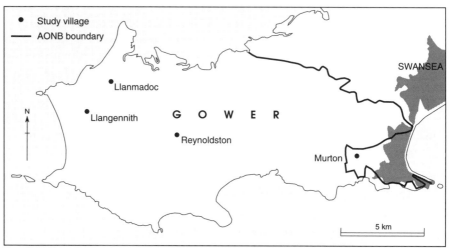

FIGURE 9.2 The Gower study villages

politically and socially colonised by Anglo-Norman feudalism with a 'marcher lordship' of Gower being established in which estates were worked by English colonists working within 'a manorial economy based on the cultivation of crops along traditional English lines' (Emery 1971: 153). This part of Gower became distinguished from much of the surrounding area in its tenurial system, its agriculture production system and in terms of the language used by its residents. The west and south of Gower was broadly feudal, arable and English speaking; the north and east less feudal, more pastoral and more Welsh speaking. A number of studies (for example, Emery 1965, 1971) have documented the reproduction of similar social, economic and linguistic boundaries within and

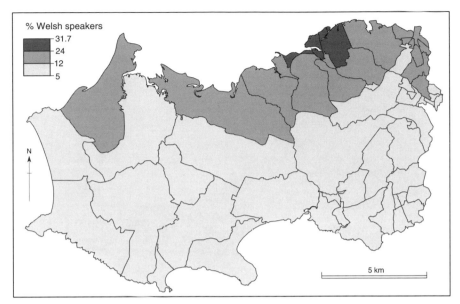

% Welsh speakers
- 31.7
- 24
- 12
- 5

N

5 km

FIGURE 9.3 Welsh speakers in Gower and surrounding areas, 1991

around Gower. Figure 9.3 shows the proportion of Welsh speakers in Gower and surrounding areas as recorded by the 1991 Census. The low degree of Welsh speaking in Gower was clearly evident in our survey, where only five percent of those interviewed could speak the language and only one person regularly used it in their workplace.

The Welsh language, whilst being a key feature in the Welsh nationalist movement, is not the only component of a Welsh identity, a point which became apparent in our study. While we found a very small number of Welsh speakers, we did find that many people residing in the Gower villages under study had been born in Wales – shown in Figure 9.4 – and many spoke of migration to Gower as a movement to a 'home area', even a 'homeland', often after a period of living and working at considerable distance from Wales and from the Gower. Figure 9.5, for example, illustrates the residential paths of people born within Gower and it can be seen that many of these 'locals' have spent at least part of their lives outside the area. Another set of locals resident in Gower were the people from the Swansea area and, as Figure 9.6 demonstrates, there were a number of people who although not born in Gower had never lived very distant from the area. Indeed, several residents and estate agents spoke of the move to Gower as the final step of a series of moves up the Swansea housing market.

In addition to these two 'local' sets of migrants we also found longer distant migrants, from both Wales and England, and also from further afield. Taken together these migrant flows raise fascinating questions about the influence of 'Welshness', 'rurality' and 'class' on the processes of social (re)composition in

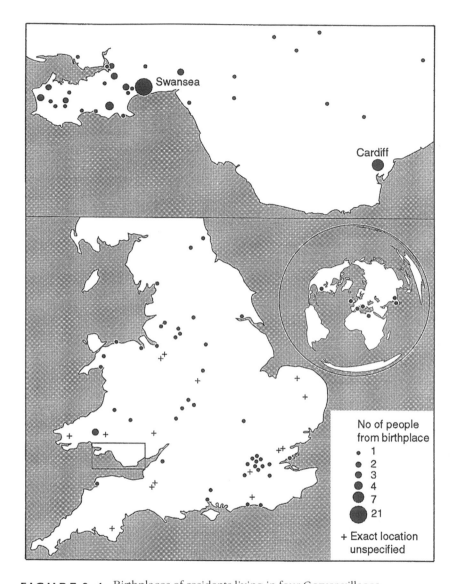

FIGURE 9.4 Birthplaces of residents living in four Gower villages

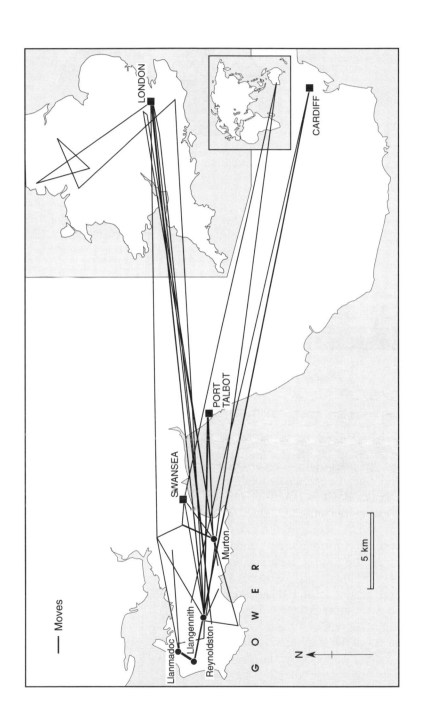

FIGURE 9.5 Residential movements of villagers born in Gower

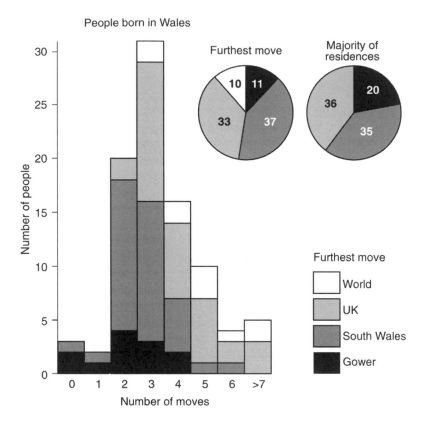

FIGURE 9.6 Residential moves of villagers born in Wales

Gower. In the remainder of this chapter we explore briefly two aspects of their interconnection: first, the role of generalised cultural textures of rurality in the processes by which Gower villages have been *colonised* by particular classes; and second, the way the cultural textures of the rural connect into the *lifestyle strategies* employed by people in the villages. With reference to the former we will argue that social constructions of rural life may (re)produce cultural textures which emphasise the happy, healthy, bucolic, self-supporting and risk-free characteristics of rurality, and colonisation may therefore represent a choice towards cultural certainty, material security and a 'safe place' for family life. With reference to lifestyle strategies we will argue that many of them seem to reflect the cultural logics as outlined by Eder in Figure 9.1 and, moreover, that the cultural texture(s) of the rural are significant in establishing collective actions within rural action and may even constitute in Eder's (1995: 180) words 'a social opportunity structure for the "making of a class"'.

COLONISATION

Introduction

In mentioning colonisation, we stand aside from a number of important technical aspects which we have dealt with elsewhere (Cloke *et al.* 1991, 1995; Phillips 1993), such as how to measure class; how different class fractions so measured are associated with particular strands of a culturally constructed idyll-ised countryside; and the mechanical processes (planning, buying, selling, market price fixing) which channel the entry of middle class into the area. We do, however, want to mention a number of particular instances in which wider-scale cultural constructions of rurality appear to interact with the localised cultural textures of rurality in the Gower villages concerned, such that they become some kind of object of desire for middle class in-migrants. Lash (1990) has suggested that houses have exchange, use and sign values. We found articulations of each in our interviews with people in Gower, who could see many clear advantages in their habitation of a rural house.

The Rural House and Exchange Value

With reference to exchange value, it was clear that housing was seen to provide a lucrative mechanism of economic accumulation for many middle class households' with the spiralling cost of rural housing in the 1980s making it a particularly attractive investment:

> 'Houses good investment, every house (I've) bought has increased in capital assets faster than interest. Resale value is important on the decision to buy' (Respondent G1).

In our overall survey of three study areas, 65 percent of respondents had traded up in the housing market in order to buy their current rural property and, while only 22 percent stated that they had purchased their residence with a specific intention to re-sell, over 86 percent considered that housing was a good investment in their area.

Moreover, several respondents in Gower perceived that there were localised features which heightened the value of their house. One person, for example, remarked that houses in Gower were a good investment because:

> 'Gower is an AONB, so planning is always strong and housing is therefore at a premium. It is also the desirable side of Swansea' (G62).

The notion that Gower housing embodied a significant degree of social positionality was most clearly demonstrated in the attempt by the Welsh Office to encourage Swansea City Council to take care that 'attractive residential areas are not spoilt by insensitive infilling' (Welsh Office, Circular 30/86; quoted in Cloke *et al.* 1991: 46).

Gentrification

The importance of exchange value was also apparent in the rehabilitation of small or run down housing stock, which was another significant feature in the Gower study area (Phillips 1993). For some, it was the lack of income accompanied by a desire for a rural residence which prompted the action. A number of instances of people spending years rebuilding dilapidated dwellings were narrated to us. In one instance, the building work lasted over eight years and involved a family living in a caravan in the garden of the dwelling because they could otherwise 'only have bought a small detached house in Port Talbot' (G23). As argued elsewhere (Phillips 1993), such people may be seen as marginal gentrifiers.

For others, gentrification was linked to the accumulation of wealth. One respondent, for example, remarked that the move to a Gower village was 'to make money by renovating the house' and that 'buying the house was simply a business venture' (G3). In such cases the improvement of housing can be interpreted as involving the investment of personal labour power, or 'sweat equity' (Smith 1979) in order to increase the exchange value of the property. It is clearly apparent that people 'gentrifying' their houses in Gower could make 'significant financial gains from selling their improved properties' (Phillips 1993: 129). One respondent, for example, had bought a house for £92 000 in 1982 that was valued at £370 000 by 1990. He had 'extensively rebuilt the house', adding a conservatory, converting the garage into a sitting room and the stable into a cottage. The house was described as now being 'an old farmhouse fully modernised inside' (G61). There was also a hint at the establishment of social status distinctions in the comment that the house had been redecorated to change the style of the house 'which before was too uniform, too utilitarian and lacking in luxury'.

As well as the utilisation of class textures in the descriptions of gentrification, many also again drew on general and local inflexions of rurality. General notions of the 'country cottage' or the 'farmhouse', as evidenced above, were often used to describe the form that gentrification activity had taken. There were also in several instances a clear local inflexion placed on the gentrification process:

> 'We were anxious that [the house] fits into the 'vernacular' style and therefore into the village... White is the traditional Gower colour, and the porch is Gower, as is the long profile... [the house is] modern design in harmony with Gower traditional' (G78).

These cultural textures were not only applied to the gentrifiers' homes, but were also used in descriptions of the homes of others:

> 'Blights in the village are dilapidated farm buildings; incongruous buildings, for example with red roof tiles; modern bungalows... the village hall could have been more in keeping with Welsh traditional buildings' (G16).

Rural Living as an Object of Desire

For Bourdieu (1984), expressions of taste are also expressions of socio-economic distinction. Hence, comments about the houses of others can be seen to be positional in both social and economic senses. However, it is not only rural housing which can be connected to such a positioning, a point clearly illustrated by a remark of one interviewee in the Bracknell study:

> 'This morning, funny enough, I was going to have you down at the sheep dip 'cos I had planned to go dipping sheep this morning with a mate of mine. . . I had sheep here but with the job commitment I had to give them up' (B96).

This interviewee was also heavily into rural pursuits such as clay shooting – which was 'all part of the game' of living in the countryside – and leisure partly dictated the reasons for his move to the countryside which was 'simply for his wife's horses'. We suggest that there is a conspicuous display of rurality going on here and evidence of a conscious attempt to purchase commodities to construct a leisured rural lifestyle. More generally, this kind of text from rural colonisers echoes Eder's ideas of class structures being both the creation of the social observer but also figuring in the discourses occurring within particular action spaces.

We would go further to suggest that many people were investing not only socially and economically but also culturally and psychologically in the countryside. Indeed, in line with the findings of Lamont, many of the people we talked to were drawing on cultural and moral as well as socio-economic boundaries when interpreting their actions of moving into the countryside. In particular, we found that the cultural investments in constituting rurality as an object of desire were, in part, connected to the construction of what Giddens (1991) terms 'ontological security' or a sense of continuity and order. Many of the people we spoke to drew on expectations of rural life which involved some notion that living in the countryside was a way of escaping or minimising the risks of modern living. In particular notions of community, family, environment and safety (particularly for children) were used frequently as reasons for moving to Gower:

> 'Llangennith is a dream place to live in – beautiful environment, great for kids, so sunny. . . and a thriving community' (G5).

> 'Wanted a nice house in a nice environment for the children' (G23).

> 'We moved for a bigger house and for the children. The village is a safe environment for kids. . . no fear of burglary. . . and good community spirit' (G30).

> 'We felt that London was not suitable for bringing up children. . . chose village because of surrounding countryside and village community' (G35).

> 'The well-being of the children was important. The school would be better and it was a nice place to grow up and play in' (G48).

Within these generalised genuflexions to the rural idyll, however, some in-migrants were clearly measuring their expectations of village life in Gower against a set of cultural constructions which referenced the *English* village. When asked to describe the positive aspects of their Gower village, one respondent answered

> 'I like the sense of community... and it has some visual interest, although it has some misfits... it has no unity, such as in a Cotswold village, although it is nice around the village green... has two village pubs, quite a good village hall and a nice community spirit' (G16).

Another respondent explained that they chose to settle in their Gower village because:

> 'It looked like an English village to us, rather than many urban-like villages north of Swansea... I suppose it's our preconception of what a village should look like' (G39).

For other respondents, however, there was a particularly localised cultural texture to middle class life in the Gower countryside. Here, there was a sense of returning to family roots or other strong personal connections with place:

> 'We wanted to live in Gower... my wife's from here... there are strong family connections' (G11).

(Note here the potential for different or multiple cultural constructions of the rural within a household, as this male respondent also suggested that he had 'looked for a place that paralleled the village [they had lived in] in Sussex'.) Other similar responses included:

> 'I moved to the village where I had lived before... I had moved to Sri Lanka and also lived in Iraq, Thames Valley, Aberystwyth, Methyr and Bishopston' (G26).

> 'I wanted to come back to Bishopston' (G32).

> 'We moved because my husband was born in the Swansea Valley... we thought that the weather was much better here – because of the Gulf Stream. Also we wanted land as the family had always kept Welsh mountain ponies and wanted to keep some' (G66).

> 'We moved at retirement and for family reasons. We are a Gower family and it was important to come back here. Also, the children will visit us in a nice place' (G78).

Such responses do indicate that for some middle class households, where labour market opportunities and life-cycle stages permit, the cultural texture of a rural object of desire is linked with localised affinity – a belonging and a sense of place in a particular part of rural Wales. This localised cultural texture will represent particular cultural life-forms which prompt individuals to act collectively, and class will impact on action through the specific production and reproduction of these life-forms. In a place like the Gower, there appear to be recognisably different strands of cultural texture which both constitute middle class presence and offer scope for conflict between middle class fractions. Equally it illustrates how many different class fractions will end up in a village for many different reasons. Unifinality must be matched with multiple symbolic and material pathways to colonisation.

MIDDLE CLASS LIFESTYLE STRATEGIES IN RURAL AREAS

We also want to suggest that there are important differences in the way in which different middle class households strategise their lifestyles having moved to a rural location such as Gower. Different reactions to cultural expectations of how to practise rural lifestyles effectively produce different embodied dispositions which iteratively reproduce different cultural textures in the same village. Our surveys showed that there were significant differences in the manner in which our interviewees interpreted the way they acted in the countryside. For example, length of residence, age, gender, previous place of residence, income, mobility, and where appropriate ethnicity, seem to interconnect with varying cultural and moral competencies to result in a variety of different accounts of what is important about rural life as experienced in their particular place of residence. We would suggest, however, that there are some significant cuts of difference in amongst these factors. These draw on Eder's interpretative schema in Figure 9.1.

- A local gentry – individuals and households with a long-standing presence in the local community and whose stake in the place was represented to us as intergenerational. They prized the connections between heritage, belonging, intimate knowledge of what life should be like in a place, and a secure position within their own construction of local community. Such people tended to cherish life-worlds and action spaces associated with community organisations, political representation, and the constitution of 'common good' in the village, although they are not necessarily drawn from traditional farmer/landowner cultures which are often held to be the heartland of the gentry. When asked about the negative attributes of the village, one respondent replied:

    'Certain groups want to maintain their hold on the village – that is family groups' (G36).

    One of the strategies of local gentry will be to maintain such a hold. We would see the local gentry as aligning with Eder's Schemas 1 and 2.

- Village regulators – individuals and households taking an extraordinarily keen interest in regulatory practices in the village, notably those involving planning controls. If the gentry see themselves as community leaders, these village regulators reflect on their role as one of guardianship of the often abstracted notion of village space. One respondent from another of our study areas, who was a 'reluctant' member of the village preservation society, complained of:

> 'the rather lax, unplanned, developments that's taking place... it's a classical no-man's-land between agricultural land and an urban area, so you only have to have an acre of land to put up a goat farm and under current legislation you call yourself an agricultural dwelling and you shove up a barn and you convert it into accommodation, and lo and behold you have a property which you have acquired on agricultural land at agricultural value and where there is no planning at all. So really the basis of the preservation society is either plan it or stop it...' (B95).

The village regulators in Gower are extremely vigilant in contesting potential breaches of public sphere codes relating to planning controls and other established place-relations. Their class-ness is not that of the gentry, but they share to some extent the gentry's ethos and interests as suggested by Eder's Schema 1. However, there is also evidence amongst different village regulators of the achievement of culture (Schema 2) and the materialism of culture (Schema 3).

- Move in and join in – individuals and households whose lifestyle strategy involved joining in with what they perceived to be the benefits of village community life. Their cultural expectation of such life tended to be related to aspects of friendliness, inclusiveness and the close-knit nature of rural life. The living out of this expectation therefore involved a strategy of joining in village-based social, cultural and political activities (although their choice of activities in which to involve themselves varied widely, and in some cases overlapped with the regulators) . What unites these strategies, however, is they represent an *outward-looking* posture from the dwelling and land which they have purchased. For example, one respondent was a community councillor, trustee of the village hall, secretary of the local Commoners Association and editor of the village magazine. This person commented that they:

> 'feel strongly on every point... I feel for the community, the environment, the people who live here, for Christianity... [I have] the feeling of doing something worthwhile... [I] feel that [but] for me being in the village lots would not happen... this brings me in contact with a lot more people in the village... develops a momentum in social life – it brings the village together, creates a community spirit' (G53).

This group of movers-in and joiners-in illustrate a mix of the interpretative traits suggested by Eder. As in-migrants they are likely to reflect a culture of achievement (Schema 2). However, their strategy of joining in suggests a life-world which does take in the cultural and public spheres (Schema 1).

- Move in for self and show – individuals and households whose imagined culture of rural life is actioned within the house and land itself rather than in the wider village community. Here, the village and surrounding countryside is an aesthetic backdrop setting to the dwelling, and a vista from it. The emphasis on lifestyle is property-based with strategies of extending the dwelling, furnishing and decorating it appropriately, landscaping the garden, and even hobby farming. Here there is a colonisation of a private place within a place, and an inward-working lifestyle strategy which may be for show, but is not a basis for joining in. Several aspects of such strategies can be seen in the following examples:

'The key factor in choice of Reynoldston was the house rather than the character of the village' (G95)

'Not really involved in village organisations although asked to belong' (G77).

'Replaced windows with replicas of old ones as far as was possible. . . architect helped design the drive' (G6).

The lifestyle strategies exhibited here combine the cognitive form of materialistic culture with the predominance of life-interests in the work and private spheres (Eder's Schema's 2 and 3).

These four strategies do not represent the only ones found amongst rural middle class residents, but they do permit a number of broad conclusions about class and culture in rural arenas. First, lifestyle strategies do appear to be aligned to some extent with those suggested by Eder. Secondly, lifestyle strategies do not, however, draw exclusively on any one class texture, and they are not connected with distinct life-worlds. Thirdly, risks to the village are spread unevenly amongst these groups. For example, risks to the village environment threaten all lifestyle strategy groups, but risk to particular community amenities or political stabilities will not affect 'move in for self and show' households. Finally, cultural textures of class and of the rural in some cases reflect class relations associated with cultural capital, bureaucracy and strategies for economic accumulation. Thus the 'village regulator' and 'move in for self and show' quoted earlier were a senior manager and a private sector service worker respectively. Their rural lifestyles may well be conditioned by their 'habitus' of bureaucratic and marketing practices in the workplace.

CONCLUSION

We are not seeking to suggest Eder's work as a template for analysing comprehensively the culture of the rural middle classes. Rather we have selected out some of his ideas which seem to inform our conceptualisation of the connections between class and culture. Eder does not problematise issues of ethnicity, gender and sexuality to the extent that we would want him to. Equally, the categories of migrants identified in our study do to some extent cut across his categories in their characteristics. However, we do argue that he offers scope for understandings of rural culture beyond those perhaps rather essentialist tools of cultural capital and positional consumption. What the study of middle classes in the Gower suggests is that the notion of cultural texture may be most helpful in clarifying the links between class and collective action in rural areas undergoing rapid social recomposition. Indeed, rurality does seem to be implicated as a contributor to class formation rather than merely being associated with the actions of particular middle classes. Eder's guidelines on class-specific cultures are also useful. However, the study shows that the specific lifestyle strategies employed by middle class rural residents do not conform directly to those suggested by Eder. Lifestyle strategies appear to draw on different interpretative schemes, take different cognitive forms, and inhabit different life-worlds. All of which, it seems to us, represents a healthy reminder to avoid essentialist tools of class analysis when studying the interconnections between class and rurality.

REFERENCES

Bourdieu, P. (1984) *Distinction*, Routledge and Kegan Paul, London.
Bowen, E. (1940) *Wales: a study in geography and history*, University of Wales Press, Cardiff.
Cloke, P., Phillips, M. and Rankin, D. (1991) 'Middle class housing choice: channels of entry into Gower, South Wales', in A. Champion and C. Watkins (eds.), *People in the countryside*, Paul Chapman, London, 38–52.
Cloke, P., Doel, M., Matless, D., Phillips, M. and Thrift, N. (1994) *Writing the rural: five cultural geographies*, Paul Chapman, London.
Cloke, P., Phillips, M. and Thrift, N. (1995) 'The new middle classes and the social constructs of rural living', in T. Butler and M. Savage (eds.), *Social change and the middle classes*, UCL Press, London, 220–240.
Cloke, P., Phillips, M. and Thrift, N. (1998) *Moving to rural idylls*, Paul Chapman, London.
Day, G., Rees, G. and Murdoch, J. (1989) 'Social change, rural localities and the state: the restructuring of rural Wales', *Journal of Rural Studies*, **5**, 227–244.
de Certeau, M. (1984) *The practice of everyday life*, University of California Press, Berkeley.
Dreyfus, H. and Rabinow, P. (1993) 'Can there be a science of existential structure and social meaning?', in C. Calhoun, E. Li Puma and M. Postone (eds.), *Bourdieu, critical perspectives*, Polity, Cambridge, 35–44.
Eder, K. (1993) *The new politics of class*, Sage, London.
Emery, F. (1965) 'Edward Lhuyd and some of his Glamorgan correspondents: a view of Gower in the 1690's', *Transactions of the Honorable Society of Cymmrodorion*, 59–114.
Emery, F. (1971) 'The Norman Conquest and the medieval period', in W. Balchin (ed.) *Swansea and its regions*, University College of Swansea, Swansea, 147–161.
Giddens, A. (1991) *Modernity and self-identity*, Polity, Cambridge.
Goldthorpe, J. (1982) 'On the service class, its formation and future', in A. Giddens and G. MacKenzie (eds.), *Social class and the division of labour*, Cambridge University Press, Cambridge, 162–185.
Lamont, M. (1992) *Money, morals and manners*, Chicago University Press, Chicago.
Lash, S. (1990) *Sociology of postmodernism*, Routledge, London.
Miller, S. (1996) 'Class, power and social construction: issues of theory and application in thirty years of rural studies', *Sociologia Ruralis*, **36**, 93–116.
Pahl, R. (1995) 'Review: *Writing the rural* and *Family, economy and community*', *Rural History*, **6**, 119–122.
Phillips, M. (1993) 'Rural gentrification and the processes of class colonisation', *Journal of Rural Studies*, **9**, 123–140.

Savage, M., Barlow, J., Dickens, P. and Fielding, T. (1992) *Property, bureaucracy and culture: middle class formation in contemporary Britain*, Routledge, London.

Smith, N. (1979) 'Towards a theory of gentrification: a back to the city movement of capital not people', *American Planning Association Journal*, **45**, 538–548.

Wright, E. (1978) *Class, crisis and the state*, New Left Books, London.

Wright, E. (1985) *Classes*, Verso, London.

10

MIDDLE CLASS MOBILITY, RURAL COMMUNITIES AND THE POLITICS OF EXCLUSION

JONATHAN MURDOCH and GRAHAM DAY

INTRODUCTION

The question of what constitutes the rural provides an implicit backdrop to many studies in the sub-disciplines of rural geography and rural sociology. This is something of a legacy, a hangover from times when rural/urban distinctions were simply common sense, taken-for-granted. These distinctions are, naturally, of long standing. Murdoch and Pratt (1993), for instance, have suggested that during the extended phase often termed 'modernism' – that period which broadly covers industrialisation and urbanisation in the West – rural and urban space came to be functionally separated into two distinct spheres. However, with a shift to what has come to be termed, rather problematically, 'postmodernism', this functional separation has broken down. The boundary between urban and rural space seems increasingly porous and so there is continuing dispute over the status of any distinction between the two. Counterurbanisation – urban-to-rural patterns of migration – has been pivotal in undermining many of the key distinctions previously assumed between the urban and the rural. It now seems that rural areas possess fewer and fewer distinctive defining characteristics as their populations come to take on more and more of the features of the urban realm.

Consequently, categorisations of rurality are now hard to substantiate: those based upon indices such as population density tend to be dismissed as static and positivist, while more complex definitions of rural economy and rural society tend to be subsumed within processes – notably migration – that evidently span both urban and rural spheres. Thus, Marc Mormont can ask 'Who is rural?' and 'How is it possible to be rural?' (Mormont 1990). He accepts that the functional separation which gave a coherence to rural space has broken down and that it is now hard to define any specifically rural economies and societies. Instead Mormont distinguishes between users of 'rural' space, stressing that these users are not necessarily local or rural but might be located in a whole variety of situations. He also discusses representations of rurality and the way these can frame uses and activities. Moreover, as Keith Halfacree (1993) has shown, these representations to some extent 'float free' from any rural reality. Again they do not provide secure grounding for definitions of the rural. Such difficulties perhaps culminate in Keith Hoggart's (1990) demand that we should 'do away' with the rural, itself an echo of John Urry's earlier (1984) claim that the rural is a 'chaotic' conception.

We take these concerns as our starting point in this chapter not because we wish to rehearse the many arguments which now surround the concept 'rural' – these have in any case become rather stale – but because we treat them as read: the rural is a deeply problematic concept that needs setting in a new context. By this we mean it can no longer be simply counterposed to the urban. The rural is far more complex than this; it has splintered into many ruralities, and it is far from clear that these have much in common with each other. Thus Chris Philo (1992) calls attention to the multiple rural realities which are lived by a whole host of varied groups and actors many of whom are situated at some distance from dominant conceptions of rurality. As Philo indicates, these multiple ruralities provide a welcome new agenda for rural studies (see Cloke and Little 1997). At the same time, however, they take us still further from any coherent conception of a singular reality which can legitimately be called 'rural'.

In this chapter we wish to illustrate how one particular version of the rural may currently be in the process of (re)construction. We propose that the rural, although the subject of many competing, and often conflicting, representations, may now be (re)gaining some coherence within sets of discourses and practices concerned primarily with nature and community. In essence our argument is that the rural is being recast as social actors seek out new forms of natural and communal stability within the context of increasingly globalised forces and relations.

We begin by asking why 'community' has become of such concern in recent times. In response, we propose that, paradoxically, the answer is given in part by reference to the forces of globalisation that might more usually be considered to be undermining the foundations of communal life. Often, in fact, these forces presage the reinvention of community in forms which derive from how we (both academics and lay people) have *imagined* it to have been in the past. As we will show, in contemporary rural contexts this is exemplified most clearly in the relationships between communities and sets of mobile middle class incomers, amongst whom an imaginary past is frequently drawn upon in a manner which mirrors all too readily their location in the social formations of the present. This type of reinvention may well be based on the desire to find elements of stability and certainty within a globalising world. We suggest that beyond the community which they are constructing these 'new communitarians' have very different identities, and are closely involved in the emerging global order, but that within the community they seek to retreat from the modern world by selectively excluding its influence. In this regard they may practise the politics of exclusion towards other social groups and categories whose presence does not 'fit' their conception of what constitutes a 'local', 'rural' community.

The community has, of course, long been a subject of concern to rural sociologists and has to some extent become a 'tainted' concept within sociological analysis (see Day and Murdoch 1993 for a brief summary of its troubled history). In this context, we wish to stress that we are not suggesting that the rural is yet again the key site for the discovery of 'real' communities. Rather, we are concerned with how social actors – i.e. members of the mobile middle class – are now redefining 'rural' communities in the likeness of 'real' communities. It is as if these actors have adopted rather outmoded sociological characterisations of the rural community – i.e. holism, consensual social relations, small-scale, and so on – and attempted to put them into practice. In so doing they have also acted upon some long-standing assumptions about rural life and the rural environment – the rural as a 'civilised retreat' (Lowe *et al.* 1995) – and have sought rather systematically to bring these into being. Thus the rural is recast within these assumptions, and related practices, as a particular type of social space, one amenable to certain conceptions of communal living. In what follows we seek to explore some of the reasons why such conceptions are now being imposed and some of the consequences that stem from such impositions.

COMMUNITY IN AN ERA OF GLOBALISATION

The idea of 'community' drops in and out of favour at regular intervals. Currently, while, on the one hand, the forces of globalisation stalk the world, rupturing communal ties in a seemingly arbitrary fashion, on the other, responses to the same forces seem to strengthen local alliances and identities, albeit in markedly new ways (Fisher and Kling 1993; Hall 1993). The increasing globalisation of social life has not, therefore, resulted in community being consigned to the 'dustbin of history' for there is currently a revival of interest in its utility and meaning (most evident in the work of Etzioni 1995). Moreover, certain commentators have interpreted the shift from modernism to postmodernism as marking the end of abstractions such as 'society' and a return to communities, the latter seen as multiple sources of agency and power. As Zygmunt Bauman (1992: 134) puts it, 'postmodernity, the age of contingency *fur sich*, of self-conscious agency, is for the thinking person also the age of community: of the lust for community, search for community, invention of community, imagining community'.

To show how the reinvention of community can be tied into accounts of globalisation in economic and social life we turn briefly to Lash and Urry's recent (1994) book *Economies of signs and space*. In this text it is argued that the contemporary global order (or, perhaps, disorder) is now best characterised as a 'structure of flows', a 'decentred set of economies of signs in space' (p. 4). These flows, which seem increasingly subject to 'time–space distanciation', in which time and space 'empty out' (Giddens 1990), consist of capital, labour, commodities, information and images. All these components are increasingly disembedded from concrete space and time as their mobility is steadily increased. Lash and Urry provide a number of examples of such flows: 24-hour world financial markets, increasingly globalised cultural industries, new information technologies, the global restructuring of manufacturing and service industries along so-called 'post-Fordist' lines, and so on. The net effect of this new structural (dis)order of flows on people seems to be a 'flattening out of economic, social and political life', as time–space compression (the speed at which the flows sweep through the world or the world is swept into the flows) both empties out meaning and creates new forms of 'ontological insecurity' and anxiety (Giddens 1991).

The story does not, however, end there, in a bleak dystopic vision of a placeless, meaningless world. Lash and Urry are keen to stress that new opportunities for social action are provided by the new world of flows:

> 'There is an ongoing process of detraditionalisation in which social agents are increasingly "set free" from the heteronomous control or monitoring of social structures in order to be self-monitoring or self-reflexive. This accelerating individualisation process is a process in which agency is set free from structure, a process in which, further, it is structural change itself in modernisation that, so to speak, forces agency to take on powers that heretofore lay in social structures themselves' (Lash and Urry 1994: 4–5).

In their view, 'reflexivity' characterises the new (post)modern period and this is of two types: firstly, 'cognitive' reflexivity which refers to monitoring of the self and of the self's socio-political roles; secondly, 'aesthetic' reflexivity which refers to both self-interpretation and the interpretation of background social practices (p. 50). Lash and Urry place great stress on the latter which they feel is evident in both consumption practices (the aestheticisation of everyday life – see Featherstone 1991) and in understandings of space (new interpretations of, emphases upon, place) and time (a widespread refusal of clock time and any sort of utilitarian calculation of temporal organisation). Moreover:

> 'Aesthetic or hermeneutic reflexivity is embodied in the background assumptions, in the unarticulated practices in which meaning is routinely created in 'new' communities – in subcultures, in imagined communities and in the 'invented' communities' of, for example, ecological and other late twentieth century social movements' (Lash and Urry 1994: 6).

People come to understand that there are many times and many spaces, not just those currently evident in their own society:

> 'To be reflexive is to have some sense of the diverse paths and patterns travelled by different societies in different periods… And… it is in a cultural sense possible now to 'travel in time', to move into the future or back into various pasts, and to simulate such periods through complex and sophisticated encounters with the cultural products, images and displays of different times' (Lash and Urry 1994: 227).

Thus, in present day England, it seems that 'nostalgia is everywhere' (p. 247), people long for 'memory with the pain taken out' (Lowenthal 1985: 8) as they turn their backs on the instantaneous times, incalculable risks and uncertain futures of the world of flows; they look to the past, to golden ages, as times of certainty and security.

As part of this nostalgic retreat there is a reassessment of place, as a resistance to both placelessness and the instantaneity of time. Places are sought out which bear distinctive traces of the past and which are 'heavy with time' (Lowenthal 1985, quoted in Lash and Urry 1994: 250). Particularly treasured places often resonate with romanticised notions of 'community'. While the (supposedly) secure and stable communities of yesteryear are now clearly of the past, they are nevertheless ripe for reinvention. Thus:

> 'to a greater or lesser extent we are not so much thrown into communities, but decide which communities to throw ourselves into. . . the invention of communities is a sort of conduct which we more frequently enter into. New communities are being ever more frequently invented, so that such invention of community, such innovation becomes almost chronic' (Lash and Urry 1994: 316).

For Lash and Urry the reinvention of community (and the associated self) arises from aesthetic reflexivity. Furthermore, although the new communities are by no means necessarily marked by the physical proximity of their members (the world of flows – communication technologies, mobility – has often rendered this past necessity redundant), in a world that comes to be characterised by increasing impersonality, face-to-face interaction may gain in desirability, becoming almost as valuable a positional good (Hirsch 1976) as landscape and environment.

More and more, then, it seems that people have the ability to choose the type of time and place that they might inhabit. However, this choice is not equally available to all. As Quilley (1995) has pointed out in his review of *Economies of signs and space*, aesthetic reflexivity almost by definition is an attribute of the middle class. Interpretation of self and social context can be, and is, conducted from within almost any culture, but such interpretation must depend, to some extent, upon the possession of sufficient cultural resources to attain some reflexive distance from the world of flows. It is, then, worth considering more closely the relationship between community and middle class in this new global (dis)order. We do this in the context of so-called rural communities, those communities where the middle class has gone in search of the timeless values and securities they believe to have been afforded traditionally by life in rural England.

REMAKING RURAL COMMUNITIES

The Rural and Community

Within this narrative of globalisation, the pressures associated with an emerging world of flows seem to be motivating members of the middle class to seek stability and security in many areas of social life. An especially powerful signifier of security and timelessness in Britain, particularly in England, has been the countryside. Affluent sections of English society have long seen the countryside as emblematic of all that is truly valuable in the national culture and psyche. As the English planner Thomas Sharpe put it in 1944: 'the English countryside may be claimed to be one of the supreme achievements of civilisation'; whilst the editor of *Country Life*, a magazine that is devoted to the maintenance of many features of this achievement, recently said: 'From the beginning *Country Life* has embodied a way of life that many people believe to be the most civilised in the world' (both cited in Lowe *et al.* 1995). The significance of rural space as a cultural arena in which the hopes, values and prejudices of dominant social groups can be played out appears to be in almost direct contrast to its economic importance (Williams 1975): as rural areas have been progressively emptied of diverse economic activities so they have become a palimpsest on which dominant representations can be imposed. Thus the rural can be reconstituted as new aspirations motivate new social practices.

Rural areas, therefore, have a traditional place in the 'bourgeois universe' as islands of stability in a frenetic capitalist world. Moreover, because such areas have lost many of their traditional economic functions, they also hold out the possibility of social recomposition for those groups seeking an improved quality of life. They provide a key arena in which the practices of aesthetic reflexivity identified by Lash and Urry can be expressed. Evidence that rural areas are currently playing this role is provided by Savage *et al.* (1992) who have demonstrated, in the course of an excellent account of middle class formation in the United Kingdom, that such areas are being used by this class to distinguish itself from others. Savage *et al.* propose that the middle-class has privileged access to the economic and cultural assets necessary to make key choices over living and working arrangements. Particularly marked in the United Kingdom, they argue, is the rise of owner occupation and the acquisition of property assets which can be transformed in turn into cultural capital. This applies not just to housing but to whole neighbourhoods, as the processes of gentrification bestow cultural and economic value on particularly favoured areas. Using available assets, the middle class seeks to create stability in an increasingly globalised environment.

Such stability, as we have intimated, can be perhaps most readily located in rural areas. Savage *et al.* (1992), drawing upon work conducted by Short *et al.* (1986) in Berkshire, argue that it is rural areas which are most amenable to being shaped in the preferred image of the middle class. Murdoch and Marsden (1994) also investigate this process in a series of land development case studies in an area close to London. They note that the processes of social and geographical mobility, first identified by Ray Pahl in the 1960s (Pahl 1966) and subsequently explored by Newby (1979), are leading to the reconstitution of many communities in the rural areas of the south of England, resulting in particular types of environment emerging which in turn prove attractive to specific social groups (while the middle class are not the only such group, they are particularly dominant in the rural areas of this region). A cumulative process is set in train whereby new residents, overwhelmingly middle class, seeking a particular form of communal life which they *believe* exists in rural areas, move into places which would seem to favour the existence of appropriately rural communities. Once established in such places these new middle class residents act to enhance, or bring into being, the qualities they value; in the process, they may indeed attempt to impose their own exclusive definitions of community upon others. For example, they create institutions which allow certain types of activities to be conducted which act to bring together many of the recent in-migrants (one of the villages studied by Murdoch and Marsden boasted more than 20 societies, ranging from a drama company to a recital group). While these institutions allow certain types of resident to participate fully in village life (the activities just mentioned are overwhelmingly middle class in character) they may also, wittingly or unwittingly, exclude others (as was the case in the village cited – see Murdoch and Marsden 1994, Chapter 4).

Communal activities in the new rural communities also extend to political action and there is now a substantial literature dealing with middle class domination of the essential informal political and social activities (see for instance, Cloke and Little 1990; Lynn and Davis-Smith 1992; Murdoch and Marsden 1994; Parry *et al.* 1992). This is by no means a new situation. The political mechanisms through which middle class influence is exercised have been examined in some detail by Lowe (1977) who argues that the rise in localistic environmental protest has been closely related to both social change and the scope for public participation in planning. The existence of the planning system, therefore, would seem to provide an arena for middle class political representation (see Abram, Murdoch and Marsden, Chapter 13, this volume). Moreover, within this arena decisions are taken which have real material effects. Planning thus provides not only a focus for middle class representation but also a means whereby these representations can be translated into actual spatial forms. Cloke and Little (1990) show that this process may well become self-reinforcing for as more middle class incomers take up residence they too will tend to become involved in local politics and will work to ensure that restrictive planning policies remain in existence. Furthermore, they argue, the planning system itself is structured in such a way as to demand a relatively high standard of education from those who choose to participate in it. Thus the middle class will be favoured as its members are likely to have the social, technical and communicative assets required to make successful representations, allowing it to dominate not just particular forms of housing, labour markets and communities, but also political institutions.

The thrust of these studies is that the middle class – through the activities of well-organised action and amenity groups – is coming to dominate the politics of rural areas. Such political activity is part of what Savage *et al.* (1992) characterise more generally as a 'defensive politics' oriented to the protection of economic, cultural and property assets. The aim is to protect the properties and neighbourhoods which form the core of middle class space from unwelcome development and, by extension, unwelcome social groups.

The movement of these residents into rural communities reflects the desire for a particular kind of living space, a space which extends beyond the house itself out into the surrounding environment. This environment is physical – aesthetically pleasing buildings, open space, countryside – and social – being part of village life, having a sense of belonging. For these middle class in-comers, rural life *means* life in a community; and if no such community exists, it will be created, as in-comers weave together the old with the new into a 'hybrid' rurality, defined in such a way as to exclude all the pernicious effects of the urban modern world that they have moved away from, such as anonymity, crime, noise, and so on. They thus reflexively assert a particular aesthetic, one which directly combines aspects of the rural environment and community. In these 'new' rural communities 'old' certainties can be renewed and security re-established; thus new rural communities serve as sites for 'anchoring' middle class identities (Cloke and Thrift 1990) as attempts are made to find shelter from the world of ever accelerating global flows. New communities play out a parody of tradition: selecting certain features deemed to be 'timeless' (such as aspects of the physical fabric) and attempting to reinstate these as emblems of a particularly valued way of life.

Community and Nature

The attractiveness of rural areas does not come, however, simply from the widely held belief that they are the location for 'real' communities. The rural is also seen as 'natural'; it has more 'environment' than urban areas. As Giddens (1994: 77) has suggested, there is still some sense in such a view, for 'nature':

'means that which lies undisturbed, that which is created independently of human activity. In one way the image is quite false, for the countryside is nature subordinated to human plans. Yet "nature" in this meaning does preserve traits long associated with its separation from human contrivance'.

While, as Giddens emphasises, nature has been brought firmly within the ambit of human systems, nature as that domain free from human contrivance is still more easily imagined in the countryside than in the urban environment and this would seem to provide a key motive for counterurbanisation amongst many middle class families.

This theme is taken up in Michael Mayerfield Bell's (1994) study of the Hampshire village of 'Childerley'. In this work Bell aims to explore the villager's social experience of nature and to relate this experience to the conduct of social life. He chooses to study a village in the south east of England because he believes it is in such a place that 'the limits of the city and the edge of nature are constant topics of discussion, for [this] is a conceptual zone which is neither raw nor cooked' (p. 6). In this village the thoughts and conversations of people return again and again to the question of whether it is really 'the country' (p. 21).

Bell notes that, as in most other Hampshire villages, the residents of Childerley are white, mainly Tory, Christian and Protestant. Yet within this homogeneity he discerns a considerable amount of diversity, coordinated along the axis of class. He argues that in fact class is central to the lives of the villagers: they move in relatively discrete 'subcommunities' and have distinct cultural orientations. Most Childerleyeans, he believes, come from what he terms the moneyed (i.e. middle and upper) classes while around 40 percent are relatively 'poor'. Drawing upon Erving Goffman's notion of 'regions', in which certain behaviours are appropriate – 'frontstage' and 'backstage' (see Goffman 1959) – Bell characterises the two groups as having distinct 'styles'. The poorer villagers have what he terms a 'back door style'. By this he means 'a style that is more informal, group-oriented, local interactive, and experiential'. The moneyed residents, on the other hand, have an opposite 'front door style' which is 'more formal, individualistic, far-flung, private and distanced' (p. 52). These styles are expressed in almost all areas of communal life, from bodily presentation, to behaviour in the pub and the arrangement of village gardens.

Having established that the village is riven by class, Bell goes on to argue that what all villagers have in common is that they 'routinely deplore that this is so' (p. 28). He believes that Childerleyeans regard class as 'morally ambiguous' (p. 78). They recognise that it structures their lives but they do not wish to be bound by this structuring:

> 'Most moneyed villagers do not enjoy thinking about themselves merely as "one of those rich people"... and the ordinary villagers do not enjoy thinking of themselves as merely the poor... What they do feel good about is being someone who lives in the country and more than that, being a "country person", a "village person", a "country girl", a "villager", or a "countryman born and bred"' (Bell 1994: 86).

In the eyes of the people of Childerley, the virtues of the country seem to be two-fold: firstly, it embodies 'nature' (as distinct from the city which is fully 'social'); and secondly, they see communities in the country as being the 'real thing'. Thus:

> 'In all their varied forms for varied villagers, nature and community are the hedgerows that bound and define countryside talk. By these landmarks, Childerleyeans know when they are in the country, and when they are not.... [Moreover,] [v]illagers often interwove themes of nature and *gemeinschaft*, passing easily from one to the other, both when they described the rural idyll and Childerley's failure to live up to it' (Bell 1994: 95, 97).

Class and country are two sides of the same coin: deploring their class identities Childerleyeans find solace in an alternative identity – the countryperson – but they express this identity in ways which are redolent of class:

> 'With a country identity comes a sense of legitimacy – of rights and motivations appropriate to country people. Such a sense is an important resource to have in

life. As country people, Childerleyeans have access not only to another language for thinking and talking about class, but also class motivations and class conflict' (Bell 1994: 108).

Through this alternative language and source of identity both the moneyed and the poorer villagers gain a secure moral foundation for their lives: the former because they do not have to feel embarrassed being country people and the latter because they gain a secure place in the 'natural order'. The security of the country identity derives, Bell argues, from pastoralism – that gradient of life forms which live close to nature and far away from nature. Through pastoralism country people and country ways of life are connected to nature. This is important because the villagers regard nature as 'free from social interests'; it is 'something that stands apart from the selfishness, greed, power, and domination they see in social life' (p. 138). However, in Bell's analysis the villagers cannot 'escape' completely from their social selves in this way for they go into nature in the same way they go into the rest of their lives: the moneyed resident goes through the front door and the poorer resident through the back door. Thus 'the villagers' 'vocabulary of nature' closely resembles their vocabulary of society' (p. 228); moneyed villagers find in nature privacy and formality while the poorer villagers see informality, liveliness and animation. The villagers bring the natural realm into line with their social selves; ultimately their understanding of each is made to correspond.

That the people of Childerley stand in such a close relationship with their environment should not surprise us, neither should the centrality of 'nature' to their conceptual schemes. It is clear by now that 'green' environments are favoured repositories of those middle class assets identified by Savage et al., ensuring that they become bound into the processes of aesthetic reflexivity to which Lash and Urry refer. Hence, once middle class members begin to establish themselves in these places, using their political and cultural resources they begin actively to mould the social and material shape of the locale, often attempting to reproduce certain dominant conceptions of the rural (Thrift 1989, Urry 1990). We can also go on to speculate that rural areas would seem particularly favoured locations for the establishment of new middle class communities in England, not only because they are viewed as 'close to nature' and therefore act as a source of moral worth – but also because they tend to be monoracial and mononational spaces (Murdoch 1995). Furthermore, rural communities appear to provide a key site for the maintenance of 'traditional' family relationships of a kind that may be seen as conducive to stabilisation; for example, Gordon and Forrest (1995: 46–47) have recently shown that lone parents and cohabitees are over-whelmingly confined to the cities while the traditional family is dominant in rural areas. Thus, this particular socio-spatial context enables the emergent middle class to re-work already existing dominant cultural discourses associated with the English countryside, characterised as 'a bucolic vision of an ordered, comforting, peaceful and, above all, deferential past' (Thrift 1989: 26), in ways which facilitate the constitution of 'new traditionalist' communities (Urry 1990).

No matter that this is a mythical rural past, for these elements can be fused into a new idyllic conception of rurality, which the middle class can then act to put into effect in its reconstituted communities.

However, the new middle class ruralites do not live the majority of their lives within the umbrella of the community. As has been noted by Charlesworth and Cochrane (1994: 1734), these residents need to look beyond the immediate rural locale because they are thoroughly embedded in wider regional and sub-regional networks. While maintaining the positional status of their own 'retreats' they seek to profit from wider sets of economic linkages. They endeavour to exclude undesirable forms of development and undesirable social formations. As Charlesworth and Cochrane (1994: 1734) say of such groups in the south east of England:

> 'In one sense they are citizens of the south-east. . . but political arrangements are such that they are able to protect their enclave within it'.

The processes employed to protect these enclaves can lead to these communities taking on ever more rigidly that white, Tory, Christian complexion that Bell discerned in Childerley. Moreover, as the economic and cultural value of these retreats increases, as it inevitably must, their class complexion will become more homogeneous as the poorer residents, the working class, are driven out, along with other marginal rural groups (for example, gypsies and other travellers). Conversely, the 'ghettoisation' of ethnic minority groups within *urban* communities can be understood in the context of the 'traditional' exclusive role accorded to the countryside as new, white, middle class communities come into being (Lowe *et al.* 1995).

CONCLUSION: WHAT IS A RURAL COMMUNITY?

It is evident that rural communities yield conflicting perspectives on the term community. They present us with, on the one hand, stable arenas in which social relations and identities can be forged in ways which exclude, to some degree, market and economic relations, while, on the other, they exhibit defensive and exclusive tendencies which reproduce some of the most pernicious forms of social closure. In general this kind of tension has been long understood and the term 'community' comes to us loaded with ambiguities (cf. Nisbet 1966). It is therefore by no means clear whether this concept belongs to a radical or emancipatory discourse. Undoubtedly, it arouses suspicion on the part of many, who discern in its usage a harking back to a more puritanical era, one where personal freedom (as manifest, for instance, in the postmodern politics of identity) was sublimated to a restrictive social whole. Iris Marion Young (1992), for instance, argues from a feminist perspective that community necessarily privileges unity over difference and limits one's understanding of others from their point of view. She warns that the:

'desire for community relies on the same desire for social wholeness and identification that underlies racism and ethnic chauvinism on the one hand and political sectarianism on the other' (Young 1992: 302).

Young's position derives from her belief that the desire to bring things into unity, to define an identity or separate off a totality always involves excluding some elements, so ensuring that certain categories or attributes will lie 'outside' or 'beyond' whatever is being defined; thus the return to a concern with community may endanger the assertion of difference, something Young sees as more practicable in the streets of the city than perhaps in the rural village.

The sense of community Young wishes to retain, while conforming to a postmodern sensibility, is weak: it merely specifies a set of guidelines which should inform social relations centred on difference. Our analysis of the trends which are leading to the reassertion of the importance of rural communities seems to indicate that the degree of openness – the postmodern celebration of difference and diversity – to which Young appears to adhere, can imply, for many who experience it, an extraordinary degree of uncertainty. In such a context, current reassertions of, and concern with, questions of 'community' and 'belonging' might be said to represent efforts to engage with the states of insecurity that arise as uncertainty becomes so prevalent in many areas of modern life. However, the outcomes of efforts undertaken to banish insecurity would seem to lend some support to Young's worries about communities in general. The 'new traditionalist' rural community is, to a considerable extent, founded on the attempt to create a distance between affluent living environments and the world of flows. As has so often been the case in England, the countryside is the place where this distance is felt to be greatest. Michael Bell's study of Childerley, for instance, showed that the village was valued by its residents for its 'natural' qualities, for its distance from the 'artificial' urban realm. The security of the country identity, as Bell emphasised, is derived from proximity to nature.

If security and solace is found in 'nature' then it is to be expected that middle class residents, having gone to some trouble to seek this out, will endeavour to protect the naturalness of their neighbourhoods against external threats. Most often this comes in the form of development, as Murdoch and Marsden (1994) have described. Residents will form new associations – action groups, amenity societies and so on – to resist any fundamental reshaping of their settlements and communities, using the state in the form of the planning system to systematically exclude any large-scale or untoward development. One, often unintended, side effect is the exclusion of certain social groups who, as members of other national (albeit 'urban') cultures, might legitimately make some claim on the countryside. Sometimes, however, the exclusion is more systematic and conscious. Murdoch and Marsden cite the case of a village school teacher who notes approvingly that parents are attracted to the village by the school because it has almost no children on free school meals and is a place where all children speak English. This accords with other aspects of rural racism which have been highlighted by the Commission for Racial Equality (Jay 1992). Thus the forms of community that are likely to emerge may bear out Young's depressing prognosis, becoming totalising, homogeneous institutions which suppress difference and exclude the unwanted.

The question remains, therefore, how communities can be prevented from travelling down an exclusionary road. There is no ready answer here. Communitarians such as Etzioni (1995) seem to hold that a national society needs to ensure that individual communities do not lock in values that are abhorrent to a wider majority, and that some higher institutions must prevent communities from turning against one another: the national community in this sense should act as a 'community of the communities'. How this is to be achieved in practice is far from clear. While national education systems, legal norms and media may spread common modes of tolerant behaviour, one key impediment to their implementation is the way in which globalising trends serve to heighten the distinctions between social groups. Not only are such trends increasing levels of anxiety, thus prompting the search for secure communal identities, but they also enable some groups to participate easily in many different social and economic arenas while others find themselves increasingly excluded from almost all. Favoured groups act to differentiate themselves from these others, and embrace associations with the like-minded and like-bodied. In short, they reflexively establish discrete communities. In the process, the rural, as an arena which is regarded as close to nature and which is seen as steeped in tradition, becomes redefined as the almost exclusive domain of the white middle class.

REFERENCES

Bauman, Z. (1992) *Intimations of postmodernity*, Routledge, London.
Bell, M.M. (1994) *Childerley*, University of Chicago Press, London.
Charlesworth, J. and Cochrane, A. (1994) 'Tales of the suburbs: the local politics of growth in the south-east of England', *Urban Studies*, **31**, 1723–1738.
Cloke, P. and Little, J. (1990) *The rural state?*, Oxford University Press, Oxford.
Cloke, P. and Little, J. (eds.) (1997) *Contested countryside cultures*, Routledge, London.
Cloke, P. and Thrift, N. (1990) 'Class and change in rural Britain', in P. Lowe, T. Marsden and S. Whatmore (eds.), *Rural restructuring*, David Fulton, London, 165–181.
Day, G. and Murdoch, J. (1993) 'Locality and community: coming to terms with place', *Sociological Review*, **41**, 82–111.
Etzioni, A. (1995) *The spirit of community*, Harper Collins, London.
Featherstone, M. (1991) *Consumer culture and postmodernism*, Sage, London.
Fisher, R. and Kling, J. (1993) *Mobilising the community: local politics in the era of the global city*, Sage, London.
Giddens, A. (1990) *The consequences of modernity*, Polity, Cambridge.
Giddens, A. (1991) *Modernity and self-identity*, Polity, Cambridge.
Giddens, A. (1994) 'Living in a post-traditional society', in U. Beck, A. Giddens and S. Lash, *Reflexive modernisation: politics, tradition and aesthetics in the modern social order*, Polity, Cambridge, 56–109.
Goffman, E. (1959) *The presentation of the self in everyday life*, New York, Doubleday.
Gordon, D. and Forrest, R. (1995) *People and place 2: social and economic distinctions in England*, School of Advanced Urban Studies, Bristol.

Halfacree, K. (1993) 'Locality and social representation: space, discourse and alternative definitions of the rural', *Journal of Rural Studies*, **9**, 23–37.

Hall, S. (1993) 'Culture, community, nation', *Cultural Studies*, **7**, 349–363.

Hirsch, F. (1976) *The social limits to growth*, Harvard University Press, Cambridge, Massachusetts.

Hoggart, K. (1990) 'Lets do away with the rural', *Journal of Rural Studies*, **6**, 245–257.

Jay, E. (1992) *'Keep them in Birmingham': challenging racism in south-west England*, Commission for Racial Equality, London.

Lash, S. and Urry, J. (1994) *Economies of signs and space*, Sage, London.

Lowe, P. (1977) 'Access and amenity: a review of local environmental pressure groups in Britain', *Environment and Planning A*, **9**, 35–58.

Lowe, P., Murdoch, J. and Cox, G. (1995) 'A civilised retreat? Anti-urbanism, rurality and the making of an Anglo-centric culture', in P. Healey (ed.), *Managing cities*, Wiley, Chichester, 63–81.

Lowenthal, D. (1985) *The past is a foreign country*, Cambridge University Press, Cambridge.

Lynn, P. and Davis-Smith, J. (1992) *The 1991 National Survey of Voluntary Activity in the UK*, Volunteer Centre, Berkhamstead.

Mormont, M. (1990) 'Who is rural? Or, how to be rural: towards a sociology of the rural', in T. Marsden, P. Lowe and S. Whatmore (eds.), *Rural restructuring*, London, David Fulton, 21–44.

Murdoch, J. (1995) 'Middle-class territory? Some remarks on the use of class analysis in rural studies', *Environment and Planning A*, **26**, 1213–1230.

Murdoch, J. and Marsden, T. (1994) *Reconstituting rurality: class, community and power in the development process*, UCL Press, London.

Murdoch, J. and Pratt, A. (1993) 'Rural studies: modernism, postmodernism and the post-rural', *Journal of Rural Studies*, **9**, 411–427.

Newby, H. (1979) *Green and pleasant land*, Penguin, Harmondsworth.

Nisbet, R. (1966) *The sociological tradition*, Heinemann, London.

Pahl, R. (1966) *Urbs in rure*, Weidenfeld and Nicholson, London.

Parry, G., Moyser, G. and Day, N. (1992) *Political participation and democracy in Britain*, Cambridge University Press, Cambridge.

Philo, C. (1992) 'Neglected rural geographies: a review', *Journal of Rural Studies*, **8**, 193–207.

Quilley, S. (1995) Review of *Economies of signs and space*, *Antipode*, **27**, 101–102.

Savage, M., Barlow, J., Dickens, P. and Fielding, T. (1992) *Property, bureaucracy and culture*, Routledge, London.

Short, J., Fleming, S. and Witt, S. (1986) *Housebuilding, planning and community action*, Routledge and Kegan Paul, London.

Thrift, N. (1989) 'Images of social change', in C. Hamnett, L. McDowell and P. Sarre (eds.), *The changing social structure*, Sage, London, 12–42.

Urry, J. (1984) 'Capitalist restructuring, recomposition and the regions', in T. Bradley and P. Lowe (eds.), *Locality and rurality*, Norwich, Geo Books, 45–64.

Urry, J. (1990) *The tourist gaze*, Sage, London.

Williams, R. (1975) *The country and the city*, London, Chatto and Windus.

Young, I.M. (1992) 'The ideal of community and the politics of difference', in L. Nicholson (ed.), *Feminism/postmodernism*, Routledge, London, 300–323.

11

NEO-TRIBES, MIGRATION AND THE POST-PRODUCTIVIST COUNTRYSIDE

KEITH HALFACREE

'Computers crashing
All around us business fails
The times are hard – or so they say
But I don't believe the Times
And I don't believe the Globe
It's spinning free enough to choose
Your way to go'
('Information Age', Damon Krukowski and Naomi Yang, 1992)[1]

INTRODUCTION

Since Findlay and Graham (1991) drew attention to what they saw as a problem of 'separate development' within population geography, the sub-discipline has begun to take on board more explicitly many recent developments within social theory (White and Jackson 1995). Such concerns have been especially pronounced within migration studies. For example, there have been calls to develop 'multi-method' research (McKendrick 1995) and a 'biographical approach' (Halfacree and Boyle 1993), and there has been renewed appreciation of the value of literary perspectives on the migration experience (King *et al.* 1995). Elsewhere, rural studies have also now largely shrugged off their 'Cinderella complex' (Cloke 1980: 171) regarding theory and have become increasingly integrated into the social science mainstream. This process, too, has involved adapting many of the broader intellectual ideas and terminology of the social sciences to the rural studies' arena (Halfacree 1996a; Phillips 1998).

This chapter contributes to this (re)integration and (re)invigoration of both migration and rural studies by beginning to explore what the French 'postmodern' sociologist Michel Maffesoli's ideas have to say about some aspects of migration to rural Britain. In particular, it employs his concept of 'neo-tribalism' to help understand the emerging but contested shape of the 'post-productivist' countryside (Halfacree and Boyle, Chapter 1, this volume).

THE NEO-TRIBES OF POSTMODERNISM

From the Social to Sociality

Michel Maffesoli has only recently been brought to the attention of English-speaking academics, thanks largely to the efforts of Zygmunt Bauman, Rob Shields and Kevin Hetherington. Maffesoli is an extremely 'postmodern' academic in that his concern is not to produce some 'heroic' modernist statements on contemporary society but with the production of more nuanced and subtle perspectives on what he terms 'sociality'. His central thesis is that sociality has increasingly surpassed the social as the organisational basis of everyday life. Some key differences between sociality and the social are illustrated in Figure 11.1. From this emphasis on sociality, Maffesoli develops a sociology of contemporary life, where the formal abstract structures of the social are played down in contrast to the nebulous 'polydimensionality of the lived experience' (Maffesoli 1989: 4) and an emphasis on the varied 'masks' we adopt in living from day to day (see also Shields 1991a, 1991b). Consequently, in Bauman's (1987) terms, the social scientist needs to be an 'interpreter' rather than a 'legislator' – to speak of mysteries rather than to provide administration (Maffesoli 1987: 76) – and to adopt an 'intellectual open-endedness' (Maffesoli 1987: 81).

From this standpoint, Maffesoli seeks to play down the role of economic (occupational) class in defining and explaining *everyday life*. For him, 'common experience' is the 'true motor of human history' (Maffesoli 1989: 4) and it is both arrogant and erroneous to attempt to reduce this experience to the experience of abstract categories such as 'class'. Indeed, he suggests that the convergence between this 'common experience' and the abstractions of the social – such as economic class – represented a contingent period of human history – modernity. Thus, class based politics, identity and everyday significance is historically relativised as being just one experiential axis for daily life. In the postmodern present, this class-based axis of *identity* is being lost, even if the *process* of class formation – capitalism – remains paramount (Harvey 1993), as we move into an era of identification. Such an understanding also relativises the individualist rhetoric of the New Right:

'It is really the understanding of the present which forces us to relativize, if not to throw overboard, the whole set of the theoretical presuppositions which corresponded to a stage when the *individual* and the *economy* (of the person and of the world) were the two great pivots of social structurations. . . . The heterogeneity of social life, in all its dimensions, is currently making a return in full force to the field of actuality' (Maffesoli 1987: 85, emphasis in original).

Moreover, although the resurgence of heterogeneity within everyday life is challenging for both the social scientist and those engaged in developing radical political projects, it suggests a *puissance* or 'will to live' (Maffesoli 1996: 31) on the part of ordinary people which is irrepressible and a celebration of humanity (see also Baudrillard 1983).

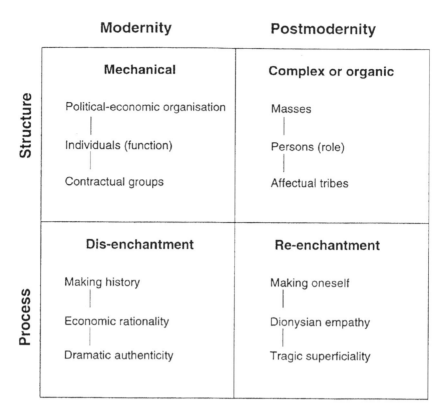

Modernity	Postmodernity
Mechanical	**Complex or organic**
Political-economic organisation	Masses
|	|
Individuals (function)	Persons (role)
|	|
Contractual groups	Affectual tribes
Dis-enchantment	**Re-enchantment**
Making history	Making oneself
|	|
Economic rationality	Dionysian empathy
|	|
Dramatic authenticity	Tragic superficiality

FIGURE 11.1 From the modern social to postmodern sociality (based on Maffesoli 1996)

Neo-tribalism

The concept of 'neo-tribalism' is central to Maffesoli's discussion of postmodern society. The 'neo-' in the term is crucial, as it allows a distinction to be made with traditional tribalism. With both abstract class-based identities and New Right individualism historically relativised as bases of action, new collectivities are emerging. These are defined in terms of a 'multitude of individual acts of *self-identification*' (Bauman 1992: 136, emphasis in original). People are gathering together to 'bathe in the affectual ambience' (Maffesoli 1991: 11) in their search for community and belonging, the loss of which – disillusion with both the Times and the Globe – appears to be the *leit-motif* of the postmodern condition (Giddens 1990; Harvey 1989). These groupings comprise the postmodern neo-tribes[2] and they differ from the 'true' Gemeinschaft communities of 'historical' tribes in that they are actively achieved rather than being something one is born into (Shields 1992: 14) – people are choosing their way to go. They also differ in that an individual can move between different neo-tribal groupings within their everyday life-worlds, as 'neo-tribalism is characterized by fluidity, occasional gatherings and dispersal' (Maffesoli 1996: 76). Hence, we have the fluidity of sociality over the fixity of the social (Figure 11.1). As such, contemporary society can all too easily be taken as the undifferentiated 'mass' so reviled by modernist political thinkers. However, this is too static a picture, as we must recognise a 'mass-tribe dialectic', with the individual being in constant movement between being a member of the mass and belonging to specific 'crystallised' neo-tribes (Maffesoli 1996: 99, 127). In this way, the individual can live a more fulfilling 'plural' existence within the 'polyculturalism' of the social body. Thus, the diversity of an individual's positionality, as stressed by postmodern theory more generally, can begin to be accommodated.

Given their 'worked at' origins and their unstable dialectical relation to the mass, neo-tribes have to be actively monitored and reflected upon by their members in order for them to exist. Indeed, the 'elective sociality' (Maffesoli 1996: 86) of the neo-tribe is one which stresses the existential rewards of just 'being together' with like-minded people, without the need for more instrumental goal-directed behaviour. Nonetheless, an 'internal morality' is apparent and necessary for the tribe to achieve some degree of coherence. Consequently, neo-tribes are unlikely to crystallise for long periods of time – they are 'essentially tragic' (Maffesoli 1996: 78) – as this constant need for self-monitoring ultimately becomes too arduous. This is unlikely to matter much to the individual, who will merely adopt a neo-tribal role elsewhere. The self-monitoring also readily exposes the impracticalities, contradictions and general insufficiency of neo-tribal beliefs. Consequently, neo-tribes are apt to 'inflame imagination most and attract most ardent loyalty when they still reside in the realm of hope' (Bauman 1992: 137).

Nonetheless, it could be argued that Maffesoli has over-stressed the ephemerality of neo-tribes. Perhaps this is because he has failed to develop fully the issue of neo-tribal geographies. On the one hand, his work *is* very geographical in its emphasis on the situatedness of everyday life (Shields 1991a: 4) and the importance he attaches to place as the 'proxemic' grounding of sociality (Maffesoli 1996: 123–148)[3]. Thus, Maffesoli emphasises how a neo-tribal group 'declares itself, delineates its territory and thus confirms its existence... [with] territorial demarcation... [forming] the structural foundation of multiple socialities' (Maffesoli 1996: 137, 141). However, he does not extend this insight much further, apart from the following hint on a future 'social logic':

'Of course, not all these groups survive; but the fact that *some of them assume the various stages of socialization* creates a social 'form' of flexible organization which is rather uneven. .... [This] new social *logic*... risks challenging a good number of our most comfortable sociological analyses. Thus, what was in the not too distant past deemed 'marginal', can no longer be described as such' (Maffesoli 1996: 143–144, first emphases added).

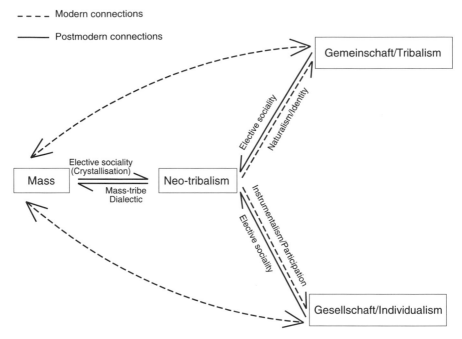

FIGURE 11.2 Locating neo-tribal identities (based on Hetherington 1990; Maffesoli 1996)

The Survival of Neo-tribes

Hetherington (1990, 1994) has described neo-tribes through the concept of the *Bund* (meaning communion/league or federation, after Schmalenbach 1977). He notes the instability of these 'new sociations', suggesting that they are liable to be transformed into either *Gemeinschaft* or *Gesellschaft* structures (Hetherington 1990: 19, 25–34). This tension between neo-tribalism and these alternate states is illustrated in Figure 11.2. Such a tension, between those people happy to move constantly with the mass-tribe dialectic and those wishing to achieve either more or less permanent crystallisations, represents a key arena of struggle within postmodern sociality/society. This contrasts with the relative fixity of the modernist dualism between class identity and individualism, where any sense of an elective sociality is bypassed.

The turn to a *Gemeinschaft* and possibly a tribal condition for the neo-tribe involves a general 're-skilling of identity' beyond neo-tribal parameters. Such a re-skilling, Hetherington suggests, will involve the growth of support networks, empowering friendships, personal fulfilment, local participation and concern, and the emergence of a distinct lifestyle. Hence, the neo-tribe becomes 'naturalised'. In contrast, a turn to a *Gesellschaft* condition involves a re-skilling of participation and a development of more abstract means of empowerment. This would involve the growth of new institutions and actions through institutions, such as the political system. In both circumstances the intensity of the initial neo-tribal arrangement is lost and replaced by routinisation, focusing on either lifestyle or purposive practice.

These first suggestions of the potential survival of neo-tribal ideas in alternative forms do not adequately deal with the geographical dimension. Yet, Maffesoli's emphasis on 'lived spaces', with their own 'emotional geographies', enables us to distinguish, at least conceptually, between emotional geographies which remain in the 'imagination' and those which become materialised 'on the ground'. Drawing on Lefebvre (1991), it can be suggested that it is in the latter case that the neo-tribe will have the greatest chance of longer-term survival, maybe even acquiring a *Gemeinschaft* condition. In short, only by producing the distinctive space suited to its own needs can a neo-tribe survive; and this space needs to be material if its associated routines and forms of behaviour are not to contradict and clash with the routines and forms of behaviour of a rival imaginative geography:

> 'Any "social existence" aspiring or claiming to be "real", but failing to produce its own space, would be a strange entity, a very peculiar kind of abstraction unable to escape from the ideological or even the "cultural" realm. It would fall to the level of folklore and sooner or later disappear altogether, thereby immediately losing its identity, its denomination and its feeble degree of reality' (Lefebvre 1991: 53).

Thus, with the mass-tribe dialectic, we must also expect to see an active tribal strategy of creating spaces which 'guarantee... sociality a necessary security' (Maffesoli 1996: 133). Such a strategy is apparent in struggles over the production of the post-productivist countryside.

NEO-TRIBALISM IN THE POST-PRODUCTIVIST COUNTRYSIDE

Dionysus, Rurality and Institutional Saturation

Maffesoli's work is of immediate relevance to rural researchers in that he recognises the revival of interest in 'things rural' which makes the post produc tivist countryside such an important arena of study. Such a recognition of the contemporary significance of rurality is part of a broader line of reasoning. Specifically, Maffesoli frequently notes how the spectre of Dionysus, the Greek god originally of fruitfulness and vegetation but more often just seen as the god of wine, hangs over his work. Indeed, the 'dionysiac form' (Maffesoli 1996: 19) appears to be his 'spirit of the times', which exists in spite of the 'swarming multiplicity of heterogenous values' (Maffesoli 1991: 12) which surround it.

Dionysus is reflected in a number of traits of postmodern society and our engagement with the postmodern experience. There is the return to a 'more carnal relation to the social world and to the natural environment' (Maffesoli 1987: 85), a more embedded and sensuous experience than the 'colder' objective distancing of modernism. In particular, there is a 're-enchantment' with the world, signified by a greater direct participation in, *inter alia*, nature, the countryside and localism (Maffesoli 1987: 85). Maffesoli talks of the 'horror of emptiness' (Maffesoli 1991: 14) and how this can be countered through the 'poetic act' of dwelling, as reflected in rural second homes and the search for roots (Maffesoli 1991: 15). Overall, the 'aesthetic aura' of postmodernity conjoins a 'communal drive', a 'mystical propensity' and an 'ecological perspective' (Maffesoli 1996: 13), all key features of the post-productivist countryside.

The transition from productivism to post-productivism itself, through which these dionysian values take hold in the countryside, reflects what Maffesoli terms the 'saturation' of the institutions and practices of the modernist social order. Saturation refers to what is regarded as the worn-out nature of our social institutions, which can absorb no more changes and new experiences, just as a saturated sponge can no longer absorb water (Maffesoli 1996: 27, translator's note). Maffesoli concentrates on the saturation of the political order, with politics 'dissolved into everyday life' (Hetherington 1990: 10), the consequence of which is to witness the emergence of:

> 'changes in values; the failure of the myth of progress; the resurgence of the qualitative; the increased devotion to hedonism; the continued preoccupation with the religious; the significance of the image' (Maffesoli 1996: 32).

These changes generate a dionysian re-enchantment of the world through neo-tribalism (see also Melucci 1989).

Aspects of such a saturation and re-enchantment are apparent in the post-productivist countryside (Halfacree and Boyle, Chapter 1, this volume). The overall change in values from seeing the countryside as a space for the rational development of a production-orientated agriculture is clear from the critiques of this model, such as those from an environmental perspective. This critique, furthermore, blends into a feeling that the changes which have taken place, during at least this century, may not reflect any linear idea of progress, given their various costs to the social and physical ecology of rural Britain. At the same time, the growth of leisure and other consumption uses of the countryside (Clark *et al.* 1994) are indicative of the emergence of both a more qualitative evaluation of the countryside and a realisation in some quarters of its hedonistic potential (for example, in its use for music festivals (Hetherington 1992)). Finally, the spirituality of much of the contemporary environmental movement (Dobson 1990) and a heightened interest in earth mysteries, such as ley lines and crop circles, suggests a renewed religious interpretation of the countryside, while all of this change is underpinned by the significance attached to competing social representations or images of the rural (Halfacree 1993), notably the 'rural idyll'.

The Neo-tribalism of the Rural Idyll

In considering the rural idyll a neo-tribal resource for re-enchantment, I examine it here with respect to four of the characteristics of neo-tribalism in general (see also Shields 1992: 15). First, as we have seen, neo-tribalism *elevates symbolic practices* of the here-and-now over goal-directed projects. For such symbolic practices, a key role is given to 'emblematic images' as reference points for activities. Such 'icons' provide 'the centre of a complex and concrete symbolic order in which everyone has a role to play in the context of an overall theatre' (Maffesoli 1996: 137). Symbols also provide the aura on which neo-tribalism depends. Such a role is played by the rural idyll, especially in the context of migration and residence, with the countryside and rural living forming a highly symbolic backdrop for this migration (see Short 1991; Williams 1973; Wright 1985).

Secondly, there is the *importance of ritual* for neo-tribalism, as compared to the more reflexive usage of rational procedures. Such ritual is associated, in particular, with initiation and renewal. Again, the rural idyll appears in this light. For example, the idea of 'retiring to the country', whether in terms of leaving (urban) work behind, or in the form of retired people moving to the countryside, is both of highly ritual significance and emphasises renewal. The association of the rural with rest, which the idea of retiring implies, belies the reality of the rural experience for many people (Cloke and Little 1997). The ritual aspect of the rural idyll is also reflected in second home owners trying to adopt a persona wholly at odds with their weekday equivalent when they travel to their cottages on Friday evenings. Finally, the link between the rural idyll and the service class, frequently made in the literature, has been explained in part by the intellectual competence needed to appreciate fully the countryside for what it is (Thrift 1987), a linkage which remains valid even if no longer linked so directly to class; in short, one has to be initiated into rurality in order to understand and appreciate it properly.

Thirdly, although in theory open to all, neo-tribalism demonstrates a *closure against the uninitiated*, through its dependency upon the relatively intangible characteristics of symbol, ritual and myth, and through its association with the production of space. This is clear in the way in which Thrift (1987) links the idyll to the service class and is apparent in the rural idyll as practised spatially in the British countryside. For a start, there is the NIMBY mentality of many new rural residents, as demonstrated in their resistance to development in the countryside and their construction of exclusivity (Murdoch and Marsden 1994). Furthermore, there is the realisation within the academic literature of the exclusivity of the rural idyll (Philo 1992), as represented in the selectivity of its appeal and its socio-cultural coverage (Agg and Phillips, Chapter 14, this volume; Cloke and Little 1997).

Fourthly, what may most strongly link the rural idyll to neo-tribalism is its *emphasis on 'community'*. Although the rural idyll may not express the more extrovert hedonism of Dionysus, it is dionysian in its emphasis on a re-enchanted world, with various elements of community forming key dimensions of the representation (Halfacree 1995). An overall theme of Maffesoli's work is this move towards such re-enchantment and of people's search for the existential warmth of community through neo-tribal associations. Hence, Maffesoli (1996: 57, 69, 97) talks of 'villages' in the city and, in his conclusion, argues:

> 'the glue of aggregation – which we could call experience, the lived, sensitivity, image – is made up of proximity and the affectual (or the emotional), which is evoked by area, the minuscule and the everyday. . . .postmodern sociality is investing in some rather archaic values to say the least. . . .*the re-actualization of the ancient myth of community*; myth in the sense in which something that has perhaps never really existed acts, effectively, on the imagination of the time' (Maffesoli 1996: 147–148, emphasis added).

Evaluating the rural idyll in neo-tribal terms, we must also consider the extent to which it has assumed a *Gemeinschaft* and/or *Gesellschaft* character (Figure 11.2). The former is to a degree undermined immediately by the very active and deliberate use of the social representation within migration to rural areas (Halfacree 1994). Whilst other factors might prove to be the stimulus to the move, such as employment considerations, the rurality of the destination tends to be striven for actively and appreciated accordingly. Thus, whilst migrants I interviewed expressed some surprise and uncertainty in answering questions about their ideas of the countryside, there was generally a high degree of discursive ability in their answers and a clear enthusiasm to discuss 'things rural' (Halfacree 1992). Rurality has not, therefore, gone so far as to become naturalised; a feature abundantly clear in the other, often distinctly 'non-rural', activities and behaviour patterns within which migrants are enmeshed. However, in contrast to any more *Gesellschaft* use of the countryside, the rural idyll also does not appear to be employed in clear, objective and tightly-bounded instrumental terms in directing migration to rural areas. For example, while capital accumulation and employment concerns have a role in explaining the residential choice, they certainly do not provide *the* answer to this trend. Instead, the instrumentality of the rural idyll appears to be more in terms of the existential search for the 'collective ambience' suggested by Maffesoli (see also Halfacree 1997).

The Tribalism of Productivism

The suggestion that the post-productivist countryside and its new residents may display neo-tribal characteristics contrasts with the situation of the productivist countryside and its inhabitants, which have more in common with tribalism. The post-1945 productivist hegemony built upon the historical role of the countryside as the locus of agricultural production, to embed and naturalise a particular set of practices and ideas. Thus, a *Gemeinschaft* tribalism stemmed from the historical sedimentation of the local farming community and its distinctive local practices. Although often over-stated, farming was in this sense a 'way of life', albeit one which was 'leaky' in respect of members of the farming community leaving that tribe – for example, to take up work in the towns and cities – and in respect of newcomers to farming, although many of the latter were likely to find it hard to be accepted by or to accept farming's tribal community.

The tribalism of the agricultural community can be demonstrated through reference to Rapport's (1993) study of 'Wanet' in the Cumbrian Dales (see also S. Fielding, Chapter 8, this volume). Rapport described some of the deeply embedded 'world views' of the Dale's inhabitants, loops of thought, 'each… like a whole world of ideas around which its owner might cognitively travel' (Rapport 1993: 80). For the Wanet community, individuals might use the same words and expressions in their individual world views but these terms were ambiguous enough to be perceived and used in quite different ways by contrasting individuals. Detailed agreement was not needed for sustained interaction to be maintained, as the world views were not explicitly and discursively subjected to examination within daily life. This social ambiguity and individual distinctiveness helped the community cohere and eliminated serious conflict. It was only the intrusion of uninitiated 'outsiders', with their different ideas and forms of behaving, which disrupted these sedimented lives. Such people failed to have the necessary 'cultural competence' (Cloke, Goodwin and Milbourne, Chapter 7, this volume). In the *Gemeinschaft* world of Wanet 'a distinction between form and meaning is of overriding import' (Rapport 1993: 158), in contrast to the neo-tribal world where the two may be seen to be more reflexively equivalent.

The post-1945 agricultural settlement in Britain consolidated the tribal status of farming, bolstering cultural and ideological ritual with official support, aided by the corporatism of bodies such as the National Farmers' Union. Of course, there was some *Gesellschaft*-like manipulation of the system, witnessed in farmers' deliberate instrumental appeal to agrarian ideology to legitimate price support and other state assistance, but a *Gesellschaft* attitude to farming and the farming community has only developed significantly within agribusiness. Hence, we can begin to understand the sense of profound shock and betrayal that the farming community has felt in the wake of the crisis of productivism, witnessed, for example, in the community's very high levels of depression and suicide.

Conflict Within the Post-productivist Countryside

Bearing in mind the Lefebvrian insight that neo-tribes require their own spaces for any long-term survival, it is not surprising that we see conflict as one of the principal features of the post-productivist countryside. In the transition from productivism to post-productivism, a space has opened up for residents associated with the rural idyll to re-'striate' (Deleuze and Guattari 1987) the countryside in their own image. The conflict generated by such a struggle occurs both between neo-tribal in-migrants and the tribal agricultural community, and between different groups of migrants.

As Rapport's (1993) study suggested, new actors on the rural scene undermine the tribal position of the agricultural community. Thus, in Figure 11.2, the *Gemeinschaft* position of agriculture is questioned. This can be illustrated in a number of ways; from Newby's (1979) identification of beleaguered 'farm-centred communities' of farmers and farm workers, to the contrast between the rural idyll's romantic image of farming and the often unflattering exposure of its contemporary reality. For example, looking at the productivism of agriculture, whilst a productive agriculture is implied in the rural idyll's landscape, it is a productivism with no negative environmental externalities. Recognition of the presence of such externalities jars harshly with the idealisation of the new rural residents (Lowe *et al.* 1986: 23–25; Ward 1993: 358–359) and fuels their critique of modern farming. All of this raises numerous questions of purpose and identity which the farming community is increasingly forced to confront, thereby undermining its embedded position.

Another more specific example of the neo-tribal versus tribal conflict concerns the rural pursuit of hunting, which recently made headlines as a result of John McFall's Wild Mammals (Protection) Bill, presented to Parliament in 1995 (*Guardian* 4 March 1995), and the emergence of the pro-hunting Countryside Movement (Keeble 1995). Hunting, as Cox *et al.* (1994) have demonstrated with respect to stag hunting in Devon and Somerset, is a very 'tribal' activity, with farmers comprising over half the economically active subscribers. Cox *et al.* showed that hunting provides a Wittgensteinian 'form of life' for those it encompasses. Thus, for example, there are the elaborate rituals of the hunt, such as dress, language and the progression through a 'meet' itself. Moreover, the hunt is not only important to its adherents on hunt days but also represents a broader social community with associated events and activities. Overall, the hunt's continuity and certainty rests on clear and well established 'powerful narratives of identity' (Cox *et al.* 1994: 204). Thus, measures such as the McFall Bill, which represents most clearly the urban and rural newcomer's perception of hunting as a cruel and archaic activity, threaten much more than just a blood-sport. Instead, they resonate with the tribal spatiality of exclusion and inclusion, with anti-hunting campaigners being especially criticised as being urban residents with little or no connection to rural life.

Besides the conflict between agriculturally based tribalism and the new rural residents' neo-tribalism, we can also see conflicts both between and within neo-tribal groupings. On the one hand, internal conflicts come about through the exclusionary character of neo-tribes and their struggle to embed themselves in space, as witnessed in NIMBY 'pulling up of the drawbridges' by in-migrant-based 'environmental' pressure groups. In their attempt to project their neo-tribal identity towards the *Gemeinschaft* position in Figure 11.2, the in-migrants are forced to confront other neo-tribal interests in the countryside (for example, leisure-based groupings), potential fellow rural residents and groups with more profit-based interests in rurality (for example, housebuilders). Conflict is also apparent between neo-tribal in-migrants and more Baudrillardian 'playful' residents, who reject the seriousness and the commitment required to embed a neo-tribal lifestyle and move it towards the tribal position in Figure 11.2. An interesting variant on this issue comes from Buller's and Hoggart's (1994: 112–113) study of British migrants to rural France, where permanent (British) residents often expressed resentment towards their fellow British second home owners for their failure to integrate into French rural society. Finally, divisions between neo-tribes can expose the political economy of neo-tribal imposition. Nowhere is this more apparent than in the clash of culture between what have now become 'conventional' migrants to rural Britain, with their adherence to the domestic and privatised rural idyll, and either non-sedentary and more public 'New Age' traveller bands (Halfacree 1996b) or the plethora of different leisure users of the countryside (Clark *et al.* 1994). The resolution of such conflicts draws attention to Harvey's (1993: 63) observation that 'in any society certain principles of exclusion have to operate', with these principles reflecting society's relations of power, a political economic perspective within which all discussion of neo-tribalism ultimately must be framed.

CONCLUSION

> 'Gods, their myths and their rites have changed names and shapes, but they continue to operate in sociality and in the environment' (Maffesoli 1987: 73–74).

As Lowe *et al.* (1993) note, the advent of the post-productivist countryside heralds new opportunities and new uncertainties. Through the use of Maffesoli's idea of neo-tribes I suggest that this new rural geography is going to be contested by the actions of groups rooted in the sociality of daily life and united by their common dionysian passion for re-enchanting the world dis-enchanted by modernism. Three such groupings have been noted here, the loosely-defined rural idyll-adopting migrants and the more specific groups of travellers and rural leisure users. Currently, the major source of tension in the creation of the post-productivist countryside is between the former of these groups and the remaining productivist agricultural community. This conflict is likely to escalate in the foreseeable future as the neo-tribal groupings strive to create the spaces for their long-term persistence. Such is the way that *Homo Aestheticus* is 'fashioning an ethic... equally as solid as those that have gone before' (Maffesoli 1991: 19) in contemporary rural Britain. The end result of these struggles remains uncertain, although underlying political economic relations of power suggest a certain outcome.

Maffesoli's ideas bring various insights to the study of the creation of this post-productivist countryside. Whilst some of these insights are not novel, the theory introduced here provides an added layer of sophistication to our understanding and appreciation of rural change. For example, Maffesoli's work draws attention to:

- The possibility that migration to rural Britain is rooted in nebulous 'common experiences' of day-to-day living, rather than being constrained as solely a reflection of the class-based structure of capitalist society. In particular, attention is drawn to the postmodern experience of institutional saturation.
- The extent to which the intensity of the struggle for a new hegemony in rural

Britain is driven in part by the precariousness of neo-tribal existence and the need to create a material space for the neo-tribe.

- How neo-tribalism is constructed by the active striving of people with common interest but how the detailed form that neo-tribalism takes is relatively open. Thus, we must recognise not only the 'affectual ambience' of the rural idyll but also equally neo-tribal alternative ruralities.

- The researcher's role as an 'interpreter', where there is a need for detailed work 'inside' the neo-tribes of the post-productivist countryside, detailing their beliefs, ways of behaving etc. A clear ethnographic moment is required (see Allan and Mooney, Chapter 15, this volume).

- An observation that whilst migration to the countryside is usually regarded in rather passive consumption terms, the operation of neo-tribalism also emphasises its productive capacity. The migration is productive with respect to the survival of the neo-tribe itself but, in particular, with respect to the building of a distinctive neo-tribal space.

- Hetherington's suggestion that neo-tribal relationships are likely to become routinised into *Gemeinschaft* or *Gesellschaft* relationships. This routinisation needs to be considered in the light of the ongoing nature of the production of the post-productivist countryside. What is the balance, within the migration stream to rural Britain, between its neo-tribal character and its naturalism or instrumentalism? In short, where is urban-to-rural migration positioned and where is it going, and what implications does this trajectory have for the ultimate shape of post-productivist countryside? If the rural idyll is becoming naturalised, attention must focus once again on the critique of 'community' (Murdoch and Day, Chapter 10, this volume; Maffesoli 1996: 97).

- Neo-tribalism's characteristic as a celebration of *puissance* and as a reaction against the existential disruption caused by the saturation of society. This suggests that migration to rural Britain may display a more radical *potential* than is often appreciated. In this respect, attention must be drawn to the way in which migration to rural Britain as a re-skilling of everyday life seeks to overcome the commodification, riskiness and space–time compression of society. Thus may the spirit of Dionysus be incorporated into efforts to 'green' the post-productivist countryside.

ACKNOWLEDGEMENTS

I would like to thank Paul Boyle and Kevin Hetherington for making some useful comments on an earlier version of this paper.

NOTES

1. From the album by Damon and Naomi (1992), 'More Sad Hits', Shimmy Disc Records, Shimmy 058.

2. 'Sports clubs, friends at the office, coffee "klatches", associations of hobbyists, the crowd of fans at a sports match, the local level of a political party, 'Neighbourhood Watch' community policing, and single-issue pressure groups' are all listed by Shields (1996: ix) as examples of potential neo-tribes when utilised in the ways suggested by Maffesoli.
3. Also of note here are Maffesoli's fellow French academics, Alain Minc – with his discussion of a centre-less 'New Middle Ages' (Lennon 1994) – and Michel Foucault.

REFERENCES

Baudrillard, J. (1983) *In the shadow of the silent majorities*, Semiotext(e), New York.
Bauman, Z. (1987) *Legislators and interpreters: on modernity, postmodernity, and the intellectuals*, Polity Press, Cambridge.
Bauman, Z. (1992) *Intimations of postmodernity*, Routledge, London.
Buller, H. and Hoggart, K. (1994) *International counterurbanization*, Avebury, Aldershot.
Clark, G., Darrall, J., Grove-White, R., Macnaghten, P. and Urry, J. (1994) *Leisure landscapes*, Centre for Environmental Change, London.
Cloke, P. (1980) 'New emphases for applied rural geography', *Progress in Human Geography*, **4**, 181–217.
Cloke, P. and Little, J. (eds.) (1997) *Contested countryside cultures*, Routledge, London.
Cox, G., Hallett, J. and Winter, M. (1994) 'Hunting the wild red deer: the social organization and ritual of a "rural" institution', *Sociologia Ruralis*, **34**, 190–205.
Deleuze, G. and Guattari, F. (1987) *A thousand plateaus*, University of Minnesota Press, Minneapolis.
Dobson, A. (1990) *Green political thought*, Unwin Hyman, London.
Findlay, A. and Graham, E. (1991) 'The challenge facing population geography', *Progress in Human Geography*, **15**, 149–162.
Giddens, A. (1990) *The consequences of modernity*, Polity, Cambridge.
Guardian (4 March 1995) 'Landmark anti-hunting vote unlikely to bring ban'.
Halfacree, K. (1992) 'The importance of spatial representations in residential migration to rural England in the 1980s. A quest for "sophisticated simplicity" in a postmodern world?', PhD Thesis, Department of Geography, University of Lancaster, Lancaster.
Halfacree, K. (1993) 'Locality and social representation: space, discourse and alternative definitions of the rural', *Journal of Rural Studies*, **9**, 23–37.
Halfacree, K. (1994) 'The importance of "the rural" in the constitution of counterurbanization. evidence from England in the 1980s', *Sociologia Ruralis*, **34**, 164–189.
Halfacree, K. (1995) 'Talking about rurality: social representations of the rural as expressed by residents of six English parishes', *Journal of Rural Studies*, **11**, 1–20.
Halfacree, K. (1996a) 'British rural geography: a perspective on the last decade', Paper presented at the British-Spanish Rural Geography Symposium, University of Leicester, 8–14th September.
Halfacree, K. (1996b) 'Out of place in the country: travellers and the "rural idyll"', *Antipode*, **28**, 42–71.
Halfacree, K. (1997) 'Contrasting roles for the post-productivist countryside: a postmodern perspective on counterurbanisation', in P. Cloke and J. Little (eds.), *Contested countryside cultures*, Routledge, London, 70–93.
Halfacree, K. and Boyle, P. (1993) 'The challenge facing migration research: the case for a biographical approach', *Progress in Human Geography*, **17**, 333–348.
Harvey, D. (1989) *The condition of postmodernity*, Blackwell, Oxford.
Harvey, D. (1993) 'Class relations, social justice and the politics of difference', in M. Keith and S. Pile (eds.), *Place and the politics of identity*, Routledge, London, 41–66.

Hetherington, K. (1990) 'On the homecoming of the stranger: new social movements or new sociations?', *Lancaster Regionalism Group, Working Paper 39*.

Hetherington, K. (1992) 'Stonehenge and its festival', in R. Shields (ed.), *Lifestyle shopping*, Routledge, London, 83–98.

Hetherington, K. (1994) 'The contemporary significance of Schmalenbach's concept of the *Bund*', *Sociological Review*, **42**, 1–25.

Keeble, J. (1995) 'Hunt, shoot, fish. . . kill', *Guardian*, 15 November.

King, R., Connell, J. and White, P. (eds.) (1995) *Writing across worlds: literature and migration*, Routledge, London.

Lefebvre, H. (1991) *The production of space*, Blackwell, Oxford.

Lennon, P. (1994) 'Prophet of a fatal drift', *Guardian*, 31 January.

Lowe, P., Cox, G., MacEwen, M., O'Riordan, T. and Winter, M. (1986) *Countryside conflicts*, Gower, Aldershot.

Lowe, P., Murdoch, J., Marsden, T., Munton, R. and Flynn, A. (1993) 'Regulating the new rural spaces: the uneven development of land', *Journal of Rural Studies*, **9**, 205–222.

Maffesoli, M. (1987) 'Sociality as legitimation of sociological method', *Current Sociology*, **35**, 69–87.

Maffesoli, M. (1989) 'The sociology of everyday life (epistemological elements)', *Current Sociology*, **37**, 1–16.

Maffesoli, M. (1991) 'The ethic of aesthetics', *Theory, Culture and Society*, **8**, 7–20.

Maffesoli, M. (1996) *The time of the tribes*, Sage, London.

McKendrick, J. (ed.) (1995) *Multi-method research in population geography: a primer to debate*, Population Geography Research Group, Manchester.

Melucci, A. (1989) *Nomads of the present*, Radius/Hutchinson, London.

Murdoch, J. and Marsden, T. (1994) *Reconstituting rurality*, UCL Press, London.

Newby, H. (1979) *Green and pleasant land?*, Wildwood House, London.

Phillips, M. (1998, forthcoming) 'Rural restructuring: social perspectives', in B. Ilbery (ed.), *The geography of rural change*, Addison Wesley Longman, Harlow.

Philo, C. (1992) 'Neglected rural geographies: a review', *Journal of Rural Studies*, **8**, 193–207.

Rapport, N. (1993) *Diverse world-views in an English village*, Edinburgh University Press, Edinburgh.

Schmalenbach, H. (1977) *Herman Schmalenbach: on society and experience*, University of Chicago Press, Chicago.

Shields, R. (1991a) 'Introduction to "The ethic of aesthetics"', *Theory, Culture and Society*, **8**, 1–5.

Shields, R. (1991b) Review of M. Maffesoli (1990) *Au creux des apparences*, *Theory, Culture and Society*, **8**, 179–183.

Shields, R. (1992) 'Spaces for the subject of consumption', in R. Shields (ed.), *Lifestyle shopping. The subject of consumption*, Routledge, London, 1–20.

Shields, R. (1996) 'Foreword: masses or tribes?', in M. Maffesoli, *The time of the tribes*, Sage, London, ix–xii.

Short, J. (1991) *Imagined country*, Routledge, London.

Thrift, N. (1987) 'Introduction: the geography of late twentieth-century class formation', in Thrift, N. and Williams, P. (eds.), *Class and space*, Routledge and Kegan Paul, London, 207–253.

Ward, N. (1993) 'The agricultural treadmill and the rural environment in the post-productivist era', *Sociologia Ruralis*, **33**, 348–364.

White, P. and Jackson, P. (1995) '(Re)theorising population geography', *International Journal of Population Geography*, **1**, 111–123.

Williams, R. (1973) *The country and the city*, Hogarth Press, London, 1985 edition.

Wright, P. (1985) *On living in an old country*, Verso, London.

12

COUNTERURBANISATION, FRAGMENTATION AND THE PARADOX OF THE RURAL IDYLL

MATTHEW GORTON, JOHN WHITE and IAN CHASTON

INTRODUCTION

This chapter considers the nature and extent of counterurbanisation as a process of reordering within and between rural localities in Britain. The first section considers counterurbanisation, together with the concurrent re-ordering processes of rural economic diversification and agricultural restructuring and their promotion of inter- and intra-rural variations. The attempts of researchers to capture and order this diversity is discussed in the second section together with a critique of the orthodox approaches taken. It will be argued that contemporary fragmentation does not mean that, historically, rural communities were homogeneous and harmonious societies – far from it – but rather that traditional dichotomies aimed at understanding rural communities and, in particular, the landed versus landless binary classification (Shoard 1987) are no longer, if they ever were, appropriate. Customary sources of power have been diluted and new forms have evolved so that the policy locality is more heterogeneous and less shapeable by traditional and individual actors. Analysis of evolving power relations will utilise David Marquand's (1988) distinction between three modes of operation: command, exchange and preceptoral. This discussion of power relationships will be used to enhance the final section which seeks to link the effects of counterurbanisation and fragmentation with the contemporary problematic of how ought individuals and communities to organise themselves and relate to one another within rural localities.

COUNTERURBANISATION AND RURAL RESTRUCTURING

Counterurbanisation

Counterurbanisation can be defined as a deconcentration of population from urban to rural areas (Robert and Randolph 1983), with two distinct forms: that within the urban–rural fringe and that arising in remote rural areas (Harper

1991). The first sizeable migrations out of urban areas began during the inter-war era and were predominately to rural areas immediately surrounding conurbations, particularly around London (Cloke and Little 1990). Until the mid-1960s growth was most extensive in the accessible countryside, within easy commuting distance of major employment centres. Since the 1970s migration flows have spread further out to remoter regions, reversing long-term trends of depopulation. Some of these gains have been substantial – in Cornwall, for example, between 1971 and 1981 there was an increase of 50 000 on a base population of 380 000 (Robert and Randolph 1983). An analysis of the 1991 Census returns shows that counterurbanisation has been sustained but that relative population gains during the 1980s were highest in these accessible peripheral counties such as Dorset. These counties are too distant for daily commuting to metropolitan centres such as London but are not the most remote localities (i.e. the Highlands and Islands of Scotland). An archetypal accessible peripheral county is Devon where for the period 1981 to 1991 the population rose by 7.3 percent – a net increase of 80 000 accounted for entirely by migration (Halliday and Coombes 1995: 434).

Counterurbanisation can be seen as having three major dimensions (Sant and Simons 1993: 124):

- Place utility: the value put on different living environments.
- Ability to move: the economic and personal attachments one has to present locations.
- Willingness to move: the desire to relocate to non-metropolitan localities.

Starting with place utlility, significant numbers of the population, particularly middle classes, have consistently placed a premium on rural residential environments. This rural idyll initially became obtainable through the growth of private transport (facilitating commuting) and the provision of reasonably cheap housing in the immediate post-war era (Pahl 1965). More recently further advances in transport infrastructure provision, rural industrialisation and improved communications have meant that urban dwellers have been able to move further from the metropolitan core and maintain the degree of mobility and service provision they desire. In addition, tight planning controls (green belt legislation) around the major cities have pushed housing pressures further out into free-standing towns and villages and more remote regions (Buller and Lowe 1990).

There has been no systematic survey comparing the characteristics of migrants who relocate to rural core and rural peripheral localities, but several separate surveys within each group have been undertaken (Dean *et al.* 1984; Jones *et al.* 1986; Harper 1991; Pahl 1965). Considering one of these surveys in detail, Dean and his associates look at the characteristics of migrants and non-migrants in the rural peripheral district of West Cornwall. Within the seven study areas examined only 22.4 percent of migrants were born in Cornwall. From the area questionnaires, migrants accounted for 43.3 percent of total respondents and around one-third were aged over 59. The migrants, when compared to non-migrants, were significantly more likely to have completed higher education courses, to be owner occupiers and to be members of socio-economic groups A and B. 'New to Cornwall migrants' also had the lowest percentages of persons aged 15 to 29, persons completing their full-time education before 17 and members of socio-economic groups C2 and D. Such migrants were disproportionately attracted to the three most environmentally attractive coastal study areas, suggesting a high degree of local selectivity, particularly for retirees, who represented 40 percent of migrants in these areas. However, although retirees were numerous, the majority of adult immigrants were economically active. While few were under 30 years of age, higher proportions of migrants compared with non-migrants fell into the 30–44 and 45–59 age groups. Importantly, there was a marked tendency for economically active migrants to be of higher occupational status than non-migrants.

The profile of new migrants is thus very different from that of established residents, increasing the diversity of rural peripheral localities. Nonetheless, while the overall profiles of the two groups are different, there is also a significant spread within each – migrants to rural areas in general include a wide range of 'mature aged middle-class households, the elderly, and even the occasional "urban drop-out" (Lewis et al. 1991: 318). In terms of Sant and Simon's place utility, the way in which the migrants value the countryside is thus multifarious and cannot be attributed to a single disposition (Bolton and Chalkley 1990).

The peripheral regions appear to gain proportionately more elderly migrants and fewer young family migrants than rural core areas (Harper 1991). The preference of elderly people for less developed, particularly coastal environments, is indicated by the clear concentration of retirees in the coastal counties of southern Britain, with a belt stretching from mid-Wales, around the South West, along the south coast and up into East Anglia (Central Statistical Office 1992).

Overall, the theme of diversity should be recognised in the study of counterurbanisation – rural areas are not 'homogeneous lumps'. The rate of population change and the characteristics of those attracted has been multifarious. Moreover, while there may be a net increase in population, rural areas may still see out-migration of key groups, particularly the young, in search of greater opportunities and to obtain higher education – a trend which is masked in the overall figures. For example, between 1971 and 1981 net population in Powys increased by 11 300 but within the age group 16–19 there was still an overall loss (Champion and Townsend 1990). This leads on to the point that counterurbanisation may in some circumstances promote depopulation, notably by increasing rural house prices so that indigenous first-time buyers have to look elsewhere for affordable property; the growth of some groups may be at the direct expense of others (Weekley 1988). Furthermore, in some of the most isolated settlements net out-migration has continued. For example, the Western Isles of Scotland experienced a population decline of 9.5 percent for the period 1981–1991 (Lloyd and Black 1993). The process of counterurbanisation and population growth within rural areas cannot be over generalised and, as a re-ordering phenomenon, it must be seen as promoting heterogeneity rather than a new form of homogeneity.

Agricultural Restructuring

Under a system of price supports, stemming from the 1947 Agriculture Act and reinforced by the Common Agricultural Policy of the European Union, agricultural production has been comprehensively increased. Britain has gone from an inter-war position of being able to produce only one-third of its domestic food requirements to being a significant net exporter of temperate foodstuffs (Marks 1989). These rises in agricultural production have been achieved by increased mechanisation, input intensification and farm amalgamation with consistent falls in the number employed – within Britain the number of farms has fallen by about one-half and the workforce has been reduced by approximately three-quarters since 1951 (Clark 1991). Three-quarters of British farms now employ no full-time hired hands (Cox *et al.* 1986). By the beginning of the 1980s, even within rural areas the percentage of the workforce engaged in agriculture (14 percent in 1981) was half that in manufacturing and construction (28 percent), and less than one-third of that engaged in services (58 percent) (Department of the Environment/Welsh Office 1988). Capital intensification accelerated during the 1980s with farming playing an increasingly subordinate role within highly complex agri-food chains (Whatmore *et al.* 1990) and with an ever diminishing role for labour. United Kingdom agriculture in 1989 accounted for only 1.2 percent of GDP (the lowest within the European Union) and only 2.1 percent of total employment (also the lowest within the European Union) (Eurostat 1992). The declining economic importance of agriculture and the achievement of post-war food supply goals have contributed to a shift in emphasis of agrarian development from a productionist ethic to a broader rural agenda. Within this agenda farmers are seen not only as food producers but as environmental and landscape managers, guardians of land as part of a post-productionist policy package (Marsden 1995).

Rural Economic Diversification

Britain's rural economy can no longer be seen as predominantly agrarian based, with the space taken up by agriculture in stark contrast to the employment opportunities it now offers. Agriculture and related industries no longer provide nearly enough jobs for the rural workforce and there is a clear need for economic diversification. This diversification has been achieved in many areas via market-led changes, such as the urban–rural shift in manufacturing and services. However, in peripheral and less attractive areas, the extent of these processes has been more limited. These peripheral localities have not attracted a large manufacturing base and thus tend to be characterised by a low skilled, poor opportunity local economy of ever decreasing agricultural demand and a service sector highly geared to part-time and seasonal work (particularly in tourism, catering and retail sectors) (Day and Thomas 1993; Gilligan 1984). Service sector growth comprises a very heterogeneous grouping, ranging from management consultancy to market stalls, and, by and large, rural peripheral areas have proportionately more of the low paid, unskilled and semi-skilled employment opportunities.

The actors responsible for the diversification of the rural economy have come principally from outside the agricultural community and encompass a whole range of economic units from small businesses to multi-national corporations. While agricultural diversification has been heavily promoted since the early 1980s at both a national and supra-national level via grants, advice, training and promotional literature (Ministry of Agriculture, Fisheries and Food 1994) the majority of farmers attempted to deal with the farming recession of the 1980s by reducing input costs (especially labour) rather than radically restructuring their businesses (Errington and Tranter 1991). Griffiths (1989) found that only 18 percent of farmers could be classified as major diversifiers (defined as being involved in two or more types of diversification, or in one which produced over 10 percent of gross farm income). Townroe and Mallalieu (1993), analysing the motivations and types of new firm founders in rural areas, found that only six percent of new businesses created could be attributed to diversification by farmers. Not only has the importance of agriculture to the rural economy been diluted but the importance of farmers as economic actors has been as well.

Studies of the establishment of small businesses in rural areas show the long-term importance of counterurbanisation. Keeble and his colleagues, (1992) in their study for the Department of the Environment, considered the origins of founders of small businesses in accessible rural, remote rural and urban localities (Table 12.1). The fact that over one-fifth of remote rural owner-managing directors moved there to set up their firms provides an unequivocally strong connection between population migration to rural areas and subsequent or contemporaneous new enterprise formation in these localities. The importance of migration, followed discontinuously by the establishment of new enterprises in rural areas, is also highlighted. This is a very different profile from urban founders, who are predominantly indigenous.

Alongside the skewed nature of small business formation can be seen the uneven form of the rural shift of multi-site actors, with accessible localities gaining both more new actors and more sophisticated plants. At the risk of oversimplifying, core localities have gained proportionately more non-routine and technologically advanced production units, while relocated plants in peripheral regions have tended to be far more involved in routine production activities. Those plants engaged in non-routine and batch production, manufacturing products at the beginning of their life cycle, tend to have far greater discretion to obtain material inputs from local suppliers (Sweeney 1987).

Table 12.1 Origins of small business founders in differing localities

	Company location		
	Remote rural (%)	Accessible rural (%)	Urban (%)
Born in the country	42.4	34.2	65.6
Moved to the country before setting up firm	36.5	52.5	25.9
Moved to set up the firm	21.1	13.3	8.6
Total	100.0	100.0	100.0

Source: Keeble *et al.* 1992: 14. Crown Copyright. Reproduced with the permission of the Controller of Her Majesty's Stationery Office.

Several authors have attempted to explain this relocation movement in terms of a single dynamic, but survey data highlight no single motive or neat compartmentalisation. Four key sets of motives, the importance of which are not uniform, can be identified: production costs (lower labour costs and more flexible employment patterns in rural areas), land-oriented decisions (availability and lower cost in rural areas), localisation (proximity to local markets, trained labour force or other specialist suppliers) and environmental considerations (attractiveness to management and other employees). Within the South East, localisation and land considerations appear as the most important factors, while in the peripheral extreme South West access to a cheap labour supply and environmental factors rank far higher (Spooner 1972). In terms of factors inhibiting movement into peripheral areas, poor transport facilities and access to major markets and key decision-makers appear paramount (Newby 1971). Choice of location cannot thus be reduced to a single factor, such as a crude (Marxist) focus on the capital–labour relationship. Businesses face a whole array of critical success factors, such as innovation and changing product technologies, which cannot simply be reduced to 'the consequences of success or failure in disciplining labour' (Morgan and Sayer 1985: 384). As a greater range of products and markets are served within contemporary capitalism one cannot see a single, ubiquitous production system or critical success factor. The polymorphous nature of modern capitalist production thus implies the rationale behind location decisions will be multi-various. In this way, predicting the future economic prospects for rural areas as a *whole* is impossible.

Finally, two key findings can be drawn out. Firstly, the effects of these reordering processes has been to increase historically prevalent intra- and interrural variations in income. For example, in April 1991, outside Greater London, the rural core counties of southern England had the highest average male gross full-time weekly earnings (£372.80 in Berkshire and £361.00 in Surrey), while the rural peripheral counties had the lowest (£246.30 in Cornwall, £260.20 in Dyfed and £268.10 in Devon) (Central Statistical Office 1992). A similar picture emerges from comparative female figures, with the lowest average figures being £178.00 in Cornwall and £174.58 in Borders (Central Statistical Office 1992). The degree of income difference is thus now much greater between rural areas than between core and peripheral urban counties. Secondly, the increasing diversity and fragmentation of rural communities has meant the dissipation of the traditional rural aristocracy and gentry hegemony, with its control over local politics, culture and economy. The dominance of agricultural interests and actors has long gone – with the new economic protagonists in rural areas coming from outside this community. This means that understanding the way in which individuals and groups appeal to each other and the claims to justice they make are vital to our comprehension of rural communities.

DIVERSITY AND CONTESTED SPACE

Recognising and Classifying Diversity

The central task facing rural commentators is thus the need to explain the diversity and heterogeneity of existence within the countryside. This is a monumental task, which would take rural scholars well outside traditional boundaries and, given contemporary production systems, will need to be truly global in its sphere of reference. In the spirit of such a project, but obviously not the completion of it, the remainder of this chapter considers some of the linkages between fragmentation, conflict and appeals to justice within rural localities. This area has been poorly considered within rural studies, under the influence of positivistic methodology with its disjunction between facts and values, and the desire to imitate the practices of natural scientists. This section now considers some of the conceptual devices previously used to capture this diversity and seeks to show the theoretical weaknesses often implicit within them, in terms of apprehending the dynamic nature of the processes detailed above and the relationships between relevant actors.

Contemporary commentators have rejected Frankenberg's (1973) morphological continuum between rural and urban modes of living in that it ignores the diversity and interpenetration between, and within, the modes. Sociological characteristics of a place cannot simply be 'read off' from its relative location on the continuum (Halfacree 1993: 25). Young and Wilmott (1957) discovered, for example, 'model rural societies' in the East End of London, while Connell (1978) and Pahl (1965) found the foundations of 'urban' societies in central Surrey and Hertfordshire respectively. The structuralist-functionalist approach similarly failed to capture the heterogeneity of existence within the range of localities – a weakness which, since Pahl (1966), researchers have sought to ameliorate (Table 12.2). Successive commentators have sought to identify and classify the various groupings (stemming from the heterogeneity of existence) which are present within rural communities and the conflicts between them.

The most ubiquitous and basic classification employed has been the disjunc-

Table 12.2 Studies conceptualising conflicts and group interests in rural communities

	Author(s)				
	Radford (1970)	Connell (1978)	Pahl (1966)	Robinson (1990)	Ambrose (1992)
Study Area	Worcestershire	Surrey	Hertfordshire	Non-retirement migrants in Cornwall	Rural-urban fringe
Groups identified in rural communities	(i) newcomers (ii) indigenous villagers	(i) newcomers (ii) locals	(i) Large property-owners / traditional landowners (ii) Salaried immigrants with some capital, often living in substantial houses (iii) Spiralists: professional employees who are highly mobile (iv) 'Reluctant commuters': forced out of the town by property prices (v) The retired: made up of both indigenous villagers and immigrants (vi) Council house tenants	(i) Career transients or 'spiralists' (ii) Commuters (iii) Professional self-employed and small business owners (iv) Small manufacturers, people seeking a 'new start' and people involved in permanent job transfers (v) Job-specific and non-specific migrants (vi) Partial employment migrants. Choose to be employed for part of the year (normally in tourist industry)	Group-interest interaction approach Each group has specific interest: (i) old landed interests: maintaining limited access to land (ii) new agriculturalists: limit access, maintain price supports and promote rationalisation (iii) housebuilders: land for development available in attractive areas (iv) conservationists: non-anthropocentric approach to the preservation and management of rural environments

				(v) central government: free market approach (vi) planning interest: 'balanced development'
				(vii) Tied cottages and other tenants in rented property (viii) Small business owners
Conceptual problems	Does not allow for inter-group differences between 'locals' or 'newcomers'. Each group seen as having pre-determined preferences living in separate worlds	Newcomers and locals must be seen as heterogeneous clusters. Functionalist	Does not explain how such diverse groups exist within the same space–time continuum	Classification presented as answer rather than as an identifying tool prior to explaining the diversity of existence it seeks to catalogue	Does not explain how groups come into existence or the motivation and rationale of individuals. Explanatory power of individual action is extremely limited

tion between newcomers and locals (Strathern 1981; Radford 1970; Connell 1978). For example:

> 'Conflict often arises between the new rural dwellers and established ones...The later group wishing to see more economic growth and employment from new industry and commercial development. The former group to preserve the country-side and refuse any development' (Strak 1989: 41).

Such a scheme, however, does not allow for differences *within* both the 'locals' and 'newcomers' categories, and sees each group with a constant and predeter-mined set of preferences living in separate, bounded worlds. It does not allow for the farmer who was anti-development prior to the 1980s who now sees diversification as vital, nor an incoming pro-development entrepreneur who on retirement becomes a fervent preservationist (Rogers 1993). The empirical evi-dence detailed above indicates that newcomers and locals must be seen as heterogeneous clusters – the realisation of which has led to the promulgation of more complex classifications, beginning with Ray Pahl (1965), who first divested of the newcomer–local dichotomy. Following his work in Hertfordshire, Pahl developed a framework comprising eight distinct elements. These attempts at capturing the heterogeneity of existence in rural localities have led to finer and finer classifications; for example, Robinson (1990) – drawing on the work of Dean *et al.* (1984), Dobson (1987) and Spooner (1972) – identifies six groups of non-retirement counterurbanites in Cornwall alone. Each of these attempts implicitly links the discovery of interacting groups and the conflicts between them. These conflicts are generalised by Peter Ambrose (1992) (see Table 12.2) in a conceptualisation which can be broadly labelled a 'group-interest interac-tion approach'.

This group interest approach does not explain, however, how such diverse groups exist within the same space–time continuum, and it is regrettable that classifications are presented as answers rather than as an identifying tool prior to explaining the diversity of existence they catalogue. Such an approach also does not explain how groups come into existence or the motivation and rationale of individuals. Why do some people become conservationists? Why are some conservationists willing to camp out for two months as a protest against a new road while others will merely add their name to a petition? Its explanatory power of individual action is extremely limited, with the same weaknesses as the 'abstract self' of rational choice (utilitarian) theory:

> 'Theories of decision making... assume the pre-existence of preferences as provid-ing a motivation for policy actors to select a particular course of action. They insist that the process of decision making can be understood by looking at actors' interests as prior attitudes to behaviour... The fundamental deficiency of this model lies in the fact that it fails to concern itself with the origins of interest. It treats the interests adopted by policy actors as self-evident, ignoring the question as to how the alignment of particular interests and actors is actually determined. Politics of interest models of decision making cannot handle the question: "how do policy actors who behave in their own best interest come to know where that interest lies?"' (Schwarz and Thompson 1990: 49).

The group interest approach is essentially static as it cannot explain how attitudes and perceptions change over time. It is also based upon conflict between groups rather than recognising that conflicts within single groups can arise. For example, small business owners are often defined as a single homogeneous group (see Pahl 1966), and they may well be united in terms of a wish to see lower Uniform Business Rates, but they are also in direct and indirect competition with each other – does the fast food restaurant want to see planning permission granted for a local 'take-away'? Finally with the demise of landowner hegemony it does not show how each of the groups and individuals appeal to each other and how they interact. If no individual grouping can see all of its demands met in the fragmented environment in which it operates, how do they argue their case to impartial others?

Marquand's Modes of Political Change

At this point it is useful to consider what David Marquand (1988), developing the analysis of Lindblom (1977), outlines as the three modes of political change: command, exchange and preceptoral (Table 12.3). Utilitarian thinking and rational choice have concentrated on the exchange mode for understanding politics. All forms of the reductionist paradigm concentrate principally on the first two conceptions of politics. Under such a system of thinking:

> 'Hobbes, in some ways the greatest of all the thinkers in the reductionist tradition, painted a marvellously coherent, if chilling, picture of a society operating by the command mode. The seventeenth-century English Whigs, and their eighteenth-century American intellectual descendants, drove out their respective rulers in the name of the exchange mode. Both modes are, of course, omnipresent; it is hard to conceive of a society in which neither played a central part. Change can come by either of them, and frequently does. Almost by definition, however, neither can generate profound cultural changes – changes of value, belief and assumption' (Marquand 1988: 228).

Crucially for the argument one develops here, it is possible to see how traditional agricultural interests have historically operated through the command and exchange modes, via their domination of the rural economy, employment opportunities and, in consequence, local political power. However, with the dilution of agricultural interests and the growing diversity of new actors, stemming from the reordering processes discussed above, the preceptoral mode has become far more important. If no single actor, or set of actors, constitutes a majority the way in which these minority actors interact and appeal to each other becomes a vital area of study. To meet individual objectives actors must appeal to others, as no single set of actors can operate solely through the command and exchange levels. This of course is not to say these modes are unimportant or that relationships between actors are somehow now symmetrical, but rather that any conceptualisation of rural politics and studies of the interaction-relevant actors must consider how the various fragmented elements appeal to disinterested

Table 12.3 Modes of political change identified by Marquand

Mode	Definition	Mechanism of change
Command	Change is ordered from the top-down.	Actors obey orders, laws or dictates
Exchange	Change through the exchange relationships of individuals	Actors pursue certain avenues because it is made worth their while
Preceptoral	Change from persuasion, discussion, indoctrination and conversion (learning)	The way in which individuals perceive and understand a situation alters

Source: adapted from Marquand 1988: 224–235.

others and how in meeting their own objectives they make them seem in line with the overall aims of the whole community.

This loss of agricultural hegemony and the growing importance of the preceptoral mode is reflected in the changing nature of rural political systems. At a national level, there has been a clear challenge to the enclosed 'holy trinity' policy community of: the Ministry of Agriculture, Fisheries and Food with its 'single minded commitment to the farmers' cause' (Cox et al. 1986:185), the National Farmers' Union and the Country Landowners' Association. With the de-emphasis of primary food production (Walford 1992) there has been a greater prominence given to questions of agricultural policy (with an increasingly well informed public opinion, a clash between free market and traditional forms of Conservatism, and a widening of the environmental agenda from visual amenity and habitat protection to a less anthropocentric view and an assertion of tentative public environmental rights). At a supra-national level the linking of the reform of the Common Agricultural Policy with *The future of rural society* (European Commission 1988) highlights the recognition of the need to manage the transition to an economic and social system in which farming is not the major employer of the rural workforce (Walford 1992). In short, agricultural policy can no longer be seen (if it ever should have been) as a synonym for rural policy. The vitality of the agricultural interests and the well-being of the rural community as a whole are more and more detached. It is the realisation of this situation which has led the challenge to two cherished freedoms: the autonomy of the Ministry of Agriculture, Fisheries and Food and the farming community in the administration and implementation of agricultural policy, and the autonomy of farmers in making production and land use decisions (Cox et al. 1986).

In local rural politics the squeezing out of agricultural interests, while patchily studied, is no less clear. Until the 1974 local government reorganisation, farmers and landed interests were grossly over-represented as councillors in rural areas (as indicated by the 1977 findings of the Robinson Committee) and especially over-represented as council leaders (Jones 1978). Up to 1945 most were 'Independents', with 'council leaders. . . [being] major landowners their offices would almost be inherited with major estates' (Elcock 1994: 81). These agricultural groups watched their absolute power base dilute in the 1970s, as the 1974 merging of town and county saw their displacement by town-based or new-comer Conservative leaders. However, it was during the 1980s and early 1990s that the major shift occurred via the changed socio-economic structure of the Conservative Party and the latter's decline in local politics. After the 1993 county elections, the Conservative Party controlled outright only a single county (Buckinghamshire) and only just over one in four county councillors belonged to the party (Rallings and Thrasher 1993). The next step in mapping out the implications of this new fragmented environment – and the importance of the preceptoral mode – is to consider how individual actors appeal to each other and what appeals to the common good to support their case can be made.

INDIVIDUALISM AND COMMUNITARIANISM: JUSTICE AND THE 'RURAL IDYLL'

Theories of Justice

A broad and inclusive dichotomy can be drawn between individualist and communitarian theories of justice (Brown 1992). The former approach contemporary normative political problems by assigning primary significance to the interests and values of individuals, whilst the latter view communities as the prime source of value. Each approach includes a myriad of different forms but, at the risk of oversimplifying, the overall debate encompasses two key controversies – a methodological and a normative discussion (see Figure 12.1). The methodological element of individualism has tended to rest on one or both of the following stances: the abstract self – a way of conceiving individuals in which the features that 'determine the ends which social arrangements are held (actually or ideally) to fulfil, whether these features are called instincts, faculties, needs, desires or rights, are assured as given, independently of a social context' (Lukes 1973); atomism – which asserts that social phenomena can only be understood with recourse to individual actions (Cell I of Figure 12.1). The normative element of this individualism tends to be an appeal to global forms of justice or a moral cosmopolitanism (Cell III).

The stances which form the grounding for utilitarianism have long been challenged by Marx, Durkheim and Veblen, amongst others, who claim that the individualist image of the self is ontologically false. To use the neo-Hegelian term of Chris Brown (1994), the self is a 'constituted construct' (Cell II). The self, and thus individuals, are constituted by the community of which they are part. The community is thus more than an aggregate of individuals and has its own intrinsic value (Avineri and de-Shalit 1992). The implication for the normative debate is that the conceptions of justice people hold will derive from the communities to which they belong – global or absolute rules are therefore problematic (Cell IV). The community is itself a common good rather than the mere environment for individual interaction.

	Individualism	Communitarianism
Methodological	(I) Abstract self Atomism	(II) The constructed self
Normative	(III) Utilitarian Moral cosmopolitanism Libertarianism	(IV) 'Moral communities'

FIGURE 12.1 Individualism and communitarianism – a framework for analysis

This debate between individualists and communitarians, briefly outlined here, can be traced back to classical philosophy, and its deep tradition in both lay and academic discourse is readily apparent. It is this divide which also lies at the heart of our competing notions as to the 'good' rural society and it is to this which we now turn.

The 'Rural Idyll': Communitarianism and Individualism

The 'rural idyll' can be defined as the collective images of what rural living should be (Newby 1985). It is argued here that normative, collective notions of rurality embrace both individualistic and communitarian theories of the good. While often appealed to, the term 'rural idyll' in itself thus does not provide a framework for dealing with competing claims on rural land-use. This fissure between communitarian and individualist thought produces mutually incompatible theories as to appropriate individual rights and systems of political decision-making. It is these debates about the appropriate nature and limitations of individual rights which form the basis of contemporary arguments.

Notions of the rural idyll focusing on the integration of the 'natural' world with social cohesion have deep roots within British culture (Newby 1985; Wiener 1986: 41–80), with the village seen as the ideal entity for fostering '*community development*':

'Few people who live and work in the village have any doubt that social integration is worth fostering. In spite of the limits imposed on behaviour, the traditionalism, narrow-mindedness and gossip, village life offers something of high value – a sense of belonging to a face-to-face group' (Crichton 1964: 9).

Thus, Victor Bonham Carter (1952) concluded his book with the appeal 'our aim must be an integrated rural community', and Richard Wollheim talked of an 'English dream' of an unalienated folk society bound together by tradition and by stable local ties, symbolised by the village (cited in Weiner 1986: 42). Elsewhere, the 1980s saw a resurgence of local community development schemes based on a 'bottom up approach', in contrast to the central role of the state within the modernisation paradigm. For the most part these notions of rural communitarianism reflect post-Enlightenment, romantic views of the rural. However, other streams of thought should not be ignored, such as the re-emerging popularity of neo-Rousseauian participatory local democracies (see also Halfacree, and Murdoch and Day, Chapter 10, this volume).

The rural idyll also embraces the heart of individualism, with rural living a 'sense of achievement' – counterurbanisation, to use Berlan-Dorque and Collomb's (1991) term, is very much about the achievement of 'private ambitions'. The economic individualism of the 1980s had a clear rural focus, with country houses and second homes key status symbols for those with high discretionary incomes (Thrift *et al.* 1987). This was merely a new form of Conservatism, the roots of which are rural. Yet other individualistic dimensions of the rural idyll also exist which do not fall into the economic individualist camp – such as several forms of environmental cosmopolitanism and Kantian naturalism.

The rural idyll thus embraces both communitarian and individualist values which are mutually exclusive. It does not in itself provide a *telos* for settling disputes between competing plans in rural localities. Crucially then, for all the long tradition of 'rural worship', there has never been a single, clear and consistent notion of what the countryside should be. Notions of what the countryside should be – rooted in both academic and lay discourse – are expressed in both individualist and communitarian terms. This reflects the deep divide in normative thinking rather than presenting a consistent normative blueprint. Consequently, there has never been a consistent benchmark by which competing notions of the rural good could be judged. Our next task is thus to map out how these theories manifest themselves in contemporary fragmented societies.

Individuals and Communities in Fragmented Localities

While the communitarian tradition has long roots in academic and lay discourse two central issues face its rural crystallisation – the question of boundaries and, derived from this, the distinction between insiders and outsiders. When studying the social boundaries of rural communities the interactionist approach outlined by Sarah Harper (1987, 1989) is of interest. She argues that some individuals confine all aspects of their lives – physical (use of settlement – work, residence and recreation), social (networks of kinship and friendship) and symbolic (past and present experiences, images of place) – within the one settlement. These individuals are termed 'centred residents'. In contrast, those who conduct little of their lives within one settlement may be described as 'partially-centred' or 'non-centred' residents. In terms of settlements one can thus distinguish between localities where the majority of the inhabitants 'centre' their lives on that settlement – 'centred' settlements – and other settlements containing mainly 'partially-' or 'non-centred' residents – 'partially-centred' or 'non-centred' settlements. Harper concludes by arguing that only those residents who centre their lives on the settlement can claim membership of that settlement, thereby proffering that a real rural person is a centred person, residing in a centred settlement.

While not herself making the connection, the increasing diversity and mobility of residents combined with contemporary production systems means that very few residents fit into the centred groups. The centred community has become more problematic. The influx of counterurbanites and the globalisation of production systems (detailed above) means that very few people will live, work and socialise in the same community. Individuals belong to more than one community (see Halfacree, Chapter 11, this volume) – a person may work in a city office, join a local action group, go sailing with old university friends, and have family ties with people who live in another region. The re-ordering of rural communities means that the density and intensity of in-group relations within specific, spatially bounded micro-communities has declined (Calhoun 1991). In short, the totally 'centred community' is dead. The ideal of spatially bounded rural communities is no longer realistic under the contemporary political-economic framework. It is this loss which is behind what Howard Newby (1990) calls 'rural retrospective regret'.

The Paradox of the Rural Idyll

Taking Newby's notion of rural retrospective regret further, one can see it as a community ideal which is desired but no longer obtainable. Paradoxically, given the multi-community belonging of new counterurbanites (and their maintenance of external contacts long after moving), these rural residents would want to be, in any case, the exception to its rule. While the (mythical) golden age of 'everybody knowing each other' and a thriving community centred on the village may be missed, individuals cannot and/or will not (and should they have to?) give up their multi-community status. At the heart of the 'village community' is thus a paradox – it is desired but rejected.

It is this 'desired but rejected' paradox which forms the final part of this chapter. As Figure 12.2 details, three dimensions or implications of this paradox can be outlined. Culturally, the prevailing notions of the rural idyll within contemporary society by being associated with dead but mourned lifestyles has led to rurality becoming *kitsch*. *Kitsch*, deriving from the German *verkitschen* or 'to make cheap' (Calinescu 1987), stands in stark contrast to the avante-guard, which seeks to replicate the very impulse of creation rather than to recreate already formed works. In opposition *kitsch* wallows in re-creation, with its very dependence upon mass consumption serving as an integral part of its definition.

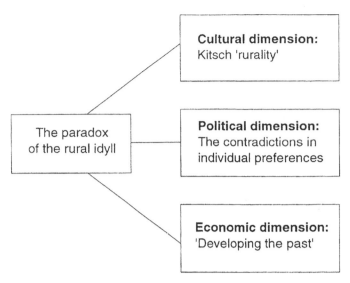

FIGURE 12.2 The paradox of the rural idyll

This paradox of the rural idyll leaves a culture constantly looking to the past – the terms rural and heritage are now almost synonymous. Within such an environment a whole industry devoted to the oxymoronic aim of 'developing the past' has emerged within a society constantly looking to preserve and recreate but without a clear notion or framework for deciding what should be preserved.

CONCLUSIONS

The breakdown of agricultural hegemony has heightened the importance of the preceptoral mode of political action within rural areas, with individuals and groups having to attract support from, convince and/or reassure others. With the growing heterogeneity of rural actors in terms of both economic and socio-demographic status, their competing claims and perspectives represent an ever widening spectrum. Indeed, there is great and growing diversity within and between rural areas, with a consequent increase in the number of potential conflicts as to the use of space. Individual and community based theories have inevitably come into play within this conflict. We are left with a fragmented social arena of competing possible uses of space but without a bounded community in which problems can be solved through consensus. The rural idyll, although often appealed to in this context, does not in itself provide an appropriate framework for evaluating between competing notions of justice. There has never been a clear and consistent historical tradition of what the countryside should be, who it is for, and what should be the rights of those living within and outside it.

REFERENCES

Ambrose, P. (1992) 'The rural/urban fringe as battleground', in B. Short (ed.), *The English rural community: image and analysis*, Cambridge University Press, Cambridge, 175–194.

Avineri, S. and de-Shalit, A. (1992) 'Introduction', in S. Avineri and A. de-Shalit (eds.), *Communitarianism and individualism*, Oxford University Press, Oxford, 1–11.

Berlan-Darque, M. and Collomb, P. (1991) 'Rural population – rural vitality', *Sociologia Ruralis*, **31**, 252–261.

Bolton, N. and Chalkley, B. (1990) 'The rural population turn-around: a case study of North Devon', *Journal of Rural Studies*, **6**, 29–43.

Bonham-Carter, V. (1952) *The English village*, Penguin, Harmondsworth.

Brown, C. (1992) *International relations theory: new normative approaches*, Harvester Wheatsheaf, Hemel Hempstead.

Brown, C. (1994) 'The ethics of political restructuring in Europe – the perspective of constitutive theory', in C. Brown (ed.), *Political restructuring in Europe: ethical perspectives*, Routledge, London, 163–186.

Buller, H. and Lowe, P. (1990) 'Rural development in post-war Britain and France', in P. Lowe and M. Bodiguel (eds.), *Rural studies in Britain and France*, Belhaven Press, London, 21–36.

Calhoun, C. (1991) 'Indirect relationships and imagined communities; large-scale social integration and the transformation of everyday life', in P. Bourdieu and J. Coleman (eds.), *Social theory for a changing society*, Westview Press, Boulder, Colorado, 95–121.

Calinescu, M. (1987) *Five faces of modernity*, Duke University Press, Durham, North Carolina.

Central Statistical Office (1992) *Regional Trends 27*, HMSO, London.

Champion, A. and Townsend, A. (1990) *Contemporary Britain: a geographical perspective*, Edward Arnold, London.

Clark, G. (1991) 'People working in farming: the changing nature of farmwork', in T. Champion and C. Watkins (eds.), *People in the countryside: studies of social change in rural Britain*, Paul Chapman, London, 67–83.

Cloke, P. and Little, J. (1990) *The rural state? Limits to planning in rural society*, Clarendon Press, Oxford.

Connell, J. (1978) *The end of tradition: country life in central Surrey*, Routledge and Kegan Paul, London.

Cox, G., Lowe, P. and Winter, M. (1986) 'Agriculture and conservation in Britain: a policy community under siege', in G. Cox, P. Lowe and M. Winter (eds.), *Agriculture: people and policies*, Allen and Unwin, London, 181–215.

Crichton, R. (1964) *Commuters' village; a study of community and commuting in a Berkshire village*, David and Charles, Dawlish.

Day, G. and Thomas, D. (1993) 'Rural needs and strategic response: the case of rural Wales', *Local Economy* **6**, 35–47.

Dean, K., Shaw, D., Brown, B., Perry, R. and Thorneycroft, W. (1984) 'Counterurbanisation and the characteristics of persons migrating to west Cornwall', *Geoforum*, **15**, 177–190.

Department of the Environment/Welsh Office (1988) 'Rural enterprise and development', *Planning Policy Guidance Note 7*, January.

Dobson, S. (1987) 'Manufacturing establishments, linkage patterns and the implications for peripheral area development: the case of Devon and Cornwall', *Geoforum*, **18**, 37–54.

Elcock, H. (1994) *Local government: policy and management in local authorities*, Routledge, London, 3rd edition.

Errington, A. and Tranter, R. (1991) *Getting out of farming? Part two: the farmers*, Study No. 27, Farm Management Unit, University of Reading.

European Commission (1988) *The future for European society*, European Commission, Luxembourg.

Eurostat (1992) *Europe in figures*, Statistical Office of the European Communities, Brussels.

Frankenberg, R. (1973) *Communities in Britain: social life in town and country*, Penguin, Harmondsworth, Revised edition.

Gilligan, J. (1984) 'The rural labour process: a case study of a Cornish town', in T. Bradley and P. Lowe (eds.), *Locality and rurality: economy and society in rural regions*, Geo Books, Norwich, 91–112.

Griffiths, A. (1989) 'Patterns of farm diversification in Devon and Cornwall', unpublished paper, Department of Geography, University of Exeter.

Halfacree, K. (1993) 'Locality and social representation: space, discourse and alternative definitions of rural', *Journal of Rural Studies*, **9**, 23–27.

Halliday, J. and Coombes, R. (1995) 'In search of counterurbanisation: some evidence from Devon on the relationship between patterns of migration and motivation', *Journal of Rural Studies*, **11**, 433–446.

Harper, S. (1987) 'Rural reference groups and images of place', in D. Pocock (ed.) *Humanistic approaches in geography*, Occasional Paper No. 23, Department of Geography, University of Durham.

Harper, S. (1989) 'The British rural community: an overview of perspectives', *Journal of Rural Studies*, **5**, 161–184.

Harper, S. (1991) 'People moving to the countryside: case studies of decision making', in T. Champion and C. Watkins (eds.), *People in the countryside: studies of social change in rural Britain*, Paul Chapman, London, 22–37.

Jones, G. (1978) 'Political leaders in local government', in G. Jones and A. Norton (eds.), *Political leadership in local authorities*, INLOGOV, Birmingham, 9–29.

Jones, H., Caird, J., Berry, W. and Dewhurst, J. (1986) 'Peripheral counter-urbanization: findings from an integration of census and survey data in northern Scotland', *Regional Studies*, **20**, 15–26.

Keeble, D., Tyler, P., Broom G. and Lewis, J. (1992) *Business Success in the Countryside: the performance of Rural Enterprise*, PA Cambridge Economic Consultants Limited for the Department of the Environment, HMSO, London.

Lewis, G., McDermott, P. and Sherwood, K. (1991) 'The counter-urbanization process: demographic restructuring and policy response in rural England', *Sociologia Ruralis*, **31**, 309–320.

Lindblom, C. (1977) *Politics and markets: the world's political-economic systems*, Basic Books, New York.

Lloyd, G and Black, S. (1993) 'Highlands and Islands Enterprise: strategies for economic and social development', *Local Economy*, **8**, 69–81.

Lukes, S. (1973) *Individualism*, Blackwell, Oxford.

Marks, H. (1989) 'Statistical survey', in A. Britton (ed.), *A hundred years of Britsh farming*, Taylor and Francis, London.

Marquand, D. (1988) *The unprincipled society: new demands and old politics*, Jonathan Cape, London.

Marsden, T. (1995) 'Beyond agriculture? Regulating the new rural spaces', *Journal of Rural Studies*, **11**, 285–296.

Ministry of Agriculture, Fisheries and Food (1994) *Success with farm diversification: a step by step guide*, Ministry of Agriculture, Fisheries and Food Publications, No. PB1689, London.

Morgan, K. and Sayer, A. (1985) 'A "modern" industry in a "mature" region: the remaking of management-labour relations', *International Journal of Urban and Regional Research*, **9**, 383–403.

Newby, H. (1985) *Green and pleasant land? Social change in rural England*, Hutchinson, Hounslow.

Newby, H. (1990) 'Revitalising the countryside: the opportunities and pitfalls of counter-urbanisation', *Royal Society of Arts Journal*, August, 630–636.

Newby, P. (1971) 'Attitudes to a business environment: the case of the assisted areas of the South West', in K. Gregory and W. Ravenhill (eds.), *Exeter essays in geography*, University of Exeter Press, Exeter, 185–199.

Pahl, R. (1965) 'Urbs in rure: the metropolitan fringe in Hertfordshire', *London School of Economics Geographical Papers No. 2*.

Pahl, R. (1966) 'The social objectives of village planning', *Official Architecture and Planning*, **29**, 1146–1150.

Radford, E. (1970) *The new villagers: urban pressure on rural areas in Worcestershire*, Frank Cass, London.

Rallings, C. and Thrasher, M. (1993) *Local elections handbook 1993: the 1993 County Council election results in England and Wales*, Local Government Chronicle Elections Centre, University of Plymouth, Plymouth.

Robert, P. and Randolph, W. (1983) 'Beyond decentralization: the evolution of population distribution in England and Wales 1961–81', *Geoforum*, **14**, 75–102.

Robinson, G. (1990) *Conflict and change in the countryside: rural society, economy and planning in the developed world*, Belhaven, London.

Rogers, A. (1993) 'English rural communities: an assessment and prospects for the 1990s', *Rural Development Commission Strategy Review, Topic Paper 3*, Rural Development Commission, London.

Sant, M. and Simons, P. (1993) 'The conceptual basis of counterurbanisation: critique and development', *Australian Geographical Studies*, **31**, 113–126.

Schwarz, M. and Thompson, M. (1990) *Divided we stand: redefining politics, technology and social choice*, Harvester Wheatsheaf, London.

Shoard, M. (1987) *This land is our land: the struggle for Britain's countryside*, Paladin, London.

Spooner, D. (1972) 'Industrial movement and the rural periphery: the case of Devon and Cornwall', *Regional Studies*, **6**, 197–215.

Strak, J. (1989) *Rural pluriactivity in the UK*, A report to the Rural Employment Group of the NEDC Agriculture Ad Hoc. Sector Group, NEDO, London.

Strathern, M. (1981) *Kinship at the core: an anthropology of Elmdon in the Nineteen Sixties*, Cambridge University Press, Cambridge.

Sweeney, G. (1987) *Innovation, entrepreneurs and regional development*, Francis Pinter, London.

Thrift, N., Leyshon, A. and Daniels, P. (1987) '"Sexy greedy": the new international financial system, the City of London and the South East of England', *University of Bristol Working Paper on Producer Services No. 8*.

Townroe, P. and Mallalieu, K. (1993) 'Founding a new business in the countryside', in J. Curran and D. Storey (eds.), *Small firms in urban and rural locations*, Routledge, London, 17–53.

Walford, N. (1992) 'Agriculture in the context of the restructuring of rural employment', in I. Bowler, C. Bryant and D. Nellis (eds.), *Contemporary rural systems in transition: economy and society*, CAB International, Wallingford, Oxfordshire, 187–200.

Weekley, I. (1988) 'Rural depopulation and counterurbanisation: a paradox', *Area*, **20**, 127–134.

Whatmore, S., Munton, R. and Marsden, T. (1990) 'The rural restructuring process: emerging divisions of agricultural property rights', *Regional Studies*, **24**, 235–245.

COUNTERURBANISATION, FRAGMENTATION AND RURAL IDYLL / 235

Wiener, M. (1986) *English culture and the decline of the industrial spirit 1850–1980*, Penguin, Harmondsworth.

Young, M. and Wilmott, P. (1957) *Family and kinship in East London*, Routledge and Kegan Paul, London.

13

PLANNING BY NUMBERS: MIGRATION AND STATISTICAL GOVERNANCE

SIMONE ABRAM, JONATHAN MURDOCH and TERRY MARSDEN

INTRODUCTION

The previous chapters have indicated that counterurbanisation is a distinctive component in the social construction of rurality. People who move from urban areas into the countryside bring with them ideas about what the rural environment is, or should be, and often attempt to mould the countryside to fit those images. Counterurbanisation is thus not a simple movement of people, but involves a re-creation of the rural that appears through developments (or through resistance to development) which are, in turn, regulated by all levels of government through land-use planning.

Yet whilst the distinctive character of counterurbanisation has been recognised, along with the social implications of migration patterns and processes, the means by which it is governed has been subject to less attention. In particular, the interrelations between statistical projections and the development of specific localities are under-researched. In this chapter we focus upon the tools used by government agencies, planners and others to conceptualise populations and migration and the role these play in shaping strategies for the governance of rural areas. In particular, we consider how the provision for development in strategic plans can shape in-migration, and how the focus on statistical projections can result in a potentially self-fulfilling planning process (see Bramley and Watkins 1995) which sidelines attempts to draw up a broad philosophy of rural development.

We take as our starting point the premise that the migration of households is mediated through the planning system at the points where houses (or, more generally, 'dwellings') are to be built, modified or serviced, or where transport facilities are developed. It is at the strategically important moments of decision-making, where spatial allocations for developments are made and where particular proposals are considered, accepted, modified or rejected, that different actors may effectively exert pressures to influence development. In particular, the expectations of new rural residents in desirable areas can be encouraged or directed when strategic and development plans are under review. To govern these 'planning moments', the fundamental strategic objectives are embodied in technical statistical models that, we will argue, may only be modified on their own terms. The ability of local residents to modify these models is therefore sharply circumscribed.

In this chapter we consider the development of statistics of rural migration within the planning system, showing their passage from local to national government, back to local government and finally into the 'public' domain. In particular, we will show how negotiations over the distribution of provision for development in rural areas – between the tiers of local, regional and national policies – lead to constraints on county-level strategic planning. We will, thus, illustrate how the planning system acts with recourse to statistical constructions to mediate and regulate the migrations described in the counterurbanisation literature. We seek to trace out how the statistical calculations and representations of migration feed into planning, how these might be contested and what effects they are likely to have.

We begin in the next section by briefly outlining how statistics have become an everyday tool in the conduct of government. We then go on to examine the use of statistics in the forward planning process, tracing the calculations at the apex of the planning hierarchy and how these are then passed down to the local level. We employ an analysis derived from research undertaken in the county of Buckinghamshire of its structure plan review process in order to illustrate how numbers are used to frame debates at the local level and show that these have real material effects in shaping both migration patterns and the nature of rural space.

STATISTICS AND GOVERNANCE

According to Rose (1991), numbers have an unmistakable power in modern political culture; indeed, 'modern political argument seems inconceivable without some numerical measure' (p. 674). The use of numbers in governance can be traced from early attempts at census-taking which effectively counted the population and their goods (for example, the Domesday project) in order to provide a basis for the conduct of effective governance. As European states consolidated themselves, so they developed new techniques of government which concentrated on regulating the economic activities of individuals and corporations (see Foucault 1991). Thus, Hacking (1990: 3, 5) describes an 'avalanche' of printed numbers throughout Europe, most notably in Germany, from the end of the eighteenth century onwards. The use of numerical methods was further bolstered by the social surveys of Booth and Rowntree in the nineteenth century, formalising a process of social representation that fed directly into the formation of the modern welfare state.

Statistical techniques provide a graphic example of how particular domains (for example, the social, the rural) can be both represented and opened up to political deliberation to form a domain of governance. By translating economic and social phenomena into numbers, they can more easily be acted upon (Latour 1987). Furthermore, once social and economic issues have been enumerated, subjects can be persuaded to regulate themselves by acting within a system of government which begins to appear self-evident. As Hacking (1990: 6) explains:

> 'enumeration requires categorisation, and [the] defining [of] new classes of people for the purpose of statistics has consequences for the ways in which we conceive of others and think of our own possibilities and potentialities'.

'Counting' leads to the articulation of 'norms' whereby people are considered 'normal' if in their characteristics they conform to the central tendencies of statistical laws; those that do not are considered 'pathological':

> 'Few of us fancy being pathological, so "most of us" try to make ourselves normal, which in turn affects what is normal' (Hacking 1990: 2).

The collection of statistics and the proliferation of inscriptions, with their technologies for classifying and enumerating, thus become effective techniques of governmentality, allowing civil domains to be rendered visible, calculable and, therefore, governable. Furthermore, they herald the advent of subjects who remain 'free' but come to calculate themselves in terms derived from the tools and techniques of governmentality (Foucault 1991). Thus we can begin to imagine how government might depend upon calculations made in one place in order to affect things in another, enabling us to illustrate how policies derive from these processes of representation.

Numbers have, therefore, become an intrinsic part of the way governance is practised. However, as numbers come to be widely accepted as a normal element of political calculation, so they purport to act as 'automatic technical mechanisms for making judgements, prioritising problems and allocating scarce resources' (Rose 1991: 674) thus; political calculation appears to be 'de-politicised'. For this reason, this aspect of government is often overlooked, as it seems to be a 'neutral' or 'objective' aspect of decision-making that resists political influence. However, the use of numbers to represent specific phenomena of population or economy (Foucault 1991) then comes to define the range of activities which are to be governed by politics. This process of enumeration captures only a partial, and often distorted, view of those phenomena. Actions then taken on the basis of the numerical representation later feed back on the phenomenon, usually through the formation of policy. In short, numbers delineate 'fictive spaces' for the operation of government, and establish a 'plane of reality', marked out by a grid of norms, on which governments can operate (Rose 1991). In the next section we outline the use of numbers in planning for migration, and show how their use has the effect of limiting the scope of policies.

PLANNING BY NUMBERS

We focus here on the statistics used in strategic planning. We will argue that, much in the same way as accounting 'seeks to align the actions of "free" individuals with specific objects by enclosing them within a particular calculative regime' (Miller 1992: 72), the system of regulation, guidance and statistical projection that provide the basis for strategic land-use planning steers the arena of debate between narrowly drawn boundaries.

The system of regulation which surrounds housing and migration patterns can be characterised as a 'pyramid', at the top of which are statistics for population growth and household formation. These figures, which are provided by the Office for National Statistics, provide the basic assumptions upon which calculations of housing needs are based. The calculations work on assumptions of population trends, household formation and likely migration patterns in particular areas, and so on. They ascertain what the likely levels of housing demand will be for a 20-year period. Further down the pyramid the provision of an 'adequate' and 'continuous' supply of housing is achieved through the following planning hierarchy (Department of the Environment 1991):

- Regional guidance and structure plans – provide overall policy targets.
- Local plans – provide criteria for the release of sites and identify potential housing sites.
- Land availability studies – identify a five-year supply of sites for housing and indicate the extent to which plan requirements are being met.

Population growth is, therefore, apparently managed through the planning hierarchy.

The management of population growth also has a regional dimension. For example, in the South East region of England (where our case study county is located), the central calculations of likely population growth and housing demand are mediated through SERPLAN, the regional planning forum. Land availability is ascertained through housing availability studies, and district-wide availability is aggregated and forwarded to the County Councils who negotiate at a regional level, as SERPLAN. SERPLAN offers regional recommendations to the Department of the Environment (DoE) for approval according to the government's development priorities. The DoE then issues guidance figures, derived from the Office of Population Censuses and Surveys population and the household projections, which are then passed back to SERPLAN to apportion to the counties. SERPLAN holds the responsibility to distribute the figures to the counties, which eventually feed into the structure plan review process. Within the structure plan, the figures are divided into district targets. It is up to the districts and county officials to find sites, through the operation of land availability studies, to meet the perceived levels of 'demand'. In short, the whole pyramid is based on, and held together by numbers. Figure 13.1 shows the initial flow of information about land availability, which is aggregated at district, county and

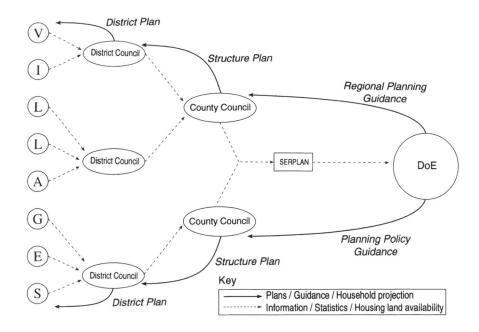

FIGURE 13.1 The passage of statistics from local to strategic level and back

regional levels, and which then flows back again through the counties and districts as dwellings projections to be incorporated into plans and, finally, to re-emerge as buildings in the landscape (here indicated as villages, for the sake of simplicity). (This pattern of aggregation and dis-aggregation of statistics is closely paralleled in the forecasts of minerals demand, where the DoE liaises via a similar 'circular' process with regional committees (Regional Aggregates Working Parties, parallel to the Regional Planning Fora) made up of Mineral Planning Authorities (who are the County Councils), minerals companies and selected clients (Murdoch and Marsden 1995: 373)).

At each stage, a certain amount of public consultation is invited, but we are concerned to show that as each round of enumeration and allocation proceeds, it becomes more and more difficult to challenge the conclusions reached. As the figures become progressively immune to dispute, the opportunity for a public challenge to them diminishes. Furthermore, challenges to the figures become less likely to result in any alteration unless they can be expressed within a specific technical discourse. The power of the planning hierarchy, as an activity of the state, lies in its regulation of remote actions such as the building of x number of houses, the building of roads, planting of trees, and so on. In this case, the writing and reviewing of local plans is the means whereby this action is effected. The structure plan review process is, therefore, in part, an attempt to legitimise the allocation of houses at the county level. In the next section we turn to the structure plan review process, to show that planning comes to play a mediating role between the hierarchies of government and the public.

THE STRUCTURE PLAN

Our case study area is Buckinghamshire, a prosperous county with a long history of middle class in-migration to the rural areas (Murdoch and Marsden 1994). The county is centrally placed within a buoyant region (the South East of England) and the tensions generated by development pressures and preservationist aspirations are intense. The potential for the development sector to reach a relatively buoyant housing market is circumscribed by acute concern amongst residents over the maintenance of areas of protection against development pressure. The south of the county is marked by Green Belt and Area of Outstanding Natural Beauty (AONB) designations which have become home to groups of residents keen to uphold the 'green' spaces that characterise their neighbourhoods. These designations play a crucial role in maintaining those idyllic conceptions of rural settlements which motivate many residents in both their search for, and behaviour in, rural environments (Thrift 1989).

In 1990, Buckinghamshire County Council began a review of its County Structure Plan. The review began from a certain number of premises, including the general acceptance of the continuation of a period of intense growth in the county, which was to be curtailed only towards the end of the 20-year plan period, and a desire to protect the southern Chiltern Hills AONB and the Metropolitan Green Belt. In preparing the Structure Plan, the County Council referred to the recommendations of SERPLAN and the regional planning guidance (RPG9). Along with the consultation draft plan (Buckinghamshire County Council 1994a), the County Council also published a justification of its housing projections, demonstrating its use of demographic models and showing how these vary according to the choice of data-set (Buckinghamshire County Council 1994b). This document detailed the variation between the levels of population, housing and dwellings produced both by the Chelmer demographic model and by the county's[1] own model of population projection when these were dwellings-led versus migration-led.

The consultation draft plan introduces housing figures by outlining the county's intention to meet the immediate demands of economic growth and development and the needs of local residents, within the constraints of the county's 'capacity' (Buckinghamshire County Council 1994a). The intention is expressed in terms of the number of dwellings to be built during the plan period. Thus, housing provision is rendered into a 'de-politicised' number. For the first half of the plan period, the county-wide provision follows the amount of housing already given planning permission, and those sites already identified in local plans (35 000 dwellings). The housing provision suggested for the remainder of the plan period follows the governmental strategy to direct more growth to the east of the region (the 'East Thames Corridor'), and the figure follows what the county calls the 'natural change' which it expects during that period and which assumes that net in-migration will cease after 2001 (26 700 dwellings). Of the total number of dwellings which might potentially be built during the plan period of 1991 to 2011, the majority have already been envisaged in particular sites, leaving a key figure of 14 700 dwellings in 'new sites' to be found during the period of the plan. Out of the 61 700 dwellings projected by the plan, it is these 14 700 which the council has opened to debate, and which were the focus of the crucial discussions on the location of the new sites.

Even in constructing this account of the progress of the plan, it is difficult to avoid representing the household projections as a fait accompli. The projections presented by the county were based on DoE household projections that selected census data, 'vacancy rates' and migration factors to reach conclusions about the number of dwellings which ought to be built, as mentioned above. However, these household projections actually hide an array of social issues, such as a trend for household sizes to diminish, the averaging of household incomes used in compiling household figures, gender assumptions made in defining 'heads of household', ethnic differences in household arrangements, wealth differentials and their correlation with household sizes, and so on. Furthermore, these projections merely extrapolate previous trends, making little, if any, allowances for complex social and economic changes. The general trend towards double-income households and away from simple nuclear family households has proved extremely problematic in the formulation of averages based on existing household models, thereby calling into question the relationship between actual household formation and statistical approximations (see Bramley and Watkins 1995). Given also that these projections are based on the Census, and that the 1991 Census excluded a significant number of people, further doubts might be expressed about the accuracy of the DoE's household projections.

Frequently used phrases in the debate on the projections in the plan, such as 'housing need' or 'demand', include crude assumptions about working practices and 'lifestyles' which can be seen to be changing, but these changes cannot be incorporated into unidirectional projections. However, the apparent 'factuality' of these figures, and their processing according to complex forecasting models, gave them an air of authority that hid the vast array of social arrangements that lay behind them. Challenges to the figures on the basis of social issues (for example, the possibility that more people may become home-based tele-workers) lacked the processed numeracy of the 'housing need' figures, and were excluded from the debate. It was the processed figures which framed the debate, effectively excluding qualitative challenges.

However, numerical challenges to the county's population and household projections, particularly from the House Builders Federation, showed that the housing projections were not as neutral or factual as the county's initial presentation suggested. The variation in projected levels between the different statistical models used, pointed out by one developer in order to undermine the county's population model (Bolton 1995), actually provided an indicator of the underlying possibility of negotiating statistics. Particularly during the review of the plan, the statistical levels of provision were not quite so inviolable as they originally appeared, but were open to negotiation, or at least to debate, on their own terms, and many of the arguments presented focused on the possibility of altering them. This was nowhere more evident than during the Examination-in-Public.

THE EXAMINATION-IN-PUBLIC: MOVEMENT INTO THE COUNTY

During the review of the Structure Plan, a quasi-public debate was held to discuss what were seen as the major issues in the plan. This 'Examination-in-Public' (EiP) was held over three weeks, approximately three-quarters of the way through the review, and one year after the first draft plan was published for public consultation. Given that apprehension about the plan concerned the level of housing provision allocated to the five districts within the county, it is not surprising that the bulk of the EiP was devoted to the discussion of population growth and housing demand. Central to this debate was the question of rural migration: how much there was to be and where it was to go.

As we have explained above, the migration statistics presented in the drafts of the plan were the result of a round of negotiation between the districts, the counties (as SERPLAN) and the DoE. During this round, the notion that the figures reflect a 'need' which is somehow 'out there' is reinforced, so that at each review stage a further layer of authority is added to 'household needs' and 'provision' These are so tightly packed that by the time the review of the Structure Plan falls open to debate, the layers are not susceptible to being peeled back. If the choice of criteria used to draw up the figures cannot be challenged, then they are only open to review in terms of their own numerical logic. In the EiP, this was recognised by representatives of the various councils and of the housebuilders. Whilst one of the village-society representatives who attended the EiP also recognised this, his repeated challenges to the assembled representatives to bring 'some real numeracy' into the debate and divulge the basis on which their models were constructed raised only the response that the figures were based on 'well established models, using DoE household projections'. This illustrates the extent to which the councils 'take on board' the figures proffered; one might say they 'believe in them' and thus find it difficult to rise to the challenge of querying them. To query the figures which provide the basis for the justification of their own projections would be to undermine planners' own status as competent technicians. Also, the complexity of the models used makes them reasonably resistant to simplistic explanation; in short, any political choices enshrined in the figures are hiden under a cloak of technicalities.

During the EiP debate on housing numbers, the House Builders' Federation

(HBF) provided a set of comparative figures and projections which gave alternative scenarios to those provided by the County Council. Putting particular emphasis on the mismatch between possible employment growth in the county and dwelling provision, the HBF plumped for a figure of 79 500 dwellings between 1991–2011, explaining that 'this is both realistic and reasonable, given the longer term intention to reduce growth'. Other developers also arrived at the EiP with their own housing projections (ranging from 64 000 to 74 000 during the plan period) and concentrated on undermining the County Council's housing projections, using alternative calculations. They attacked the figures from a number of directions – the Regional Guidance figures were too low, there was an excessive and unrealistic reliance on the east–west shift (the so-called East Thames Corridor), high levels of in-migration would continue, there was a mismatch between jobs and homes (linked to the issue of sustainability and the need to reduce commuting), and so on. The vacancy rates used by the County Council in their calculations were also criticised as too modest, thereby leading to a low overall figure.

The dense language used by the planning consultants during the EiP further emphasised the technical character of the debate. The following extract from the presentation made by one such planner during the EiP's discussion of the total figures proposed for Aylesbury Vale illustrates this:

'Now, background paper 1 usefully tells us that, in table 2, that migration in the twenty year period 1970 to 1991 was actually 20 000 persons, that's 1 000 persons per annum, 63 percent of the total population change. The period of 83 to 93, there was completions taking place at an annual rate of about 992 per annum. When you look at 1986 to 1993, . . . you are seeing an average rate of 935 completions per annum. . . . If you look at the approved structure plan, policy 5, structure plans alteration number 3, you will see provision for 11 200 dwellings in the district and that works out about 745 completions over the whole of the approved Structure Plan period. . . so for the period of 86 to 96, you are looking at a slightly higher figure than the average and that was presumed to be 810 completions. . . .'.

Any effective challenge to the Structure Plan policies had to confront this discourse and, moreover, had to adopt numerical terms. Qualitative remarks were sidelined as arguments proceeded on the basis of 'hard facts'.

Effectively, the professional planning consultants – and other representatives who spoke for the housebuilders – had the task of opening up the plan to scrutiny from a technical standpoint. Using alternative numerical calculations they sought to undermine the county's own figures and argued for increased dwellings figures on the basis that in-migration patterns would be higher. In this they were partially successful, for the EiP Panel concluded that net-in-migration would be higher than the County Council had allowed, particularly in the latter half of the period. It also noted that the County Council had used a figure of 4.1 percent vacancy rates for 1991 declining to 3.0 percent in 2011. The Panel concluded that a rate nearer 4.0 percent than 3.0 percent would be more appropriate and calculated that a higher completion rate could be expected between 2001 and 2006. The total number of houses to be provided during the plan period was raised. The housebuilders had thus won a minor victory and the scope for in-migration was slightly increased.

The housebuilders' success, it might be argued, derived from their grasp of the figures and the calculations that lay behind them. They could therefore undermine the county's own calculations. Participants who did not have their 'own' figures were not so well equipped to conduct the appropriate arguments. When the EiP Panel came to write its report, the chair admitted that much of the content of the plan and of the EiP consisted of conflicting opinions on the shape and appearance of the county, whereas the only point on which the Panel could make an apparently definitive contribution was on the numerical issue of housing projections, balancing the different equations put forward during the review. Those participants who expressed deep reservations about the validity of the statistics, the assumptions about the 'need for growth', and so on, but who did not put forward a thorough numerical analysis suggesting alternative calculations, were not able to make an impact on the final projections accepted. For example, the Council for the Protection of Rural England (CPRE) argued that levels of growth were too high, as this exchange during the EiP makes clear:

> *CPRE representative*: 'We questioned the need for Bucks as a whole and particularly Aylesbury Vale in this case to grow at the rate that it is projected to grow at. . . we would like to press our point that we don't believe that Bucks should be growing at the rate it is and some of the problems that we're talking about today [infrastructure, transport, sustainable development] could be solved in that way'.
> *Chair*: 'And of course, by implication, you see no reason why Aylesbury Vale should have to accommodate another 14 600 [dwellings]'.
> *CPRE representative*: 'Exactly'.

The CPRE did put forward an alternative total, but did not provide a numerical model to justify their figure. For the panel, this was the expression of a 'feeling' that was to be expected from CPRE. Without numerical indices on which to base calculations, however, it could not be mathematically reasoned alongside the arguments of the County Council or the HBF.

THE CASE OF THE IMAGINARY MIGRATION: MOVEMENT WITHIN THE COUNTY

In the review of the plan, a great deal of effort was expended in explaining the distribution of the county's development, namely the allocation of a number of dwellings to each of the districts. If the county was to plan to build an extra 14 700 dwellings during the plan period, and these were not to violate the protected areas in the south of the county, they would have to be located in the north of the county. Whilst there were housing 'needs' identified for the southern districts, through what was termed 'natural' or 'indigenous' growth, the housing allocations for these districts were much lower than the levels of 'need' projected for the plan period, leaving a shortfall in housing provision. The housing allocations in the plan provided for extra dwellings in the north of the county to compensate for the shortfall in the south, thus arithmetically matching the population forecasts to the housing provision. However, implicit in the plan was the assumption that the forecast growth in population in the south could be housed in the north of the county through a certain degree of movement from south to north.

A few salient points can be made here. The north of the county is dominated by the new town of Milton Keynes, which continues to grow, although at a declining rate. Across the county, there is a great deal of demonstrative public objection to building in the open countryside and public attention is well focused on this issue. In contrast to the very vocal representation from the rural areas, there is little public representation from the inhabitants of Aylesbury town, which is not parished and therefore has no statutory representative. As a further source of pressure for development on the northern areas, house prices in the south of Buckinghamshire are extremely high and little 'affordable housing' is available. During the debate, it was repeatedly asserted that the lack of development in the south was compensated for by the high levels of development in the north, particularly in Milton Keynes and Aylesbury. It was asserted by both the county and the southern districts that Buckinghamshire as a whole was fulfilling its regional responsibilities by providing housing in the north, the implication being that if people in the south could not afford to buy houses in their neighbourhoods, they were able to move northwards and buy there; thus a migratory trend was established.

However, this logic was flawed: census data provided at the EiP by Milton Keynes Borough Council suggested that the number of households which had moved from the southern districts of Chiltern and South Buckinghamshire northwards into Milton Keynes during 1990/1991 totalled a net −10. Migration from Wycombe district, slightly further north, totalled 13 households, whereas the net in-migration from the more northern district of Aylesbury Vale, which neighbours Milton Keynes, was given as 102. (The migration flows in and out of north and south Buckinghamshire are shown in Figure 13.2.) The imaginary south to north migration reveals the fictions included in the distribution of housing between districts within the county, and raises questions about the meaning of 'housing need'. While developers were using the concept of 'housing need' to press for permission for more building, it was apparent that the few new houses to be built in the south of Buckinghamshire were not providing homes for those who 'needed' them, but for those who 'demanded' them and had the wealth to purchase property in this desirable area. Those in need of housing, i.e. those concealed or newly formed households with low incomes, were not actually moving into the housing available in Milton Keynes. While the county justified its housing allocations by arguing that housing was provided in the north for people in the south, this argument worked only as a persuasive strategy to legitimise its plan. It was not reflected in the movement of households.

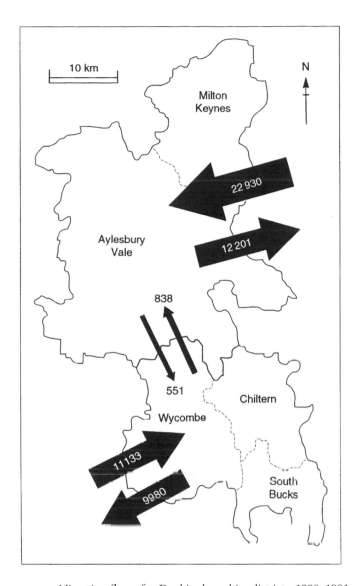

FIGURE 13.2 Migration flows for Buckinghamshire districts, 1990–1991

The supposed migration also illustrates the multivalency of the housing statistics. The spatial capacity for development in the county is translated into a statistical measure of the number of dwellings which could be built, through the process outlined above. However, the total has meaning not only as a lump sum of housing to be built in the county. Implicit within this quantity is a spatial distribution, i.e. the figure is an aggregate whose parts have individual values appropriated to the different districts within the county and to the particular growth points identified. Furthermore, the value of these separate statistical quantities must be seen in relation to one another as it is the relative quantities of development allocated to the different districts within the plan that form the political agenda of the plan, i.e. the regional strategy.

The explanation given at the EiP and the justifications written into the text of the plan for the concentration of growth in Milton Keynes and Aylesbury, with its reliance on a fictional notion of south to north migration, can be understood as a discursive strategy for managing the statistical problem of migration and housing provision. Clearly, migrants move into Milton Keynes from places outside Buckinghamshire and residents of South Buckinghamshire move out of the county to find affordable housing (for instance, to Slough, Berkshire, from the south), but the county's insistence on maintaining a strict limit on growth in the south whilst still fulfilling its responsibilities under the regional regime leads it to a contradiction between its stated aims and the activities it proposes to reach them. This is then rationalised using the fictional migration.

The buildings which result from the rounds of strategic and local planning activity are distributed around the county but the point at which the statistical quantities become housing on the landscape is dispersed throughout the process, each decision as to location relying on the preceding one. Once the housing is built and occupied, the fictions as to who would live in them, migrants from the south, from outside the county, or the 'natural growth' of the 'indigenous population', are no longer important. What matters during the negotiations about the current plan is balancing the calculations which lead to the desired total, and this may rely on anomalies such as the imaginary migration.

CONCLUSIONS

We have illustrated how public consultations and discussions of strategic planning policy tend to be structured by the statistics used initially to develop the policy. This is clearly visible in the narrow confines of discussions about planning policies, which are dependent on statistical forecasts and targets and we have shown how the particular use of statistical data discourages questions about the assumptions and implications used to compile them. Debate is thus confined to a discussion of numerical limits that can be measured, since dwellings, for example, can be counted and the quantities compared with the figures in the policies. Without the element of measurability, proposed policies can be dismissed as 'wishful thinking'.

This reveals a requirement for a local, effective forum for discussion of strategic planning policy, where the participants all have access not only to the information used to prepare the policies, but to the forms of knowledge that constitute their basis. Thus the numbers might be set in a broader context of wider issues. Although 'quality of life' is discussed in strategic planning policies, it is only in quantifying a measure such as amount of traffic or level of noise that policy is made effective. Qualities such as 'community' remain resistant to quantification and, thus, to manipulation and governance. Development poli-cies, whatever their direction, are written after an initial counting of 'how things stand', consideration of the possibilities for change based on numerical models and projections, and a set of calculations which move from the former to the latter. Thus we may argue that migration can be regulated and governed in terms of its quantity, and in some of its qualities (such as the wealth of migrants), but not in its sentiments (such as feelings of belonging or neighbourliness). These methods are not confined to migration projections. We can see the same trajectory being followed in efforts to incorporate the environmental agenda into strategic planning, legitimising and establishing environmentalism through the adoption of environmental audits and strategic environmental assessments, and in the process of so doing, reinforcing the model by increasing the volume of statistics and the authority of such methods of calculation.

If the use of numbers and numerical calculations clearly inhibits debate, we can also speculate that there may be a worse fate than being captured by numbers: that of being neglected by them. To illustrate this point, we can contrast the thorough (numerical) debate over the projected development of 'dwellings' with that around another related but quite different issue: Gypsy sites. At the EiP, a spokesperson for Buckinghamshire Council for Voluntary Services (BCVS) objected to the lack of provision in the plan for 'Gypsy sites'. Although the government had just removed the duty for councils to provide sites (the week prior to the debate), the BCVS spokesperson stressed that:

'whilst [the new legislation] removes the duty, it doesn't remove the power and Bucks CVS would very, very strongly support any encouragement that the plan can give to Bucks County Council to empower authorities to provide sites for travellers in the county'.

The Structure Plan did include a policy on 'travelling people', although it was further narrowed to 'Gypsy sites' reflecting an ongoing debate within the county and elsewhere over the nature of 'real Gypsies' (see Okely 1983: 28–37; Halfacree 1996: 54) as opposed to presumably inauthentic 'New Age Travellers' – namely that it should continue to provide sites for 'Gypsy families' (Buckin-ghamshire County Council 1994c. 37). However, in contrast to its policies on built homes, no statistical consideration of the level of provision required was put forward. Indeed, no debate was held on this issue at all. Could it be that the lack of definite enumeration of the requirements for travellers left the issue without any focus? One might also suspect that the lack of definite, enumerated commitment to such sites reflected the County Council's estimation of their importance.

Councils are used to working with housebuilders to organise their require-ments for development through the calculation of future demand pressures and so on. The policies in the plan reflect this by setting out requirements and intentions in a form which suits cooperative working patterns (which Shuck-smith (1991) criticises as verging on a 'corporatist' relationship). In contrast to the household projections, the moral and social obligations on the county to provide sites for travellers (whom we might venture to include as rural migrants) were not so clearly structured. In fact, they were so closed to questioning that the county were not prepared to engage in a discussion about them in the context of the Structure Plan Review; they were effectively 'hidden' from view.

In conclusion, we have highlighted the role of planning in mediating the counterurbanisation migrations described and analysed by others, in this volume and elsewhere. Although it might be argued that people are apparently at liberty to move around the country as they wish, it should be remembered that, quite apart from financial and social barriers (including gender and ethnicity), the whole process is governed and this governance is conducted by numbers. The process of abstraction which is 'thinking in numbers' is a specialised form of knowledge that is, by definition, inaccessible to non-specialists. In particular, those members of the public who choose to involve themselves in planning consultation exercises may well have neither access to this knowledge, nor the resources to make use of it. Members of the public enter such exercises in the belief that they can influence decision-making but, as we have shown, the technical processes used to make planning decisions are relatively impervious to non-specialist scrutiny. They consist of technical calculations and representations which appear to be de-politicised. However, these calculations have deep and lasting implications which go to the heart of conflicts in planning, development and rural migration.

ACKNOWLEDGEMENTS

This chapter is based on research carried out under the auspices of the ESRC Local Governance research programme. The authors should like to express their thanks to the participants in the Buckinghamshire County Council Structure Plan review and EiP, particularly to Chris Kenneford, Gordon Cherry and Chloe Lambert for their cooperation. Further thanks are expressed to Nick Gallent of University of Wales, Cardiff for his suggestions. This chapter is dedicated to the memory of Gordon Cherry who tragically died shortly after our fieldwork ended.

NOTES

1. References to 'the county' refer to Buckinghamshire County Council's Planning and Transportation section.

REFERENCES

Bolton, R. (1995) *Submission to the EiP for Buckinghamshire Replacement Structure Plan*, Development Land and Planning Associates, Aylesbury.
Bramley, G. and Watkins, C. (1995) *Circular projections*, CPRE Publications, London.
Buckinghamshire County Council (1994a) *The new Buckinghamshire County Structure*

Plan 1991 to 2011. Consultation draft, Buckinghamshire County Council, Aylesbury.

Buckinghamshire County Council (1994b) 'Population, labour supply, households and dwellings projections', Technical Paper, Buckinghamshire County Council, Aylesbury.

Buckinghamshire County Council (1994c) *The new Buckinghamshire County Structure Plan 1991 to 2011. Deposit draft*, Buckinghamshire County Council, Aylesbury.

Department of the Environment (1991) *Housing land availability*, HMSO, London.

Foucault, M. (1991) 'Governmentality', in G. Burchell, C. Gordon and P. Miller (eds.), *The Foucault effect: studies in governmental rationality*, Harvester Wheatsheaf, Hemel Hempstead, 87–104.

Hacking, I. (1990) *The taming of chance*, Cambridge University Press, Cambridge.

Halfacree, K. (1996) 'Out of place in the country: travellers and the "rural idyll"', *Antipode*, **29**, 42–71.

Latour, B. (1987) *Science in action: how to follow scientists and engineers through society*, Open University Press, Milton Keynes.

Miller, P. (1992) 'Accounting and objectivity: the invention of calculating selves and calculable spaces', *Annals of Scholarship*, **9**, 61–86.

Murdoch, J. and Marsden, T. (1994) *Reconstructing rurality: class, community and power in the development process*, UCL Press, London.

Murdoch, J., Abram, S. and Marsden, T. (1996) 'Modalities of planning: arenas, actors and strategies of persuasion in the development plan review process', *Working Paper Series*, CPLAN, University of Wales, Cardiff.

Okely, J. (1983) *The traveller Gypsies*, Cambridge University Press, Cambridge.

Rose, N. (1991) 'Governing by numbers: figuring out democracy in accounting', *Organisations and Society*, **16**, 673–692.

Shucksmith, M. (1990) *Housebuilding in Britain's countryside*, Routledge, London.

Thrift, N. (1989) 'Images of social change', in C. Hamnett, L. McDowell and P. Sarre (eds.), *The changing social structure*, Sage, London.

14

NEGLECTED GENDER DIMENSIONS OF RURAL SOCIAL RESTRUCTURING

JENNY AGG and MARTIN PHILLIPS

INTRODUCTION: RURAL SOCIAL CHANGE, RURAL RESTRUCTURING AND THE NEGLECT OF GENDER

In recent years there have been significant changes in the study of rural social change. While for many years emphasis had been on the demographic structure of rural areas and universalistic notions of rural depopulation and counterurbanisation, recent work has begun to take a more 'critical' focus (Phillips 1994), examining the power relations which are bound up in the ability to move into the countryside and in the practices adopted by those living in the countryside. One of the key drives in this reorientation of rural social studies has arguably come from class analysis which has elaborated notions of class *colonisation* and class *restructuring of rurality* (Cloke *et al.* 1991, 1995; Cloke and Thrift 1987, 1990; Murdoch and Marsden 1994; Phillips 1993; Thrift 1987). Basically, the former relates to the ability of some social groups to gain entry into the countryside for residence because of the assets associated with their class position, while the latter refers to the way that social groups may actively mould the environments in which they live, both consciously and through their unconscious impacts on their localities. Thrift succinctly summarises these processes as they may relate to service class members:

> 'Members of the service class have a strong predilection for the rural ideal/idyll. . .
> more than other classes, they have the capacity to do something about that
> predilection . They can exercise choice in two ways. First of all, they can attempt to
> keep the environments they live in as 'rural' as possible. Such a process can operate
> at a number of scales. Homes can be covered with Laura Ashley prints and fitted
> out with stripped pine furniture. Developments which do not gel with service class
> tastes can be excluded in the name of conservation. . . Second, they can colonise
> areas not previously noted for their service class composition. . . and mould these
> in their image' (Thrift 1987: 78–79).

While we feel the notions of class colonisation and class restructuring of rurality are highly significant, we also feel that rural class analysis has so far tended to neglect gender issues. This has been at a time when other work, notably that of Little (1987) and Whatmore (1991), has highlighted the importance of gender issues within rural studies. There has, however, been little integration of these arguments with studies of migration and the social recomposition of rural communities. In the wider context of studies of social stratification, on the other hand, the relationship between gender and other axes of social stratification has been the subject of increasing debate, with the integration of gender and class having been described both as being of central importance (Massey 1995; Witz 1995) and as being largely an irrelevance (Goldthorpe 1983). In this chapter we provide some reasons why the former view should be adopted in studies of rural recomposition and restructuring, and provide some initial ideas about how the issues of gender and class may be integrated within the study of contemporary villages. The chapter is structured into four sections: first, we use some results from a study of social change in Leicestershire and Warwickshire[1] to argue that there are important gender dimensions to the processes of class colonisation of the countryside; second, we argue that there is a clear gender division of labour spanning the official money economy and the unofficial economy of domestic work in at least some rural areas; third, we suggest that many rural images are highly, and quite specifically, gendered; fourth, we explore how gendered identities may be connected into processes of class colonisation and into rural lifestyle activities, although we also claim that these processes of class recomposition and restructuring of ruralities are, at the same time, a process of composing and recomposing gender orders in the countryside.

GENDER AND CLASS COLONISATION

Reasons for Ending the Neglect

As mentioned above, much of the work on class colonisation appeared to be rather gender blind. For instance, there has been a tendency in rural class analysis to talk in genderless terms: to talk about rising numbers of middle or service class 'people' and the migration of middle or service class 'members' into the countryside. There are at least three objections that can be raised about such a neglect of gender.

Firstly, empirical work on the number of men and women in the so-called service class has highlighted clear gender differences. For instance, a number of studies (for example, Boyle and Halfacree 1995; Crompton and Sanderson 1986) have remarked that service class employment for women is growing and there has been a rise in 'dual career households' whose combined consumption power may surpass households with a single high earner. Nonetheless, it is easy to over-emphasise the degree of gender change. For example, while the percentage of economically active women in service class employment grew by some seven percent between 1981 and 1991, the percentage of economically active men in these jobs still grew by six percent (Boyle and Halfacree 1995: 46). Furthermore, men appear from the 1991 Census to hold over 60 percent of service class jobs (Boyle and Halfacree 1995: 46), and there is clear gender differentiation within service sector employment, with much of the growth of female service sector employment being in 'servicers of the service class' (Crompton 1986; Crompton and Sanderson 1990) (secretarial, catering and caring occupations). Gender differentiation in class positions is clearly still very significant.

A second set of objections that can be raised against the neglect of gender relations relate to a number of more theoretical studies which suggest that gender relations are themselves key components of class formation. In a recent review of this theoretical debate Witz (1995) has suggested that there have been three specific foci of attention:

- The role of gender relations in establishing class positions within occupations in the official, market, economy; for example, Crompton and Jones (1984), Crompton (1986, 1992), Pringle (1989) and Witz (1990, 1992).
- Extending the notion of class across the boundary of the official money economy and into the area of domestic or 'reproductive labour'; for example Delphy (1981), Foord and Gregson (1986) and Walby (1986).
- The socio-political consequences of gender and class relations, such as how class-based political movements in part derived solidarity through the mediation of gender (and ethnic) identities; for example, Cockburn (1983), Mark-Lawson et al. (1985), G. Rose (1988, 1989) and Savage (1985, 1987). Also, how gender identities formed in the public sphere of politics and the media may actively constitute, as opposed to reflect, gender and class relations.

There are considerable differences in emphasis between each of these approaches. Part of the failure of class analysis to take on board the issues of gender may stem from people failing to recognise the different foci of attention, and more arguably from not seeking to integrate the insights from each perspective. This certainly appears to be the position of Witz who argues that there is a need for:

> 'a three-pronged gendered dynamic in class theory: gender mediated class-practices and socio-political class formation; gender, the family and socio-demographic class analysis; and gender, the occupational order and socio-structural class formation' (Witz 1994: 7; see also Witz 1995).

Simplifying, Witz is arguing that class and gender relations can be interconnected with reference to:

- Political – and we would add cultural – practices;
- Practices operating at the household level with regard to participation in the official and unofficial, domestic, economies.
- Practices within workplaces in the official economy.

We feel that there is much to be gained from employing such a multidimensional perspective both in understanding the interrelationships of class and gender, and also in understanding the colonisation and construction of ruralities.

A third objection to the genderless conception of class colonisation of the countryside stems from its emphasis on individuals, and in particular on 'male heads of household'. Most rural in-migration involves not single individuals but households: people tend to migrate with partners, with children, with relatives of some form. This was certainly the case within our study of social change in Leicestershire and Warwickshire. An initial stage of this research was to conduct questionnaires in five villages which spanned a range of different rural localities from relatively isolated and enclosed settlements to much larger ones which bordered quite closely onto urban settlements. Use was also made of the 1981 and 1991 Censuses to select settlements which had experienced a range of levels and forms of recent social changes related not only to class but also related to female employment and age structure. Across these villages over 200 in-depth questionnaires were conducted, wherever possible with all adult members of households, followed later by more informal interviews and focus group discussions. Within the questionnaire sample, some 95 percent of the people who had moved into the area had migrated as a household of more than one person.

Despite such evidence, much of the discussion of class colonisation still focuses on the seemingly genderless individual: talk is of rising numbers of members of particular classes, as if it makes no difference to the analysis if these class members are male or female. We suggest that it may very much matter, and that there may be very significant gender dynamics involved in class colonisation. Indeed, much of the current content of rural class analysis may be rather more reflective of the experiences of one gender. One of the causes of this may well be official statistics: the Census, for example, still emphasises the class position of the 'male head of household'. However, it can be suggested that there is a need to recognise both that members of households are involved in their own individual sets of class relations, and that some of these relations will run through the household and connect with other household members (see Acker 1973; Dale *et al.* 1985; Erikson 1984; Stanworth 1984). Theoretically, this may mean, as Wright (1989a, 1989b) has argued, that one needs to recognise how class positions are often combinations of what he terms 'direct' and 'mediated' class relations. Methodologically this means that all individuals should be ascribed a class position, or positions, and that it is important to explore the interconnection of class positions of individuals within households.

The significance of classifying all class positions is illustrated in Figure 14.1, based upon respondents to the questionnaire survey. The results suggest that there are important differences in class distributions between men and women. The prevailing orthodoxy in rural studies is that most of the people living in villages are middle class, even predominantly service class. Some studies (for example, Cloke *et al.* 1994b, 1995) have recently come to question this view. Phillips (1993), in particular, has argued that using Wright's (1978) class classification gives the impression of considerable class diversity in rural areas, with a

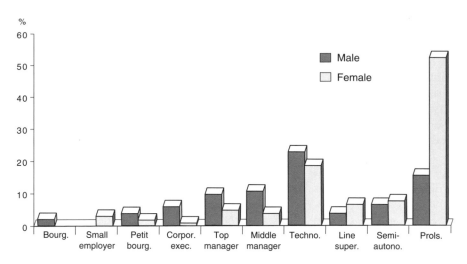

FIGURE 14.1 Class positions by gender: results of a survey of five villages in Leicestershire and Warwickshire

significant number of people being classed as working class or 'proletariat'. Our results reinforce the suggestion that there may be a gender dynamic to this diversity, with many of the people classed in the proletariat being women (Phillips 1993).

The significance of considering the interconnection of the class positions of individual household members has been highlighted by the notion of 'household gender–class symmetry' (see Bondi 1991). Households may be described as being 'symmetrical' when there is little difference in the class positions of men and women in the household. The existence of 'household gender–class asymmetry' in a rural population has been confirmed by Phillips's (1993) study of gentrification in four Gower villages, which found that women often had a much more proletarianised class position than their male partners. The present study of five villages in Leicestershire and Warwickshire produced similar results (Figure 14.1).

In the questionnaire we asked respondents about their work situation. The results confirmed the impression of a gender differentiation in class positions. As Table 14.1 illustrates, a large number of women in the survey were working or had last worked in paid employment in jobs which gave them very little control over their work conditions. Occupations associated with such work conditions included shop assistant, secretary, waitress, receptionist – all illustrations of the servers of the service class category of occupations – as well as some rather more traditional proletariat type jobs such as driver and warper. A higher proportion of women in the sample were in part-time employment, and women in general received lower remuneration and appeared to have lower career expectations than did men. Qualitative comments lend further weight to the suggestion of gender differentiations of work situations. While many men spoke of work

T A B L E 1 4 . 1   Gender differences in work situations

Aspects of work situation	Men (%)	Women (%)
In part-time employment	1	16
Have no control over daily work tasks	22	37
Cannot alter work rate	12	28
Cannot decide work tasks	36	63
Have no recognised career path	40	60
Average number of hours worked (per week)	45	34
Contribute under 25% of household income	1	66
Contribute over 75% of household income	43	8

Figures based on number of men and women in 'remunerative employment' (i.e. paid employment or self-employed).

being enjoyable, of forming a large component of their lives and even giving meaning to their lives, many of the comments by many women were much more downbeat: 'it's a means of existing'; 'there was no job satisfaction, I did it entirely for the family'; 'it gave me some pin money'.

These findings raise at least two important questions for those studying rural social change: firstly, what are the causes of the gendered asymmetry in the class composition of households living in rural areas, and, secondly, what are the consequences of this on interactions within the village and thereby on the constructions of rurality? In the remainder of this chapter we begin to address these two complex issues, but first we position ourselves with respect to some general debates about class and gender.

Gender: A 'Compositional Approach'

The causes of gender differences and inequalities and their relationship to class have been a subject of considerable debate (see Walby 1986). In this chapter we adopt what we term, drawing on the work of Connell (1987), a 'compositional approach'. Connell, in his book *Gender and power*, suggests that gender relations should not be seen as centred on any single 'structure' – be that capitalism or patriarchy – but instead are an 'historical composition' created, as in a musical 'composition', by 'a tangible, active and often difficult process of bringing elements together in connection with each other and thrashing out their relationships' (Connell, 1987: 116). He argues that gender analysis – indeed much of social science – operates with too big, and too static, a concept of structure. He argues, for instance, that the 'dualist theory' of structure and agency developed by Giddens, makes 'the link of structure and practice a "logical" matter, a requirement of social analysis in general' (Connell 1987: 95) and views all structures as being analogous to the structure of language. Connell argues that both points are wrong: practices do not always accord with the current structural forms, although they will be influenced by them; and what people describe as structures may vary considerably. In particular he argues that the structures of labour allocation, of domination, and of sexuality are quite different, although each is significant for the creation of gender relations. Gender relations become the historical outcome of practices which affect these, and possibly other, social relations. Their current form, so Connell (1987: 159) argues, generally consists of:

- A gendered separation of reproductive labour from the money economy and the political world.
- Heavily masculinised power regimes in 'core' social institutions and more 'open textured' regimes in 'peripheral' institutions.
- Institutionalised heterosexuality of a highly masculine form; all of which together sustain:
- A 'sexual politics' in which men dominate women.

Connell adds, however, that each aspect of the contemporary order has its own crisis tendencies and may be subject to change, albeit perhaps at present only within a particular social and geographical milieu: namely, within the younger intelligentsia of large Western cities.

The ideas of Connell appear to us to be of value in considering the causes and consequences of the gendering of class colonisation of the countryside. In particular, they raise at least three significant questions: are rural areas characterised by a dominant 'gender order'; if so, what are the processes sustaining this order; and, are there any signs of change in the gender order?

Rural Colonisation and Gendered Divisions of Labour

One of the strongest strands of the feminist critique of social science is that it has tended to ignore the gendered separation of 'reproductive labour' from the 'official economy' of money and state power. Thus, human geography has been criticised for focusing on the official economy and ignoring the role that the unofficial sphere can play in constituting major social transformations including those involving the migration of people. For example, the role of reproductive labour has been highlighted in feminist interpretations of such processes as urban gentrification and suburbanisation (see Bondi 1991; McDowell 1983; McKenzie 1988; Women in Geography Study Group 1984). In the case of suburbanisation, it has been suggested that the movement of population to the periphery of cities involved the creation of a gendered and spatialised division of labour in which men worked in the 'official economy' of the city centre and women in the 'unofficial economy' of the suburban home. Interestingly, this argument has not really been applied to the process of counterurbanisation: for example, gender relations are a notable omission from Champion's (1989) list of alternative explanations of counterurbanisation. This omission is despite the process of counterurbanisation often being conceived as being, at least in part, an extension of the same processes of dispersal which created suburbanisation (Keinath 1982; Robert and Randolph 1983).

Boyle and Halfacree (1995) have, however, recently claimed that much of the population decentralisation of the 1970s may indeed have a gender dimension. From the argument that counterurbanisation is related to the residential migration of service class members, they suggest that there are important differences in the migration patterns of male and female service class members, with the former often moving either from metropolitan to non-metropolitan regions or between non-metropolitan regions, while female service class movement was more often towards metropolitan areas such as London. Significantly, Boyle and Halfacree also remark that differences in migration patterns which seem to relate to gender also have a clear age dimension, with female migrants younger than their male counterparts. We suggest that the associations of gender, age and residential migration patterns may be indicators of the role of a dominant 'patriarchal' gender order in relations between householders. In other words, many young independent women are attracted to the job opportunities and facilities of the city centre where they can minimise journey-to-work costs and the costs of household production, and substitute market-produced commodities for household labour (Markusen 1981; D. Rose 1989; Warde 1991). Older women who are linked into a conjugal household with children, on the other hand, may have severed their personal participation in the official economy, and have hence lost any official marker of class except their husband's occupation. Such women become hidden migrants in the analysis of Boyle and Halfacree, yet they may also be the hidden agent in their male-centred process of counter-urbanisation. Pahl and Pahl (1971), for example, argued that the residential choices of married managerial men were greatly influenced by their wives. They also made the more general claim that the wives straddle both the official and unofficial spheres and that key moments of change, such as a change in residence, are created in the context of the interconnections between these spheres.

The results from our study suggest that the five villages in Leicestershire and Warwickshire share many of the features associated with gender division of labour within suburban areas. As Table 14.1 showed, there was a marked gender difference in the number of hours worked in the official economy', with men on average working 11 more hours per week than women. The demands of male employment also seem to play a major role in decisions over residential locations. As Table 14.2 illustrates, men cited their jobs as a reason for moving more often than women and, even more significantly perhaps, women were over five times more likely to cite their partner's occupation as an influence on their residential location than were men.

There were also clear gender differences in the performance of domestic labour, differences which furthermore seemed to accord closely with what might be rather stereotypical views of the performance of domestic labour. For example, women appeared to do most cooking, cleaning, ironing and shopping for food. Men, on the other hand, appeared to lavish particular attention on the car, to deal with the bank more often and to be much more likely to change

TABLE 14.2 Stated reasons for moving to present residence

Reasons	Frequency of mention (%)		
	Men	Women	Total
Occupation	24	12	36
Partner's occupation	8	42	50
Well-being of children	15	34	49
Changes in household structure	17	24	41

plugs! While some of these differences may appear rather amusing – they certainly raised a few smiles when we were asking the questions, particularly when the respective contributions clearly added up to more than 100 percent – the results also have a serious side. In particular, while there were aspects of domestic work which men were apparently more likely to perform than women, looking across the range of tasks it was clear that women, on the whole, were contributing far more to the performance of domestic tasks. This was often the case even when both partners were in employment.

Overall, the clear impression from our study was that there were very stark gender divisions of labour spanning both the official and unofficial economies. Women appeared to be seriously disadvantaged in the official economy both financially and in terms of their work conditions and promotion prospects. Women were also likely to be bearing an unequal proportion of domestic work. Taken together it appears that many rural households could be characterised as being 'patriarchal' in the sense that the interests of women seem to be subordinated to the interests of men.

It is interesting to note that within the urban literature the patriarchal, conjugal household is often portrayed as a household under threat, particularly because of the rising participation of women in the official economy. The process of urban gentrification which is often seen as the reversal of suburbanisation is, for example, often related to the formation of new divisions of labour created in association with rising female participation in the official economy (for example, D. Rose 1989). There is, however, considerable debate as to how one should account for this rise. Some writers (for example, Braverman 1974; Massey 1984; McDowell and Massey 1984) provide capital-centred accounts of the change: women are seen as an element of a reserve army of labour who are drawn into the workforce when required. Others (for example, Miller 1983) point to changes in the technology of reproductive labour – the vacuum cleaner, washing machine, dishwasher – and the ability of some households to buy in services. Another factor which has been identified is change in the state provision of welfare which makes women less able to gain sufficient finance to work exclusively in the unofficial economy (for example, McDowell 1991). Finally, a number of commentators (for example, Connell 1987; McDowell 1991) have pointed to more social and cultural explanations. Particular attention has been paid to an apparent decline in the significance of the 'conjugal family', with men and women delaying marriage and childbirth, having fewer children, living on their own for longer, not marrying, divorcing frequently, and acting as single parents more often. The existence of non-heterosexual households is also increasingly recognised, and indeed the issue of the gender divisions of labour is increasingly being linked in discussions to 'cathexis', the sexually charged relations between people.

The debate over the origins of rising female participation in the official economy is not only of relevance for those seeking to explain urban gentrification, but also serves to problematise further the processes of counterurbanisation. So far the argument has been that movement into the countryside might in part be constituted as part of a spatialised and gendered separation of productive and reproductive labour. The evidence from our survey certainly seems to confirm that there is such a spatial and gendered division of labour. The debates over urban gentrification can be seen to demonstrate that the gender division of labour was itself constructed in relation to changes lying beyond what is generally taken to constitute the economic. Phillips (1994) has recently suggested that rural studies has often been restricted by 'public'/'private' and 'official'/'unofficial' distinctions and that there is a need to think across these distinctions. This point is clearly demonstrated with respect to understanding the changing composition of the gender division of labour. Suggested explanatory factors have ranged from the official public spheres of the state and the mass media through to the unofficial spheres of the social reproduction of labour power and cathexic interpersonal relations. We suggest that a recognition of such a wide range of factors will be equally necessary to account for gender relations in the rural sphere.

Discussion of the full range of factors remains beyond the scope of this chapter. Instead we take one slice through the composition of the rural gender order by exploring the links between 'gender identities' circulating in the 'official public sphere' of the mass media, the constitution of the division of labour within the 'private spheres' of the official and unofficial economies, and actions in the 'intermediate public sphere' of the rural community (see Phillips 1994: 97–107 for clarification of these distinctions).

IMAGES OF THE RURAL AND GENDER IDENTITIES IN THE MASS MEDIA

Rural geography, like much of the social sciences, is undergoing something of a cultural turn. Attention is increasingly being paid within rural studies to the images of and meanings attached to the countryside (see Bell and Valentine 1995; Cloke et al. 1994a; Cloke and Milbourne 1992; Halfacree 1993, 1995; Jones 1995; Short 1991). Studies such as those of Cloke and Thrift (1987, 1990), Cloke et al. (1995), Halfacree (1994) and Thrift (1987) have suggested that images of the rural are central to the processes of colonisation and construction of rurality. In particular, it has been suggested that 'the rural' may act as a 'class marker', as a way of establishing social distinction between people. Detailed attention has been paid to the way that living in the countryside can be seen as a 'positional commodity' (Cloke *et al.* 1991; Cloke and Thrift 1987, 1990; Newby 1987; Phillips 1993; Thrift 1989). We feel that whilst these arguments are important, there are at least two further points that should be considered. Firstly, the 'cultural textures' (Cloke, Phillips and Thrift, chapter 9, this volume) of the rural are connected into class formation in other ways than through the establishment of social distinction. Many of the impressions of the rural are, for example, conveyed through images of landscape and it is therefore important to consider the claims of Cosgrove (1984) that landscape images are a 'viewpoint of control' which are closely connected to the establishment of property relations over land. In addition, as the work of Barrell (1980, 1992) has highlighted, many images of the countryside, to use the words of Thompson (1990), act to 'dissimulate' or hide social groups rather than to 'fragment' them by establishing social distinctions.

A second argument we wish to advance in relation to rural images and other cultural texts is that they may act both to form and to fragment relations of class. This fragmentation may occur when the processes of cultural circulation expand the orbit of 'the rural' beyond both the locality of the countryside (Halfacree 1993) and beyond the powers of middle class petty-capital. It may also occur because the cultural textures are linked into other constellations of social practices and relations which are able to exert a rather different influence. One such constellation of social relations and practices may well be those of a patriarchal gender order. For example, a number of feminist writers have argued that landscape paintings – such as Gainsborough's image of Mr and Mrs Andrews – embody a heterosexual masculinism:

> '*Mr and Mrs Andrews*. . . is a symptom of capitalist property relations. . . However, the painting. . . can also be read in other ways. In particular, it is possible to prise the couple – 'the landowners' – apart and to differentiate between them. Although both figures are relaxed and share a sense of partnership. . . their unity is not entire: they are given rather different relationships to the land around them. Mr Andrews stands, gun on arm, ready to leave his pose and go shooting again. . . Meanwhile, Mrs Andrews sits impassively, rooted to her seat. . . her upright stance echoing that of the tree directly behind her. If Mr Andrews seems at any moment able to stride off into the vista, Mrs Andrews looks planted to the spot. . . these two people are *not* both landowners – only Mr Andrews owns the land' (Rose 1993: 91–93).

Rose argues that this image, many other landscape images and many images of villages in the countryside reflect a heterosexual masculinism in that they emphasise and naturalise the conjugal family, bodily differences between men and women, the power of men in the official sphere and the importance of women in the unofficial sphere.

The problematic nature of such essentialism and naturalism has been clearly spelt out by a number of feminists. One of the foremost critics of the notion of 'essential' and 'natural' gender divisions has been Connell (1983, 1987) who, as mentioned before, sees gender divisions as being an historical construction. For Connell, there is no natural basis for the divisions between men and women. Instead, there are multiple male and female identities which are currently constructed in relation to two particular gender identities, namely 'hegemonic masculinity' and 'emphasised femininity'. These gender identities share common roots in heterosexuality and thereby involve each other in their own construction. Hegemonic masculinity, as the name implies, is a dominant identity, both in relation to emphasised femininity and to other male and female identities. The identity emphasises male power and is an identity which is often constructed through an emphasis on physical strength and body power, although its construction is also mediated through associating men with technological prowess, economic success, authoritative practices, violent behaviour and phallic sexuality. Emphasised femininity, on the other hand, draws associations between women and activities such as nurturing, caring, compliance and sexual receptivity. All these features are, Connell argues, located in a subordinate position to the supposed characteristics of men. As a result emphasised femininity is 'a femininity... orientated to accommodating the interests and desires of men' (Connell 1987: 183).

Connell suggests that these two gender identities dominate the contemporary mass media. It is certainly possible to see these gender identities within many contemporary media images (see Jackson 1991), including many of those which also draw upon images of the countryside (see Brandth 1995). Such images, for example, often emphasise and naturalise the conjugal family: this form of household appears frequently in rural imagery and this household form is portrayed as relaxed and at peace, seemingly in its 'natural' setting (Figure 14.2). Furthermore, Mills (1992) has argued that many of the magazines which Thrift (1989) identified as promoting service class lifestyles also promoted the image of feminine domesticity. We also suggest that there are other ways in which country magazines reinforce the dualism of hegemonic masculinity and emphasised femininity. For example, the magazine *Country Life* is not only full of advertisements for dream houses but has for many years contained what may be seen as a full page advertisement for the institution of marriage (Figures 14.2 and 14.3). These images have a clear emphasis on the feminine: looking at issues of *Country Life* for the period 1986 to 1988, for example, we found that only 10 out of 143 marriage announcements used a photograph which included the husband. The rest were images of exclusive women: in both the gender and class sense.

The significance of the dualism of hegemonic masculinity and emphasised femininity is not just in the imagery but also connects to the 'material', often quite literally. Connell (1987), for example, argues that the body is quite literally clothed with the gendered identities of hegemonic masculinity and emphasised femininity. He claims that these identities require the construction, both symbolically and materially, of men and women as being distinct categories and that one way in which this can be achieved is by 'converting average difference into a

COUNTRY LIFE

Vol. CLXXXII No. 6   FEBRUARY 11, 1988

MISS AMANDA ELIOT-COHEN AND MR SAM BULLARD
Miss Amanda Eliot-Cohen, younger daughter of Mr and Mrs Christopher Eliot-Cohen, of Ramsbury, Wiltshire,
is to be married to Mr Sam Bullard, youngest son of Mr and Mrs Gerry Bullard, of Gressenhall, Norfolk. They
are pictured with their black labrador, Plover.

FIGURE 14.2 The conjugal family in its 'natural' setting

categorical difference' (Connell 1987: 80). Hence, while on average men may be taller and physically stronger than women, this does not mean that all men are taller or stronger than women. Yet, symbolically and materially, bodies are often clothed as if they are. 'Men's clothes' are constructed as if, or to give the image that, men are larger and tougher than women. These categorical differences are constructed even when there appears to be little real need for them. Take for example, the classic 'country' clothing markers of class, the Barbour jacket and 'green wellies'. Several of the advertisements for these reproduce categorical gender difference even when advertising a supposedly unisex product (Figure 14.4). There are other examples of a gender dimension to the portrayal and construction of clothing for use in the countryside. Much of the advertising for outdoor clothing, for example, reproduces the dualisms of hegemonic masculinity and emphasised femininity by portraying men as larger, stronger and more powerful than women, and women as smaller, in need of protection and support (Figure 14.5). Instances such as this suggest that there is as much a

FIGURE 14.3 Advertising the institution of marriage

People who know the country know why they need **Barbour**® COUNTRY CLOTHING

The best British clothing for the worst British weather

FIGURE 14.4 Gendering the unisex product

gender dimension to rural imagery as there is a class dimension, and indeed the two are often conjoined in a mutually reinforcing way.

GENDER IDENTITIES AND THE COLONISATION AND RESTRUCTURING OF THE COUNTRYSIDE

Gender Identities and the Colonisation of the Countryside

As previously mentioned, Connell suggests that the gender identities of hegemonic masculinity and emphasised femininity are particularly significant in the mass media. He notes that their prevalence in the mass media may tempt people to think that they only exist as a mass media image, particularly when Connell himself suggests that these gender identities do not necessarily correspond with the gender identities of individual people: very few men act like John Wayne or Rambo. However, recognition of the difference between public sphere identities and individual personalities does not mean that you can ignore the public

FIGURE 14.5 Hegemonic masculinity and emphasised femininity

identities. On the contrary, Connell suggests that individual identities are structured very much in relation to, but do not necessarily replicate, public identities. So, for example, while individual men may not act like Rambo, some men may at times fantasise about acting like him. Equally, others may choose to distance themselves from these images. Whichever is the case, the official public sphere image may significantly influence the attitudes and beliefs of individuals (see Bourdieu 1984, Appendix 4, for similar arguments).

With respect to the interaction between the gender identities of the official public sphere and rural colonisation and restructuring, we present four argumentative sketches of how rural images in the public sphere, constructed through the dualisms of hegemonic masculinity and emphasised femininity, can be connected into the processes of class colonisation of the countryside.

Firstly, gender identities may be involved in the processes of class formation by creating gender closure around particular class positions. This point has been made by Connell himself, who mentions a number of gender identities and discusses how these may be significant in constituting class positions. It is

TABLE 14.3 Occupations and gender identities: some illustrations

Occupations	Gender identities	Form of gender relation	Case study
Professional/ managerial	'Rational man'	Emotional ties must be minimised. Men divorced as far as possible from emotional ties of childcare and domestic work. Women marginalised in workplace	Pahl and Pahl (1971)
Professional/ managerial	'Paternal man'	Management based on authority which was seen to rely on discretion and autonomy from supervision. Abilities seen to be product of age and a stable home life. Managerial posts therefore often restricted to married men with families	Savage (1992) Halford and Savage (1995)
Craft worker	'Versatile man'	Prepared to be flexible and to move with the job. Partner must be willing to stay or go as required	Connell (1987)
Office worker	'The secretary'	Must be able to fuse technical competence with interpersonal skills, attractiveness and compliance	Griffin (1985) Pringle (1989)
Industrial factory worker	'Violently heterosexual man'/'The lads'	Involves a 'cult of masculinity' centred on physical and heterosexual power. Used to deprecate non-manual workers and managers	Lippert (1977) Willis (1977, 1979)

possible to expand on his remarks and to suggest some loose connections between gender identities and occupations in the official economy (see Table 14.3). It is important to note that some occupations are associated with a number of gender identities. This may reflect the complexity of gender relations in these areas, or alternatively and arguably more likely, it reflects the greater degree of attention paid to the constitution of gender identities present in middle class occupations. Either way, all the gendered identities here appear to be structured in accordance with the dualism of hegemonic masculinity and emphasised femininity: certainly none seem to question the notion of essential difference between men and women, nor the differential power relations associated with being masculine or feminine.

The significance of these studies is that they may well imply that gender identities may be crucially involved in the processes by which people gain assets which they can use to effect the colonisation of rural areas. The migration of a professional and managerial service class, which has been seen as a major constituent of counterurbanisation, might hence involve the migration of 'rational men' or 'paternal men', as well as middle class men. The processes of class colonisation which give rural areas a particular class composition may hence be equally a process of composing and recomposing the gender order of rural areas.

A second connection between gender identities and class colonisation may be in the establishment of propensities to move. The mobility of sections of the middle class has been seen as an important constituent of counterurbanisation. This was epitomised in Pahl's (1965a, 1965b) notion of the 'spiralist': the transient owner occupier who lived in any one village for only a short time as they sought to rise up the career ladder by responding to the dictates of capital to be flexible and spatially footloose. A few years later, Pahl worked with his wife on a project of managers and their wives and the Pahls state explicitly that the origins of this project lay in the earlier study of Hertfordshire. The aim of the new project was to understand the role of managers and their wives in the process of spiralling (Pahl and Pahl 1971: 6). The Pahls argued that while women sometimes acted as a brake on the career spiralling of their husbands, they were also often a key agent enabling such spiralling and, indeed, saw their own identities as closely connected to the spiralling of their husband.

Gender identities may also influence propensities to move at a more general level. Massey (1995), for example, has argued that the division of labour between 'conceptualisation' and 'execution', and the accompanying socio-economic status and power accorded to those whose work is perceived to have a high abstract content, corresponds to a 'masculinist' valuation of 'Reason' and 'mind' over 'non-Reason' and 'body'. She notes that the work of Fielding (1995) reveals that the professionals and managers of the service class evidence greater spatial mobility than do other classes and speculates that different social classes might exhibit distinct spatial powers. This later part of her argument fits quite well with the suggestions made by Crompton (1992) and Savage (1988) that there are different occupational careers with distinct 'mobility propensities' built into them. Putting the arguments of Massey together with these points suggests that gender identities may be critically involved in the formation of propensity to move through occupational career structures. It is also interesting to note the debate between Crompton and Jones (1984), who suggest that the increasing participation of women in some occupations may lead to changes in their career structures, and Halford and Savage (1995), who suggest that occupational restructuring is not associated with any fundamental shift in gender identities. These arguments suggest that while all instances of class colonisation have associated gender dynamics, this does not necessarily mean that a change in the class composition of in-migrants will lead to a change in the gender order. Similarly, it is possible that rural gender orders may change without changing class composition, perhaps in association with changes in the cultural politics of gender.

A third point to make about the constitution of the rural gender order is that it might be quite resistant to change because there may be some aspects of rural lifestyles which encourage re-creation of the patriarchal identities. In particular, the current structure of rural areas may encourage the establishment of patriarchal identities through enabling a more rigid separation of the official economies and the unofficial economy of the village and the home. Living in rural areas makes combining roles in official and unofficial economies hard. Work in the official economy is often located outside the village and may involve considerable travelling time, particularly if car transport is unavailable. Studies have also demonstrated the impact of poor child care facilities in rural areas and how this has acted to reduce female participation in the official economy (see Little 1991; Little *et al.* 1991; Stone 1990). In our study villages all these factors appeared to play a part in naturalising the gender divisions of labour.

A fourth route-way linking the gender identities of hegemonic masculinity and emphasised femininity is through the motivation that people have to live in the countryside. A number of recent rural studies have highlighted the significance of the cultural constitution of the rural within migration studies (see Cloke and Milbourne 1992; Halfacree 1993, 1994) and within the explanation of processes of class colonisation (see Cloke, Phillips and Thrift, this volume). It has been suggested that the rural can be seen as a means of class identification, as an arena of class actions, and even as a cultural determinant of class formation (Cloke *et al.* 1995). Equally, one can suggest that the rural can be seen as a means of gender identification, as an arena of gender action, and as a cultural determinant of gender identity. Gender identification in particular may be of some significance with respect to rural colonisation. For example, a number of studies have highlighted the interconnection of the rural with the migration of conjugal households to the countryside and have suggested that migration to the countryside may be associated with ideas over the desirability of the country location for the raising of children (see Cloke *et al.* 1994b; Halfacree 1993; Phillips 1993). The significance of these arguments was confirmed in the present study, which suggested that women, in particular, were likely to connect rural residence with changing household structure and the upbringing of children (see Table 14.2). Qualitative comments gained during the research reveal this association to be deeply felt and at times to override other lifestyle factors:

> 'Moved. . . because I didn't want them [the children] to grow up in such an [urban] environment'.

> 'I wanted a good area, even if it's a small house, as the schooling of children is very important'.

> 'I wanted to stay in. . . [the village] after the break up of my marriage, as I had a lot of friends here and I didn't want to disrupt the children's schoolwork'.

Although these quotes were all made by women, and despite women as a whole mentioning more frequently than men that the well-being of their children was a factor in their decision to move, it is important to recognise that many men expressed very similar feelings about raising a family in the countryside. The gender identification of rural space may stem rather less from gender differences in views about the suitability of such spaces for child-rearing and have rather more to do with the gendered differentiations of roles in the official and unofficial economies associated with rural spaces. Moving to the country-side to start a family frequently entailed women leaving employment in the official economy and accepting, seemingly on the whole reasonably willingly, a social situation centred on the unofficial economies of the home, and subse-quently for some, on the village. In this sense, the desire to live in the country was being constituted according to the dualisms of hegemonic masculinity and emphasised femininity.

Gender Identities and the Construction of Ruralities in the Unofficial Public Sphere

In the final section of the chapter we explore whether the gender identities of hegemonic masculinity and emphasised femininity circulating in the 'official public sphere' (Phillips 1994) of the media and of advertising play any role in the way rural residents live out their lives in the countryside. In particular, we focus on the role of these identities in leisure activities and in participation in rural community organisations.

A number of studies have recently highlighted the relationship between class and rural leisure (Clark et al. 1994; Cloke and Thrift 1990; Harrison 1991; Savage et al. 1992; Urry 1990, 1995a, 1995b). As well as having serious reservations about the over-emphasis on culture as capital (see Cloke et al. 1995, and Cloke, Phillips and Thrift, Chapter 9, this volume), we also feel that there are distinct gender identities within leisure pursuits. Interviewees were asked to indicate which leisure activities they pursued. These were then classified as to whether the pursuit drew upon notions of hegemonic masculinity or emphasised femi-ninity. Activities were classified as hegemonically masculine if they appeared to promote identities of masculine body power – man the hunter, man the protec-tor. Activities were classified as emphasised feminine if they seemed to draw upon notions of women as housekeepers, homemakers or body trimmers. There were a number of activities which we felt had little gender identity, such as doing crosswords, bell ringing and walking. There were also a number of activities which can be seen to have either identity, as least within the context of the general descriptions of leisure activity we were given. Examples included horse riding, which is often portrayed as a highly physical, masculine activity – as in horse racing – but is also often associated with the demure and the childlike – as in dressage and the Pony Club. Activities with little gender identity, or with an ambiguous identity, were for the purposes of this analysis classified together as 'other leisure activities'.

Figure 14.6 shows the frequency of men and women undertaking leisure pursuits classified according to their gendered identity. The results show that there is a clear division between the leisure activities pursued by men and women, with men favouring masculine leisure pursuits over feminine and

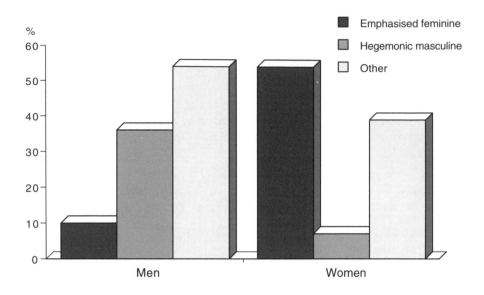

FIGURE 14.6 Gender identities in leisure activities

women favouring the feminine. However, there were important differences in the patterning of activities. The most frequent leisure activities of men were not hegemonically masculine but were in the gender neutral or gender ambiguous category. The leisure activities of women, on the other hand, appeared to be starkly gendered: over 50 percent of the stated leisure activities had an 'emphasised feminine' identity, with the most common of these activities being embroidery, knitting, sewing, cooking, flower arranging and needlework.

As well as looking at the gendered character of leisure activities amongst the residents in the study villages, we also looked at the spatial location in which these activities were conducted. We expected that many of the feminine activities would be located in the village, as in such locations they would reinforce their connection with feminised activities, such as work in the home and in the community, and they would be accessible to women without personal transport. There was some evidence that this was the case with, for example, flower arranging, needle craft and keep fit being held during the week in village halls. One might argue that in a sense, therefore, villages are being structured as a feminine space. Having said this, it is important to note two caveats to this. Firstly, the decline of services in some of the villages appears to be undermining the association of rural space with emphasised feminine activity. Several women complained of the unavailability of activities such as craftwork classes and coffee mornings in the villages, which was forcing them to travel to neighbouring towns to participate in what they clearly felt were rural activities. The second caveat to the notion that villages are being constructed as emphasised feminine spaces was the existence of clearly hegemonically masculine places. The classic example is the local public house and, in particular, the public bar. Our survey suggested that there were significant differences in the frequencies with which women and men visited their village public houses, with a larger number of women than men stating that they never visited those in the village.

We also examined whether there were any gender differences with regard to participation in village institutions. Again, the results were suggestive that this was the case (Figure 14.7). For example, while men and women were both very involved in organisations such as the parish council and residents associations which seemed to be predominantly concerned with planning and the conservation of the village form – a point which reinforces the notion that a perception of village life as being at risk is a uniting feature of contemporary rural life (see Cloke *et al.* 1995, and Cloke, Phillips and Thrift, Chapter 9, this volume) – women appeared to be involved in a much wider range of village institutions. Furthermore, many of the emphasised feminine institutions – such as the Women's Institute and the Mums and Toddlers (it was given this title in all the villages, as opposed to the less gendered title of Parent and Toddlers)– were well supported by women, as were institutions relating to heritage and nature. This point is particularly interesting given that nature and heritage have often been described as being clear markers of the service class. The findings of our survey suggest that these cultural textures are associated with women, many of who work at the base of the service sector. Indeed, we found clear examples where gender associations were overriding class-based ones. Several middle class women appeared to have decided quite consciously to integrate working class women into their groups.

CONCLUSIONS

This chapter has sought to explore rural social restructuring from a critical perspective and with regard to the social relations of gender. It was suggested that while there is much to be gained from adopting some form of class analysis when investigating rural social change, it is also important to consider the role gender relations play both in influencing the processes of colonisation and in construction of ruralities. The chapter began by noting that there appear to be clear differences in the class positions of men and women living in villages, a feature which appears to be largely overlooked in many class-based studies. It also found that these differences in the official economy appear to be broadly mirrored (reflected but reversed) in the unofficial, domestic, economy. Here women appear to be the predominant, if not necessarily the dominant, participants.

It was then suggested that these differences in official and unofficial economies might correspond to the dualistic gender identities of hegemonic masculinity and emphasised femininity outlined by Connell. The chapter explored these identities as constructed within some rural images before considering how these two gender identities might be linked in with processes of social recomposition

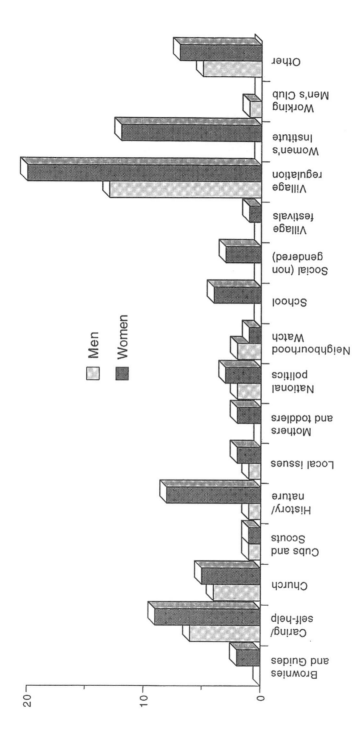

FIGURE 14.7 Participation in institutions

through the migration of the professional and managerial middle classes. We reiterate that we are not saying that these identities are unconditionally tied to class positions. Indeed, the classes which may have once been key vehicles of the re-creation of a patriarchal gender order may also be amongst the most likely vehicles of change. However, the rural gender order, at least within the five villages under study, still appears quite patriarchal. This gender order may reflect some current realities of rural life which reinforce the division of official and unofficial economies. Such an argument does not, however, really explain why this division is so evidently gendered: why it is that men predominate in the official economy and women in the unofficial economy.

A partial explanation of the gender order may be the significance in the official public sphere of images of hegemonic masculinity and emphasised femininity. In the chapter we explored four ways that these gender identities may be influencing the colonisation of the countryside – namely by being involved in the establishment of gender closure around particular class positions, thereby influencing the ability of people to buy into the countryside; by being involved in establishing propensities to move and to stay; by reinforcing a separation of official and unofficial economies within the countryside; and by being involved in the constitution of the rural as an object of desire. We then explored how these gender identities are being enacted in the way people live in the countryside.

NOTES

1. The study of 'Recent social change in the Leicestershire and Warwickshire Countryside' was funded by Coventry University and undertaken in collaboration with the Leicestershire and Warwickshire Rural Community Council.

ACKNOWLEDGMENTS

Thanks are due to J. Barbour and Sons, Morris, Nicholson, Cartwright Ltd, Ursy Barnard and Rosalind Mann for permission to reproduce their photographs and advertisements.

REFERENCES

Acker, J. (1973) 'Women and stratification: a case of intellectual sexism', *American Journal of Sociology*, **78**, 936–945.

Barrell, J. (1980) *The dark side of the landscape: the rural poor in English painting 1730–1840*, Cambridge University Press, Cambridge.

Barrell, J. (1992) 'Sportive labour: the farmworker in eighteenth century poetry', in B. Short (ed.), *The English rural community*, Cambridge University Press, Cambridge, 105–132.

Bell, D. and Valentine, G. (1995) 'Queer country: rural lesbian and gay lives', *Journal of Rural Studies*, **11**, 113–122.

Bondi, L. (1991) 'Gender divisions and gentrification: a critique', *Transactions of the Institute of British Geographers*, **16**, 190–198.

Bourdieu, P. (1984) *Distinction: a social critique of the judgement of taste*, Routledge, London.

Boyle, P. and Halfacree, K. (1995) 'Service class migration in England and Wales, 1980–1991: identifying gender-specific mobility patterns', *Regional Studies*, **29**, 43–57.

Brandth, B. (1995) 'Rural masculinity in transition: gender images in tractor advertisements', *Journal of Rural Studies*, **11**, 123–133.

Braverman, H. (1974) *Labour and monopoly capital: the degradation of work in the twentieth century*, Monthly Review Press, New York.

Champion, A. (1989) *Counterurbanization: the changing pace and nature of population deconcentration*, Edward Arnold, London.

Clark, G., Darrell, J., Grove-White, R., MacNaughten, P. and Urry, J. (1994) *Leisure landscapes*, Council for the Protection of Rural England, London.

Cloke, P. and Milbourne, P. (1992) 'Deprivation and lifestyles in rural Wales – II. Rurality and the cultural dimension', *Journal of Rural Studies*, **8**, 359–371.

Cloke, P. and Thrift, N. (1987) 'Intra-class conflict in rural areas', *Journal of Rural Studies*, **3**, 321–333.

Cloke, P. and Thrift, N. (1990) 'Class change and conflict in rural areas', in T. Marsden, P. Lowe and S. Whatmore (eds.), *Rural restructuring*, David Fulton, London, 165–181.

Cloke, P., Doel, M., Matless, D., Phillips, M. and Thrift, N. (1994a) *Writing the rural: five cultural geographies*, Paul Chapman, London.

Cloke, P., Milbourne, P. and Thomas, C. (1994b) *Lifestyles in rural England*, Rural Development Commission, London.

Cloke, P., Phillips, M. and Rankin, R. (1991) 'Middle-class housing choice: channels of entry into Gower, South Wales', in T. Champion and C. Watkins (eds.), *People in the countryside: studies of social change in rural Britain*, Paul Chapman, London, 38–51.

Cloke, P., Phillips, M. and Thrift, N. (1995) 'The new middle classes and the social constructs of rural living', in T. Butler and M. Savage (eds.), *Social change and the middle classes*, UCL Press, London, 220–238.

Cockburn, C. (1983) *Brothers: male dominance and technological change*, Pluto Press, London.

Connell, R. (1983) *Which way is up? Essays on class, sex and culture*, George Allen and Unwin, Sydney.

Connell, R. (1987) *Gender and power: society, the person and sexual politics*, Cambridge University Press, Cambridge.

Cosgrove, D. (1984) *Social formation and symbolic landscape*, Croom Helm, London.

Crompton, R. (1986) 'Women and the "service class"', in R. Crompton and M. Mann (eds.), *Gender and stratification*, Polity, Cambridge, 119–136.

Crompton, R. (1992) 'Patterns of social consciousness amongst the middle classes', in R. Burrows and C. Marsh (eds.), *Consumption and class: divisions and change*, Macmillan, London, 140–165.

Crompton, R. and Jones, G. (1984) *White-collar proletariat: de-skilling and gender in the clerical labour process*, Macmillan, London.

Crompton, R. and Sanderson, K. (1986) 'Credentials and careers', *Sociology*, **20**, 25–42.

Crompton, R. and Sanderson, K. (1990) *Gendered jobs and social change*, Unwin Hyman, London.

Dale, A., Gilbert, N. and Arber, S. (1985) 'Integrating women into class analysis', *Sociology*, **19**, 384–408.

Delphy, C. (1981) 'Women in stratification studies', in H. Roberts (ed.), *Doing feminist research*, Routledge and Kegan Paul, London, 114–128.

Erikson, R. (1984) 'Social class of men, women and families', *Sociology*, **18**, 500–514.

Fielding, T. (1995) 'Migration and middle class formation in England and Wales, 1981–91', in T. Butler and M. Savage (eds.), *Social change and the middle classes*, UCL Press, London, 169–187.

Foord, J. and Gregson, N. (1986) 'Patriarchy: towards a reconceptualisation', *Antipode*, **18**, 186–211.

Goldthorpe, J. (1983) 'Women and class analysis: a defence of the conventional view', *Sociology*, **17**, 465–478.

Griffin, C. (1985) *Typical girls?*, Routledge and Kegan Paul, London.

Halfacree, K. (1993) 'Locality and social representation: space, discourse and alternative definitions of the rural', *Journal of Rural Studies*, **9**, 1–15.

Halfacree, K. (1994) 'The importance of "the rural" in the constitution of counterurbanization: evidence from England in the 1980s', *Sociologia Ruralis*, **34**, 164–189.

Halfacree, K. (1995) 'Talking about rurality: social representations of the rural as expressed by residents of six English parishes', *Journal of Rural Studies*, **11**, 1–20.

Halford, S. and Savage, M. (1995) 'Restructuring organisations, changing people: gender and careers in banking and local government', *Work, Employment and Society*, **9**, 97–122.

Harrison, C. (1991) *Countryside recreation in a changing society*, TMS Partnership, London.

Jackson, P. (1991) 'The cultural politics of masculinity: towards a social geography', *Transactions of the Institute of British Geographers*, **16**, 199–213.

Jones, O. (1995) 'Lay discourses of the rural: development and implications for rural studies', *Journal of Rural Studies*, **11**, 35–49.

Keinath, W. (1982) 'The decentralisation of American economic life: an economic evaluation', *Economic Geography*, **58**, 343–357.

Lippert, J. (1977) 'Sexuality as consumption', in J. Snodgrass (ed.), *For men against sexism*, Times Change Press, Albion, California, 207–213.

Little, J. (1987) 'Gender relations in rural areas: the importance of women's domestic role', *Journal of Rural Studies*, **3**, 335–342.

Little, J. (1991) 'Women in the rural labour market: an evaluation', in T. Champion and C. Watkins (eds.), *People in the countryside: studies of social change in rural Britain*, Paul Chapman, London, 96–107.

Little, J., Ross, K. and Collins, I. (1991) *Women and employment in rural areas*, Rural Development Commission, London.

Mark-Lawson, J., Savage, M. and Warde, A. (1985) 'Gender and local politics: struggles over welfare policies, 1918–1939', in Lancaster Regionalism Group (ed.), *Localities, class and gender*, Pion, London, 195–215.

Markusen, A. (1981) 'City spatial structure, women's household work, and national urban policy', in C. Stimpson, E. Dixler, M. Nelson and K. Yatrakis (eds.), *Women and the American city*, Chicago University Press, Chicago.

Massey, D. (1984) *Spatial divisions of labour: social structures and the geography of production*, Macmillan, London.

Massey, D. (1995) 'Reflections on gender and geography', in T. Butler and M. Savage (eds.), *Social change and the middle classes*, UCL Press, London, 330–344.

McDowell, L. (1983) 'Towards an understanding of the gender division of urban space', *Environment and Planning D: Society and Space*, **1**, 59–72.

McDowell, L. (1991) 'Life without father and Ford: the new gender order of post-Fordism', *Transactions of the Institute of British Geographers*, **16**, 400–419.

McDowell, L. and Massey, D. (1984) 'A women's place?', in D. Massey and J. Allen (eds.), *Geography matters*, Cambridge University Press, Cambridge, 128–147.

McKenzie, S. (1988) 'Balancing our space and time: the impact of women's organisation on the British city, 1920–1980', in J. Little, L. Peake and P. Richardson (eds.), *Women in cities: gender and the urban environment*, Macmillan, London, 41–60.

Miller, R. (1983) 'The Hoover® in the garden: middle class women and suburbanisation, 1850–1920', *Environment and Planning D: Society and Space*, **1**, 73–88.

Mills, C. (1992) 'For home and country: the cultural constructions of femininity and rurality in England', paper presented at the 88th Annual Conference of the Association of American Geographers, San Diego, USA.

Murdoch, J. and Marsden, T. (1994) *Reconstituting rurality: class, community and power in the development process*, UCL Press, London.

Newby, H. (1987) *Country life: a social history of rural England*, Wiedenfeld and Nicholson, London.

Pahl, J. and Pahl, R. (1971) *Managers and their wives: a study of career and family relationships in the middle class*, Allen Lane, London.

Pahl, R. (1965a) 'Class and community in English commuter villages', *Sociologia Ruralis*, **5**, 5–23.

Pahl, R. (1965b) *Urbs in rure*, Geographical Paper No. 2, London School of Economics, London.

Phillips, M. (1993) 'Rural gentrification and the processes of class colonisation', *Journal of Rural Studies*, **9**, 123–140.

Phillips, M. (1994) 'Habermas, rural studies and critical social theory' in P. Cloke, M. Doel, D. Matless, M. Phillips, and N. Thrift, *Writing the rural: five cultural geographies*, London, Paul Chapman, 89–126.

Pringle, R. (1989) *Secretaries talk: sexuality, power and work*, Verso, London.

Robert, S. and Randolph, W. (1983) 'Beyond decentralisation: the evolution of population distribution in England and Wales, 1961–1981', *Geoforum*, **14**, 75–102.

Rose, D. (1989) 'A feminist perspective on employment restructuring and gentrification: the case of Montréal', in J. Wolch and M. Dear (eds.), *The power of geography: how territoriality shapes social life*, Unwin Hyman, London, 118–138.

Rose, G. (1988) 'Locality, politics and culture: Poplar in the 1920s', *Environment and Planning D: Society and Space*, **6**, 151–168.

Rose, G. (1989) 'Locality-studies and waged labour: an historical critique', *Transactions of the Institute of British Geographers*, **14**, 317–328.

Rose, G. (1993) *Feminism and geography: the limits of geographical knowledge*, Polity, Cambridge.

Savage, M. (1985) 'Capitalist and patriarchal relations at work: Preston cotton weaving 1890–1940', in Lancaster Regionalism Group (ed.), *Localities, class and gender*, Pion, London, 177–194.

Savage, M. (1987) *The dynamics of working class politics: the labour movement in Preston 1880–1940*, Cambridge University Press, Cambridge.

Savage, M. (1988) 'The missing link? The relationship between spatial mobility and social mobility', *British Journal of Sociology*, **39**, 554–577.

Savage, M. (1992) 'Women's expertise, men's authority: gendered organization and the contemporary middle classes', in M. Savage and A. Witz (eds.), *Gender and bureaucracy*, Blackwell, Oxford, 124–151.

Savage, M., Barlow, J., Dickens, P. and Fielding, T. (1992) *Property, bureaucracy and culture: middle class formation in contemporary Britain*, Routledge, London.

Short, J. (1991) *Imagined country: society, culture and environment*, Routledge, London.

Stanworth, M. (1984) 'Women and class analysis: a reply to John Goldthorpe', *Sociology*, **18**, 159–170.

Stone, M. (1990) *Rural childcare*, Rural Development Commission, London.

Thompson, J. (1990) *Ideology and modern culture*, Cambridge University Press, Cambridge.

Thrift, N. (1987) 'Manufacturing rural geography', *Journal of Rural Studies*, **3**, 77–81.

Thrift, N. (1989) 'Images of social change', in C. Hamnett, L. McDowell and P. Sarre (eds.), *The changing social structure*, Sage, London, 12–42.

Urry, J. (1990) *The tourist gaze: leisure and travel in contemporary societies*, Sage, London.

Urry, J. (1995a) *Consuming places*, London, Routledge.

Urry, J. (1995b) 'A middle-class countryside?', in T. Butler and M. Savage (eds.), *Social change and the middle classes*, Routledge, London, 205–219.

Walby, S. (1986) *Patriarchy at work*, Polity, Cambridge.

Warde, A. (1991) 'Gentrification as consumption: issues of class and gender', *Environment and Planning D: Society and Space*, **9**, 223–232.

Whatmore, S. (1991) *Farming women: gender, work and family enterprise*, Macmillan, London.

Willis, P. (1977) *Learning to labour: how working class kids get working class jobs*, Saxon House, London.

Willis, P. (1979) 'Shop floor culture, masculinity and the wage form', in J. Clarke, C. Critcher and R. Johnson (eds.), *Working class culture*, Hutchinson, London, 185–198.

Witz, A. (1990) 'Patriarchy and professions: the gendered politics of occupational closure', *Sociology*, **24**, 675–690.

Witz, A. (1992) *Professions and patriarchy*, Routledge, London.

Witz, A. (1994) 'Gender and service class formation', paper presented at the Social Change and the Middle Classes conference, Danbury Park, Chelmsford.

Witz, A. (1995) 'Gender and service class formation', in T. Butler and M. Savage (eds.), *Social change and the middle classes*, UCL Press, London, 41–57.

Women in Geography Study Group (1984) *Geography and gender*, Hutchinson, London.

Wright, E.O. (1978) *Class, crisis and the state*, New Left Books, London.

Wright, E.O. (1989a) 'Rethinking, once again, the concept of class structure', in E.O. Wright (ed.), *The debate on classes*, Verso, London, 269–348.

Wright, E.O. (1989b) 'Women and the class structure', *Politics and Society*, **17**, 35–66.

15

MIGRATION INTO RURAL COMMUNITIES: QUESTIONING THE LANGUAGE OF COUNTERURBANISATION

JANE ALLAN and ELIZABETH MOONEY

INTRODUCTION

The preceding chapters have outlined the mechanisms, theories and arguments surrounding counterurbanisation in a British and international context. This chapter focuses upon some of the terminology that underpins investigation into the impacts of counterurbanisation in rural Scotland. To do this we will consider our experiences of carrying out fieldwork in rural Scotland[1] and emphasise the importance of direct contact with people in rural places. As such we are not involving ourselves in the debates on the mechanisms that contribute to counterurbanisation in Scotland. The nature, mechanisms and reasons for counterurbanisation, such as lifestyle preferences and changes to employment structure, have been well documented elsewhere (Boyle 1995; Forsythe 1980a; Gray 1993; Jedrej and Nuttall 1996; Jones 1982, 1992; Jones *et al.* 1984, 1986; Mooney and Gray 1994). Rather, we start from the premise that there are important changes taking place in the Scottish countryside, and it is the ways that we articulate and conceptualise these changes that we wish to consider. This requires an exploration of the terms used both by researchers and by those living in the countryside when talking about counterurbanisation.

It is important, however, to recognise that our questioning of the language of counterurbanisation reflects, and is part of, the changing nature of British rural geography. This reflects moves within social studies to question the relationships between researchers, fieldwork and the texts they construct (for example, Katz 1992; Keith 1992; Mooney 1994; Rapport 1993). Recent studies of rural geography have problematised and theorised upon the nature of the rural and representations of rurality (Halfacree 1993, 1995; Hoggart 1990; Pratt 1989) and have started to integrate reflexivity into studies of the countryside (for example, Agg 1996; Cloke *et al.* 1994a; Mooney 1993; Woodward 1996). While we accept that there is a need to consider our textual strategies as researchers, it is equally important to understand the language used by the people we research. This requires an understanding of the conceptualisations held by ourselves and other(s) and the ways in which we 'visualise' and 'vocalise' (Fielding 1995) notions of the changing countryside. We believe that an important part of this process involves direct experience with people in 'place'.

Scotland's rural areas are varied and dynamic and are experiencing (and have experienced in the past) important social, cultural and economic changes (Allan and Mooney 1995; Gray 1993; Jedrej and Nuttall 1996; Shucksmith *et al.* 1996). These changes are characterised by competing forces: the development of tourism (Burnett 1995; Hunter 1995); conservation and preservation (Cairngorms Working Party 1992; Holbourn and Baisley 1994); and a changing social arena. Counterurbanisation has also been an important force in Scotland's changing countryside (Pacione 1995), and recent evidence (Boyle 1995; Hunter 1995; Scottish Office 1996) suggests that the process of migration into the Highlands and Islands of Scotland has continued into the 1990s:

> 'No other predominantly rural area in the European Union has recently been gaining population as fast as the Highlands and Islands [of Scotland]' (Hunter 1995: 17).

While it has been shown that counterurbanisation has a varied impact on different rural areas (Gray 1993; Mooney 1993; Mooney and Gray 1994), the language used in portraying the impacts of counterurbanisation presents an ambiguous image of the processes involved. On the one hand, movement into the countryside has been presented as a rural renaissance, bringing with it new blood (Shucksmith *et al.* 1994, 1996; Stephenson 1984) and opportunities. On the other hand, deprivation, rural decline and polarisation, and age-selective migration out of rural areas continue to be problematic issues. For example, in a study of Ford (a village in mid-Argyll), Stephenson (1984) identifies that young people 'have been leaving the area since the beginning of the nineteenth century' (p. 82) because of a lack of opportunities. The Scottish Office (1996) indicate that rural Scotland experienced a 3.5 percent growth[2] in population between 1981 and 1991, while Scotland as whole experienced a 1.4 percent decline. In-migration, rather than natural increase, was largely responsible for the increasing populations. Forsythe (1980a) explains that on the Island of Stormay (a pseudonym for one of the Orcadian Islands) migrants replaced labour that was lost through depopulation. However, the increased competition for housing resulted in inflated house prices. Among others counterurbanisation is interpreted as the colonisation of the countryside by groups who threaten 'traditional' life and appropriate existing structures[3] (Gray 1993; Rapport 1993; Shucksmith *et al.* 1994, 1996; Stephenson 1984).

Each of these perspectives has produced a particular vocabulary associated with counterurbanisation in which terms such as 'locals', 'incomers' and 'settlers' have become common parlance. The use of the terminology reflects implicit assumptions about social organisation in the countryside. However, the boundaries around these groups are not clearly defined. The language of counterurbanisation has embraced terminology relating to problematic and fluid boundaries between a non-specific but indigenous 'rural' grouping (the local) and an 'other' who does not belong and/or who differs in some way (the incomer). Despite detailed discussion elsewhere[4], the terminology remains problematic and continues to result in perceived dichotomies within the countryside. These dichotomies, however, are far from clearly defined and do little to inform us of the processes of social change in the countryside. Rather they homogenise and oversimplify the complexity of the motivations and experiences of those who move into the countryside and those affected by counterurbanisation.

In this chapter we make some attempt to redress the balance by re-examining our own experiences of this language in rural Scotland. By drawing upon examples from the field we illustrate the complexity involved in the use of the routine language of counterurbanisation. Furthermore, we reflect upon our own field experiences to illustrate the extent to which our text is grounded within particular experiences, perspectives and relationships.

A PROBLEMATIC RURAL SCOTLAND?

'In Scotland the dimensions of meaning involved in the use of the terms such as "local" and "incomer" are a function of the inescapable experience of asymmetries in social relationships' (Jedrej and Nuttall 1995: 188).

Within the Scottish context, studies of the changing social structure of the countryside have adopted a language in which differences between groups of rural dwellers are expressed through the use of specific terms, in particular the use of 'local' versus 'incomer'[5]. This language is commonly used by people in rural places and has been appropriated by the media, political activists and academics when discussing the impacts of counterurbanisation. For example, groups such as 'Scottish Watch' and 'Settler Watch' have projected images of harmonious rural life which is being disrupted and destroyed by incoming populations. In this context, the term 'incomer' has been imbued with ethnic connotations: incomer has been interpreted as meaning English. The use of the term 'White Settler', in particular, conveys feelings of colonisation[6] where local culture is interpreted as being usurped by a more dominant 'English' culture. Even where incomers are not regarded as synonymous with English, the terminology is worryingly ethnocentric and xenophobic. 'Incomers', it seems, are held responsible for various social problems in the countryside and often act as convenient 'scapegoats' (Newby 1979; Shucksmith *et al.* 1994, 1996) for problems that have continued over the years. Incoming populations have been targeted as the cause of a variety of socio-economic problems in the Scottish countryside:

'In particular Scottish Watch have attempted to advance the argument that English people in Scotland are pushing up property prices and therefore taking the best housing, that in employment Scots are forced to take second best, and that in political and cultural terms the English people in Scotland are distinctly English in their values and opinions' (Dickson 1994: 114).

Stephenson (1984) identified an anti-English sentiment in the use of the term 'White Settler' in Ford which, he suggests, is 'a term of harsh derision'[7] (p. 130). However, he also suggests that the division between Scots and English in the village is neither explicit nor is it necessarily a useful means of understanding the social structures of the village:

'"The division" is too ill-constructed to be workable, spreading out as it does in some cases, to include recent incomers of every nationality, placing an artificial wedge between otherwise natural friendships and working relationships. The stereotype is too awkward to be useful at close quarters in everyday life in a small village' (Stephenson 1984: 134).

With regard to ethnicity, it has been shown that the incoming populations are not exclusively English (Boyle 1995). In fact many of the new residents in rural Scotland originate from urban Scotland and other rural areas (Jedrej and Nuttall 1996; Stephenson 1984). Indeed it seems that 'anglo-phobia' is unwarranted. For example, Dickson (1994: 131) has argued that for English people in Scotland:

'there is more evidence to support the idea that English born people have in many respects assimilated themselves into many aspects of Scottish life, not open to them in England, for example in politics and religion. From this, it could be argued that the broader English population in Scotland has experienced some form of "Scottishing" effect'.

Despite the rhetoric and strong feelings, the evidence suggests that rural problems are not necessarily attributable to incoming populations (Gray 1993; Mooney 1993). Weekley (1988) outlines a paradox, in that counterurbanisation can be interpreted both as a solution to and as a cause of rural depopulation (for example, by increasing the competition for housing). In the Scottish context, Shucksmith et al. (1996: 471) suggest that 'the counterstream migrant "problem" masked, and detracted attention from, the fundamental problems of housing, employment and poverty in rural areas' While reviews of counterurbanisation in the early 1980s (for example, Jones et al. 1984; Perry et al. 1986) associated urban to rural migration with something of a rural renaissance, it can be argued that in many rural areas in-migration occurred whilst existing problems persisted, and that rural decline and age-selective depopulation (Jedrej and Nuttall 1996; Shucksmith et al. 1996[8]) has continued over recent years.

Unfortunately, there is also a distinct lack of information relating to rural poverty and disadvantage in Scotland which makes it difficult to comment on overall trends[9]. Shucksmith et al. (1994, 1996) have drawn attention to this inadequacy and problematise some of the traditional wisdoms relating to notions of 'disadvantage', 'poverty' and 'change' within small and dispersed populations. They identify that deprivation and disadvantage tend to be thought of as urban phenomena and that indices of multiple deprivation based upon urban indicators fail to reveal the extent of disadvantage in rural areas. The limited evidence that is available suggests lower than average income levels in rural Scotland but higher prices (Scottish Office 1996; Shucksmith *et al.* 1994, 1996). The lack of information at a sub-district level means that understanding of issues such as wealth, income and employment is problematic. When discussing the perceived problems resulting from what they term 'counter-stream' migration, Shucksmith *et al.* (1994) indicate that these issues are extremely complex and relate to issues such as class, status and power, especially as they manifest themselves in inequalities in housing and employment opportunities.

In the English context, Cloke *et al.* (1994b) identified that there are important problems of low income and poverty in many rural areas. These patterns, they suggest, may be reproduced by in-migration of lower income migrants. However, there is also evidence of areas with high income profiles attracting wealthier migrants. In this way, migration into the countryside reproduces social and economic relations in the countryside. Conversely, new rural residents can be heralded as the 'cause' of 'rural renaissance' and a panacea for rural decline as they bring new life into communities and become involved in the countryside by taking a proactive role in community involvement (MacNee 1994). Whatever the interpretation of the effects of counterurbanisation, it is clear that these new rural inhabitants are only part of more general rural transformations and that the effects of counterurbanisation are as varied and complex as the communities themselves (Mooney and Gray 1994).

Counterurbanisation not only involves movement of people, but when combined with ongoing processes such as out-migration it has a social and cultural impact upon the communities which receive the flow of population. Despite the complexity of counterurbanisation, popular dialogue still tends to be based upon the premise that there are two main groups of people living in the countryside: those who are indigenous and have a '*bona-fide*' link with the village (the 'local') and those who move into rural Scotland (the 'incomer'). In this context, the local population are often presented as a group upon whom the impacts of these processes (whether negative or positive) are imposed. However, research has shown that rural populations are heterogeneous and that division into these discrete units is problematic (Allan 1995; Allan and Mooney 1995; Burnett 1995; Frankenberg 1957; Jedrej and Nuttall 1996; Mooney 1993; Rapport 1993). This, in turn, impacts upon the ways in which we conceptualise and articulate changes associated with counterurbanisation. This is complicated by the fluidity of the terms used to identify groups of people within the countryside and it is to the problematic nature of the disparate groups of people living in the countryside that we now turn our attention.

SCOTTISH RURAL VOICES: LOCALS VERSUS INCOMERS?

Despite the varying evidence, the language of 'incomers' and 'locals' is bound into everyday discourse about rural areas and rural problems and it is to this that we now turn our attention. The language is a stylised and stereotypic portrayal of social distinctions in rural Scotland which has been perpetuated by national level discourses (for example, media, political campaigns), and this has resulted in oversimplification of actual changes within particular rural places. Furthermore, it fails to give due attention to place and how social organisation will vary throughout rural areas in Scotland. Moreover, it highlights the need to consider the context within which research is undertaken. That is, the study of rural social change is positioned within an unavoidable language of 'locals' and 'incomers', and this often entails tacit characteristics of those people in each group. This must be recognised when undertaking field enquiry. The language of 'locals' and 'incomers' not only oversimplifies the nature of social change in the countryside but neglects the fluidity of the terms . At the broad scale these terms seem to suggest discrete boundaries between groups of people but on closer inspection it becomes clear that the boundaries are far from well defined. Rather they have different connotations depending upon the context in which they are used, and can be both inclusionary and exclusionary. 'Locals' and 'incomers' are not, therefore, existential realities (Jedrej and Nuttall 1995), nor are they two mutually exclusive groups. The complexity of the terminology is best explained by direct reference to field evidence.

The most simple explanation of 'incomer' is a person who, without prior local connection, has migrated into a rural community. In this sense, then, an incomer is distinct from an indigenous local. The term incomer can also evoke a feeling of 'invasion' and 'colonisation' (Mewett 1982; Jedrej and Nuttall 1995, 1996) by different cultures. In the case of the Scottish countryside, this is often perceived as invasion by a dominant English culture (whether or not incomers are in fact English; see Stephenson 1984). In this sense an 'incomer' is interpreted as someone who usurps, invades and erodes existing cultures. Consider, for example, the following quotes from fieldwork – see Figure 15.1 for the location of the study areas – which refer to negative perceptions of 'incomers':

'The incomers, all the English folk, have bought up the shops. That's why they don't keep them open on a Sunday' (resident in Craigellachie);

'The other disadvantage is the price [of houses], that would be the major disadvantage because of incomers coming into the area putting the prices up, it's very difficult for somebody, a local who works in the area to get a good standard house at a price he's [sic] able to pay because basically everybody around here is building bungalows and things like that for retired pensioners from the South of England. . . or even retired pensioners from the Central Belt of Scotland' (resident in Argyll).

In each case, 'incomers' are presented as a distinct 'other' who are fundamentally different and who have a negative impact upon the communities into which they move. In the first example, incomers are identified as 'the English folk'. Difference between the two groups is conveyed through concrete practice, in this case closing shops on a Sunday. In the second example, 'incomers' have a detrimental effect on people's ability to gain access to housing. The quotes

FIGURE 15.1 Location of the study areas

imply that there is difference between 'locals' and 'incomers' and that these two groups think and behave in different ways. These boundaries are also upheld by 'incomers' who identify their 'significant other': the 'locals' (Burnett 1995; Shucksmith *et al.* 1994[10]; Stephenson 1984).

However, the use of the term 'incomer' can also be used to refer to someone who has been accepted into the 'local' community (Allan 1995) and can, therefore, be used in an inclusionary sense. Indeed, 'incomers' can be seen to have a positive impact on rural communities (Shucksmith *et al.* 1994, 1996):

'Every day you go out, there's somebody working on something. That sort of vitality has got a lot to do with incomers' (resident in Tomintoul).

'I think it's good in a way as well because they bring a new lease of life into the place and a bit of get up and go' (resident in Craigellachie).

Furthermore, locals can also be perceived negatively: a perception more commonly attributed to 'incomers':

'And the people that are locals tend to feel that incomers are taking over their village, but the thing is that quite often they don't do anything about it themselves' (resident in Tomintoul).

As previously mentioned, an initial reading of rural research suggests that there are two distinct groups of people in the countryside living in a dichotomous relationship. Frankenberg (1957) found that kinship had an important role in maintaining the exclusivity of village life. Likewise, Phillips (1986) identifies kinship as 'one of the central markers of difference in Muker' (p. 143) and that locals often stressed their link to other families in the area when talking about the community. In a similar vein, Allan and Gloyer (1996) and Smith (1993) identify that lineage is an important marker in participation of village festivals. The importance of kinship, however, extends beyond the concerns of those who may be exclusively 'local'. When reconstructing the housing histories of older people who had moved to Argyll (Figure 15.1), Mooney (1996) found that family had an important role in explaining people's household movement. Informants used family 'ties' to explain why they had arrived in particular rural places and fall into Forsythe's (1982) category of 'connected migrants'[11]:

'So when I heard there was a vacancy in Ardrishaig which is where all my folks come from and eh the kiddies were about knee high and that's how we moved up' (resident in Argyll).

'My father belonged to Ardrishaig you see that's why they moved back to this area' (resident in Argyll).

Family not only influenced movement to these rural places but also provided an explanatory variable in explaining attachments to and relationships with rural places:

'So then after [establishment of district council headquarters] and all the explosion of houses and everything, so many strangers moved into the area that the whole feeling and character of the village has gone and you go down the street and I mean, there's still well ones that are a bit older than myself, we greet each other like long lost friends because the bulk of people you haven't a clue who they are . . . They don't know you and they're not basically interested in the old village, you know, or the old families because they've got no real connection with the place' (resident in Argyll).

Jedrej and Nuttall (1996) also identify the role of 'roots' in defining who is local. Furthermore, they explain that people's discussion of 'others' reflects their own self-image. In the quote above , the informant uses the term 'strangers' to identify incomers/outsiders. The influx of these people resulting from the establishment of employment and housing in the area is identified as having a significant impact on the changing nature of the village. The informant explains that 'they' (the strangers) have no interest in the old village nor are they interested in the 'old families' because 'they've got no real connection with the place'. By default, this informant implies that she is not a stranger since she has a 'real' connection (in this case family) and has an interest in the village. She clearly locates herself within a perceived minority who are not strangers. She, in effect, defines herself by describing what 'they' – the 'strangers' – are not (Gilligan 1987). This relationship and sense of belonging is, however, complex. This woman is not local in the sense that she is indigenous to the village (she was born and spent the first 18 years of her life elsewhere). Her father's family were originally from the area and it is to this part of the family that she refers.

It has been suggested within rural studies (Gilligan 1987; Smith 1993) that village festivals and events crystallise social distinctions and, therefore, help clarify the nature of 'local–incomer' relationships and the diversity of rural experience. Susan Smith's (1993) account of the Beltane festival in Peebles notes that at this time of year:

> 'the distinction between "gutterbluids" [born within the Burgh] and "stoorifoots" [or "incomers"] is sharpest, lineage is most valued and spatial metaphors most often punctuate the language of public life' (Smith 1993: 293).

In the 1991 Beltane festival in Peebles, the boundaries of locals/insiders and outsiders were activated by a charge of racism in the 'golliwog affair' (Smith 1993). Protest followed a request by an outsider (a woman who, although born in Peebles, was resident elsewhere) for the withdrawal of 'golliwog' costumes from the festival. Arguments ensued in which the charge of racism was interpreted as a challenge from outside to the local traditions and meanings associated with the Beltane[12]. The 'golliwog affair' clearly identified racism as a Scottish rural problem but can also be read as an example of conflict between locals and outsiders. It exemplified:

> 'the extent to which the festival is not simply a mainstream statement about the niceties of local traditions and values. It is, crucially, a vehicle which reproduces those ideals and guards them against the perceived challenge of outside forces' (Smith 1993: 300).

The protests were, however, also situated within the context of a changing rural community threatened by counterurbanisation (by commuters and retirement migrants), age-selective outward migration and deindustrialisation of the local labour market (Smith 1993). Likewise, Gilligan (1987) observes that the definition of what constitutes a 'Padstonian' in Padstow, Cornwall, is clearest and most exclusive on May Day. It is implied that such 'local' events throw into focus more sharply social divisions which exist in the community.

Research by Allan and Gloyer (1996) on the Burghead Clavie (an annual fire festival held on 11 January) in north east Scotland (Figure 15.1) has highlighted that while a first reading of the Clavie suggests that the boundaries between 'local' and 'incomers' appear clear, the nature of 'local' is, in itself, problematic. Traditionally, the people who directly participate in the Clavie[13] must be male 'Brochers': those born and raised in Burghead. People in the village are aware of this tradition, and on first reading it appears that the meaning of 'Brocher' is made explicit through the Clavie procession:

'You can come to the pubs and that and everyone's welcome, but when you get to the Clavie, it's crunch time, and you get the Clavie this and the Clavie that, and the Clavie everything, and you're still an outsider'.

'That's one good thing about it... you'll never get an Englishman carrying the Clavie... maybe inside the barrel!'.

'There's a bit of animosity, like, 'cos you've got to be born in Burghead'.

Nonetheless, Allan and Gloyer (1996) found that by focusing on the 'Brocher' versus 'incomer' status, other features of the ritual are overlooked. The procession itself is gendered: one must be a male 'Brocher' to participate directly in the procession. As in the Peebles Beltane, lineage is also important, with membership of the Clavie crew commonly inherited by members of the same families (the oldest and most established families in the Broch). Furthermore, concentrating on the procession itself does not take into account overall involvement in the event. Some so-called 'incomers' are dominant in, for example, hosting parties and show more vigorous participation in the event year after year. Level of involvement in the festivities is, therefore, determined by factors other than Brocher status and it became apparent that one could achieve the status of 'local' without being a 'Brocher'. 'Local' status had more to do with behaviour and assimilation of, rather than challenging, community practices and residential qualifications (Condry 1980). Likewise, Phillips (1986: 151) identified that in Muker parish, North Yorkshire:

'the practice of "mucking in" also served to either overcome or actively use differences between locals and incomers in ways which engender community solidarity and the continuity of local ways'.

In a similar vein, Forsythe (1980a) found that one of the perceived boundaries created between locals and incomers on Stormay was due to different styles of public behaviour in which socialisation among Orcadians 'is in effect socialisation for independent but non-leadership behaviour' (p. 295), whereas 'the urban migrants... are used to a more assertive, explicit style of communication, and to the more formal methods of decision-making' (p. 296). More recently, Allan (1996) found in Morayshire that acceptance into the village community was based upon appropriate behaviour and/or attitudes rather than residential status:

'Some folk are accepted right away and other folk aren't. I think it is just the way you are, just the way you view the world and things like that. It doesn't matter what your politics are or anything, but your attitude has got to be right'.

'They have to realize that if they're going to stay in this area they have to fit in with the community. I mean, again that's a fault of a small rural place because every-body gets on wi'it without making a big fuss or noise. . . Some people come in and blow their own trumpet and still do nothing, but they think they're part of the community, and sometimes that disnae work'.

It is apparent, therefore, that boundaries between 'locals' and 'incomers' are neither based solely upon length of residence nor are they necessarily clear cut. However, it is also evident that divisions between 'locals' and 'incomers' are not insurmountable[14].

The preceding paragraphs indicate that the definition of who and what is 'local' is problematic. Even if we demarcate the boundaries of 'local' as being indigenous it does not inform our understanding of rural problems and neglects human actions and social interaction. In practice it is difficult to identify who is and is not a 'local':

'This distinction [between locals and incomers] entails a notion of cultural bound-ary: one either belongs as a born-and-bred local *of* the parish, or one is an immigrant who has *settled* in the locality but whose roots lie elsewhere. The boundary between locals and incomers, however, is anything but hard and fast. Nor are the characters, or stereotypic markers, for expressing the idea of a cultural boundary fixed in their meaning. Rather, the boundary is flexible; and this is so because the markers whereby local identity is symbolised are several, and their significance varies in and through time depending on the context of social interac-tion' (Phillips 1986: 141).

In the Scottish context, this difficulty can be exemplified by looking at a study of housing histories of young households originating from rural Scotland (Mooney 1993). In an attempt to understand a popularised version of the locals versus incomers dichotomy in the rural housing market, and the ways in which people negotiate access to housing, this study involved the reconstruction of the housing histories of individuals who completed their secondary education in rural Scotland. For analytical purposes participants were initially divided into two broad groups: 'locals' and 'non-locals'. People whose entire housing his-tories were within the village or town in which they were born were classified as 'locals'. 'Non-locals' were identified as individuals who were located in the village or town due to a parental move prior to leaving school. Thus, the essential difference was based upon whether or not these people were indigen-ous to the community. This crude division was then further broken down to reflect whether individuals had remained in the same town or district or had migrated elsewhere. However, as the analysis progressed it emerged that people's relationships with place were extremely complex. Some individuals moved into communities at a very young age and would, therefore, be classified as non-'local' under the above scheme, but to all intents and purposes may regard themselves as 'local' because they attended school and had many friends in the area. The complexity of people's relationships with place were sufficient to require an alternative method of identifying analytical categories of inform-ants[15]. Furthermore, the study concluded that incoming populations were not necessary to the cause of rural housing problems. Rather, it was suggested that they may exacerbate the problematic nature of the Scottish rural housing market. Similarly, Jedrej and Nuttall (1996) identify that while incomers are commonly scapegoated for housing problems[16], with many young people forced to leave the area (Gairloch) or live in caravans while they wait for an offer of housing, incomers cannot be entirely blamed for the lack of suitable accommodation and high house prices:

> 'As has been noted, some local people themselves are selling out to incomers, or are owners of holiday homes which they let out to tourists in the summer. There are numerous examples where locals own several houses' (Jedrej and Nuttall 1996: 77)[17].

The boundaries for defining 'localness' can also vary according to scale and the issue in hand. In studies undertaken in the villages of Tomintoul and Craigellachie in Moray district in north east Scotland (Figure 15.1), it was possible to identify communities within communities (Allan 1995). People referred to inhabitants of neighbouring villages by using the especially distancing (Gilligan 1987) term 'outsiders' when convenient; for example, in relation to crime. In this case the villages studied became unitary social organisations in so far as all residents were regarded as 'local' to the village, regardless of residential status, and crime was committed by outsiders. Closer investigation, however, revealed complex social organisation within the villages. Whilst at certain levels the notion of a village represented a singular bounded locale, where all residents 'within' are local, at a smaller scale the definition of a local or outsider was once again altered. At one instance, an outsider was someone from a neighbouring village (an individual physically non-resident), but it was found that an outsider could also be an individual within the village who had moved in from elsewhere (an in-migrant or incomer). In other words, the emphasis and implications of such terms were constantly altering, and open to (re)interpretation, depending upon the context and inference. For example, the village of Craigellachie has experienced extensive new-build housing just outside the limits of the original parish boundary. These new houses have been referred to by residents as 'up the back'. The physical boundaries of the village have been redrawn to encompass the new housing but an imagined social boundary persists between the two parts of the 'Craig':

> 'The hill just up the back is really just housing and there are a lot of new families who've moved up there, who really dinna contribute much to the actual village' (resident in Craigellachie).

Field evidence, however, has shown that there are people living 'up the back' who not only feel part of the village but actively contribute to village affairs through involvement with the community association. The boundaries between locals and incomers are, therefore, not fixed. They are open to negotiation by people who are indigenous to villages and people who migrate into villages.

Regardless of the connotations and difficulties associated with the terms, 'local' and 'incomer' continue to be used when discussing social change within a rural environment. The terms, however, do not identify concrete groupings of people but incorporate altering social relationships that are associated with, and contained within, counterurbanisation processes. These are changes that can be interpreted as positive or negative depending on one's perspective:

> 'while representations such as "locals", "incomers", "lairds", "crofters", "white settlers", "the English", "absentee property holders", "Highland culture", and so on, are agreed upon, the reality to which they refer is elusive and contested. Everyone agrees that there are "locals" and "incomers", but it is not easy to find a consensus about who they are or what is "Highland culture" and "the ancient way of life" that incomers threaten' (Jedrej and Nuttall 1996: 4).

> 'Counterstream migrants were perceived to be a powerful force in rural society: by the end of the research project counterstream migrants and new rural residents had been blamed for *all* the ills affecting changing rural societies. It was, however, clear that the inflamed rhetoric about new rural residents rarely related to the lived experience of relations between migrant and the indigenous rural people' (Shucksmith *et al.* 1996: 470–471).

We have tried to show that reflection upon different voices from the field helps identify the complexities of the terms and references used to describe the impacts of counterurbanisation in the Scottish countryside. This detailed consideration of the terms 'locals' and 'incomers' suggests that the impacts of counterurbanisation cannot be accepted at face value. Rather, when trying to understand counterurbanisation, we need to unpack the terminology that we commonly associate with it and contextualise the wider processes within the dynamics of the communities involved[18]. However, bearing in mind that our evidence comes from our informants in the field, and that the field itself together with the texts we produce are socially constructed, we must consider how our own encounters in the field contribute to our understanding of the impacts of counterurbanisation. In other words, we need to reflect upon our own positionality within the rural realm and the ways in which this shaped our interpretations of social changes in the countryside and the subsequent texts we produce(d).

ACCESSING RURALITY: REFLECTIONS AND REINTERPRETATIONS

Recent studies of rural Britain and counterurbanisation have tended to be approached in one of two particular ways. Firstly, there has been description and explanation of counterurbanisation through the use of statistical accounts of general population trends (for example, Boyle 1995). Secondly, analysis of rural change has been based on theoretical discussion, and a particular element of this has been renewed debate regarding the nature of rural. Most notably, this has centred around conceptualisations of the rural idyll, and its role in the changing countryside (Halfacree 1996; Mooney and Gray 1994). More recently, a new body of rural studies has begun to emerge: studies which involve the analysis of field experience in rural localities (for example, Agg 1996; Allan 1995, 1996; Cloke *et al.* 1994a; Fielding 1995). This type of work reflects established concerns in other areas of the social sciences such as community studies within anthropological and sociological literature (Cohen 1986, 1990; Geertz 1988; Mason 1990; Rapport 1993), and it is within this body of work that we wish to position ourselves.

Throughout this chapter our arguments have been based upon experience and discussions we have had, both during and subsequent to our fieldwork. As a result of these experiences we have come to question the extent to which the multiplicity of meanings embedded within 'talk' about counterurbanisation would have become so evident to us without direct contact with people in place. However, this necessitates reflection on our own preconceptions about the field. This reflection is, in itself, problematic. Our own biographies[19] inform how we conduct and interpret our fieldwork. It is difficult to provide an account of 'how it was' at the time of conducting fieldwork (see Cloke *et al.* 1995: 356). The texts we produce are inevitably retrospective, constructed in the light of hindsight and informed by the texts we read and by our encounters both within and outside the field.

We chose our field locations for a variety of reasons: long-term interest in rural affairs, previous experience in the areas and convenience of access to the field. In doing this we mobilised a particular definition of 'rural'[20] and identified what we accept as part of rural Scotland. We accept that the rural is a social construction and that the imagined 'rural' is subjectively defined (Cloke 1994). As a consequence, we suggest that attempting to differentiate between 'imagined' and 'real' rurals can inform but not necessarily explain the changing countryside. We have started from the premise that the rural exists, whether or not it is real or imagined, and in an attempt to understand how people feel about rural places we have turned our attention to the ways in which people articulate their experiences and beliefs about the rural. In so doing, we acknowledge that the idea of a rural Scotland exists only in so far as we hold notions of a uniquely urban dimension, and that individual perceptions and experiences of the urban and rural vary. In other words, rural and urban become convenient nomenclature which are used to summarise and simplify, in a relational sense, people's identity to place. Beynon and Hudson (1993: 82) suggest that:

'people have often become profoundly attached to particular places, which come to have socially endowed and shared meanings that touch on all aspects of their lives, helping shape *who* they are by virtue of *where* they are'.

If this is the case, fieldwork can be an essential component of understanding relationships with place and the changing countryside.

Our thoughts upon the ways in which rural studies are conducted leads us to question our own fieldwork practices. We must reflect upon our presence in the study areas. As our fieldwork progressed we discovered increasingly complex relationships between people and became aware of our naivety about some of the aspects of our research aims. Research in remote areas is fraught with difficulty. Rapport (1993) reports, in detail, on the ways in which he gained access to the field and his informants. Even in situations which do not involve prolonged field contact, the field continually changes. Researchers in rural areas are extremely conspicuous. From our first interviews, we each became aware that we had become part of the 'local' networks and that our very presence was causing speculation and changes round about us. Our informants themselves exchanged information about us. This inevitably had an influence on our relationships with informants and the communication of ideas.

In addition to the above, we assumed that people in rural communities would inform us about the multiple rural associations and negotiations that exist. In both of our studies, we remained outsiders to the rural locality by concentrating on tactics which involved detailed interviewing rather than prolonged experience in situ. In relying upon information from interviews we have assumed that our informants have information that can be both articulated and understood. In each study access to the field was negotiated via a series of gatekeepers (for example, members of community associations). This inevitably resulted in a filtered 'sample', that is, judgements about who would be an appropriate informant was taken out of our hands. In our fieldwork there was no satisfactory alternative to gaining access. In addition, our informants 'opted-in' to the studies – they agreed to participate. Others did not wish to take part in the studies and their stories will always remain hidden from us[21]. Nevertheless, we still have a significant role in shaping the data that emerged from the interviews and their subsequent representations. The role of the researcher in shaping the dynamics of field relations and the data produced from these encounters is widely documented (for example, Henslin 1990; Keith 1992; Mason 1990; Punch 1994; Rapport 1993).

As individuals interested in the 'rural', 'locals' and 'incomers' have emerged as important issues in the literature we have read, and in our discussions with our informants, between and within our(selves), with other 'rural' researchers and with contacts in the field. To some extent, the ways in which rural issues are presented (for example, the debate over access to housing) predisposed us to thinking that there are distinct groups in the countryside; specifically, 'those who have lived in a place before and those who have not' (Hoggart et al. 1995: 209). This may make it inevitable that we looked for these distinctions in the texts from our interviews. On closer examination we found that the distinctions between different groups of rural people are blurred and that the importance of these divisions varies with context. In other words, the impacts of counterurbanisation are not necessarily measurable in terms of the effect on 'incomers' and 'locals' – whatever we believe these two groups of people to be.

CONCLUSION

'The effects of demographic change upon the culture and identity of a community are often underemphasised in statistical demographic data. But it is these which are experienced by those who are actually involved in the increase and decrease of population' (Symonds 1990: 21).

'While the complex we have called "incomer" is a metaphor for change and that of "local" for stability, the reality is ambiguous and does not make for a straight forward analysis' (Jedrej and Nuttall 1996: 144).

Micro-scale studies of counterurbanisation, involving direct field experience, allow greater insight into the impact and consequences of migration than statistical accounts of population change. This chapter has touched upon the nuances of the information that can be revealed by this fieldwork and it is clear that such qualitative studies disclose a rich variety of responses and detail which often remains hidden in statistical studies. However, it is apparent from our discussion that micro-scale studies can also be problematic, particularly because of the everyday language that is used to discuss counterurbanisation. As a result of this, we must question what we see and hear whilst undertaking fieldwork. Throughout this chapter we have attempted to show that locals and incomers in the Scottish countryside are not two mutually exclusive groups. Rather, as Gilligan (1987), Jedrej and Nuttall (1996) and Phillips (1986) identify, the categories are ambiguous and change according to context and situations. Phillips (1986) proposes that the categories exists as 'scalar qualifications' in which people can range 'from real "Yorkshire dalesfolk" at one pole to "people from away" at the other' (p. 144). He further explains that there are a variety of categories along this scale, including old and new incomers, where old incomers may have become regarded as 'local' due to their continuous long-term contact with a place. It is, therefore, as Phillips argues, the 'now' that is important where constant and continued experience of, and interaction with, a place reinforces local identity. If this, is the case, then it may explain why some of our respondents who had lived in our study villages for a long time identified themselves as being distinct from more recent incomers[22]:

'The key point about all social identities, including national ones, is that they are not given once and for all, but are negotiated. People's claims to an identity have to be recognised to be valid and operative' (Brown *et al.* 1996: 209).

Another key element that has been discussed in this chapter is the need for us, as researchers, to reflect upon our own role(s) in the fieldwork process. If we are to question the language used to describe and analyse counterurbanisation, then we must reflect upon our own position in the production and study of this language. Field observation and interpretation involves complex relationships and the evidence from our interviews is the result of specific social interactions in time and space. These interactions are influenced by our biographies, our perceptions, opinions and attitudes before, during, and after fieldwork. This will obviously influence the outcome of the interview process and impact upon subsequent representations of the rural.

This chapter has, therefore, considered some of the problems involved when analysing the counterurbanisation phenomenon. Those who migrate into rural communities are not, necessarily, a clearly identifiable group. It is also important to acknowledge that we, as researchers, hold particular preconceptions about the nature of changing rural social relations, and that this is influenced by the discursive language used to describe counterurbanisation. As a result of our fieldwork experiences, we have come to recognise the fluidity of the terms 'local' and 'incomer' and we acknowledge that these reflect complex social relationships in rural Scotland. Thus, despite considerable attention, the terminology used by people when discussing social and cultural change in the countryside remains ambiguous and problematic. As a result, we must exercise due care when analysing and writing about this change. Migration and counterurbanisation are integral parts of the changing countryside, and there is a need to 'unpack' the language used by both researchers and those people who are part of our research. Problematising this language need not be negative, but rather it indicates a need to contextualise it within the context of the places and people that we study. Significantly, it reinforces the importance of fieldwork and reflection upon our activities as researchers.

ACKNOWLEDGEMENTS

We would like to thank the people who were interviewed in the course of the research projects. Special thanks to Mandy Gloyer for allowing us to use the information from research conducted in Burghead. Thanks also to Alan Murie for allowing us to use the data from the ESRC Housing Histories project (Housing Histories, Tenures and Strategies, Award No. R000233461). Special thanks also to the editors, Paul Boyle and Keith Halfacree, for their help in writing this chapter.

NOTES

1. The data in this chapter are drawn from four separate studies: Mooney's (1993) investigation into housing histories in rural Scotland, Allan's (1996) investigation into identity in rural Scotland, Allan and Gloyer's (1996) study of the Burghead Clavie, and Murie and Mooney's (1995) investigations into the life experience of housing.
2. The complexity of the impacts of counterurbanisation is also highlighted by Rapport (1993), who indicates that in the village of 'Wanet' in Cumbria, north west England, it is debatable whether the rise in tourism has provided more jobs for local people.

Furthermore, he explains that the migrants' search for 'village harmony' combined with National Park preservation may have thwarted industrial development. While the population figures for Wanet showed some stability between 1971 and 1981, they disguised the fact that 'young people in search of work are being replaced by the retired or those commuting to jobs elsewhere' (p. 20). Similarly, Jones (1993: 330) refers to the 'exodus of native Welsh from rural communities in the search for jobs' as the 'other half of the "incomer problem"'.

3. In discussing the world-views of one of the informants in his study, Rapport provides the following account as part of presenting 'Sid' (who although born in Wanet, has moved around the area) as a 'local'. It pulls together many of the negative characteristics attributed to counterurbanisation:
'In recent years, however, Wanet has been invaded by outsiders. First the offcomers sent their spies in to reconnoitre. Then these went and brought more. Now they all wander round Wanet as if they owned it, ignoring the locals, – not even acknowledging them when they bump into them. They get busy buying up all the houses and land, then they begin sticking their oars into all parts of local life, swamping the pubs, even usurping local Wanet committees' (Rapport 1993: 109).

4. Discussion of terms such as incomers and locals has a long history in community studies and social anthropology (for example, Forsythe 1980a; Phillips 1986). The debate surrounding this nomenclature is more recent within rural geography, particularly in the context of counterurbanisation, which has been approached largely from the macro rather than the micro scale.

5. Here we are using the word 'incomer' as an all-embracing term for words such as 'settler' and 'outsider'.

6. See Jedrej and Nuttall (1996) for a detailed discussion of the meanings and connotations of the term 'White Settler'.

7. Stephenson (1984) also explains that while the term 'White Settler' is frequently heard in Ford, 'it is not a term used or appreciated by all or even most long-term residents' (p. 130), nor would it be used directly towards an English incomer.

8. The study by Shucksmith *et al.* (1996) on disadvantage in rural Scotland found that respondents identified youth out-migration 'as one of the main problems affecting rural areas' (p. 465).

9. Pacione (1995) provides a descriptive analysis of the incidence of rural deprivation in rural Scotland, while the Rural Disadvantage study (Shucksmith *et al.* 1994, 1996) is based upon detailed household surveys. In the context of England and Wales, the Rural Lifestyles project and related publications (for example, Woodward 1996) provide important insights into life in the countryside.

10. Shucksmith *et al.* (1994) comment that new rural residents identified themselves as incomers.

11. Forsythe (1982: 94–95) outlines a categorisation of migrants in 'Stormay', Orkney: natives or other Orcadian migrants, "connected migrants" who are related by kinship or marriage to at least one Orkney family' (p. 94), and '[by] virtue of this connection, connected inmigrants are recognised by locally-born inhabitants as belonging to the community' (Forsythe 1980b: 25), and incomers who have no Orcadian connection.

12. Smith explains that race relations problems have been interpreted by some (the Scottish Press) as an English urban problem. In this context a justification of the 'golliwog' costume was presented as resistance to challenge from outside forces. Smith, however, clearly states that:
'for the most part, I disagree with the justifications put forward for the golliwog protest. For me, the display was as much about racism in Scotland and about the marginalisation of black people in Britain as about the significance, integrity and value of local tradition' (Smith 1996: 303).

13. During the procession, the Clavie barrel is carried by a group of about 10 men. The Clavie Crew is headed by the Clavie King.
14. Jedrej and Nuttall (1996: 77) comment for the townships of Gairloch in north west Scotland 'the consensus is that incomers who fit in are generally accepted'.
15. Shucksmith *et al.* (1996) found that the term 'White Settler' in their study areas was so random that it was not of analytical use.
16. The shortage of affordable housing in rural Britain is a widely recognised problem (for example, Alexander *et al.* 1988; Mooney 1993; NACRT 1987; Newby 1979; Shucksmith 1984, 1991; Shucksmith *et al.* 1994, 1996). Gilligan (1987) identifies that in Padstow, Cornwall, the competition for second homes has caused house prices to escalate 'beyond the reach of most Padstonians' (p. 78), while Bell (1994) quotes a resident of Childerley blaming 'yuppies' for driving 'country people out of the village' (p. 110).
17. Lumb (1980) identified that the social significance of incomers is not linked to their presence in terms of absolute numbers. Furthermore, Jedrej and Nuttall (1996) indicate that there is a long history of scapegoating 'incomers' as the cause of rural housing problems.
18. Likewise, it has been suggested that studies of rural deprivation should be considered in relation to local social, economic and political conditions (Pacione 1995; Marsden *et al.* 1993).
19. See Punch (1994) for the role of personal characteristics and beliefs in qualitative research.
20. The areas in these studies fall within local authority areas classified as 'rural' by Randall (1985). This classification is widely accepted but there are limitations in that it excludes some rural areas of Scotland and includes some large centres of population (Pacione 1995).
21. This differs from the experiences of ethnographers who can, to some extent, choose their informants. In our cases we had limited opportunities to use our own judgements about who to speak to.
22. Likewise, Gilligan (1987: 80) explains that there is a 'sliding scale of exclusiveness' among the people of Padstow in Cornwall. This includes incomers who are long-term residents and who are considered to be 'naturalised' and are, therefore, considered different from more recent in-migrants.

REFERENCES

Agg, J. (1996) 'Sensitising rural research: tapping into others' realities', paper presented at the Annual Conference of the Institute of British Geographers, University of Strathclyde, Glasgow, January.

Alexander, D., Shucksmith, M. and Lindsay, N. (1988) *Scotland's rural housing: opportunities for action?*, Shelter, Edinburgh.

Allan, J. (1995) 'Reconstructing ruralities: community identity and change in Speyside', paper presented at the Annual Conference of the Institute of British Geographers, University of Northumbria, January.

Allan, J. (1996) 'The changing geographies of Scotland's countryside: towards an understanding of identity and meaning', *Scotlands*, **3**, 56–69.

Allan, J. and Gloyer, A. (1996) 'Streets of fire: casting the torch on the Burghead Clavie', paper presented at the Annual Conference of the Institute of British Geographers, University of Strathclyde, Glasgow, January.

Allan, J. and Mooney, E. (1995) 'Incomers, outsiders, non-native speakers: towards understanding the impact of migration into peripheral communities', paper presented at the Migration in Rural Areas Conference, University of Swansea, March.

Bell, M.M. (1994) *Childerley: nature and morality in a country village*, Chicago University Press, London.

Beynon, H. and Hudson, R. (1993) 'Place and space in contemporary Europe: some lessons and reflections', *Antipode*, **25**, 177–190.

Boyle, P. (1995) 'Modelling population movement into the Scottish highlands and islands from the remainder of Britain, 1990–1991', *Scottish Geographical Magazine*, **111**, 5–12.

Brown, A., McCrone, D. and Paterson, L. (1996) *Politics and society in Scotland*, Macmillan, London.

Burnett, K. (1995) 'Rat Race escapees or rural resource? Representations of Hebridean Incomers, Scotland', paper presented at the XVI Congress of the European Society for Rural Sociology, Prague, Czech Republic, 31 July–4 August.

Cairngorms Working Party (1992) 'Common sense and sustainability: a partnership for the Cairngorms', Report of the Cairngorms Working Party to the Secretary of State for Scotland, Scottish Office, Edinburgh.

Cloke, P. (1994) '(En)culturing political economy: a life in the day of a "rural geographer"', in P. Cloke, M. Doel, D. Matless, M. Phillips and N. Thrift, *Writing the rural: five cultural geographies*, Paul Chapman Publishing, London, 149–190.

Cloke, P., Doel, M., Matless, D., Phillips, M. and Thrift, N. (1994a) *Writing the rural: five cultural geographies*, Paul Chapman Publishing, London.

Cloke, P., Milbourne, P. and Thomas, C. (1994b) *Lifestyles in rural England*, Rural Development Commission, London.

Cloke, P., Goodwin, M., Milbourne, P. and Thomas, C. (1995) 'Deprivation, poverty and marginalization in rural lifestyles on England and Wales', *Journal of Rural Studies*, **11**, 351–365.

Cohen, A. (ed.) (1986) *Symbolising boundaries: identity and diversity in British cultures*, Manchester University Press, Manchester.

Cohen, A. (1990) 'The British anthropological tradition, otherness and rural studies', in P. Lowe and M. Bodiguel (eds.), *Rural studies in Britain and France*, Belhaven Press, London, 203–221.

Condry, E. (1980) '"You're not a Sassenach if you live the way we do'. Cultural assimilation: an example from the Western Isles', in A. Jackson (ed.), *Way of life: integration and immigration*, North Sea Oil Panel Occasional Paper No.12, Social Science Research Council, London, 59–69.

Dickson, M. (1994) 'Should auld acquaintance be forgot? A comparison of the Scots and English in Scotland', *Scottish Affairs*, **7**, 112–134.

Fielding, S. (1995) '"Aren't we the fourth?": culture, enclavement and the local', paper presented at the Annual Conference of the Institute of British Geographers, University of Northumbria, Newcastle, January.

Forsythe, D. (1980a) 'Urban incomers and rural change: the impact of migrants from the city on life in an Orkney community', *Sociologia Ruralis*, **20**, 287–307.

Forsythe, D. (1980b) 'Urban-rural migration and the pastoral ideal: an Orkney case', in A. Jackson (ed.), *Way of life: integration and immigration*, North Sea Oil Panel Occasional Paper No.12, Social Science Research Council, London, 22–45.

Forsythe, D. (1982) 'Gross migration and social change: an Orkney case study', in H. Jones (ed.), *Recent migration in northern Scotland: pattern, process and change*, North Sea Oil Panel Occasional Paper No. 13, Social Science Research Council, London, 90–104.

Frankenberg, R. (1957) *Village on the border*, Cohen and West, London.

Geertz, C. (1988) *Works and lives: the anthropologist as author*, Polity Press, Oxford.

Gilligan, J. (1987) 'Visitors tourists and outsiders in a Cornish town', in M. Bouquet and M. Winter (eds.), *Who from their labours rest? Conflict and practice in rural tourism*, Avebury, Aldershot, 65–82.

Gray, D. (1993) 'Counterurbanisation and the perception of quality of life in rural Scotland: a postmodern framework', unpublished PhD Thesis, Department of Geography, University of Glasgow, Glasgow.

Halfacree, K. (1993) 'Locality and social representation: space, discourse and alternative definitions of the rural', *Journal of Rural Studies*, **9**, 23–37.

Halfacree, K. (1995) 'Talking about rurality: social representations of the rural as expressed by residents of six English parishes', *Journal of Rural Studies*, **11**, 1–20.

Halfacree, K. (1996) 'Trespassing against the rural idyll: the Criminal Justice and Public Order Act 1994 and access to the countryside', in C. Watkins (ed.), *Rights of way*, Pinter, London, 179–193.

Henslin, J. (1990) 'It's not a lovely place and I wouldn't want to live there', in R. Burgess (ed.), *Studies in qualitative methodology, volume 2, reflections on field experience*, Jai Press, London, 51–76.

Hoggart, K. (1990) 'Let's do away with rural', *Journal of Rural Studies*, **6**, 245–257.

Hoggart, K., Buller, H. and Black, R. (1995) *Rural Europe, identity and change*, Edward Arnold, London.

Holbourn, I. and Baisley, L. (1994) 'Community, the people and the land', Report from Community Conference, Highlands and Islands Forum, Drumossie, March.

Hunter, J. (1995) 'The Highland challenge', *The Herald*, Saturday, July 15, 17.

Jedrej, M. and Nuttall, M. (1995) 'Incomers and locals: metaphors and reality in the repopulation of rural Scotland', *Scottish Affairs*, **10**, 112–126.

Jedrej, M. and Nuttall, M. (1996) *White Settlers, the impact of rural repopulation in Scotland*, Harwood Academic Publishers, Luxembourg.

Jones, H. (1982) 'The spatial pattern of recent migration in northern Scotland' in H. Jones (ed.), *Recent migration in northern Scotland: pattern, process, impact*, North Sea Oil Panel Occasional Paper No. 13, Social Science Research Council, London, 7–26.

Jones, H. (1992) 'Migration trends for Scotland: central losses and peripheral gains', in J. Stillwell, P. Rees and P. Boden (eds.), *Migration processes and patterns. Volume 2: population redistribution in the 1980s*, Belhaven Press, London, 100–114.

Jones, H., Ford, N., Caird, J. and Berry, W. (1984) 'Counterurbanisation in a societal context: long distance migration to the Highlands and Islands of Scotland', *Professional Geographer*, **36**, 437–444.

Jones, H., Caird, J., Berry, W. and Dewhurst, J. (1986) 'Peripheral counter-urbanisation: findings from an integration of census and survey data in northern Scotland', *Regional Studies*, **20**, 15–26.

Jones, N. (1993) *Living in rural Wales*, Gomer Press, Llandysul, Dyfed.

Katz, C. (1992) 'All the world is stages: intellectuals and the projects of ethnography', *Environment and Planning D: Society and Space*, **10**, 495–510 .

Keith, M. (1992) 'Angry writing: (re)presenting the unethical world of the ethnographer', *Environment and Planning D: Society and Space*, **10**, 551–568.

Lumb, R. (1980) 'Integration and immigration: some demographic aspects of Highland communities', in A. Jackson (ed.), *Way of life: integration and immigration*, North Sea Oil Panel Occasional Paper No.12, Social Science Research Council, London, 46–58.

MacNee, K. (1994) *Literature review of rural issues*, Scottish Office Central Research Unit, Edinburgh.

Marsden, T., Murdoch, J., Lowe, P., Munton, R. and Flynn, A. (1993) *Constructing the countryside*, UCL Press, London.

Mason, K. (1990) 'Not waving but bidding: reflections on research in a rural setting', in R. Burgess (ed.), *Studies in qualitative methodology, volume 2, reflections on field experience*, Jai Press, London, 99–117.

Mewett, P. (1982) 'Exiles, nicknames, social identities and the production of local consciousness in a Lewis crofting community', in A. Cohen (ed.), *Belonging: identity and social organisation in British rural cultures*, Academic Press, London, 222–246.

Mooney, E. (1993) 'Housing experiences and housing outcomes: an application of the housing histories methodology to rural Scotland', unpublished PhD Thesis, Department of Geography, University of Strathclyde, Glasgow.

Mooney, E. (1994) 'Representing and (re)presenting field experience in human geography', discussion paper from the Social and Cultural Geography Study Group of the Institute of British Geographers one day conference, Manchester University, February.

Mooney, E. (1996) 'Some preliminary thoughts on the life experience of housing: evidence from Argyll', paper presented at the Institute of British Geographers, Rural Geography Study Group workshop on Ethnography and Rural Research, University of Nottingham, July.

Mooney, E. and Gray, D. (1994) 'The Scottish rural idyll and counterurbanisation: the myth and reality of community change', paper presented at the Annual Conference of the Institute of British Geographers, University of Nottingham, January.

Murie, A. and Mooney, E. (1995) 'Housing histories, tenures and strategies', end of award report to the ESRC, Award No: R000233461.

NACRT (1987) *Village homes for village people*, National Agricultural Centre Rural Trust, London.

Newby, H. (1979) *Green and pleasant land?*, Hutchinson, London.

Pacione, M (1995) 'The geography of deprivation in rural Scotland', *Transactions of the Institute of British Geographers*, **20**, 173–192.

Perry, R., Dean, K. and Brown, B. (1986) *Counterurbanisation: case studies of urban to rural movement*, Geo Books, Norwich.

Phillips, S. (1986) 'Natives and incomers: the symbolism of belonging in Muker parish, North Yorkshire', in A. Cohen (ed.), *Symbolising boundaries: identity and diversity in British cultures*, Manchester University Press, Manchester, 141–154.

Pratt, A. (1989) 'Rurality: loose talk or social struggle?', paper presented at the Annual Conference of the Rural Economy and Society Study Group, Bristol, December.

Punch, M. (1994) 'Politics and ethics in qualitative research', in N. Denzin and Y. Lincoln (eds.), *Handbook of qualitative research*, Sage Publications, London.

Randall, J. (1985) 'Economic trends and support to economic activity in rural Scotland', *Scottish Economic Bulletin*, **31**, 10–20.

Rapport, N. (1993) *Diverse world-views in an English village*, Edinburgh University Press, Edinburgh

Scottish Office (1996) *Scottish rural life update*, HMSO, Edinburgh.

Shucksmith, M (1984) 'Scotland's rural housing: a forgotten problem', Rural Forum Discussion Paper, Rural Forum, Perth.

Shucksmith, M (1991) 'Still no homes for locals? Affordable housing and planning controls in rural areas', in T Champion and C. Watkins (eds.), *People in the countryside*, Paul Chapman Publishing, London, 53–66.

Shucksmith, M., Chapman, P. and Clark, G., with Black, S. and Conway, E. (1994) 'Disadvantage in rural Scotland: how is it experienced and how can it be tackled?', Department of Land Economy, University of Aberdeen, Aberdeen (Summary report commissioned by Rural Forum and Scottish Consumer Council).

Shucksmith, M., Chapman, P. and Clark, G., with Black, S. and Conway, E (1996) *Rural Scotland today. The best of both worlds?*, Avebury, Aldershot.

Smith, S. (1993) 'Bounding the borders: claiming space and making place in rural Scotland', *Transactions of the Institute of British Geographers*, **18**, 291–308.

Stephenson, J. (1984) *Ford. A village in the west Highlands of Scotland*, Paul Harris Publishing, Edinburgh.

Symonds, A. (1990) 'Migration, communities and social change', in R. Jenkins and A. Edwards (eds.), *One step forwards? South and West Wales towards the year 2000*, Gomer Press, Llandysul, 21–32.

Weekley, I. (1988) 'Rural depopulation and counterurbanisation: a paradox', *Area*, **20**, 127–134.

Woodward, R. (1996) 'Deprivation and the rural: an investigation into contradictory discourses', *Journal of Rural Studies*, **12**, 55–67.

16

MIGRATION INTO RURAL AREAS: A COLLECTIVE BEHAVIOUR FRAMEWORK?

PAUL BOYLE and KEITH HALFACREE

FROM EACH END A NEW BEGINNING?

This book began by problematising the terms 'migration' and 'rural' and will end by problematising further the conceptualisation of migration to rural areas as it has conventionally been presented in the academic literature. Specifically, we suggest that there is some scope for, and indeed value in, 'reinventing' the way we express the problematic of migration to rural areas. This is illustrated here through one such reinvention – migration into rural areas as an example of collective behaviour – an extension of the biographical approach to migration research which we have advocated elsewhere (Halfacree and Boyle 1993). This chapter's structure, we feel, provides a fitting ending to this collection on a subject for which there is still far to go before a satisfactory closure, and hence any sense of conclusion, can be reached.

The various and diverse contributions in this book have illustrated some of the ways through which migration is integral to the formation of the networks of power which are bringing about often dramatic changes within the more rural parts of many developed countries; what was termed, in Chapter 1, the creation of a post-productivist countryside. The economy, state policies, class, gender, culture, questions of identity, planning, and even the very language we and those we research use, have been shown to mesh together into the processes of rural change in which migration is so heavily implicated. A broad distinction between micro-level behavioural influences (Berry 1976) and structural factors (T. Fielding, Chapter 3, this volume) that influence migration into rural areas is well-established but such is the diversity of issues and research foci covered in this book alone that we may indeed ask ourselves just what is the value of synthesising such a range of theoretical studies of 'migration into rural areas'? Can the whole idea of rural in-migration, which can appear so straightforward when expressed in general, aggregate, statistical terms, be salvaged from being labelled one of social science's 'chaotic conceptions', whereby we:

'arbitrarily divide the indivisible and/or lump... together the unrelated and the inessential, thereby "carving up" the object of study with little or no regard for its structure and form' (Sayer 1984: 127)?

Given the diversity of issues covered in this collection, is this not the way that 'migration into rural areas' appears?

Fundamental attention must be given to how the idea of migration into rural areas can hold together conceptually. As Champion (Chapter 2, this volume) observes, there is still much to be done in disentangling the role of in-migration in the whole counterurbanisation process. One response, which has been suggested by one of the present authors (Halfacree 1994, 1997), is to focus on the significance of migrants' ideas of the 'rural' and the 'urban' in explaining this migration. Such a significance has also been suggested by many of the chapters of this book. Alternatively, but at a more descriptive epistemological level, in our ongoing search for an answer to the conceptualisation question, the present authors arrived at the idea that such diverse migration could be integrated through reinventing and representing it as an example of 'collective behaviour'. In other words, rather than just presenting what is taking place empirically as the spatial movement of persons from point A to (rural) point B over a specified time period (Halfacree and Boyle, Chapter 1, this volume), we have sought a more 'social' overview. This alternative is developed here. First, however, it is necessary to say something about the idea of re-invention.

Much of academic life is concerned with *re*invention and *re*presentation rather than with 'original' production *in senso stricto* (see Skeldon's 1995 comments on some of our own work, for example). Of course, such a result in many ways is to be expected if we take seriously the decentring claims of intertextuality raised through poststructuralism, and postmodernism's rejection of the idea of teleological progress. Consequently:

'the *real* "truth" of the human world... [is] that it is constituted of nothing but fragmented clouds of communication bound together by nothing but garbled dialogues between peoples who do not (who cannot) properly understand one another' (Cloke *et al.* 1991: 193, after Lyotard 1984).

Thus, while our biographical perspective (discussed below) overlapped with methodological approaches adopted in the developing world, we maintain that the underlying theoretical rationale was innovative, even though it inevitably drew upon the work of others (for example, Giddens, Shotter, Thrift). The condensations around 'geography' which occur in these clouds of communication provide our here-and-now as academics through a physics determined as much by historical and cultural context, force of personality, chance, and so on, as by any clear sense of progress. It is here that the scope for reinvention lies.

THE STUDY OF COLLECTIVE BEHAVIOUR

As Marx and McAdam (1994) emphasise from the outset, the study of collective behaviour is an extremely diverse and interdisciplinary tradition within social

TABLE 16.1 Dimensions of the emergence–cultural specification distinction

Does culture specify:
1. Where an episode will occur?
2. When and how it will begin and end?
3. Who will participate and, where applicable, how participants arrive and disperse from the scene?
4. What the goals are?
5. What rules will govern behaviour (including decision-making)?
6. What resources and facilities will be used?
7. Where applicable, what the division of labour will be and who will play what role?
8. What will happen in general or specific terms?
9. Where applicable, the means whereby behaviour will diffuse to other persons or places?
10. What attitudes and emotions are expected?

Source: Marx and McAdam 1994: 9.

science. However, as its name suggests, the primary focus is on the behaviour of groups: 'It is social and involves persons responding to each other or the same stimulus' (Marx and McAdam 1994: 11). Moreover, this focus is not on group behaviour which can be 'read off' from the group's culture but on behaviour ultimately irreducible to that culture, what is termed 'emergent' behaviour, since 'the openness of culture. . . creates a vacuum' (p. 18). Group behaviour is ranged on a continuum from emergence to cultural specificity, with the study of collective behaviour focusing on that which falls towards the former pole. Table 16.1 presents a number of questions which can be employed to assess whether or not a particular type of behaviour should be classed as emergent. Whilst collective behaviour tends to be highly dynamic and often ephemeral, and is typified by having those involved display a high level of personal commitment, it can arise and flourish in otherwise highly organised settings as well as in the classic case of the crowd.

Collective behaviour is typically impulsive and results from some form of social interaction. A number of social psychological experiments have shown that individuals often act differently when they are part of a group, where anonymity and diffused responsibility contribute towards more radical and less cautious behaviour. Much of this work stems from LeBon's (1895) original supposition that members of a crowd may give up their individual consciousness and take on a 'collective mind', almost as if they had become a single organism; this he described as the 'law of mental unity of crowds'. A classic demonstration of this was the extraordinary effect that Orson Welles's Halloween night 1938 radio dramatisation of H.G. Wells' *War of the Worlds* had on its American listeners, 28 percent of whom thought that an invasion from Mars had occurred (Cantril 1940)!

It is important to recognise, however, that there are many examples of social situations where the collectiveness has far more subtle effects than that found in volatile crowds. Genevie (1978) outlines a continuum which ranges from 'panic' to the 'public', where the former includes extreme group reactions to events such as natural disasters and the latter involves groups of like-minded individuals coming together in the name of a particular cause or issue. Communication among such a public exists but it is not necessary for individuals to meet directly and they are not necessarily an organised group. Blumer (1978) distinguishes more broadly between the 'crowd', the 'public' and the 'mass', with the latter providing a broader conception of collective behaviour which – importantly for our purpose – includes events such as mass migrations:

> 'the mass is represented by people who participate in mass behaviour, such as those who are excited by some national event, those who share in a land, those who are interested in a murder trial which is reported in the press, or those who participate in some *large migration*' (Blumer 1978: 72; emphasis added).

The classic contribution of Park and Burgess (1924) had earlier described migration as the most elementary example of mass movement:

> 'The migration of a people, either as individuals or in organised groups, may be compared to the swarming of a bee-hive. Peoples migrate in search of better living conditions, or merely in search of new experiences' (Park and Burgess 1924: 869).

Actors in these migrating masses do not necessarily come from similar backgrounds – they are an anonymous body – there is little exchange of experiences among them and they are a loosely organised group:

> 'The form of mass behaviour, paradoxically, is laid down by individual lines of activity and not by concerted action. These individual activities are primarily in the form of selections... which are made in response to the vague impulses and feelings which are awakened by the object of mass interest' (Blumer 1978: 73).

Thus, various migration episodes may be identified as examples of collective behaviour. Examples from the United States over the past 150 years alone include the great migrations towards California during the Dust Bowl era, the Klondike gold rush, the Oklahoma land boom, the Irish emigration to North America during the potato famine, and the south-to-north migration of black people in the early twentieth century. Typically, these migrations involved individuals from quite heterogeneous backgrounds and there was little or no discipline or order in their movement.

SMELSER'S MODEL OF COLLECTIVE BEHAVIOUR APPLIED TO RURAL IN-MIGRATION

A well known and rigorous model of collective behaviour is that proposed by Smelser (1962). He emphasised the logic of 'value-added', where each of his six stages of the unfolding of an episode of collective behaviour combines in a definite pattern, such that the type of episode in question becomes increasingly specific (Table 16.2). According to Smelser's admittedly over-rigid and hierarchi-

TABLE 16.2 Smelser's model of collective behaviour

Stage	Summary
1. Structural conduciveness	The general social conditions that enable or encourage collective behaviour. Such conditions make collective behaviour possible, but by no means necessary.
2. Structural strain	Tensions or contradictions in the social environment which produce conflicts of interest. Expressed as uncertainties, anxieties, or direct goal conflicts.
3. Spread of a generalised belief	The influence of distinctive ideologies which tend both to crystallise grievances and to suggest a remedial course of action.
4. Precipitating factors	Specific, usually dramatic and unpredictable, events or incidents which trigger action.
5. Mobilisation of participants for action	The participation of a group of individuals in a collective behaviour episode, with some kind of leadership, direction and resources.
6. Operation of social control	Factors that prevent, interrupt or deflect episodes of collective behaviour; typically via the state.

Source: Giddens 1993: 644–645, after Smelser 1962.

cal analyses of collective behaviour, there is a need to acknowledge the importance of each stage and how they combine to produce a particular episode. Once collective behaviour occurs, relatively crude processes of communication, such as contagion, rumour and diffusion, are deemed important.

An attempt has been made by Campbell and Garkovich (1984) to apply Smelser's model to migration into rural areas of the USA. Drawing on their fitting of what they term 'turnaround migration' to the collective behaviour model, we consider each of the six stages in turn:

- *Structural conduciveness.* Factors which aided the mobilisation of rural in-migrants included increasing economic prosperity in the 1960s, industrial relocation into more peripheral areas, the growth of a rural retirement infrastructure, an improved telecommunications and transportation infrastructure, and the growth of the recreational industry of rural areas. In addition we found a sustained – especially as popularly perceived (for example, the 'rural idyll') – distinction between rural and urban residential environments, and the normative position of migration for economic and other forms of betterment. These factors combined, in many countries, to provide a suitable social environment for rural in-migration to occur. The importance of these factors have been identified by many authors: Cross (1990) discusses the role of retirees in migration into peripheral areas; T. Fielding, Kontuly, and Frey and Johnson, (Chapters 3, 4 and 5, this volume) emphasise the significance of industrial restructuring; Hugo and Bell (Chapter 6, this volume) note the role which can be played by welfare benefits; and Urry (1995) draws attention to changing rural leisure practices.

- *Structural strain.* Tensions and strains are rife within the (urban) social environment, with contradictions emerging continuously. In the light of these strains, within many developed nations there has developed a growing disenchantment with urban living and its perceived associated problems of crime, pollution and public unrest. For example, Frey and Johnson (Chapter 5, this volume) suggested how immigrants to United States cities economically 'displaced' low-skill native-born residents, who turn towards the non-metropolitan areas for jobs and lifestyles. More generally, surveys repeatedly cite what are perceived to be the negative aspects of urban living – as well as the positive aspects of rural living – as causes of rural in-migration. As Campbell and Garkovich express it, there has been a shift in the 'balance sheet' of the net benefits of urban and rural living in favour of the latter. The city has shifted from being perceived as a place of promise for the future (Jerusalem) to being seen as a corrupted Babylon (Short 1991: 81). 'Community' has been lost in the city but is felt by many to remain in the countryside (Murdoch and Day, Chapter 10, this volume).

- *Spread of a generalised belief.* The grievances represented above have, as already suggested, become crystallised in an ideological belief which pits the 'rural' against the 'urban'. Here, attention is being focused on the 'social representation' of the countryside (Halfacree 1993) commonly known as the 'rural idyll'. This idea has been long represented in one form or another in many developed world cultures (for example, Bunce 1994; Hadden and Barton 1973; Williams 1973). For example, Thomas (1973: 14) argues that:

  > 'the preoccupation with nature and rural life is. . . certainly something which the English townsman (*sic*) has for a long time liked to think of as such; and much of the country's literature has displayed an anti-urban bias'.

  In the United States, various expressions of the moral, aesthetic and political virtues of rural life have also been apparent for some time; Jefferson's sturdy yeoman and Turner's frontier thesis are examples (Nash 1973). The belief in the benefits of rural over urban living can be seen directly to fuel rural in-migration episodes (Halfacree 1994, 1995, and Chapter 11, this volume). Critical to this process is the spread of this belief through its marketing via the mass media. Many argue (for example, Agg and Phillips, Chapter 14, this volume; Goldman and Dickens 1983; Lash and Urry 1994; Thrift 1989) that images of the idyllic rural are constantly produced by the media and marketing agencies, such that they have become commonly accepted by people from various backgrounds. Those who have moved into rural areas often display evidence of their rural lifestyles in the clothes they wear and the pursuits they engage in. A belief has been commoditised and successfully marketed across class boundaries, becoming involved in the behaviour of a very wide range of people in numerous countries (Kontuly, Chapter 4, this volume).

- *Precipitating factors.* Immediate critical factors bringing about rural in-migration are less easy to identify. However, attention can be drawn to the riots, disturbances or uprisings which periodically flare up in many large developed world cities. For example, the USA had the Watts Riots (1965) and the disturbances following the acquittal of the police officers responsible for the beating of Rodney King (1992), both in Los Angeles; whilst in Britain there have been several urban uprisings since the early 1980s. Other crises, such as the virtual bankruptcy of many United States cities in the 1980s and 1990s, also have a strong urban focus, as do many of the key negative features of economic restructuring (Frey and Johnson, Chapter 5, this volume). Of note here is the racialising of many of these crises, which is reflected in the 'whiteness' of the rural idyll (Agyeman and Spooner 1997); an immediate suggestion of how 'selective', and paradoxical – given its mass character in other respects – the collective behaviour discussed here is (Murdoch and Day, Chapter 10, this volume).

- *Mobilisation of participants for action.* Whilst no 'leader' *per se* is apparent in this type of collective action, there are key resources which serve as markers or guides in rural in-migration, also legitimating the decisions of those doing the migrating. Attention here can be given to the vast 'rural' literature, such as magazines (*Country Life, Country Living, The Countryman,* and so on in Britain; see Agg and Phillips, Chapter 14, this volume; Newby 1980) and other media and artistic representations of rural life (Fish 1997; Short 1991; Youngs 1985). An interesting example here is the leadership role played by the popular writer Peter Mayle in directing English migrants to rural France (Buller and Hoggart 1994) with his books *A year in Provence* (1989) and *Toujours Provence* (1990). Whilst migration to rural areas is seemingly an individualistic event for the household involved, opinions about rural life spread through the media and among friends and colleagues. Ultimately, we might ask whether the same numbers of people would have migrated into rural areas during the last few decades if their friends and colleagues had not, or if various elements of the mass media had not portrayed life in rural areas in such a positive light?

- *Operation of social control.* Since it is not an oppositional form of collective action (cf. Cohen 1973) being highly conducive to the support of many key features of a patriarchal capitalist society, it is perhaps not surprising that the state has generally not sought to deflect or prevent rural in-migration taking place. Indeed, state policies have often facilitated migration to rural areas (Hugo and Bell, Chapter 6, this volume). However, particularly in certain nations, such as Britain, the operation of planning laws and regulations do play a critical managerial role. For example, they may serve to restrict housing and industrial growth in the periphery. It also requires certain kinds of abilities and resources on the part of the (potential) rural in-migrants both to gain a place in the country and to defend that country home against environmental changes which would devalorise it in some form or another (Abram, Murdoch and Marsden, Chapter 13, this volume; Murdoch and Marsden 1994). More fundamentally still, recurrent recessions bring into question the (rising) costs of long-distance commuting and long-term societal prosperity, and keep in check the spread of industry throughout rural areas. Finally, the idea of control also operates within the rural environment, with migrants requiring a degree of 'cultural competence' to live 'successfully' in such areas (Cloke, Goodwin and Milbourne, Chapter 7, this volume). Such cultural competence can be shown to have a degree of class embeddedness (Cloke, Phillips and Thrift, Chapter 9, this volume).

Overall, therefore, from this brief skeleton of some indicative points, there seem to be some benefits conceptually to be gained from positing migration into rural areas as a form of collective behaviour as expressed by Smelser's model. However, there are flaws with this model which merit further consideration.

BEYOND THE PASSIVE MODEL

As Giddens (1993) points out, Smelser's model of collective action has a number of faults. Two particularly concern us here. Firstly, collective behaviour can occur without the presence of a particular precipitating action. Secondly, and following from this, rather than collective actions emerging from societal contra-dictions, these actions may bring into the fore and intensify hitherto hidden strains. Both of these issues seem pertinent with respect to migration into rural areas. There is the sheer (if uneven) ubiquity – across both time and space – of this migration trend, as stressed in numerous chapters of this volume. Such migration is also often linked to the consolidation of societal strain, especially within the rural environment (Abram, Murdoch and Marsden, Chapter 13; Cloke, Goodwin and Milbourne, Chapter 7; S. Fielding, Chapter 8; Murdoch and Day, Chapter 10, this volume).

The two key problems arise because Smelser's model fits into the 'strain' school of explanation for the development of collective action and social movements (Marx and McAdam 1994)[1]. In Smelser's case, the argument is that rapid social change disrupts society, causing uncertainty and anxiety amongst its members. In this case, the collective action is a coping mechanism driven by what Smelser terms 'wish-fulfilment', for example. Similarly, there are other models – mass society models – that posit social isolation rather than rapid change as the cause of alienation. However, in contrast to such 'breakdown theories' (Maheu 1995), which often lead to the conclusion that the resulting collective behaviour was in many ways an irrational response, there are expla-nations of collective action which have a more proactive emphasis.

One of these alternatives is known as resource mobilisation theory (McCarthy and Zald 1973, 1977), which contends that actors in collective behaviour are not spurred into action by time-specific strains and grievances; rather they are mobilised as resources allow, with the tendency towards action being under the surface all along. A shared culture of interests, norms and values is presupposed, but expression of this support only occurs when the resources become available or the unease with the situation reaches a particularly acute level. The uneven distribution of resources – hence, issues such as class – is therefore the key variable in explaining collective action and the participants are not assumed to be acting irrationally. A further perspective on the basis of collective action is provided by political-process theory (Marx and McAdam 1994). Here, the group action is seen very much as an organised and focused political activity. Whilst this approach might be criticised for losing some of the 'banalities' which characterise the fads which feature so strongly in collective action, it does get us away from the idea of passive participants. A good example of this approach is Gamson's (1990) distinction between 'members' and 'challengers', with the former having routine access to power whilst the latter do not. Only in periods of abnormal crisis do the challengers have a chance to gain the upper hand, and this is achieved through directed collective action.

In reflecting on these debates in the context of migration to rural areas, we agree that there is a need to take a less deterministic line than that suggested in Smelser's work. Even if rural in-migration can be seen as a response to either rapid societal change or increasing individual isolation (issues which we cannot tackle here), we do not see the action as a relatively passive response. It may be 'wish-fulfilment'[2] (Campbell and Garkovich 1984) but this in itself suggests a degree of agency (Halfacree, Chapter 11; Murdoch and Day, Chapter 10, this volume); indeed, Gorton, White and Chaston (Chapter 12, this volume) stress the role of persuasion in the creation of the post-productivist countryside. However, it is also problematic, especially given the lack of 'leadership', that the majority of such migration can be understood in terms of a distinct political project, even if an opening for potential 'challengers' has appeared in the context of the advent of the post-productivist countryside (Halfacree and Boyle, Chapter 1, this volume). Moreover, whilst resource mobilisation theory has the potential for recognising both the selectivity of rural in-migration and the investment which can go into such a move, it tends to overemphasise the acquisition of resources to the neglect of movement goals and the motives of the participants who are involved. It goes 'too far in nearly abandoning the social-psychology analysis of social movements' (Klandermans 1984: 583–584) and the exclusion of values, norms, ideologies and culture (Cohen 1985) is especially invalid when dealing with mass migrations. Resource mobilisation fails to grapple with the sense of 'we' that may exist among participants (Melucci 1989). In line with the arguments of Cloke, Phillips and Thrift (Chapter 9, this volume), the manifestation of a collective identity can be seen in the cultural icons and artefacts, such as style of dress, displayed by those who embrace it (Gamson 1992). What we wish to emphasise fundamentally, however, is the need to regard those migrating not as passive irrational dupes (of the rural idyll?) but as 'responsible' human agents.

TOWARDS A BIO-DISCOURSE METHODOLOGY?

In his work, Smelser (1962) acknowledged that many instances of collective behaviour are difficult to measure, cannot be controlled experimentally and are difficult to predict. Consequently, it may be unsurprising that convincing evidence for the role of collective behaviour at the decision-making level in the mass migration of people into the countryside has yet to have been produced. Representational models, such as the one proposed by Smelser, may be suggestive (see above) but at the level of the migrant's processes things remain most uncertain. Therefore, this final section of the chapter reflects a little on the way we may go about studying migration to rural areas as a 'responsible' collective action. Specifically, the present authors (Halfacree and Boyle 1993) have argued that a 'biographical approach' might be considered in migration research which moves away from the assumption that migration is stress induced, stimulated purely by particular events and circumstances. In line with Shotter's (1984, 1989) emphasis on social accountability, migration should be recognised as a responsible action but one which occurs within the 'hurly-burly' of everyday life; decision-making cannot be assumed to occur outside this messiness. Such an approach does not fall prey to the 'intellectual fallacy', part of the 'theoretical purification of practical orders' (Thrift 1996: 5), whereby human agents are treated as acting rationally according to a series of abstracted and decontextualised discrete promptings.

Drawing notably from Giddens' work (for example, Giddens 1984), the notion of 'practical consciousness' was acknowledged as a key issue in the biographical approach to migration. This level of thought lies between unconscious decision-making, which is unacknowledged by the participant, and discursive decision-making, which includes that which is 'actively thought about'. Instead, practical consciousness involves decision-making that is largely taken for granted, such that individuals may find it quite difficult to elaborate upon it. Practical consciousness lies in the realm of common sense. It was also argued that seeking one or two 'causes' for a migration event is inadequate as a large number of issues, admittedly of varying importance, will influence the migration decision; the identification of a single, recent stress event as the key to migration behaviour ignores the stream of consciousness and variety of influencing factors that have a role to play.

However, while the biographical approach allows for a more realistic interpretation of the multiple currents that influence migration decision-making, our account did not acknowledge satisfactorily how *collective behaviour* may have an important, and to now largely ignored, role in many migration events. Attention needs to be directed at the production of what is now seen to be rather a static idea of 'common sense' as it exists within practical consciousness, and to its articulation within the migration decision-making process. In particular, within this emphasis on its structuration, common sense has to be unpacked if we are to identify the role of collective behaviour. Considering common sense according to different social scales suggests a range from embedded knowledge derived primarily from direct individual experience to knowledge derived from a more distanciated or 'remote' learning of the normative currents within society. Referring back to the idea of collective behaviour as being emergent (Table 16.1), migration to rural areas underpinned by common sense located towards the direct experience pole is more likely to fit the collective behaviour model, as compared to more socially normative common sense migration, which more closely resembles the cultural specificity model.

Elucidating the relative role of collective behaviour in migration to rural areas requires a methodology that penetrates the responses from an individual and draws out any suggestions that collective behaviour was relevant in the decision-making process. While social psychologists have identified the effects of collective behaviour in controlled experiments (for example, Zimbardo 1970), it is much more difficult for respondents themselves to identify its presence in migration decision-making; by its very nature it is a social effect that they may be aware of but find hard to explain or acknowledge voluntarily. Thus, researchers investigating the potential role of collective behaviour in migration require a means of teasing it out from the respondent's words. One possibility is to make use of a technique that is becoming increasingly popular in social psychology. Discourse analysis (for example, Gilbert and Mulkay 1984; Potter and Wetherell 1987) involves the direct investigation of the very language of respondents. Rather than concentrating solely on respondents' answers to specific questions or on meanings that can be derived from deeper qualitative passages, this approach advocates treating the language itself as a data resource. Discourse analysts are therefore concerned with talking and conversation as a subject of study in its own right and advocate the use of ethnographic methods to generate samples of talk. Explanations that may be 'hidden' in more formal approaches can be teased out with the help of this form of analysis; common sense can begin to be unpacked.

Integrating discourse analysis within the biographical approach would provide a biographical-discourse, or 'bio-discourse' methodology. This would accept, firstly, that migration decision-making is more than simply a 'rational' reaction triggered by some stress event because it is bound up in the long-term goals and aspirations of individuals, whether as a cultural expression or as an example of collective behaviour. Secondly, it would require a deeper, much more involved, analysis of the texts that are derived from individual respondents. Evidence for both emergent and culturally embedded decision-making can be sought in the terminology used by respondents (see Allan and Mooney, Chapter 15, this volume). Clues might include references to apparently generally held views that rural living is preferential to urban living. Comments which use statements such as 'it is generally known that. . .', or 'most people aspire to. . .' may point to decision-making that is influenced by the apparent culture of a social group, rather than decision-making at the individual level. We might also ask respondents to explain the meanings of labels and other cultural symbols. In seeking a collective behaviour understanding, we are seeking evidence that respondents have been 'swept along' by a common response to structural changes occurring within society which have either triggered or enabled migration to rural areas. In contrast, a cultural explanation sees a response more delineated by determinants of culture (class, ethnicity, gender, and so on).

CONCLUSION: THE LIMIT OF THE COLLECTIVE ACTION MODEL

Just as Halfacree (Chapter 11, this volume) discusses how 'neo-tribal' identifications can easily slip to become either *Gemeinschaft* identities or *Gesellschaft* instrumentalities, so can collective behaviour lose its emergent status and become increasingly culturally specified. Indeed, this potential – clear in models such as that of Smelser – provides a limit to our re-invention of migration into rural areas as an example of collective behaviour. As suggested in the previous section, the extent to which migration to rural areas has now lost its emergent status and become thoroughly encultured is a key issue to address. Hence, Cloke, Phillips and Thrift (Chapter 9, this volume), amongst others, can embed the migration to rural areas within class-related cultural textures. Perhaps this is to be expected given the class-infused structural conditions in which the counterurbanisation trend has been located (T. Fielding, Chapter 3; Kontuly Chapter 4, this volume). Certainly, if migration into rural areas has ceased to resemble emergent collective behaviour and has become culturally normalised – as Champion's (Chapter 2, this volume) overview also suggests – then perhaps a study to follow from this one could pay greater attention to the detailed transformations being wrought upon rural areas (see Marsden *et al.* 1993; Murdoch and Marsden 1994) rather than to the agents of that transformation. In this respect, Allan and Mooney's and S. Fielding's accounts (Chapters 15 and 8, this volume) of attempts by 'native' rural people to locate themselves within the emerging post-productivist countryside are a useful initiation. A further informative leaping-off point is Gorton, White and Chaston's (Chapter 12, this volume) observation of the contradiction in the rural idyll between communitarian and individualistic elements; can these two dimensions be reconciled in counterurbanisation? 'Migration into rural areas' sets us a rich research agenda.

NOTES

1. A 'strain' school of migration research can be similarly critiqued (see Boyle *et al.* 1998: Chapter 3).
2. An interesting example of this wish-fulfilment element with respect to migration to rural areas was uncovered by Halfacree (1995). In a study of migrants to rural parts of England, respondents often indicated that they realised that the rural idyll was a myth but they still maintained this representation as a 'blueprint', an ideal of what the rural should (could?) be.

REFERENCES

Agyeman, J. and Spooner, R. (1997) 'Ethnicity and the rural environment', in P. Cloke and J. Little (eds.), *Contested countryside cultures*, Routledge, London, 197–217.

Berry, B. (1976) 'The counterurbanization process: urban America since 1970', in B. Berry (ed.), *Urbanization and counter-urbanization*, Sage, Beverly Hills, California, 17–30.

Blumer, H. (1978) 'Elementary collective groupings', in L. Genevie (ed.), *Collective behavior and social movements*, F.E. Peacock Publishers, Itasca, Illinois, 67–87.

Boyle, P., Halfacree, K. and Robinson, V. (1998) *Exploring contemporary migration*, Longman, Harlow.

Buller, H. and Hoggart, K. (1994) *International counterurbanization. British migrants in rural France*, Avebury, Aldershot.

Bunce, M. (1994) *The countryside ideal. Anglo-American images of landscape*, Routledge, London.

Campbell, R. and Garkovich, L. (1984) 'Turnaround migration as an episode of collective behaviour', *Rural Sociology*, **49**, 89–105.

Cantril, H. (1940) *The invasion from Mars*, Princeton University Press, Princeton, New Jersey.

Cloke, P., Philo, C. and Sadler, D. (1991) *Approaching human geography. An introduction to contemporary theoretical ideas*, Paul Chapman Publishing, London.

Cohen, J. (1985) 'Strategy or identity: new theoretical paradigms and contemporary social movements', *Social Research*, **52**, 663–716.

Cohen, S. (1973) *Folk devils and moral panics*, Granada Publishing, St Albans.

Cross, D. (1990) *Counterurbanisation in England and Wales*, Avebury, Aldershot.

Fish, R. (1997) 'The production and reception of popular media images of the countryside', paper presented at the Royal Geographical Society – Institute of British Geographers Annual Conference, University of Exeter, January.

Gamson, W. (1990) *The strategy of social protest*, Wadsworth, Belmont, California.

Gamson, W. (1992) 'The social psychology of collective action', in A. Morris and C. McClurg Mueller (eds.), *Frontiers in social movement theory*, Yale University Press, New Haven, 53–76.

Genevie, L. (1978) 'Introduction', in L. Genevie (ed.), *Collective behaviour and social movements*, F.E. Peacock Publishers., Itasca, Illinois, xv–xxii.

Giddens, A. (1984) *The constitution of society*, Cambridge University Press, Cambridge.

Giddens, A. (1993) *Sociology*, Polity Press, Cambridge, 2nd edition.

Gilbert, G. and Mulkay, M. (1984) *Opening Pandora's Box: a sociological analysis of scientists' discourse*, Cambridge University Press, Cambridge.

Goldman, R. and Dickens, D. (1983) 'The selling of rural America', *Rural Sociology*, **48**, 585–606.

Hadden, J. and Barton, J. (1973) 'An image that will not die: thoughts on the history of anti-urban ideology', *Urban Affairs Annual Review*, **7**, 79–116.

Halfacree, K. (1993) 'Locality and social representation: space, discourse and alternative definitions of the rural', *Journal of Rural Studies*, **9**, 23–37.

Halfacree, K. (1994) 'The importance of 'the rural' in the constitution of counterurbanization: evidence from England in the 1980s', *Sociologia Ruralis*, **34**, 164–189.

Halfacree, K. (1995) 'Talking about rurality: social representations of the rural as expressed by residents of six English parishes', *Journal of Rural Studies*, **11**, 1–20.

Halfacree, K. (1997) 'Contrasting roles for the post-productivist countryside: a postmodern perspective on counterurbanisation', in P. Cloke and J. Little (eds.), *Contested countryside cultures*, Routledge, London, 70–93.

Halfacree, K. and Boyle, P. (1993) 'The challenge facing migration research: the case for a biographical approach', *Progress in Human Geography*, **17**, 333–348.

Klandermans, B. (1984) 'Social psychology expansions of resource mobilization theory',

American Sociological Review, **49**, 583–600.

Lash, S. and Urry, J. (1994) *Economies of signs and space*, Sage, London.

LeBon, G. (1895) *The crowd*, Viking Press, New York, 1965 edition.

Lyotard, J-F. (1984) *The postmodern condition – a report on knowledge*, Manchester University Press, Manchester.

Maheu, L. (1995) 'Introduction', in L. Maheu (ed.), *Social movements and social classes: the future of collective action*, Sage, London, 3–17.

Marsden, T., Murdoch, J., Lowe, P., Munton, R. and Flynn, A. (1993) *Constructing the countryside*, UCL Press, London.

Marx, G. and McAdam, D. (1994) *Collective behavior and social movements*, Prentice Hall, Englewood Cliffs, New Jersey.

Mayle, P. (1989) *A year in Provence*, Hamish Hamilton, London.

Mayle, P. (1990) *Toujours Provence*, Hamish Hamilton, London.

McCarthy, J. and Zald, M. (1973) *The trend of social movements in America: professionalization and resource mobilization*, General Learning Press, Morristown, New Jersey.

McCarthy, J. and Zald, M. (1977) 'Resource mobilization and social movements: a partial theory', *American Journal of Sociology*, **82**, 1212–1241.

Melucci, A. (1989) *Nomads of the present: social movements and individual needs in contemporary society*, Temple University Press, Philadelphia.

Murdoch, J. and Marsden, T. (1994) *Reconstituting rurality*, UCL Press, London.

Nash, R. (1973) *Wilderness and the American mind*, Yale University Press, New Haven.

Newby, H. (1980) 'A one-eyed look at the country', *New Society*, **53**, 324–325.

Park, R. and Burgess, E. (1924) *Introduction to the science of sociology*, University of Chicago Press, Chicago.

Potter, J. and Wetherell, M. (1987) *Discourse and social psychology*, Sage, London.

Sayer, A. (1984) *Method in social science. A realist approach*, Hutchinson, London.

Short, J. (1991) *Imagined country*, Routledge, London.

Shotter, J. (1984) *Social accountability and selfhood*, Oxford University Press, Oxford.

Shotter, J. (1989) 'Realism and social constructionism', paper presented at the 'Realism and the social sciences' conference, Manchester Polytechnic, August.

Skeldon, R. (1995) 'The challenge facing migration research: a case for greater awareness', *Progress in Human Geography*, **19**, 91–96.

Smelser, N. (1962) *Theory of collective behaviour*, Free Press, New York.

Thomas, K. (1973) *Man and the natural world, 1500–1800*, Allen Lane, London.

Thrift, N. (1989) 'Images of social change', in C. Hamnett, L. McDowell and P. Sarre (eds.), *The changing social structure*, Sage, London, 12–42.

Thrift, N. (1996) *Spatial formations*, Sage, London.

Urry, J. (1995) 'A middle-class countryside?', in T. Butler and M. Savage (eds.), *Social change and the middle classes*, UCL Press, London, 205–219.

Williams, R. (1973) *The country and the city*, Chatto and Windus, London.

Youngs, M. (1985) 'The English television landscape documentary: a look at Granada', in J. Burgess and J. Gold (eds.), *Geography, the media and popular culture*, Routledge and Kegan Paul, London, 144–164.

Zimbardo, P. (1970) 'The human choice. Individuation, reason, and order versus deindividuation, impulse, and chaos', in W. Arnold and D. Levine (eds.), *Nebraska Symposium on Motivation 1969*, Lincoln, University of Nebraska Press, 237–307.

ILLUSTRATIONS

TABLES

CONTRIBUTORS

Simone Abram Department of City and Regional Planning, University of Wales, Cardiff, UK

Jenny Agg Department of Geography, Coventry University, Coventry, UK

Jane Allan Directorate of Environmental Strategy, Scottish Environmental Protection Agency, Stirling, UK

Martin Bell Department of Geography, University of Adelaide, Adelaide, Australia

Paul Boyle School of Geography, University of Leeds, Leeds, UK

Tony Champion Department of Geography, University of Newcastle-upon-Tyne, Newcastle-upon-Tyne, UK

Ian Chaston Plymouth Business School, University of Plymouth, Plymouth, UK

Paul Cloke Department of Geography, University of Bristol, Bristol, UK

Graham Day School of Sociology and Social Policy, University of Wales, Bangor, UK

Shaun Fielding Evaluation, Development and Research Unit, Tavistock Institute, London, UK

Tony Fielding Centre for Urban and Regional Research, University of Sussex, Brighton, UK

William H. Frey Population Studies Center, University of Michigan, Ann Arbor, USA

Mark Goodwin Department of Geography, University of Wales, Aberystwyth, UK

Matthew Gorton Wye College, University of London, Wye, Ashford, UK

Keith Halfacree Department of Geography, University of Wales, Swansea, UK

Graeme Hugo Department of Geography, University of Adelaide, Adelaide, Australia

Kenneth M. Johnson Department of Sociology, Loyola University-Chicago, Chicago, USA

Thomas Kontuly Department of Geography, University of Utah, Salt Lake City, USA

Terry Marsden Department of City and Regional Planning, University of Wales, Cardiff, UK

Paul Milbourne   Countryside and Community Research Unit, Cheltenham and Gloucester College of Higher Education, Cheltenham, UK

Elizabeth Mooney   Department of Social Sciences, Glasgow Caledonian University, Glasgow, UK

Jonathan Murdoch   Department of City and Regional Planning, University of Wales, Cardiff, UK

Martin Phillips   Department of Geography, Leicester University, Leicester, UK

Nigel Thrift   Department of Geography, University of Bristol, Bristol, UK

John White   Department of Marketing, University of Plymouth, Plymouth, UK

Country index

Subject index